OUR WAY TO GOD

OUR
way to god

A Book of
Religious Self-Education

DR. FRANZ MICHEL WILLAM

Translated by RONALD WALLS

THE BRUCE PUBLISHING COMPANY
MILWAUKEE

NIHIL OBSTAT:

JOHN A. SCHULIEN, S.T.D.
Censor librorum

IMPRIMATUR:

✟ WILLIAM E. COUSINS
Archbishop of Milwaukee
May 28, 1964

This work is translated from a German edition published by Verlagansanstalt Tyrolio, Innsbruck, Austria. James Clark & Co., Ltd., London, England, is the Licensee for the English language editions.

Library of Congress Catalog Card Number: 64–22859

PREFACE TO THE ENGLISH TRANSLATION

FATHER FRANZ MICHEL WILLAM is numbered among the leading figures in the catechetical renewal. His writings are marked by a deep grasp of the "good news" of salvation, of the central core of the Christian message. The present work is a translation of *Unser Weg zu Gott,* written by Father Willam as a book of religious instruction for adults. In preparing this volume, Father Willam's purpose was to lead the adult Christian to an encounter with his Lord, present *now* in the Church, actively at work in building up the people of God, the living stones of the temple of the New Covenant, worshiping with them, through the Spirit, the heavenly Father. To communicate this message Father Willam has drawn on the living sources of Christian faith, the Bible and the liturgy, wherein we encounter the living Word of God. For Father Willam the life of a Christian is one characterized by commitment and responsibility and joy — joy in the Lord whose saving acts we *celebrate* in the liturgy of His Church.

Perhaps the best way to introduce Father Willam's work to the English-speaking world is to cite Father Martin Ramsauer, S.J., Professor of Dogmatic Theology and member of the East Asian Pastoral Institute in Manila, himself a leading catechist. Father Ramsauer writes:

> Father Willam lets *God Himself* speak to us, as He spoke to us through the prophets and His own Son. Our generation has found new interest and esteem for the Word of God. We want to hear above all *Him.* The word of the human writer shall lead to a fuller understanding of God's own teaching: "One only is your teacher" (Mt 23:8). Willam follows this advice of Christ. In his book God's Word is not used to "confirm" assertions and explanations by the author, but as the very source and fountain of all teaching. This manner of presentation does justice to the fact that our teaching

comes from God, and that our faith is the answer to God's revelation. This "primacy" given to the Word of God results in a dignity and unction and also forcefulness throughout the whole text, touching the reader in a personal, intimate way.

Another characteristic of Willam's book is the masterly *union* into which all the "ramifications" of Catholic life are brought. The understanding of God's Word makes us perceive first of all the inner coherence and deep union which exists among the various parts of Catholic teaching and leads furthermore with inner consequence to applications in our private and social life as well as to an intelligent and active participation in the liturgy. The fact that the explanations are interwoven with excerpts from the Fathers of the Church, with facts from Church history and contemporary life makes the content of the book very concrete, rich, and interesting; and still — thanks to the masterly pedagogy of Professor Willam — it does not destroy the clarity and unity.

Furthermore we do not miss a useful *apologetical orientation* which the adult Catholic needs, living in the community of so many Christian and non-Christian beliefs, and from which the convert and inquirer too will greatly profit. And we are glad to observe how Willam puts more stress in preparing the adult for his apologetical task, by giving him a proper understanding of Catholic teaching rather than by providing him with ready-made answers which generally show more "brilliance" than true satisfaction.

The book, finally, is not only for reading and study. The skillful selection and abundant use of Scripture texts, the excellent quotations from the Fathers, and that comprehensive and unifying view under which all the details of, and applications for the Christian life are seen, invite spontaneously *reflection and meditation*. And it is perhaps by this characteristic that the book will exercise its greatest influence: by letting our faith grow — in an almost imperceptible manner — into the adult maturity of a responsible Catholic life.

Citations from the New Testament are taken from the version by Fathers James Kleist and Joseph Lilly. Quotations from the Old Testament are taken from the new Confraternity translation except for a few passages from books not as yet released in the Confraternity version. For these the Douai has been used.

FOREWORD

THE THEOLOGICAL EDUCATION of the reader is the aim of this book. Nothing is presupposed except his willing cooperation. The book bears, therefore, the subtitle "A Book of Religious Self-Education." Today there seems to be a readiness to study Holy Scripture. Men find their way to God and to the sources of grace most easily through those words which God has spoken to men and about men. An exposition which keeps close to the Bible leads inevitably to Christ; and it enables the reader to share the experience of how our Lord established the new redemptive order by which He gave Himself to mankind.

The author acknowledges the help and encouragement in this work of His Excellence Bishop Dr. Paul Rusch of Innsbruck, of the Right Reverend Dr. Josef Andreas Jungmann, S.J., of Innsbruck, and of the Right Reverend Dr. Alois Wurm of Munich.

DR. FRANZ MICHEL WILLAM

CONTENTS

Preface to the English Translation v
Foreword vii

PART I

THE MESSAGE OF THE LOVE OF GOD TO MAN MADE KNOWN THROUGH HIS SON JESUS CHRIST

BASIC INTRODUCTION

GOD BREAKS INTO HUMAN HISTORY BY REVELATION
THE CHURCH IS COMMISSIONED TO PROCLAIM
THE REVELATION

1. Revelation: The Message of the Love of God . . 3
2. The Apostles' Creed 7

EXPOSITION IN DETAIL

THE APOSTLES' CREED, THE FIRST DOGMATIC
COMPENDIUM OF REVELATION AFTER ITS
CONCLUSION WITH THE DEATH OF THE APOSTLES

First Article of the Creed (3–9)

3. God, the Uncreated Creator of All Created Things . 12
4. The Attributes of God: Ways to Knowledge of God . 17
5. The Army of Invisible Spirits, Companions of Men . 23
6. Man, Appointed by God to Be Lord of the Earth; His Share in the Divine Life 27
7. The Sin of Our First Parents 33

ix

x   Contents

8. God's Sentence Upon Satan and Upon the Parents of
   the Human Race   36
9. The History of Man From the Expulsion From Paradise
   Until the Appearance of the Redeemer .   .   .   40

Second Article of the Creed (10)

---

10. Jesus Christ the Son of God, the Mediator Between God
    and Man   44

Third Article of the Creed (11–14)

---

11. The Incarnation of Christ the Son of God, the New Union
    Between Heaven and Earth   48
12. The Birth of the Redeemer Jesus Christ in the Stable at
    Bethlehem   52
13. The Baptism of Jesus: The Mystery of the Most Holy
    Trinity Revealed   56
14. The Public Appearance of Jesus, the Mediator Sent From
    the Father   61

Fourth Article of the Creed (15)

---

15. The Sacrificial Death of Jesus Upon the Cross, Atonement
    for the Sin of the World   65

Fifth Article of the Creed (16)

---

16 The Risen Jesus, Victor Over Sin and Death   .   .   70

Sixth Article of the Creed (17)

---

17. The Ascension of Jesus Into Heaven: The Inauguration
    of His Kingdom   75

Seventh Article of the Creed (18)

---

18. The Future Judgment of Mankind by Jesus Christ   .   78

Eighth Article of the Creed (19)

---

19. The Holy Spirit Who Leads Men to Christ and the Father   82

Ninth Article of the Creed (20–25)

---

20. The Visible Structure of the Church Built by Christ Upon
    the Foundation of the Apostles   88

Contents

21. The Atoning Death of Christ, the Spiritual Foundation of the Church 92
22. The Sending of the Holy Spirit, the Beginning of the Autonomous Life of the Church 97
23. The Marks of the Church Founded by Christ . . 102
24. The Church, the Place of Salvation in Jesus Christ . 106
25. The Communion of Saints: The Participation of All the Faithful in the Treasures of Salvation Through Christ . 109

Tenth Article of the Creed (26)

26. The Power of Forgiving Sins — Transmitted From Christ to the Church 115

Eleventh Article of the Creed (27)

27. The Consummation of the Kingdom of God: The Resurrection of the Dead 117

Twelfth Article of the Creed (28)

28. The Entry of the Blessed Into Heaven: The Consummation of the Kingdom 122

PART II

THE NEW COVENANT BETWEEN THE BLESSED TRINITY AND MAN, ESTABLISHED THROUGH JESUS CHRIST WITHIN THE CHURCH, THE MOTHER OF ALL THE FAITHFUL

BASIC INTRODUCTION

MAN SHARES AGAIN IN THE DIVINE LIFE THROUGH THE GRACE OF JESUS CHRIST

1. Sanctifying Grace: Man Shares in Divine Life . . 127
2. God's Cooperation With Man: Actual Grace . . 133

EXPOSITION IN DETAIL

MAN'S COMMUNION WITH THE TRINITY: BY PRAYER, IN THE SACRAMENTS, AND IN THE SACRIFICE OF THE NEW COVENANT

Section 1: The Prayer of the Christian (3–8)

3. Before the Appearance of the Redeemer. Prayer to God the One and Only 140
4. Prayer Since Christ's Ascension Into Heaven. The Mediation of Jesus Christ 143
5. What Jesus Demands of His People at Prayer: Humility and Trust 147
6. The *Our Father*: The Prayer in the Name and in the Spirit of Jesus 150
7. The *Hail Mary*: Asking for Mary's Intercession With Her Son 155
8. Jesus at Prayer: The Model of Prayer for His People . 160

Section 2: The Sacraments, Except the Holy Eucharist (9–18)

9. The Sacraments: Man's Companions Along the Road of Life 164
10. Baptism: The Sacrament of New Birth . . . 168
11. Confirmation: The Sacrament of Individual Responsibility 171
12. The Sacrament of Penance: The Sacrament Which Renews Reconciliation in the Atoning Blood of Christ . . 174
13. The Five Parts of the Sacrament of Penance: Examination of Conscience; Repentance; Purpose of Amendment; Confession; Satisfaction 178
14. Indulgences: Remission by the Church of Temporal Punishment Due to Sins 185
15. The Anointing of the Sick: Christ Beside the Sick . 187
16. The Sacrament of Marriage: The Consecration of Parenthood 189
17. Self-Discipline: The Indispensable Preparation for Marriage 195
18. The Sacramentals: The Incorporation of Nature in the Blessing of Redemption 198
19. Holy Orders: Solemn Dedication as a Representative of Christ 202

Section 3: The Holy Eucharist (20–28)

20. Sacrifice Under the Old Covenant; Sublime Yet Limited 206
21. The Sacrifice of the New Covenant, Perfected by Christ, Is Made Known 210

Contents

22. The Last Supper: The Sacrifice of the New Covenant Is Instituted 215
23. Christ's Sacrifice Upon the Cross: The Once-For-All Blood Sacrifice of the New Covenant 219
24. The Holy Sacrifice of the Mass: The Bloodless Food Offering With a Sacrificial Meal as the Sacrifice of the New Covenant 223
25. The Sacrificial Meal, Holy Communion . . . 227
26. Offering the Holy Sacrifice of the Mass . . . 230
27. The Liturgical Year: The Re-presentation of the Work of Redemption Through the Liturgical Year; the Presence of Jesus in the Tabernacle 240
28. The Consummation of the Christian Life in Death; The Homecoming to Christ and the Father . . . 245

PART III

THE EXALTATION AND FULFILLMENT
OF NATURAL LIFE IN THE COMMUNITY
OF GRACE WITH JESUS CHRIST

BASIC INTRODUCTION

THE DOCTRINE OF THE TWOFOLD WAY

Conscience and the Fundamental Rules for
Conscience Revealed by God (1–3)

---

1. Conscience and Man's Sense of Moral Obligation . 251
2. The Ten Commandments of God: Ten Fundamental Rules for Conscience, Revealed by God . . . 256
3. The Ten Commandments of God — Commandments of Christ 261

Life With and In God (4–6)

---

4. The Theological Virtues: Faith, Hope, and Charity, The Fundamental Forces in Striving Toward God . . 265

5. The Four Cardinal Moral Virtues: Prudence, Justice, Fortitude, Temperance — The Four Basic Principles Governing All Human Action 269

6. The Law of Love: The Summary of All Man's Duties . 275

Life Without and Against God (7–9)

7. Sin: Man's Disobedience to God . . . 281
8. Temptation: The Mysterious Warfare Within the Soul . 285
9. The Seven Capital Vices: Seven Roads to Destruction . 289

EXPOSITION IN DETAIL

THE COMMANDMENTS OF GOD AND OF THE CHURCH,
AND THE DUTIES OF ONE'S STATION IN LIFE
AS THE FULFILLMENT OF THE ONE SUPREME
COMMANDMENT TO LOVE GOD AND OUR NEIGHBOR

The First Commandment (10–11)

10. God: Man's Chief End 294
11. God, Exalted Above All Things. The Adoration of God 300

The Second Commandment (12–13)

12. Keeping the Name of God Hallowed . . . 303
13. God in Human Conversation 306

The Third Commandment (14–15)

14. Keeping the Lord's Day Holy 310
15. Hearing the Word of God: A Duty for All the Faithful 314

The Fourth Commandment (16–18)

16. The Law of God and the Family 318
17. The Law of God and the State 323
18. The Law of God and the Church . . . 332

Contents

The Fifth Commandment (19–20)

19. The Law of God and Life on Earth . . . 335
20. The Law of God and the Life of Grace in the Soul . 341

The Sixth Commandment (21–22)

21. The Law of God and the Generative Powers of Father and Mother 345
22. Preserving the Spirit's Control Over the Senses . . 351

The Seventh Commandment (23–25)

23. The Law of God and Private Property, Its Rights and Obligations 356
24. The Law of God and Working for Others . . 360
25. Unlawful Gain and Restitution 364

The Eighth Commandment (26–28)

26. The Inner Desire for Truth, the Prerequisite of All Truthfulness 369
27. The Law of God About Speaking and Keeping Silent . 374
28. The Law of God and Keeping Faith in Confidences and Contracts 377

The Ninth and Tenth Commandments (29)

29. The Law of God in the Realm of Desires . . 380
30. The Commandments of the Church: The More Precise Regulations for Carrying Out the Various Commandments of God 384
31. Duties of Vocation and Station: The Command to Love One's Neighbor Applied to Particular Spheres of Activity 390
32. The Priestly and Religious State: The Special Vocation to Serve Christ and His Church 394
33. Awaiting Christ the Lord 398

PART I

THE MESSAGE OF THE LOVE OF GOD TO MAN MADE KNOWN THROUGH HIS SON JESUS CHRIST

BASIC INTRODUCTION

GOD BREAKS INTO HUMAN HISTORY BY REVELATION

THE CHURCH IS COMMISSIONED TO PROCLAIM THE REVELATION

In many fragmentary and various utterances, God spoke of old to our ancestors through the prophets; at the present time, the final epoch, he has spoken to us through his Son, whom he has appointed heir of the universe. Through him, too, he made the world (Heb 1:1–2).

1. REVELATION: THE MESSAGE OF THE LOVE OF GOD

"WITH AGE-OLD LOVE I have loved you; so I have kept my mercy toward you" (Jer 31:3).

These words of God, which apply as much to the community as to the individual, are the key to our understanding of what God has done for the salvation of man.

When we are far from those we love we write letters to them. To insure perfect understanding of our message, we may even send the letter by a messenger who can explain and fill out its substance. If such a letter is sent to a group of people, the reception of the letter binds them to one another as well as to him who sent it; and if anyone refused to listen to the message he would be cutting himself off both from the sender and from the rest of those to whom it was sent.

What men do out of love for one another, the love of God does likewise. God sends His messengers to tell what His love has done for men, and how they can embrace His love and return it. And likewise, God has given these messengers who proclaim His love a letter to take with them which they must deliver and explain. This letter is the longest one the world has known; its writing extended from the time of Moses in the thirteenth century before Christ to the last days of the Apostles as the first century of this era was drawing to a close. It is collected in the writings of the Old and New Testaments.

Just as people who receive an earthly messenger with his letter become a community, so too those who receive God's message become a community; and, as he who rejects the earthly messenger with the letter cuts himself off both from the sender and from those who receive it, so he who will not accept the message of God separates himself both from God and from those who receive God's message.

Faith consists in acceptance of that message which God in His

3

love makes known to men, generation by generation, through His appointed messengers. In the Epistle to the Romans, St. Paul says:

There is the same Lord of all, generous toward all who call upon him, since "whoever calls on the name of the Lord shall be saved."
How, then, are people to call upon him in whom they have not attained faith? And how can they attain faith in him whom they have not heard? And how are they to hear if no one preaches? And how are men to preach unless they be sent? As it is written,
"How welcome is the coming of those who
proclaim the Good News."
But not all have submitted to the Good News. So Isaias says,
"Lord, who has believed our preaching?"
Faith, then, depends on hearing, and hearing on Christ's teaching (Rom 10:12–17).

All men of goodwill long for a revelation from God and believe that God will not leave man, the creature of His own hand, all to his own devices. This dim awareness is the preparation for faith.

In his encyclical *Humani Generis* (1950) Pope Pius XII attributed the following capacities to human knowledge in the sphere of religion: (1) Human reason is able to reach sure and certain knowledge of the existence of a personal God from creation and the voice of conscience. (2) It can trace correctly the law which the Creator has put into the hearts of men. (3) From the ancient historical records and the miracles described in them it is able to recognize that, since the Fall, God has revealed Himself to men in a special manner. (4) In a limited yet highly fruitful way, it is able to grasp the mysteries of faith.

The most significant things in world history are these:

After the Fall in paradise, God resumed the outward union with man and made Himself known to him in word and deed.
This new message of the love of God is called the revelation of God; its proclamation is entrusted to the Catholic Church. That revelation is communicated in Scripture and the living tradition of the Church.
Holy Scripture is the collection of those books which were written by inspiration of the Holy Spirit and given to the Church by God Himself, and which are now preserved and explained without falsification by the Church, relying on the support of the Holy Spirit.

The Life of the Individual. By the power of faith man receives a new spiritual vision. The spiritual vision which grace supplies certainly does not consist in enabling people of "average endowment" to know as much about secular matters by the help of grace as do "great minds" without it. Yet everyone who looks upon the world and into his own being with the eye of faith sees deeper and farther than does the person whom faith passes by. Judging by the light of faith, fishermen, mountain peasants, and street laborers know more about the ultimate questions of life than the greatest philosopher who approaches the same questions only with his own insight.

In Psalm 118, the song in praise of God's revelation as the guide of man, is found the exultant declaration that a man who holds fast to the Commandments is wiser than the sages of this world who do not know them or dispense with them. The psalmist says:

> I have more understanding than all my teachers
> when your decrees are my meditation.
> I have more discernment than the elders;
> because I observe your precepts (Ps 118:99–100).

The Life of the Church. The Holy Scripture of the Old Covenant comprises 45 books; the Holy Scripture of the new, 27. All of these books of Holy Scripture contain the Word of God. If, in spite of this, one wishes to distinguish between the important and the less important, then we must give first place to the four Gospels — the Gospels according to St. Matthew, St. Mark, St. Luke, and St. John.

The origin of the Gospels is bound up in the closest possible way with the first proclamation of the glad tidings of the Redemption through Jesus Christ. The introduction which Luke prefixes to his Gospel provides direct evidence of this; "Many an attempt has been made before now to present the drama of events that have come to a climax among us, so as to accord with the tradition which the original eyewitnesses and ministers of the gospel have handed down to us. And, therefore, Theophilus, I, too, after accurately tracing the whole movement to its origin, have decided to write a consecutive account for your excellency. It is my aim that you should appreciate the certainty on which the oral instruction you have already received is grounded" (Lk 1:1–4).

This opening sentence of the Gospel according to St. Luke — completed about A.D. 63 — discloses the following facts.

The Gospels received only those statements about the "events" — i.e., the public activity, sacrificial death and glorification of Jesus — which came from "original eyewitnesses and ministers of the gospel." The Gospels presuppose a "ministry of the word," a preaching; and their purpose is to provide a written record both for those who proclaim and also for the faithful who hear.

Between the time of Moses, whose personality and work dominate the Pentateuch or Torah of the Old Testament, and the time when the final book of the New Testament was composed — that mysterious revelation which came to the Apostle John — is a space of almost 1500 years. In spite of this, Holy Scripture is the work of a single author — the Holy Spirit; and the various authors who, during those 1500 years, each contributed his own part, all wrote under the inspiration of the one Holy Spirit. As Leo XIII wrote in his encyclical on biblical studies, the Holy Spirit inspired and moved them to write, "with a supernatural power, and supported them while writing in such a way that they understood all of what He commissioned them to write — and only that — and also wrote it down faithfully and expressed it with infallible accuracy."

The operation of the Holy Spirit did not, however, suspend the mental capacities and personal traits of the writers; nor did it exclude natural stimulus but rather enlisted that in the supernatural purpose, and even when making a definite pronouncement, the authors of the books did not have to be aware that they were writing under the influence of the Holy Spirit.

Whatever individual authors wrote down, they did so in the language and in the manner of thought of the time to which they belonged. It follows from this that we who live many thousands of years later cannot now without effort comprehend all that was written. For this reason Christ has committed the preaching of the revelation to the Church and has promised her that until the end of the world the Holy Spirit will preserve her from all error. It is the selfsame Holy Spirit whose influence brought the Holy Scripture into being who provides for the correct exposition of the Holy Scripture within the Church.

2. THE APOSTLES' CREED

WITH THE DEATH AND RESURRECTION of the Lord, the legal status of the people of Israel changed. Until then the Jews had had an absolute monopoly in preaching the good news of the kingdom of God; now the day dawned when this was to be withheld no longer from other nations.

Before His Ascension, Jesus commanded His Apostles to invite the non-Jews to enter the kingdom of God:

> As for the eleven disciples, they betook themselves to the mountain in Galilee to which Jesus had ordered them. When they saw him, they adored him, although at first they had doubts. Jesus then came closer to them and spoke to them the following words:
> "Absolute authority in heaven and on earth
> has been conferred upon me.
> Go, therefore,
> and make all nations your disciples:
> baptize them in the name
> of the Father
> and of the Son
> and of the Holy Spirit,
> and teach them to observe
> all the commandments I have given you.
> And mark:
> I am with you at all times
> as long as the world will last" (Mt 28:16–20).

Jesus introduces His command to the Apostles with a "therefore." Because all power has been given to Him in heaven and on earth, He gives instructions to the Apostles to teach and to baptize all peoples. The Apostles were to "make all nations their disciples," i.e., followers of Christ, dedicated to the work of Jesus. Only those who had already become disciples of Jesus, that is, who had already come to have faith in Him, could be baptized. Anyone who wished to be admitted to baptism had to have sufficient previous instruction to under-

7

stand what baptism signified and effected, and had to desire this sacrament in faith.

It was only natural that the Apostles, as preachers of the Word of God, very soon summarized the principal truths of faith, the central core of their preaching, in a series of propositions which a candidate for baptism had to acknowledge and remember. Thus arose the first "apostolic" Creed.

God the One and Only had revealed Himself as the Trinity. Jesus Christ, the Son of God, had appeared as a man among men, and after His return to heaven had sent, from the Father, the Holy Spirit. Therefore, this Creed first presents truths about God the Father; then truths about Jesus, the Son of God; and finally, truths about the Holy Spirit.

In this way the Creed becomes a short history of the world with a first section on the period from the creation of the world until the appearance of Jesus, a second on the period when Jesus was on earth, and a third embracing the period from the coming of the Holy Spirit until the end of the world.

In its origin, the Creed provides an official collection of truths of faith to which the newly baptized had to assent.

When this was handed for the first time to the candidate for baptism, the bishop gave a solemn discourse, which explains also the nature of this ancient prayer. The bishop said:

> Beloved, you have here a short compendium of your faith, the text of the Creed, compiled not according to the rules of ordinary language, but inspired by God. Each one is able to understand and to hold these doctrines.

> For here it is proclaimed that Father and Son are one in being and equal in power, that the only-begotten Son of God was born, taking flesh from the Virgin Mary through the co-operation of the Holy Spirit; here is proclaimed His crucifixion, His burial, His resurrection on the third day, and His ascension; here we confess that He sits at the right hand of the Father of all power and majesty, and that one day He will come to judge the living and the dead.

> To the Holy Spirit is attributed the same indivisible divine being which is attributed to the Father and the Son. Here we are taught about the natural vocation of the Church, the remission of sins and the resurrection of the body.

> Beloved, you who once were like the old Adam are now to renew

yourselves after the image of the new man, Jesus! from being fleshly you are to become spiritual, from being earthly men, you are to become heavenly men.

Believe firmly and unshakably that one day the resurrection of Christ will be fulfilled in all of us; for what has happened to the Head will be accomplished in the members also.

The Holy Spirit, who inspired the first teachers of the Church with the sacred words, has embodied the sacred doctrines of faith in clear and precise expressions, so that those things which you are to believe and to make the object of your constant meditation should not remain dark to your understanding and wearisome to your memory.

After saying the Creed, aloud, the bishop added:

Now, my dear ones, you have heard the confession of the Catholic Faith. After you leave this holy place, fix it in your memory without altering one syllable of it. All things are possible with the mercy of God; may it lead you who thirst to faith and to holy baptism, and permit us who taught, along with you who heard the divine mysteries, alike to arrive at everlasting life. Through the same Lord Jesus Christ who lives and reigns for ever and ever. Amen.

For Catholic Christians of all countries, the Apostles' Creed still has the same meaning as in the early centuries. Therefore the words just quoted hold good for us too.

Apart from Holy Scripture, the Apostles' Creed is the most precious document of Christendom.

I believe in God, the Father Almighty, Creator of heaven and earth; and in Jesus Christ, His only Son, our Lord; who was conceived by the Holy Spirit, born of the Virgin Mary, suffered under Pontius Pilate, was crucified, died and was buried. He descended into hell; the third day He rose again from the dead; He ascended into heaven; sitteth at the right hand of God, the Father Almighty; thence He shall come to judge the living and the dead.

I believe in the Holy Spirit, the Holy Catholic Church, the Communion of Saints, the forgiveness of sins, the resurrection of the body, and life everlasting. Amen.

In the Apostles' Creed one professes before God and man one's belief in the truths which it contains and commits oneself to them.

The Life of the Individual. The articles of the Creed always begin with the phrase, "I believe," not "we believe." The individual does not become lost in the crowd, rather, he must stand up for himself and profess: "I believe before the world; I believe before God."

Knowledge through faith is knowledge received from God; because God's knowledge is superior in certainty to all human knowledge, so is knowledge by faith high above all human knowledge in certainty.

The Life of the Church. The Faith contained in outline in the Creed is more fully developed in Holy Scripture; hence it is by studying Scripture that our knowledge of the Faith is deepened. In his encyclical on Holy Scripture, *Divino Afflante Spiritu* (1943), Pope Pius XII urged the bishops, as responsible leaders of the Church, to "take every measure to foster and increase this veneration among the faithful committed to their charge, by promoting all those undertakings through which men of apostolic zeal are laudably striving to arouse and encourage among Catholics the knowledge and love of the Sacred Books. Let them favor and assist those pious associations whose object is to circulate copies of the Bible, and especially of the Gospels, among the faithful, and to encourage Christian families in the habit of reading them devoutly every day."

To read Holy Scripture only for its exciting stories is not to read it as a Christian. As Pope Pius noted: "God has not given the Sacred Books to men to satisfy their curiosity or to provide material for work and research. Holy Scripture is supposed, rather to 'instruct to salvation by the faith which is in Christ Jesus' 'that the man of God may be perfect, furnished to every good work' (2 Tm 3:15, 17)."

Whoever reads Holy Scripture in the spirit of faith will prepare himself inwardly to receive its lessons. He will be aware of the fact that in reading the Holy Scripture he enters into union with the Holy Spirit, the author of the Scripture. And he will follow the Church's advice to become recollected and pray to the Holy Spirit before reading the Scripture. Whoever reads Holy Scripture in this disposition will find it a source of real blessing.

St. Gregory the Great commended Holy Scripture to Theodore, the private physician of the emperor, in these words: "I pray you, take trouble each day to consider the words of your Creator. Come to know the heart of God from His words in order that you may strive more eagerly for that which is eternal, in order that you may long more deeply for the joys of heaven."

EXPOSITION IN DETAIL

THE APOSTLES' CREED, THE FIRST DOGMATIC COMPENDIUM OF REVELATION AFTER ITS CONCLUSION WITH THE DEATH OF THE APOSTLES

Bestow great care upon learning the Creed which we now teach you as we once were taught it. Do not write it upon a fading page, but upon the parchment of your hearts (an early Christian liturgical text).

3. GOD, THE UNCREATED CREATOR OF ALL CREATED THINGS

EAST OF THE MEDITERRANEAN SEA, the desert stretches out endlessly toward Mount Sinai. For years, Moses had wandered about this desert as the shepherd of his father-in-law Jethro, following a fixed rule according to the changing of pastures. And so once again he had come close to Mount Sinai. While there he experienced God. Listen to the account given of this experience in the Old Testament book of Exodus:

> Meanwhile Moses was tending the flock of his father-in-law, Jethro, the priest of Madian. Leading the flock across the desert, he came to Horeb, the mountain of God. There an angel of the Lord appeared to him in fire flaming out of a bush. As he looked on, he was surprised to see that the bush, though on fire, was not consumed. So Moses decided, "I must go over to look at this remarkable sight, and see why the bush is not burned."
>
> When the Lord saw him coming over to look at it more closely, God called out to him from the bush, "Moses! Moses!" He answered, "Here I am." God said, "Come no nearer! Remove the sandals from your feet, for the place where you stand is holy ground. I am the God of your father," he continued, "the God of Abraham, the God of Isaac, the God of Jacob." Moses hid his face, for he was afraid to look at God. But the Lord said, "I have witnessed the affliction of my people in Egypt and have heard their cry of complaint against their slave drivers, so I know well what they are suffering. Therefore I have come down to rescue them from the hands of the Egyptians and lead them out of that land into a good and spacious land, a land flowing with milk and honey, the country of the Chanaanites, Hethites, Amorrites, Pherezites, Hevites and Jebusites. So indeed the cry of the Israelites has reached me, and I have truly noted that the Egyptians are oppressing them. Come,

12

now! I will send you to Pharao to lead my people, the Israelites, out of Egypt."

But Moses said to God, "Who am I that I should go to Pharao and lead the Israelites out of Egypt?" He answered, "I will be with you; and this shall be your proof that it is I who have sent you: when you bring my people out of Egypt, you will worship God on this very mountain."

"But," said Moses to God, "when I go to the Israelites and say to them, 'The God of your fathers has sent me to you,' if they ask me, 'What is his name?' what am I to tell them?" God replied, "I am who am." Then he added, "This is what you shall tell the Israelites: I AM sent me to you."

God spoke further to Moses, "Thus shall you say to the Israelites: The Lord, the God of your fathers, the God of Abraham, the God of Isaac, the God of Jacob, has sent me to you. This is my name forever; this is my title for all generations" (Ex 3:1–15).

Moses was a man of exceptional intellectual gifts, and, moreover, had been instructed in all the wisdom of the Egyptians at the court of Pharaoh. He was no ignorant herdsman.

Because God gave Himself a "name" in this revelation, this is equivalent to a description of His innermost being. He said of Himself: "I am who am," that is, compared with all other things in the world, I have a special kind of being: I am from Myself; there exists between Me and other things a great wall of partition: these have been created by Me and are dependent upon Me their creator; I am self-sufficient and unchangeable, while all other things have been created by Me and are changeable.

The statement that God created all things and is Lord of all will be true in the same sense forever; but man's knowledge of the creation and his insights into the laws governing nature and the mental and bodily life of man will alter.

For example, at the time when the Israelites were in the wilderness, men did not know about radio or the atom bomb but, had they known of these things, they would have remained firm in their affirmation that even these powers of nature come from God — man is able only to discover and apply the already existent powers of nature, he cannot create new ones.

Because in the world around him man is constantly finding paths which lead him toward God, there have been, even in heathen times, great men who have borne amazing witness to God. Euripides the Greek playright says: "In vain does human cleverness pit itself against God — what our fathers have bequeathed to us from olden time — that remains in order, no sophistry can overturn it — even if the mind were to storm the summit of knowledge."

Cicero, the great Roman orator, says: "The question as to whether or not there is a God, as it appears to me at least, admits of no discussion. For what can be so plain and clear as the truth, that there must exist an all-wise and intelligent being by whom all things are ruled? If someone asserted that he did not understand this, then I should as easily believe that he doubted the existence of the sun."

Likewise, in the modern age of scientific research there have been men who were at once men of science and men of faith. For example, Justus von Liebig, the pioneer teacher in the sphere of chemistry, in his book *Chemistry in Its Application to Agriculture and Physiology* (1840), writes thus: "Truly, the greatness and wisdom of the Creator will only be genuinely recognized by him who makes the effort to read the thoughts of God in that great book which we call nature."

The study of nature, which leads honest men to God, can mislead men of frivolous or proud mind into regarding themselves as lords of the powers of nature. These, through idolatry of nature, lose all sense of God. To these apply the words of Scripture:

> For all men were by nature foolish who were in ignorance of God, and who from the good things seen did not succeed in knowing him who is, and from studying the works did not discern the artisan; but either fire, or wind, or the swift air, or the circuit of the stars, or the mighty water, or the luminaries of heaven, the governors of the world, they considered gods. Now if out of joy in their beauty they thought them gods, let them know how far more excellent is the Lord than these; for the original source of beauty fashioned them. Or if they were struck by their might and energy, let them from these things realize how much more powerful is he who made them. For from the greatness and the beauty of created things their original author, by analogy, is seen (Wis 13:1–5).

Because the world, as the creation of God, has no permanence in itself, God must uphold and guide it every moment with the same omnipotence by which He created it.

God is the Uncreated Creator, Lord and Sustainer of all created things. Without Him no one can be completely happy. He is our Father in heaven.

Even the great heathen minds recognize that the questions about God and immortality are more important than all others. Aristotle, the Greek philosopher, says: "The slightest knowledge of the Divinity is higher than the greatest knowledge of all other things."

Revealed truth and true scientific knowledge can never contradict one another. It is possible, however, that in individual cases the ultimate relationship between the results of scientific study and individual truths of faith are not yet or never will be capable of clarification. In these cases they must be stated with caution.

The Life of the Individual. Nature does not lead man automatically into the realm of spiritual truth, but by the observation of nature, man can reach it. Man must not merely seek out laws (that is the task of science) but must reflect upon nature and its laws, inquiring about the ultimate cause. The famous physicist Max Planck drew attention to this fact, which is all too frequently overlooked, when he said that the natural sciences may well be able to establish countless isolated facts but can never make any statement about how all these things came into existence.

The Life of the Church. The Church declared emphatically at the First Vatican Council that the existence of God can be known from the created world. By doing this it insisted that all those objections which obstruct man's approach to God, overemphasizing difficulties and making the proofs of God's existence seem inadequate, are answerable, the results of a one-sided and pessimistic appraisal of human intelligence. It must always be remembered that man's own weakness will incline him to be deceived by a kind of atheism. Apropos of this, Pope Pius XII, in his encyclical *Humani Generis,* says:

> In the abstract, to be sure, man's reason is genuinely capable of apprehending certain truths by its own natural power, its own natural light. It can have well-grounded and certain knowledge about the existence of one God, a personal Being, who watches over and controls the world of His providence; about the existence of a natural

law written in our hearts by Him who created us. But this inborn faculty — can it be used effectively, can it produce results? There are many obstacles, to be encountered. The truths we have to learn about God and man are truths which wholly transcend this visible order of things, and truths of that kind, if they are to be translated into human action, call for self-surrender and self-sacrifice. Meanwhile, the human mind is hampered in the attaining of such truths, not only by the impact of the senses and of the imagination, but by disordered appetites which are the consequences of the Fall. What wonder if men who are faced by such problems persuade themselves, all too readily, that any conclusion which is unwelcome to them personally is groundless, or at best uncertain?

We have to admit, then, the moral necessity of a revelation from God. Without that, religious and moral truths, which of their own nature lie within the scope of human reason, cannot be apprehended promptly, with full certainty, and without some alloy of error, in the state of mankind.

It is the same with the Catholic faith. It is, sometimes, not without difficulty that a man makes up his mind in favor of its credentials. True, God has provided us with an amazing wealth of external evidence by which the divine origins of the Christian religion can be brought home without question, even to the unaided light of reason. But a man may be so blinded by prejudice, so much at the mercy of his passions and his animosity, that he can shake his head and remain unmoved; not only the evidence of external proofs, which is plain to the view, but even the heavenly inspirations which God conveys to our minds, can go for nothing.

4. THE ATTRIBUTES OF GOD: WAYS TO KNOWLEDGE OF GOD

IN NATURE there are things which man cannot immediately grasp in their unity and greatness. For example, man cannot take in the measureless expanse of the ocean at one glance. How much more must the greatness of God baffle his intellect! All that he can ever contemplate are isolated attributes of God. On the other hand, many things point back to God as the author of all being.

1. Certain attributes of God can be traced from nature which surrounds us and from the laws which we see ruling therein — the great solar systems which fill the universe, and the atom which again represents a kind of solar system, the flight-mechanism of the mosquito and the wax cell of the bee, the tissue of a stem and the laws of crystallization. These all point to the omnipotence, the wisdom, and the beauty of God.

God certainly could have created a much simpler world. He could have created only one kind of rock, one plant, one animal; and to all alike — including man — He could have given but the one color, gray for example. But, as the Greeks said, God created the world as *Kosmos,* as something which, in its complexity and unity, manifests a beauty to which everything contributes.

Hence the Psalmist declares:

> Praise him, sun and moon;
>   praise him all you shining stars.
> Praise him, you highest heavens,
>   and you waters above the heavens.
> Let them praise the name of the Lord,
>   for he commanded and they were created.
>
> (Ps. 148:3–5)

Jesus points to the order and beauty of the created world as something which leads us to God, when He says: "Observe the lilies in the field! How they grow. They do not toil or spin; and yet, I tell you, even Solomon in all his glory did not dress like one of these" (Mt 6:28).

2. Conscience enables man to know from within the holiness and justice of God.

Man has an immediate knowledge that there are things which are good and things which are evil. The heathen poet Sophocles says: "There are compelling laws which, although not written down, persist."

God is this lawgiver; He is the Holy One. He has nothing to do with sin, into which man sees himself to have fallen.

3. When, through revelation God made contact with men, He spoke of Himself. He confirmed first of all those attributes which man had been able to recognize from creation and from conscience. Over and above this, He made known to man those attributes of His nature, which move man especially to love and trust in his Creator. God revealed Himself as the most true, the most faithful, the kindest and most merciful God.

The passages from Holy Scripture which follow indicate a series of attributes to which God Himself testifies.

The Eternity of God

> Before the mountains were begotten
> and the earth and the world were brought forth,
> from everlasting to everlasting you are God.
> (Ps 89:2)

The Unchangeableness of God

> Of old you established the earth,
> and the heavens are the work of your hands.
> They shall perish, but you remain
> though all of them grow old like a garment,
> Like clothing you change them, and they are changed,
> but you are the same, and your years have no end.
> (Ps 101:26–28)

The Omnipresence of God

> If I go up to the heavens, you are there,
> if I sink to the nether world, you are present there.

If I take the wings of the dawn,
if I settle at the farthest limits of the sea,
Even there your hand shall guide me,
and your right hand hold me fast.
(Ps 138:8–10)

The Omniscience of God

More tortuous than all else is the human heart, beyond remedy; who can understand it? I, the Lord, alone probe the mind and test the heart, to reward everyone according to his ways, according to the merit of his deeds (Jer 17:9–10).

The Omnipotence of God

O Adonai, Lord, greatest art thou, and glorious in thy power, and no one can overcome thee.

Let all thy creatures serve thee, because thou hast spoken, and they were made. Thou didst send forth thy spirit, and they were created, and there is no one that can resist thy voice (Jdt 16:16–17).

The Wisdom of God

How manifold are your works, O Lord!
In wisdom you have wrought them all —
(Ps 103:24)

The Holiness of God

After the model of the Holy One who called you, become yourselves holy in your entire conduct. So it is written, "You shall be holy, because I am holy" (1 Pt 1:15–16).

The Justice of God

But as you are just, you govern all things justly; you regard it as unworthy of your power to punish one who has incurred no blame (Wis 12:15).

The Goodness of God

Can a mother forget her infant, be without tenderness for the child of her womb? Even should she forget, I will never forget you. See, upon the palms of my hands I have written your name; your walls are ever before me (Is 49:15–16).

The Faithfulness of God

Heaven and earth will fail; my words will never fail (Mt 24:35).

The Mercy of God

As I live, says the Lord God, I swear I take no pleasure in the death of the wicked man, but rather in the wicked man's conversion, that he may live. Turn, turn from your evil ways! (Ez 33:11.)

The climax of the revelations which God has given is the incarnation of the Son of God in Jesus the Redeemer of mankind. The revelations of the old Covenant are not complete in themselves, but are intended to prepare for the appearance of the Son of God in the world; He was the completion of the old and with Him the end of time began. St. Paul, therefore, contrasts the old and new Covenants in these words:

In many fragmentary and various utterances, God spoke of old to our ancestors through the prophets; at the present time, the final epoch, he has spoken to us through his Son, whom he has appointed heir of the universe. Through him, too, he made the world. This Son is the radiant reflection of God's glory, and the express image of his nature, conserving all things by his mighty command. After he had cleansed us from sin, he took his seat at the right hand of the Majesty on high (Heb 1:1–3).

God has revealed to men only those mysteries whose knowledge brings salvation. The mysteries of faith are, therefore, interrelated; they constitute the divine order of salvation. Although men cannot comprehend the various mysteries, they are able to recognize how these supplement one another and form a unity, surrounding the innermost being of God like luminous clouds.

The most important mysteries of faith are these:

1. The mystery of the Holy Trinity
2. The mystery of grace
3. The mystery of sin
4. The mystery of the Incarnation
5. The mystery of Redemption
6. The mystery of the presence of Christ in the Holy Eucharist.

The knowledge of the attributes of God from creation, from the voice of conscience, and from the revelation of God Himself, combines to form a living unity in the man of faith.

Man can attain to knowledge of God in various ways:
Observation of the creation shows men the omnipotence, wisdom, and
beauty of God.
The experience of his own conscience convinces man of the holiness
and justice of God.
God Himself has testified that He is most kind, most merciful, most
true and faithful.
The climax of the revelations comes with the incarnation of the Son
of God in Jesus Christ, the Redeemer, who is the "interpreter" of
the Father (Jn 1:18).

The Life of the Individual. In nature there are things which we
cannot explain; they present, as we say, mysteries. But it is a fact
that things which remain a mystery can be of great importance to men
and come to have an immediate bearing upon their lives. There is no
scientist, for instance, who can create a single grain of wheat from
which a stalk bearing ears of corn could sprout. Although the wheat
germ which hides life within itself remains a mystery, no one imagines
that it is something worthless.

The same is true of many other mysteries of nature. Men cannot
answer the questions: What is electricity? What is light? What is
matter? What is plant life? What is animal life? But the inability to
answer these questions does not in the least prevent men from valuing
these things and using them all for their own ends.

For the inner life of man the mysteries of faith assume an importance similar to that of the mysteries of nature for the natural
world. We will always be incapable of comprehending the mysteries
of faith; even after their revelation by God they remain beyond our
comprehension. In spite of this, those mysteries provide the source
from which man's spirit draws nourishment, just as his bodily life
receives the mysterious gifts of nature.

As has been said, man can draw near to God in several ways,
but the knowledge which he thus gains is integrated in a single insight.
Thus when a man moves from unbelief to belief, there is in one
moment a coalescence of various equally valuable insights, impressions,
and experiences, which he has gained over a period of years.

On the other hand, when a man first calls himself an unbeliever, we have the result of many deeds and omissions, whose significance would become clear to him only if he again returned to the Faith.

The Life of the Church. In the world the Church has the strangest task imaginable. To the most gifted intellect and to the most backward child in a school for mental defectives, it must proclaim those truths which are inexplicable mysteries.

The Church, therefore, teaches the mysteries of revelation to the faithful, not so much by scholarly lectures as through those *events* in Holy Scripture in which they were revealed. Even in the construction of its worship the Church keeps to this rule; it desires to fill men not with cold knowledge but with respect and love for God.

The idea of God which simple people who attend the worship of God regularly have may very often surpass that of educated people who set aside the directions of the Church on this matter. Our Lord Himself alluded to this when He said:

> "I praise you, Father, Lord of heaven and earth, for hiding these things from wise and prudent men and revealing them to little ones!" (Mt 11:25.)

5. THE ARMY OF INVISIBLE SPIRITS, COMPANIONS OF MEN

BEFORE CREATING MAN, God had already created countless other beings. These resembled men, having intelligence and free will; but they also differed from men, being pure spirits without bodies.

These creatures are the angels. The word "angel" derives from a Greek word meaning *messenger*.

Angels are not omniscient; but they do comprehend things much more quickly and thoroughly than any man ever can. Similarly, their will is much stronger than man's. Whatever an angel wills, he wills with immense strength. In a manner appropriate to spirits, angels are beautiful beyond anything we can imagine. Light, with its magnificent play of color, is the nearest comparison we can make to this beauty. Therefore angels are said to appear to men in a gleam of splendid light.

We do not know how angels converse with one another. But it is clear that their manner of communication is far more perfect than that of men, and that they influence one another much more effectively than is possible with men. Men have to make themselves understood through external means, through speech and gestures.

In addition to their natural beauty, God gave the angels a supernatural beauty. He permitted them to participate in His divine life; but they were to earn the bliss to which He had destined them by an act of obedience.

Many theologians put forward the view that God allowed them to see Jesus as the Son of God in human form, and demanded that they worship Him as Lord of the creation. However that may be, many angels disobeyed God. And so the angels are divided into good and bad. On account of their strong will, the good angels were forever confirmed in goodness; and the wicked were given over forever to evil.

From the beginning, God had appointed the angels as messengers between Him and men. After the division into good and bad angels, the original vocation of the angels changed. The good angels became messengers of God, the bad angels became servants of Lucifer, the first of all the fallen angels.

Man, therefore, is never quite alone. Good and bad spirits are at his side. The good urge him to fulfill the will of God: the bad try to seduce him into rejection of God. In doing this, the latter keep their purpose secret: they make it appear that they have a greater concern for men than God has; that they will grant him more freedom and joy. In return for renunciation of God, they treacherously promise him a happiness which is greater than that to be found in the service of God.

Jesus speaks in deadly seriousness of the power which the devil can gain over man. He says to the Pharisees:

> "The father whose sons you are is the devil, and you are bent on carrying out the wishes of your father. He proved himself a murderer at the very beginning, and did not loyally stand by the truth; in fact, there is no spark of truth in him. Whenever he gives utterance to his falsehood, then he gives expression to his real character; for he is a liar and the father of lies" (Jn 8:44).

God has given the good angels a special task. They are not placed merely at the service of men in general. God appoints a particular angel to guard over each man from his birth until his death. Jesus speaks expressly of the angels who accompany the "little ones" and who "look continually upon the face of my Father in heaven" (Mt 18:10).

During his exile on the Isle of Patmos, the evangelist St. John had a vision in which the relationship of the angels to men was revealed. John narrates:

> Then war broke out in heaven. Michael and his angels had to fight the dragon; the dragon fought, and so did his angels. But they were defeated, and a place was no longer found for them in heaven. That huge dragon, the ancient serpent, was hurled down, he who is called the devil and Satan, he who leads the whole world astray. He was hurled down to earth, and his angels were hurled down with him.

Then I heard a loud voice in heaven. "Now the salvation which God brings about," it said, "his power and royalty, and the authority of his Christ have been established because the accuser of our brothers has been hurled down, he who accused them before our God day and night. But they conquered him by means of the blood of the Lamb and the word of their testimony, and because they despised life even to the point of being willing to die. Therefore, be glad, O heaven, and you who dwell there. Perdition to you, O earth and sea, because the devil has gone down to you in a great rage, since he knows how brief is the time he has" (Ap 12:7–12).

In this picture the following things are set before us: the good angels stand by God's side and pledge themselves to the honor of God. They consider men their brothers, being creatures of God closely related to themselves because they have will and intellect. Consequently they show themselves bound to men in fervent love.

The bad angels stand united as a hostile power against God. They hate and envy men with all the strength of their will; and, summoning up all of their insight into the nature of man in general and into the situation of each individual, they seek to injure man. But as they are not permitted to go about their business openly, they work by fraud and deception.

Man is not so alone in the world as would appear:

Before creating man, God created countless spiritual beings. The spirits which persevered in obedience to Him are called angels: the spirits who rose up against Him and who, as a result, were thrust down to hell, are called devils.

All men are susceptible to the influence of both *good* and *bad* spirits. Concerning *good spirits* — God has appointed to each man an angel to accompany and protect him. Holy Scripture warns us against the snares of the *bad spirits* in the words:

Be sober, watchful! Your adversary, the devil, like a roaring lion, prowls about looking for someone to devour (1 Pt 5:8).

The Life of the Individual. Why is it that so many men no longer think of their guardian angels nor call upon them more frequently for help in temptation? It can only be because they have ceased to take these truths of faith seriously.

The Life of the Church. As incarnate Son of God, Jesus is not merely Head of all creation but is also Head of the angels. Therefore, at every celebration of the holy Sacrifice of the Mass, the Church unites the faithful with choirs of angels, and brings them into joint homage before God. Many Prefaces, therefore, conclude with the words: "through Christ Our Lord. Through Whom the angels praise Your Majesty, the Dominations worship it, the Powers stand in awe. The heavens and the heavenly hosts together with the blessed Seraphim in triumphant chorus unite to celebrate it. Together with them we entreat You, that You may bid our voices also to be admitted, while we say in lowly praise: Holy, holy, holy, Lord God of Sabaoth! Blessed is He who comes in the Name of the Lord! Hosanna in the highest!"

6. MAN, APPOINTED BY GOD TO BE LORD OF THE EARTH; HIS SHARE IN THE DIVINE LIFE

THE DIFFICULTY of understanding the biblical narratives becomes greater the farther removed we are from the times in which they were written. It is natural, therefore, that the interpretation of the early sections of Holy Scripture which tell of the creation of the world, of paradise, of the Fall and of the first promise of the Redeemer, turns out to be specially troublesome.

The meaning of these sections of Holy Scripture shines out most clearly if we imagine a father in days long past telling his children about God. The narrative runs thus:

In the beginning God created the heavens and the earth; the earth was waste and void; darkness covered the abyss, and the spirit of God was stirring above the waters.

God said, "Let there be light," and there was light. God saw that the light was good. God separated the light from the darkness, calling the light Day and the darkness Night. And there was evening and morning, the first day.

Then God said, "Let there be a firmament in the midst of the waters to divide the waters." And so it was. God made the firmament, dividing the waters that were below the firmament from those that were above it. God called the firmament Heaven. And there was evening and morning, the second day.

Then God said, "Let the waters below the heavens be gathered into one place and let the dry land appear." And so it was. God called the dry land Earth and the assembled waters Seas. And God saw that it was good. Then God said, "Let the earth bring forth vegetation: seed-bearing plants and all kinds of fruit trees that bear fruit containing their seed." And so it was. The earth brought forth vegetation, every kind of seed-bearing plant and all kinds of trees that bear fruit containing their seed. God saw that it was good. And there was evening and morning, the third day.

And God said, "Let there be lights in the firmament of the heavens to separate day from night; let them serve as signs and for the fixing of seasons, days and years; let them serve as lights in the firmament of the heavens to shed light upon the earth." So it was. God made the two great lights, the greater light to rule the day and the smaller one to rule the night, and he made the stars. God set them in the firmament of the heavens to shed light upon the earth, to rule the day and the night and to separate the light from the darkness. God saw that it was good. And there was evening and morning, the fourth day.

Then God said, "Let the waters abound with life, and above the earth let winged creatures fly below the firmament of the heavens." And so it was. God created the great sea monsters, all kinds of living, swimming creatures with which the waters abound and all kinds of winged birds. God saw that it was good, and God blessed them, saying, "Be fruitful, multiply, and fill the waters of the seas; and let the birds multiply on the earth." And there was evening and morning, the fifth day.

God said, "Let the earth bring forth all kinds of living creatures: cattle, crawling creatures and wild animals." And so it was. God made all kinds of wild beasts, every kind of cattle, and every kind of creature crawling upon the ground. And God saw that it was good.

God said, "Let us make mankind in our image and likeness; and let them have dominion over the fish of the sea, the birds of the air, the cattle, over all the wild animals and every creature that crawls on the earth."

God created man in his image. In the image of God he created him. Male and female he created them.

Then God blessed them and said to them, "Be fruitful and multiply, fill the earth and subdue it. Have dominion over the fish of the sea, the birds of the air, the cattle and all the animals that crawl on the earth." God also said, "See, I give you every seed-bearing plant on the earth and every tree which has seed-bearing fruit to be your food. To every wild animal of the earth, to every bird of the air, and to every creature that crawls on the earth and has the breath of life, I give the green plants for food." And so it was. God saw that all he had made was very good. And there was evening and morning, the sixth day.

Thus the heavens and the earth were finished and all their array. On the sixth day God finished the work he had been doing. And he rested on the seventh day from all the work he had done.

God blessed the seventh day and made it holy because on it he rested from all his work of creation (Gn 1:1–2:3).

We must realize that this description of creation is poetic and not scientific. The author, illumined by the Holy Spirit and using the language of those far-off days, presents first and foremost the basic fact that man possesses an inward soul which gives him a resemblance to God.

For Adam and Eve in paradise, the command not to eat from the tree of the knowledge of good and evil signified a religious trans-action which constituted a sacrifice. At that time Adam and Eve fed on the fruits of the garden. If they left untouched the fruit of any particular tree this implied that God, and not themselves, was Lord of all. In their situation how could Adam and Eve have made a sacrifice in any other way?

> The Lord God planted a garden in Eden, to the east, and he put there the man he had formed. The Lord God made to grow out of the ground all kinds of trees pleasant to the sight and good for food, the tree of life also in the midst of the garden, and the tree of the knowledge of good and evil (Gn 2:8–9).

> The Lord God took the man and placed him in the garden of Eden to till it and to keep it. And the Lord God commanded the man thus, "From every tree of the garden you may eat; but from the tree of the knowledge of good and evil you must not eat; for the day you eat of this you must die" (Gn 2:15–17).

The following basic facts hold of the relation of God to man and of man to God:

God created heaven and earth, with all of the laws operating in them, in perfect freedom and out of nothing; therefore He is described as the Creator of heaven and earth.

It follows from the intimate relation of the Creator to the world which He has Created that God sustains and rules all things with that same omnipotence and wisdom by which He created them.

God has appointed the human race as a whole to be the lords of the earth and of all its blessings, treasures, and powers.

Man's *natural dignity* consists in his having been created in the image of his Creator and in particular, in being an intelligent and free moral agent, a person.

Man's soul is immaterial and immortal; we know this from God's revelation and from reason.

Man's *supernatural dignity* consists in his having been raised by sanctifying grace to the status of an heir of God.

At first Adam and Eve lived in paradise; there they enjoyed special privileges; they were exempt from suffering and their bodies were immortal.

The Life of the Individual. In various ways men forget the consequences of the fact that they did not create themselves but are *creatures of God*. Many erroneous conceptions have their ultimate, hidden root in this; and men overlook something else too: the fact *that the love which God has for the creatures, which His own omnipotence has made, must be of a depth and power of which man has no conception.*

An old folktale recounts how a father who had to inflict a burn on his child in order to save it from poisoning, first of all thrust the glowing iron into his own arm. What this tradition tells is a dull reflection of what God has done. In order to make His love comprehensible to men He used human speech and caused Himself to suffer the greatest possible pain. He sent His Son into the world and allowed Him to die as the Redeemer upon the cross so that, at the sight of this supreme suffering, all impious murmuring before God would cease in the hearts of all men whom pain terrifies.

The Life of the Church. In *Humani Generis* Pope Pius XII drew up the following guiding statements for the exposition of the first eleven chapters of the Bible: "The first eleven chapters of Genesis, although it is not right to judge them by modern standards of historical composition, such as would be applied to the great classical authors, or the learned of our own day, do nevertheless come under the heading of history; in what exact sense, it is for the further labors of the exegete to determine. These chapters have a naive, symbolical way of talking, well suited to the understanding of a primitive people. But they do disclose to us certain important truths, upon which the attainment of our eternal salvation depends, and they do also give a popularly written description of how the human race, and the chosen people in particular, came to be. It may be true that these old writers of sacred history drew some of their material from the stories current among the people of their day. So much may be granted; but it must be remembered on the other side that they did so under the impulse of divine inspiration, which preserved them from all error in selecting and assessing the material they used."

According to this, then, a distinction is clearly to be made between the statements concerning the *origin of the body* and those concerning the *creation of the soul*, which we find in the Creation story.

The question now arises: How are we to understand what is said about the formation of the body of the first man? In an address (1943) Pope Pius XII expressed the attitude of the Church to this question in these words: "On the part of the Church, it has not yet been finally settled, what the relevant passages of Scripture affirm; on the other hand, science has not succeeded in explaining the question unequivocally from its side, and we may well have to wait some time before we have results which are ascertained and recognized on all sides. As long as investigators are not unanimous the Church cannot make their assumptions the basis for the interpretation of a Scriptural text which is still not quite clear. On the other hand, because of this, the way is open for every Catholic scholar to busy himself with the investigation of this problem." The same principle was stated in *Humani Generis* in the following words: "Thus the Church leaves the doctrine of Evolution an open question, as long as it confines its speculations to the development, from other living matter already in existence, of the human body. (That souls are immediately created by God is a view which the Catholic faith imposes on us.) In the present state of scientific and theological opinion, this question may be legitimately canvassed by research, and by discussion between experts on both sides." The encyclical emphasizes, however, that such investigations must be undertaken with due seriousness and moderation and maintains that this study is guilty of neglect if the established evidence and the conclusions drawn from it are treated as exhaustive proof of such a kind that it can be harmonized without further ado with the words of Holy Scripture.

"However the still disputed question be settled, the basic facts remain as the Church's settled teaching: the first man, as a being consisting of body and soul, came into existence through the immediate operation of God's creative power, and each human soul is created directly by God in that moment when the mother conceives the child in her womb.

"Resembling the question of the creation of the human body is that of *the age of the human race*. No definite sequence of years can be produced from holy Scripture from the time of Adam and Eve down to the present day; there are marked variations among present-day scientists in their estimates of the age of the human race. Besides this, the discoveries of atomic study show us that our notion of the evolution of the world after the creation can suddenly change. It is quite possible that sometime in the future the age of the human race will be reliably determined.

"It was the *soul* which was 'breathed into' the first man. In this way, in the language of those for whom the narrative was written, the soul is described as something invisible, as a spirit created directly by God.

"To conclude from the fact that the condition of the brain affects the process of thought, that the brain generates thoughts as mists are formed over warm water, is totally invalid. Foerster says rightly: 'The independence of the soul can neither be proved nor yet denied in the laboratory. Or is materialism already proved if the physiologist demonstrates to us that in the moment when the cortex degenerates or a particular part of the brain tissue is removed by the surgeon's knife the corresponding mental function is extinguished? May we deduce from this fact that mind is only a function of matter? No, nothing is proved by this physiological fact except that in this earthly life the soul's powers can only affect the material world through the mediation of nerve tissue. If these mediating organs are disturbed, whether by surgical operation or by the degeneration of disease, then the spiritual function too is naturally interrupted — but it would be utterly unscientific to conclude from that disturbance, that the mind's power is merely a product of brain matter.' "

7. THE SIN OF OUR FIRST PARENTS

WE MUST PICTURE Adam and Eve either as gifted but inexperienced adults or as grownup children. The command which God gave them suited their condition. But the devil, too, considered their condition when he tempted them. Holy Scripture relates:

> Now the serpent was more cunning than any beast of the field which the Lord God had made. He said to the woman, "Did God say, 'You shall not eat of any tree of the garden'?" The woman answered the serpent, "Of the fruit of all the trees in the garden we may eat; but 'Of the fruit of the tree in the middle of the garden,' God said, 'you shall not eat, neither shall you touch it, lest you die.'"
> But the serpent said to the woman, "No, you shall not die; for God knows that when you eat of it, your eyes will be opened and you will be like God, knowing good and evil." Now the woman saw that the tree was good for food, pleasing to the eyes, and desirable for the knowledge it would give. She took of its fruit and ate it, and also gave some to her husband and he ate. Then the eyes of both were opened, and they realized that they were naked; so they sewed fig-leaves together and made themselves coverings (Gn 3:1-7).

Satan put his first question so as to fill Eve with distrust of God. Adam and Eve were permitted to eat from every tree with one exception: but the devil's question suggested that this was the only tree which really counted. The trap worked. By allowing herself to see all things out of perspective, Eve felt aggrieved and saw in this small prohibition an indication that God did not love them. And so in her heart she had already turned away from God.

Now the devil could risk a blatant lie; he said, "No, you shall not die; for God knows that when you eat of it, your eyes will be opened and you will be like God, knowing good and evil."

"God envies you!" said the devil, himself devoured with envy. And today he does the same thing.

Eve ate and gave to Adam. The longing to be like God came over

33

him. If the serpent's promise were true, then he, Adam, would become the real God of this world.

Immediately after sinning, Adam and Eve knew that they themselves had changed. Evil exercised a new power over them: it was like a piece of themselves. They knew that it was wrong, and yet they loved it.

Holy Scripture tells all this very briefly and points to a single case of the way sin showed its effect. After the fall, Adam and Eve were ashamed of their nakedness; they were no longer inwardly sure of themselves as formerly.

The human race still forms a unity in Adam. Just as an assurance made to a father has its significance for his children also, so Adam's obedience and disobedience has decisive significance for his posterity. As Adam could have won for all: so now he lost for all.

The sin of our first parents in paradise is the root and prototype of all the sins of men.

The devil was a *murderer from the beginning.* Jesus Himself describes him thus, because in paradise he tempted the first man to sin and thereby snatched away man's birthright at its source.

The preliminary to the first sin was distrust of God; distrust is the preliminary to every sin.

The strongest urge in Adam and Eve to consent to sin was the longing to be equal to God, that is — pride. In every sin that is committed lurks an element of pride.

The Life of the Individual. The first impulse toward sin in paradise consisted in Adam and Eve's allowing themselves to be duped by Satan into thinking that what God had forbidden could still turn out to be good. Such fateful self-deception will ever provide the first impulse to sin.

Bearing this fact in mind we reach the conclusion that the battle against temptation consists first and foremost in protecting ourselves against self-deception. The propensity to self-deception is, however, so deep in every man that his idea of what his own true life should be is often the product of deceitful fantasy. Therefore everyone who wishes to guard against self-deception must wholeheartedly surrender his whole self. Jesus puts it this way: "He who wins a reprieve from death must part with his life at any rate; but he who freely parts with his life for my sake will win it in the end" (Mt 10:39).

The Life of the Church. In the course of the centuries the Church has several times had to defend the doctrine of the cooperation of God's grace with man's free will against erroneous theories. This happened first of all in the time of St. Augustine. Pelagius and others at that time said that the human will could perform supernatural acts of itself. According to Pelagius, grace does not make possible a new kind of action but only makes easier that action which man is already able to do by himself.

In the Middle Ages, several theologians overemphasized the power of evil passions to obstruct grace. This led to heresies about the relation between grace and the will. At the Council of Trent the Church opposed these errors with the traditional doctrine of justification which is set out clearly.

In more recent times the Church has condemned Quietism which presents the Christian's spiritual life so exclusively as a work of the Holy Spirit that men's cooperation seems to be entirely unnecessary.

The necessity for man to cooperate with the grace of God is indicated by the following words from Pope Pius XII's encyclical on the Mystical Body of Christ: "But the unremitting perseverance of men in works of holiness, their eager progress in grace and virtue, and their strenuous efforts, not only to reach the summit of Christian perfection themselves but also, in the measure of their power, to spur others to a similar achievement — all these effects the heavenly Spirit will not produce unless those men do their part with constant and energetic application. 'Divine blessings,' says St. Ambrose, 'are not granted to those that sleep but to those that watch.' If the members of our mortal body gain strength and vigor from continual exercise, still more is this so in the social Body of Jesus Christ, in which each member retains his own liberty, conscience, and way of acting. And therefore the same Paul who said: 'True, I am living, here and now, this mortal life; but my real life is the faith I have in the Son of God,' said also: 'Only by God's grace I am what I am, and the grace he has shown me has not been without fruit; I have worked harder than all of them, or rather, it was not I, but the grace of God working with me' (1 Cor 15:10)."

8. GOD'S SENTENCE UPON SATAN AND UPON THE PARENTS OF THE HUMAN RACE

WHOEVER TAKES THE STORY of the Fall to heart and asks himself what Adam and Eve should have done immediately after this misfortune befell them will say: Why did Adam and Eve not immediately confess their sin with sorrow and ask forgiveness?

The man who sins is himself under the law of sin. He is inwardly deformed by the sin which he commits; he tries every possible way of justifying himself and of representing himself as not really sinful. Holy Scripture tells us:

But the Lord God called the man and said to him, "Where are you?" And he said, "I heard you in the garden, and I was afraid because I was naked; and I hid." Then he said, "Who told you that you were naked? You have eaten then of the tree of which I commanded you not to eat." The man said, "The woman you placed at my side gave me fruit from the tree and I ate." Then the Lord God said to the woman, "Why have you done this?" The woman said, "The serpent deceived me and I ate."

Then the Lord God said to the serpent: "Because you have done this, cursed are you among all animals, and among all beasts of the field; on your belly shall you crawl, dust shall you eat, all the days of your life. I will put enmity between you and the woman, between your seed and her seed; he shall crush your head, and you shall lie in wait for his heel."

To the woman he said: "I will make great your distress in child-bearing; in pain shall you bring forth children; for your husband shall be your longing, though he have dominion over you."

And to Adam he said, "Because you have listened to your wife, and have eaten of the tree of which I commanded you not to eat: Cursed be the ground because of you; in toil shall you eat of it all the days of your life; thorns and thistles shall it bring forth to you, and you shall eat the plants of the field. In the sweat of your brow you shall eat bread, till you return to the ground, since out of it you were taken; for dust you are and unto dust you shall return" (Gn 3:9–19).

God's sentence of judgment upon sin is passed in a form which simply cannot be ignored. First, God turns to the prime mover of temptation, to the serpent, that is, to the devil, and tells him that in spite of this fall mankind will be raised up a second time to the state of sanctification and of adoption by God. What God announces at this time to Satan in a veiled manner, we recognize in retrospect as the first allusion to Mary, the Immaculate Conception, and to Jesus the Son of God who took human nature from her. Just as Satan's dominion originated in Eve's disobedience, so the foundation of man's redemption which was to be completed in the sacrificial death of Jesus on the cross was laid in Mary's obedience in the incarnation of the Son of God.

Not until this promise has been made and Adam and Eve have received the assurance that God would not give the human race over irrevocably to Satan's power, does God pronounce judgment upon Adam and Eve. Once the promise has been made, then the judgment follows. Sin has destroyed not merely man's relationship with God but also the relationship of men to each other. The impulse of love is no longer pure: the love of a mother for her children is no longer sheer joy; a man's work for his dependents is now a battle for existence; and the end of it all will be death.

The sin of our first parents embraced the whole human race in its consequences:

Adam and Eve and their descendants lost participation in the divine life and the right to behold God in heaven; their knowledge became uncertain and their will weak; they lost their special privileges, became subject to suffering and death, and had to leave paradise.

Adam's sin has harmed all men because by this sin the head of the race forfeited his appointed heritage and so was unable to transmit it to his posterity. We call this sin "original sin."

Before pronouncing the sentence of punishment God gave men a comforting promise that sometime Satan's power over the human race would be broken. This came about through Jesus Christ the Redeemer, the Son of God, born of Mary the Virgin.

The Life of the Individual. The man of today inclines to think morality has developed alongside culture in general. On this view, men of ancient times could have known little about God and the distinction between good and evil. If one thinks thus, then the story of the Fall cannot possibly be understood.

What Pope Pius XII had to say of the first eleven chapters of Genesis holds good in even greater measure of this story. We are here concerned with historical events in the true sense: but these are presented in language suited to the people of that far-off time. The chief characteristic of this language is its pictorial imagery. For example, the devil is quite simply described as a serpent. Jesus Himself indicates that we are to see the devil beneath the image of the serpent when He refers to the story of the Fall and describes the devil as the murderer of men from the beginning, as a liar and the father of lies (cf. Jn 8:44).

The Life of the Church. Many non-Catholics think that the Church would keep many old adherents and gain many new ones if she would only give up the doctrine of original sin or at least keep it more in the background. The Church cannot follow such counsels. Even if she did, the supposed good effect would not be produced; for then the Church could no longer explain why man, the lord of creation, is forever pursuing schemes which are doomed to end in catastrophe.

The meaning of the doctrine of original sin, which gives man back his dignity and assures him of new possibilities of rising up, has been impressively expressed by Pascal. According to him, only that religion can be true which is able to explain both man's obvious greatness and his obvious misery. He says: "The greatness and misery of man are so plain that true religion must give an explanation both of the cause of his mighty greatness and of his overwhelming distress. If it would make man happy it must show him that there is a God whom he is bound to love; it must show him that our true blessedness consists in being united with Him, and our sole misfortune in being separated from Him; it must insist how we are full of darkness which hinders us from knowing and loving Him, and how as a result we are full of unrighteousness when it should be our duty to love this God from whom we are estranged by our concupiscence.

"In short, true religion must give an account of the cause of our contrariness to God and our own good. And accordingly it must specify the remedies which correct these incapacities and must explain the means by which we obtain these remedies.

"Let us test all the religions of the world by these conditions and see if any other than the Christian religion fulfills these requirements."

Searching Scripture closely, we come upon places in the Gospels in which the Savior points out that in the last resort it is Satan who is behind the struggle in which His enemies rage against Him. In the great discourse with the scribes and Pharisees which took place on the Feast of Tabernacles He speaks of His adversaries as "children of the Devil, who was a murderer of men from the beginning," and He describes the scribes and Pharisees as the devil's accomplices who assist him to carry out his plan to oppose the Messiah. Before being taken prisoner He told the same adversaries that now their hour and the power of darkness was come and also that it was the time when the devil was going to achieve his end, the death of the Messiah, through them (cf. Lk 22:53).

9. THE HISTORY OF MAN FROM THE EXPULSION FROM PARADISE UNTIL THE APPEARANCE OF THE REDEEMER

AFTER THE FALL man's whole behavior assumed a new pattern. It was not long until many forgot the true God and put in His place idols made of earthly materials, and lifted up their hands to them in prayer, offering, sacrifice.

Men made the first discoveries; but because their hearts were more inclined toward self-assertion, lust for power, and hate than toward the service of others and love, the use of these discoveries took an evil turn. They were not used by men to help one another but to destroy one another. Hate triumphed over love.

Holy Scripture recounts only isolated cases of this trend, and as a rule these few cases are briefly mentioned without comment on the relation to original sin. But in this way Holy Scripture points out two of the most terrible consequences of original sin: the decline of the family and the emergence of war.

Men forgot about God.

But God did not forget about men.

God saw to it that faith in Him and hope for the promised Savior did not die out among men. He called Abraham out of Ur in Chaldea and made a promise to him, that from him the promised Savior, the Founder of the new kingdom of God, would proceed. With the people who had Abraham for their patriarch God made a special covenant, and gave the sons of this race careful instructions how they were to pray to Him and present sacrifice to Him, the true God. At the same time, through the prophets, God uttered oracles which, with ever increasing precision, described the coming Savior. Their prophecies spoke of Christ as a man of mysterious, divine origin, possessing divine might and priestly powers, who in His death would found a kingdom upon earth — the kingdom of God which will know no end.

The proof of God's faithfulness runs through all the Scripture of the old Covenant. In the Psalms, God is celebrated in praise, thanksgiving, and petition as the One whose mercy and faithfulness know no end; no matter how often or how deeply men go astray from Him, He does not forget them; He is forever ready to help them if only they are humbly willing to be helped. In Psalm 116, all men without exception are commanded, therefore, to praise God for His mercy and His faithfulness. It runs:

> Praise the Lord, all you nations;
> glorify him, all you peoples!
> For steadfast is his kindness toward us,
> and the fidelity of the Lord endures forever.
> (Ps 116:1–2)

The Church still sings this psalm in thanksgiving for the Redemption during the first solemn Easter service on Holy Saturday and on several great feasts of our Lord.

The temptation of paradise, the temptation of man to make himself lord of the earth and to supplant God's laws by laws of his own devising, is renewed today through the possibilities which the development of technology presents.

Each new machine increases in some way or other the material power of man, and so increases his capacity for good and for evil. As man becomes stronger, so also he becomes more terrible. If he is to keep his equilibrium he must at the same time become better day by day. Now even the most biased advocate of technology will not dare to assert that technical skill can make man not merely *stronger* but also *better*. If man is not to be hurled along by his machines from one calamity to the next, he must receive a stimulus by virtue of which he also becomes morally better. The rescue of human society from that which threatens it depends therefore upon a moral and ultimately upon a religious renewal.

It has become customary to talk of "the problem of technology." The phrase is very misleading. Technology is certainly in no way problematic; there is no sphere where everything is so accurately calculated by number, measure, and weight as in technology. The truth is that with the progress of technology the "problem of man," which was always present, becomes manifest in a degree which corresponds to the possibilities of modern technology. The "problem of man," however, consists in his not knowing for certain what is good for him; and when he does recognize what is good, in his not being able to act accordingly.

Certain dark features in man's history can be adequately explained only by original sin:

Original sin has worked itself out in the history of man so that man has time and again allowed himself to be led astray by self-love and selfishness and has placed discoveries and inventions not at the service of brotherly love, but at the service of inordinate self-love and hate. Marriage and the family declined, murder and warfare began.

The old temptation of man to make himself lord of the earth in such a way as no longer to have God over him as supreme Lord renews itself today in the possibilities which arise from the development of technology.

The Life of the Individual. Following its own scheme, Holy Scripture gives only a brief sketch of the religious development of mankind from Adam until the calling of Abraham. From the time of Abraham on, it comments several times on the great civilizations of Asia and Egypt; but it does this only insofar as these people come into contact with the people of Israel.

In recent times science has made discoveries which confirm the biblical narrative:

1. Ethnology has established that belief in God is not governed by the same law of development as human culture; it has not undergone an *evolution* which advances from the immature to the perfect; on the contrary, faith in one God, the Creator of the world, reveals itself as a primeval possession of mankind. Belief in many gods arose only upon the dissolution of monotheistic belief.

In the Tamina valley of Switzerland human settlements of the Stone Age were found in a cave in the so-called "Dragon-hole." In these caves were found reliable signs that men of that remote time brought sacrifices of thanksgiving to God out of their firstfruits.

The record of the Bible and the results of the study of the relationship of primitive man to God thus coincide.

2. The second place in which science has made valuable discoveries of this kind is in the Euphrates-Tigris region and in the region of the Nile. The reason why the history of these peoples has special significance for the interpretation of Holy Scripture is that the land of Israel lay between these regions and that in their cultural development the Israelites had always been influenced by the peoples who dwelt there.

The Life of the Church. In its attitude to sin, the Church differs from the world in a threefold way: (*a*) The Church knows of no reconciliation with sin in the sense of a truce. (*b*) In the battle against sin the Church possesses powers which are hers alone by which she is able to combat and expose evil. (*c*) The Church does not wait to judge sin when its evil results begin to be admitted by all. For example, she rejected both unrestrained capitalism and all forms of totalitarianism whether Fascist or Communist, at a time when many people still hoped for an earthly paradise through their means.

For the Church, it is always the removal of inward spiritual evil — sin in man's heart — which is of primary importance.

10. JESUS CHRIST THE SON OF GOD, THE MEDIATOR BETWEEN GOD AND MAN

IN JESUS CHRIST, the Second Person of the Trinity appeared on earth as man. This fact determines the Catholic Faith. Jesus Christ is not merely the wisest, the kindest, the holiest of men — He is the Son of God; He is wisdom, goodness, and holiness; He is the beginning and the end.

On one occasion three Apostles, Peter, James, and John, had a glimpse of the heavenly life of Jesus in the majesty of His Father from whom He had been sent into the world so that mankind might not be lost but might have eternal life (cf. Jn 3:15–16).

Holy Scripture tells us:

> Six days later, Jesus took Peter, James, and John with him and led them up a high hill to be in a group by themselves. Here he changed his appearance before their eyes: his garments became an exceedingly brilliant white, such as no dyer on earth can produce by bleaching. Moreover, Elias and Moses were seen by them, and they were conversing with Jesus. Then Peter felt moved to say to Jesus: "Rabbi, it is well that we are here. Let us put up three tents — one for you, one for Moses, and one for Elias." Really, he was at a loss for appropriate words: they were so afraid. Then a cloud formed and enveloped them, and a voice rang out in the cloud: "This is my beloved Son. Listen to him!" Suddenly looking round, they saw no one but Jesus alone with themselves.
>
> As they were going down the hill, he enjoined them not to tell anyone what they had seen till after the Son of Man should have risen from the dead (Mk 9:2–9).

But after many years St. Peter can still speak in awe about the

44

Transfiguration upon the mountain as the incident in which the divinity
of Jesus had revealed itself before them and when it had been testified
by the heavenly Father.

We were certainly not following cunningly devised myths when
we made known to you the power and coming of our Lord Jesus
Christ. On the contrary, we were eyewitnesses of his majesty. The
fact is, he received from God the Father honor and glory when
out of majestic splendor there came this voice:
"This is my beloved Son,
    with him I am well pleased."
We ourselves heard this very voice as it came from heaven when
we were with him on that holy mountain.
We have besides the firmly established message of the prophets.
You do well to be attentive to it. It is like a lamp shining in a dark
place until the day dawns and the morning star rises in your hearts
(2 Pet 1:16–19).

Several times Jesus Himself mentioned that He had been sent by
the Father. This occurred, for example, when Nicodemus the member
of the Sanhedrin came by night to Jesus and listened to His words
with hesitant caution. In front of him, Jesus asserted that He knew
the mysteries of God from His own experience because He came
from heaven.

"I tell you the plain truth: we speak what we know, and testify
to what we have seen; but you all refuse to accept our testimony!
If I have told you of earthly things and you refuse to believe, how
will you believe if I tell you of heavenly things! Of course, no one
has ever ascended into heaven; but mind — there is one who has
come down from heaven, the Son of Man, whose home was in
heaven!
"And just as Moses lifted up the serpent in the desert, so the
Son of Man must needs be lifted up, that everyone who believes in
him may have eternal life." So marked, indeed, has been God's love
for the world that he gave his only-begotten Son: everyone who
believes in him is not to perish, but to have eternal life. The fact is,
God did not send the Son into the world to condemn the world.
Not at all; the world is to be saved through him. He who believes
in him is not liable to condemnation, whereas he who refuses to
believe is already condemned, simply because he has refused to
believe in the name of the only-begotten Son of God. And this is
how the sentence of condemnation is passed: the light has come

into the world, but men loved the darkness more than the light, because their lives were bad (Jn 3:11–19).

In the moment of His Incarnation, the Son of God at once became the Head of the human race — capable of suffering. In this role He took it upon Himself to offer a sacrifice of reconciliation for the whole human race. He willed that His own life, His own body, should be the victim for this sacrifice. This humiliation to which He subjected Himself voluntarily was followed later by His exaltation by the Father.

Therefore St. Paul sums up the redemptive work of Jesus Christ in these words:

> He is by nature God, [yet] did not consider his equality with God a condition to be clung to, but emptied himself by taking the nature of a slave, fashioned as he was to the likeness of men and recognized by outward appearance as man. He humbled himself and became obedient to death; yes, to death on a cross. This is why God has exalted him and given him the name above all names, so that at the name Jesus everyone in heaven, on earth, and beneath the earth should bend the knee and should publicly acknowledge to the glory of God the Father that Jesus Christ is Lord (Phil 2:6–11).

Original sin became the circumstance which revealed the love of God to men in a new way.

God the Father showed His love for men after the sin in paradise by sending His Son into the world as Head of the human race, to free all men from sin and to call them through grace into a life of interior union with God.

The Life of the Individual. On His entering into the world, the love of Jesus was already directed to humanity not merely as to a great family, but toward each individual. When Paul says of himself that Jesus "loved me and sacrificed himself for me" (Gal 2:20), the saying applies to all men without exception.

St. Gregory the Great expresses the thought of the love of God which extends both to the individual and to all, in the words: "God's providence reaches out to a soul as well as to a whole city; to a city as well as to the whole human race. The Lord cares for each individual as though He had nothing else to bother about, and at the same time cares for all as though He were not bothering about the individual."

Truly, a Christian may never yield to despondency, complaining that no one loves him. A Christian may never show a halfhearted trust in God, as though God's love had still to prove itself.

The Life of the Church. Since the days of the Apostles the Church has resolutely maintained faith in the divinity of Christ. This faith is the foundation of her preaching and the soul of her prayer. All of those religious societies which separated themselves from her in earliest times concur in belief in the divinity of Christ. For this faith the Sign of the Cross became the symbol of Christianity and has remained so until this day.

11. THE INCARNATION OF CHRIST THE SON OF GOD, THE NEW UNION BETWEEN HEAVEN AND EARTH

JESUS, the only-begotten Son of God, could have become man, suddenly appearing upon earth as an adult. Among the people of Israel there were in fact those who maintained that the Redeemer would be let down upon the temple court from heaven and from there would establish the new kingdom of David.

As Holy Scripture says, however, the Son of God was to become like man in everything except sin. Thus He was to have a mother within whom He should begin life. And so an individual, the mother of Jesus, took up an interior and an exterior relationship to the redemption of man.

Of that hour, when this came to pass, Holy Scripture tells us:

> In the course of the sixth month, the angel Gabriel came with a message from God to a town in Galilee called Nazareth. He was to speak to a virgin espoused to a man named Joseph, a descendant of David. The name of the virgin was Mary. On coming into her presence, he said: "Greetings! child of grace! The Lord is your helper! You are blessed beyond all women!" But she was profoundly disturbed by the address, and debated within herself what this greeting might mean. So then the angel said to her: "Do not tremble, Mary! You have found favor in the eyes of God. Behold: you are to be a mother, and to bear a son, and to call him Jesus! He will be great: 'Son of the Most High' will be his title, and the Lord God will give to him the throne of his father David. He will be king over the house of Jacob forever, and to his kingship there will be no end!"

Then Mary replied to the angel: "How will this be, since I am a virgin?"

In explanation the angel said to her: "The Holy Spirit will come upon you, and the power of the Most High will overshadow you. For this reason the child to be born will be acclaimed 'Holy' and 'Son of God.' Note, moreover: your relative Elizabeth, in her old age, has also conceived a son and is now in her sixth month — she who was called 'the barren'! Nothing indeed is impossible with God." Then Mary said: "Regard me as the humble servant of the Lord. May all that you have said be fulfilled in me!" With that, the angel left her.

In those days Mary set out in haste to go into the mountains to visit a town of Juda. There she entered the home of Zachary and greeted Elizabeth. The moment Elizabeth heard the greeting of Mary, the babe in her womb leaped, and Elizabeth, inspired by the Holy Spirit, exclaimed in a ringing voice: "Blessed are you beyond all women! And blessed is the fruit of your womb! How privileged am I to have the mother of my Lord come to visit me! Hear me now: as the sound of your greeting fell upon my ears, the babe in my womb leaped for joy! Happy is she who believed that what was told her on behalf of the Lord would be fulfilled!" (Lk 1:26–45).

The angel commanded Mary to give the Redeemer the name *Jesus.* Jesus, in Hebrew, means: Savior, Redeemer, Bringer of Salvation, Rescuer. For Mary it was, therefore, as though the angel were saying, "You are to call him the *Redeemer.*"

The angel declares two things about the Redeemer: " 'Son of the Most High' will be his title," and "to his kingship there will be no end."

Mary's consent, "Regard me as the humble servant of the Lord. May all that you have said be fulfilled in me!" contains an unreserved surrender to the office of motherhood. Just as a faithful servant carries out all of her master's orders as they come, so Mary accepts in advance all that the office of motherhood of the Redeemer will mean.

Her cousin Elizabeth was the first person to greet the mother of the Redeemer, and the Redeemer Himself. On this occasion, enlightened by the Holy Spirit, she spoke of the Child and again of the mother as of a unity. Mary and Jesus are God's Blessed Ones in a world of sinners.

Elizabeth was also the first to describe Mary as the Mother of God when she said: "How privileged am I to have the mother of my Lord come to visit me!" And the Lord she spoke of was God.

By taking upon herself the motherhood of Jesus the Son of God for the sake of the Redemption, Mary, in the moment of her consent, entered into a spiritual relationship with all who are in need of redemption and became at the same time the spiritual mother of all who were to be redeemed.

All the graces which Mary received from the first moment of her life were for herself and also for her office as the mother of the Redeemer and spiritual mother of all the other children of Eve.

Holy Scripture speaks of a special decree of the love of God (Eph 1:3–5) which we understand to be the mystery of the Incarnation of Christ.

In a miraculous way the Son of God took flesh of the Virgin Mary by the power of the Holy Spirit. This constituted the beginning of the *Self-emptying* of the Son of God. In this hour there dawned for the world the fullness of the time when all things in heaven and on earth were to be gathered together in Christ as their Head (cf. Eph 1:10).

The *Self-emptying* of the Son of God by His Incarnation destroys the very worldly conception of the Redeemer as an earthly potentate. The true Savior redeems souls.

God the Father has placed Mary beside the divine Redeemer of mankind, as a companion (Pius XII). As she was preserved from original sin at the beginning of her life, so at its end she was assumed, body and soul, into heaven.

By her consent to be the mother of Jesus the Redeemer, Mary entered also into a relationship with all the redeemed, and became their spiritual mother (Pius X) who accompanies them on their way to heaven and to Christ.

The Life of the Individual. By her assent to the Incarnation, Mary has become our mother also. The love with which she did this became apparent on Calvary when her Son offered up His life, a sacrifice upon the cross. In these hours of suffering she suffered along with Jesus for our sake; moreover, for our sake she consented to the sacrificial death of Jesus, thus denying her own rights as a mother. A mother who has accepted so much for our sake will never forget us; it is she who suffers when we forget her. Therefore we should persevere faithfully in remembering her and asking her to make intercession for us with her Son.

The Life of the Church. In devotion to Mary two features are found alongside one another. First, Mary was sent from God to be the mother of Jesus. She thus stands in the closest union with Jesus. Yet Mary is still a creature like other men; her response to the message of the angel Gabriel should be ours too: "Regard me as the humble servant of the Lord."

Second, Mary was taken, body and soul, to heaven. Thus she occupies the first rank among men, and all honor is hers. In the *Magnificat,* Mary herself foretold this kind of veneration when she said: "Behold, from this age onward age after age will call me blessed."

Finally, the article of Faith concerning Mary's bodily assumption into heaven provides protection against the prevailing mood of our time, when the belief in progress which characterized the nineteenth century has turned to despair. In certain forms of Existentialism, this despair of finding a higher meaning in life has found philosophic dress. According to this philosophy, man's greatness consists in his coming to terms with the meaninglessness of life which reveals itself in the vain attempt to make a paradise of the world. The Church, or rather the Holy Spirit within the Church, points out across the present darkness of the world to Mary, who was taken up, body and soul, into heaven. Man is destined in body and soul for an eternal life and for a glory which exceeds all the joys of an earthly paradise.

12. THE BIRTH OF THE REDEEMER JESUS CHRIST IN THE STABLE AT BETHLEHEM

THE EARLY HISTORY of Jesus as handed down in the Gospel according to St. Luke is controlled by the thought that according to God's plan the Redeemer was to come into the world and grow up as a member of a family. For this reason the mother of God consented to accept motherhood, being at the time betrothed to St. Joseph. St. Joseph thereafter took Mary along with her Child into his home on the basis of lawful marriage.

Externally these events are woven into the political life of the times.

The Romans had taken over many administrative practices from the Egyptians. One of these was the custom of compiling a new census periodically; and the ancient records of Egypt show that this numbering was usually done after the harvest. In Palestine, the harvest fell in October. The enrollment was made, as Luke observes, not according to the place of residence, but according to the place of clan affiliation; and so St. Joseph had to report with Mary at Bethlehem. Thus the word of the prophet was fulfilled:

> But you, Bethlehem-Ephratha, too small to be among the sons of Juda, from you shall come forth for me one who is to be ruler in Israel (Mi 5:1).

While they were in Bethlehem the Redeemer was born: the birth took place during the first night.

The evangelist St. Luke writes:

> Long before that day a decree had been issued by order of Caesar Augustus that a census of the whole world should be taken. This census was the first to take place while Cyrinus was in charge of Syria.
>
> Accordingly, the people went, each to the city of his ancestor, to be registered; and so Joseph, too, being a member of the house and

family of David, went up from the town of Nazareth in Galilee to David's town in Judea, called Bethlehem, in order to be registered. He was accompanied by his espoused wife Mary, who was with child. In the course of their stay there, the time came for her delivery; and she gave birth to her first-born son. She wrapped him in swaddling clothes, and laid him in a manger, because there was no accommodation for them in the lodging.

In the same region shepherds were camping in the open and keeping watch over their flocks by night. Suddenly, an angel of the Lord stood facing them, and the glory of the Lord shone round about them, so that they were struck with terror. "Do not fear," the angel said to them. "Listen: I am bringing you good news of great joy which is in store for the whole nation. A Savior, who is the Lord Messias, was born to you today in David's town! And this will serve you as a token: you will find an infant wrapped in swaddling clothes and cradled in a manger." All of a sudden, the angel was joined by a crowd of the heavenly host, praising God with the strain:

"Glory to God in the heavens above,
and on earth peace to men of good will" (Lk 2:1–14).

On the slope near the Church of the Nativity, there are caves still used by nomadic people as dwellings. The position of the church makes it appear very probable that the stable was situated in the park which still belongs to the hospice.

The adoration which Mary offered up to the Child was mankind's first greeting to its Redeemer. Because Mary assumed the motherhood of the Redeemer for the sake of all mankind, she greeted Jesus, mindful of all who were to be redeemed by Him.

The shepherds to whom the angels brought the glad tidings of the Savior's birth were men who regularly spent the night in the open with their flocks.

At the angel's command, Joseph fled with Mary and the Child into Egypt shortly after the appearance of the wise men. When danger was past they returned to Nazareth — now the secret hub of the universe — and Jesus grew up there. He became an ordinary trades-man and then, at the age of about thirty, began His public ministry.

The earthly life of Jesus began in lowliness and obscurity.

Jesus was born at Bethlehem in a stable.

The Son of God continued the Self-emptying which began with His

Incarnation and birth by following the trade of an artisan until His thirtieth year, in order to be like men in all things. The Son of God lived like countless numbers of ordinary people.

The Life of the Individual. We can repeat a hundred times that Jesus lived for thirty years as a carpenter in a little Palestinian town, but in spite of that we still do not think about it enough. Those who live in the same circumstances, and for that reason are best able perhaps to imitate the Lord, think all too little about it. On the other hand, those also think too little about it who are better off, and who should let themselves be taught by the example of Jesus, learning that it is not the sort of work but the spirit in which it is done which is important in God's sight.

The Life of the Church. On December 25, the Church celebrates the feast of the Nativity of Christ, emphasizing the adoration of the shepherds. This festival goes back to about A.D. 300 when the Roman Church, after heathen worship of the sun as *Sol invictus* had declined, began to defer the birthday of Christ, the "Sun of Righteousness," until the winter solstice.

The second Christmas festival, the Epiphany, puts the coming of the three wise men from the East into the center of the picture. On the evidence of Clement of Alexandria, this feast was already known in A.D. 200. From the fourth century the feast of the Epiphany was kept in the West also. In the East Christmas was adopted about A.D. 400.

Originally the festival of Christmas supplanted the heathen festival of the solstice in southern lands and thus became integrated with the natural solar year. Today the danger is more or less present everywhere that in the celebration of Christmas, the Christian idea of the feast will be supplanted by an excess of secular spirit. We do well, therefore, to learn from a Preface, dating from the time of the introduction of the feast of Christmas, how the early Christians allowed that wonderful happening, the birth of Christ, to rule over the darkness of nature's night and to become a spiritual light. This is the text of the Preface: "O God, Thou hast blessed this coming night, which is to be holy above all nights, with the message of the angel, for the joy of heaven and the renewal of earth, so that in the incarnation of Thy Son our Lord Jesus Christ, both the great and the humble alike may rejoice.

Look down, therefore, upon Thy family who entreat Thee: protect the people who sing praise unto Thee and let them watch through the solemnities of the approaching night, that with faithful hearts we may be counted worthy to know the day of our Lord's birth. For He who in His essence is invisible has now appeared in our flesh: He who is one with Thee, who was not created in time, who is not less perfect in His nature than Thou, has come to us, being born in time. Through Him we have forgiveness of sins, and the resurrection is no longer denied us. Therefore, as is most justly due, the whole world adores and praises Thee. Thee also the highest heavens praise, and the angelic powers unceasingly cry out: Holy! Holy! Holy!"

13. THE BAPTISM OF JESUS: THE MYSTERY OF THE MOST HOLY TRINITY REVEALED

THE RELIGION OF ISRAEL, the people of the revelation, was vastly superior to the religions of neighboring peoples — the Assyrians, the Babylonians, and the Egyptians. Nevertheless the Israelite conception of God still made God seem distant and unapproachable. A change appeared for the first time with the New Covenant in the "fullness of time."

In the introduction to his Gospel, St. John clearly expresses the immense difference between the revelation of God in the old and new Covenants. In this solemn, poetic introduction he speaks of the Incarnation of the Son of God:

> When time began, the Word was there,
> and the Word was face to face with God,
> and the Word was God.
> This Word, when time began,
> was face to face with God.
> All things came into being through him,
> and without him there came to be
> not one thing that has come to be.
> In him was life,
> and the life was the light of men.
> The light shines in the darkness,
> and the darkness did not lay hold of it.
> There came upon the scene a man,
> a messenger from God,
> whose name was John.
> This man came to give testimony —
> to testify in behalf of the light —
> that all might believe through him.
> He was not himself the light;
> he only was to testify in behalf of the light.

Meanwhile the true light,
  which illumines every man,
  was making its entrance into the world.
He was in the world,
  and the world came to be through him,
  and the world did not acknowledge him.
He came into his home,
  and his own people did not welcome him.
But to as many as welcomed him
  he gave the power to become children of God —
  those who believe in his name;
who were born not of blood,
  or of carnal desire,
  or of man's will;
  no, they were born of God.
And the Word became man
  and lived among us;
  and we have looked upon his glory —
  such a glory as befits
  the Father's only-begotten Son —
  full of grace and truth!
John testifies in his behalf,
  and the cry still rings in our ears:
    "This is the one of whom I said:
    'The one expected to follow me
    takes precedence over me,
    because he was in existence before me.'"
And of his fullness
  we have all received a share —
  yes, grace succeeding grace;
for the Law was granted through Moses,
  but grace and truth have come
  through Jesus Christ.
On God no man ever laid his eyes;
  the only-begotten Son,
  who rests in the Father's bosom,
  has himself been the interpreter (Jn 1:1–18).

By "interpreter" St. John means one who initiates us into the being of God as though previous knowledge had been somewhat superficial. The new knowledge which Jesus interprets leads into the innermost being of God.

The first revelation of the mystery of the Most Holy Trinity took

place at the baptism of Jesus, immediately, that is, before the start
of His public ministry.

St. Matthew relates:

> At that time Jesus arrived from Galilee to meet John at the
> Jordan and be baptized by him. John tried to stop him. "It is I who
> should be baptized by you," he said, "and you come to me?" Jesus
> remonstrated. "Let me have my way for the present," he said to
> him; "after all, it is only so that we fulfill, as is proper for us, all
> just demands." Then he let him have his way.
>
> No sooner was Jesus baptized, than he came up out of the
> water, and there and then the heavens opened to his view: he saw
> the Spirit of God descend in the shape of a dove, and alight on
> him. And a voice rang out upon the air:
> "This is my Son, the beloved,
> with whom I am well pleased" (Mt 3:13–17).

A revelation of the mystery of the Most Holy Trinity had become
necessary. Without knowledge of this mystery, the course of the
Redemption could not be understood at all. Only because there are
three Persons in the Godhead was redemption of man possible by the
Incarnation of the second Person of the Godhead, who thereby became
the Head of the human race and thus made atonement for all and
canceled the sin of the world. In this way the mystery of the Trinity
represents not only the mystery of God's intrinsic nature, but also
the mystery upon which is constructed the divine order of salvation
which raises man up to share once more by grace in the divine life.
Through Jesus, man's life is drawn up into the life of the Most Holy
Trinity. Inspired by this thought, the evangelist St. John breaks into
this utterance in his first letter:

> We proclaim what was from the beginning, what we have heard,
> what we have seen with our own eyes, what we have gazed upon,
> and what we have embraced with our own hands. I refer to the
> Word who is and who imparts life. Indeed, this Life has mani-
> fested himself. We ourselves have seen and testify and proclaim
> that Eternal Life which was with the Father and has manifested
> himself. To you we proclaim what we have seen and heard, that
> you may share our treasure with us. That treasure is union with
> the Father and his Son, Jesus Christ. I write this to you that we
> may have joy in the fullest measure (1 Jn 1:1–4).

He who has no love does not know God, because God is love. God's love was made manifest among us by the fact that God sent his only-begotten Son into the world that we might have life through him. This love consists not in our having loved God but in his having loved us and his having sent his Son as a propitiation for our sins (1 Jn 4:8–10).

The deep mystery of the Most Holy Trinity has to be revealed before the Redemption can be understood. The mystery of the Most Holy Trinity was first revealed at the baptism of Jesus.

God the Father called out from heaven over Jesus: "This is my Son, the beloved, with whom I am well pleased." *God the Son* allowed himself to be baptized by John. *The Holy Spirit* came down upon Jesus in the form of a dove.

In God, there are three Persons. The three divine Persons are called the Father, the Son, and the Holy Spirit; together the three divine Persons are called the Trinity. Each divine Person is true God, but there is only one God.

In the Sign of the Cross we acknowledge our belief in the Most Holy Trinity and in Redemption through Jesus Christ, the second Person of the Trinity.

The prayer in praise of the Most Holy Trinity is: "Glory be to the Father and to the Son and to the Holy Spirit, as it was in the beginning, is now and ever shall be, world without end."

The Life of the Individual. Do you sign yourself with the Sign of the Cross every morning and every evening? What are your secret thoughts as you make it? Do you make the "Glory be" a prayer of thanksgiving and praise?

The Sign of the Cross with the invocation of the Most Holy Trinity is a sign of our belief. Today, the Sign of the Cross is joined with the words: "In the Name of the Father, and of the Son, and of the Holy Spirit. Amen." But in the Liturgy there are isolated formulae from olden times which are still in use. An example of this is the association of the Sign of the Cross with the verse of the Psalm, "O God, come to my assistance, O Lord, make haste to help me," with which all of the Church's prayer offices begin.

The speed with which the use of the Sign of the Cross became common in the daily life of Christians is shown by a saying of Tertullian (A.D. 200): "Going out and coming in, putting on our clothes or our shoes, washing, at table, on lighting the lamp, on going to sleep, and at every sort of work which we perform, we impress the Sign of the Cross upon our foreheads."

The Life of the Church. The Sign of the Cross, as the sign of the Most Holy Trinity, accompanies a man from the cradle to the grave. In the Name of the Father and of the Son and of the Holy Spirit he receives Baptism. In the presence of death the Church prays: "If he has sinned, yet has he not denied You, the Triune God." At the open grave the Church prays: "With heavenly dew may God refresh your soul, with heavenly fragrance may He nourish it, in the Name of the Father and of the Son and of the Holy Spirit."

Every Sunday is a day of the Most Holy Trinity. This is expressed, among other ways, by the Church giving praise to the Trinity, God, Father, Son, and Holy Spirit, in the common Preface for most Sundays of the Christian year. The Preface in honor of the Most Holy Trinity runs thus:

It is truly meet and just, right and available to salvation, that we should always, and in all places, give thanks to You, O Lord, holy Father, almighty, eternal God. Who together with Your only-begotten Son and the Holy Spirit, are one God and one Lord: Not in the singleness of one Person, but in a trinity of one substance. For what we believe of Your glory as You have revealed, the same we believe of Your Son, and of the Holy Spirit, without any difference or distinction. That in the confession of the true and eternal Deity may be adored a distinction in the Persons, a unity in the essence, and an equality in the majesty.

14. THE PUBLIC APPEARANCE OF JESUS, THE MEDIATOR SENT FROM THE FATHER

AFTER HIS BAPTISM Jesus took to the wilderness and in fasting and prayer prepared Himself for His public ministry.

The public activity of Jesus began with His preaching the good news of the coming of the Kingdom of God. This coming consisted in His destroying the power of Satan, thus enabling everyone to free himself from sin and to serve God, his true Master.

From the first days of His appearance Jesus describes Himself as the "Son of Man." Jesus chose to describe Himself by this name, which the prophet Daniel had conferred upon Him as Redeemer, because it denoted the Messiah.

In the course of His public ministry Jesus began to speak more plainly about Himself. He claimed divine power, power to forgive sins; He called Himself Lord of the Sabbath; He called God His Father in a way which no ordinary man could: "I and the Father are one."

The sermons of Jesus did not affect all in the same way. The good clung to Him, the hardhearted opposed Him from the start and persecuted Him with growing hatred.

Throughout the whole land of Israel, the appearance of Jesus caused great spiritual excitement. What to think of Jesus became a public issue. The dominant feeling of the time is expressed in the following sentences by the Apostle John:

> But when the Jewish feast of Tabernacles was near, his brothers said to him: "Quit this part of the country and go to Judea. Your disciples, too, should see what you are doing. Nobody, surely, acts in secret and, at the same time, wants to be in the public eye. Since you are having such success, show yourself before the world."

61

Even his brothers, by the way, did not believe in him.

"My time," replied Jesus, "is not yet at hand; but your opportunity is always ready to hand. The world cannot hate you. It does hate me, because I expose its wickedness. You may go to the feast; I am not going up to this feast; my time has not quite come as yet." After saying this, he himself tarried in Galilee.

However, when his brothers had gone up to the feast, then he, too, went up, not so as to attract attention, but incognito. The Jews, therefore, made search for him at the feast. "Where is this man?" they asked. There was also much whispering among the crowds. Some said: "He is a good man." Others said: "Not at all; he leads the masses astray." No one, however, expressed his opinion of him openly, because of their fear of the Jews.

By the time the feast was half over, Jesus went up to the temple to teach. The Jews were puzzled. "How is it," they said, "that this man is able to read? He has had no regular schooling!" In explanation, therefore, Jesus said to them: "My teaching is not my own invention. It is his whose ambassador I am. Anyone in earnest about doing his will can form a judgment of my teaching, to decide whether it originates with God, or whether I speak my own mind. He who speaks his own mind is looking for his personal glory; but he who looks for the glory of him whose ambassador he is, is truthful and not given to deception" (Jn 7:2–18).

Jesus confirmed His teaching by miracles and prophecies. There was a distinctive quality about them when compared with the miracles and prophecies of earlier men of God. While the prophets acted through prayer and in the name of God, Jesus relied upon His own power. He commanded the wind and the waves. "I will: be clean," He said to the leper. "Young man, I tell you arise," He commanded the widow's dead son. More than this, the miracles of Jesus are very much an expression of His sacred humanity; they reveal His kindness, love, and mercy.

What is said of the miracles of Jesus applies also to His prophecies. Jesus knew the secrets of men's hearts: from His own knowledge He announced coming events and here, too, the prophecies issued from the love of His Sacred Heart.

Even the prophecy of the destruction of Jerusalem and of the Last Day arose from His love.

The way in which Jesus performed His miracles in order to confirm that He had been sent from the Father, and the way in which men remained free, in spite of these miracles, to accept or reject His teaching, all becomes clear, for example, on the raising of Lazarus.

Then Jesus, his inmost soul shaken again, made his way to the tomb. It was a cave, and a stone lay against the entrance. "Remove the stone," Jesus said. "Master," Martha, the dead man's sister, said to him, "his body stinks by this time; he has been dead four days." "Did I not tell you," replied Jesus, "that, if you have faith, you will see the glory of God?" So they removed the stone. Then Jesus lifted up his eyes and said: "Father, I thank you for listening to me. For myself, I knew that you always hear me; but I said it for the sake of the people surrounding me, that they might believe that I am your ambassador."

Having said this, he cried out in a strong voice: "Lazarus, come forth!" And he who had been dead came forth, wrapped hand and foot with bands, and his face muffled with a scarf. Jesus said to them: "Unwrap him and let him go" (Jn 11:38–44).

All who were present at the raising of Lazarus, and all who heard of the miracle, were beside themselves with astonishment. And yet it was this very miracle which incited the Scribes and Pharisees to the highest pitch of hatred.

Why did some not believe Jesus? After the death of Jesus this question exercised the mind of St. John the evangelist until the end of his life.

As an old man St. John saw both in the opposition of enemies and in the devotion of the disciples an expression of response to Jesus.

Struck by the mystery of man's opposition to God he then wrote:

"And this is how the sentence of condemnation is passed: the light has come into the world, but men loved the darkness more than the light, because their lives were bad. Only an evildoer hates the light and refuses to face the light, for fear his practices may be exposed; but one who lives up to the truth faces the light, so that everybody can see that his life is lived in union with God" (Jn 3:19–21).

What happened in Jesus' own time repeats itself from generation to generation, from year to year, from Sunday to Sunday. It is repeated in vaulted cathedral and in little chapel. As long as the teaching of Jesus is preached there will be people who are inwardly touched by it because they are men of goodwill, and there will always be people who seek to avoid it because they refuse to refrain from evil.

The hidden life of Jesus at Nazareth was followed by His public activity:

Jesus began His public activity at about thirty years of age.

Jesus testified to the truth of His teaching by His holy life, His miracles, and His prophecies.

The words and miracles of Jesus compelled men to decide either to declare themselves for Him or against Him. Jesus Himself made this plain in the words: "He who is not with me is against me and he who does not gather with me scatters" (Lk 11:23).

According to Jesus' teaching, the world as it stands is *neither completely perfect nor completely ruined and lost.* Jesus knows about the evil in the world and its power; but He also knows that victory is with God and with those who are on His side. The Christian view of life is thus neither *optimistic* nor *pessimistic* but *realistic.*

The Life of the Individual. Every man has the capacity to accept the Word of God or to reject it. As a remedy against slipping back into the state of separation from God, Jesus has specially provided the Blessed Sacrament. Of this Jesus declares simply and categorically: "Unless you eat the flesh of the Son of Man and drink his blood, you have no life in you. . . . He who eats my flesh and drinks my blood is united with me, and I am united with him" (Jn 6:54, 56).

To insure that we never become separated from God, we must remain in union with Jesus Christ.

The Life of the Church. Since Pentecost, when it began its outward career, until the present day, the Church has always displayed the same characteristics as marked Jesus throughout His life. Before the end of the world, according to the Apocalypse, the time of antichrist will come. In the eyes of the world, the Church will appear to be destroyed. But as His individual desolation on Good Friday was followed by the victory of His Resurrection on Easter so will the time of the Church's humiliation be followed by the final triumph of Christ in His Church.

15. THE SACRIFICIAL DEATH OF JESUS UPON THE CROSS, ATONEMENT FOR THE SIN OF THE WORLD

THE SUFFERING OF JESUS is a mystery: it is beyond our full understanding because it is part of the mystery of the sacred humanity of Jesus.

It is true that Jesus endured His suffering in the most perfect, the most sensitive human nature: but He took it upon Himself not as a human being but as the second Person of the Trinity. Hence these sufferings can never be compared with the sufferings of any man, however extraordinary he may be.

Furthermore, Jesus bore His suffering with a readiness which is impossible for other men. For Him, the Son of God, living in eternity and from all eternity, every moment of earthly existence depended upon His own consent. Each pain which He accepted was, therefore, something He underwent of His own free will.

The Gospels show that Jesus described His suffering, death, and glorification, to His enemies and friends alike, as those events which were to constitute the spiritual climax of His life.

The way in which Jesus spoke about it to His enemies and to His friends is certainly different. The proclamations to His enemies bear a note of warning; in the announcements to His friends, on the other hand, we observe how Jesus is preparing them spiritually for the day of His Passion.

Jesus addressed His opponents, the Scribes and Pharisees:

"Brood of vipers! How can you say anything good when you are wicked! After all, a man's speech is but the overflow of his heart. A good man dispenses what is good from his store of good things, and a wicked man dispenses what is wicked from his store of wicked things. I tell you, moreover, that of every loose and random word which men speak they must give an account on Judgment Day. Yes, by your word you will be pronounced innocent, and by your word found guilty."

Some of the Scribes and Pharisees were provoked. "Rabbi," they said to him, "we want to see you give a proof of your claims." He answered their challenge by saying: "A headstrong and adulterous nation demands a proof of my claims! But a proof will not be given it except the proof which Jonas gave; just as Jonas spent three days and three nights in the belly of the sea monster, so the Son of Man will spend three days and three nights in the heart of the earth.

"Ninevites will rise at the Judgment together with this nation and put it in the wrong, for on the preaching of Jonas they changed their evil ways. And observe, there is something more than Jonas here! A queen of the South will rise at the Judgment together with this nation and put it in the wrong, for she came from the ends of the earth to listen to the wisdom of Solomon. And observe, there is something more than Solomon here!" (Mt 12:34–42.)

According to the Gospels, during the second half of His public life Jesus spoke three times in the presence of His friends the disciples, predicting His suffering and death. Matthew records these three announcements in the following words:

1. Prophecy of suffering:

From that time on Jesus began to make plain to his disciples that it was necessary for him to go to Jerusalem, suffer much at the hands of the elders, high priests, and Scribes, be put to death, and on the third day rise again (Mt 16:21).

2. Prophecy of suffering:

They were still wandering about in Galilee when Jesus said to them: "The Son of Man is to be betrayed into the hands of men: They will put him to death and he will rise again on the third day" (Mt 17:22–23).

3. Prophecy of suffering:

As Jesus was going up to Jerusalem, he took the twelve disciples aside for the sake of privacy, and on the way said to them: "Listen!

We are going up to Jerusalem, where the Son of Man will be betrayed to the high priests and Scribes, and they will condemn him to death, and hand him over to the Gentiles to mock and scourge and crucify; but on the third day he will rise again" (Mt 20:17-19).

During His suffering, Jesus time and again gave proof that He stood above His suffering and willingly took it upon Himself as a great work to which He was devoted with His whole soul. With authority He showed the soldiers on the Mount of Olives that He could prevent His capture. Then, voluntarily, He endured the scourging, the crowning with thorns, the crucifixion, and again voluntarily He hung, as St. Mark expressly points out, for three hours upon the cross (cf. Mk 15:25, 33). As death drew near He looked back upon His Passion as a work which the Father had given Him to do and cried out: "It is now completed" (Jn 19:30).

The suffering and death of Jesus in atonement for men was carried out in the form of a solemn act of expiation, in the form of a sacrifice. This had been announced in advance by John the Baptist when he said: "Behold the Lamb of God who takes away the sin of the world." Jesus Himself had declared that He would lay down His life for many, that is, for all men (cf. Mt 20:28).

In the first days of Christianity the word "redemption" had quite a different effect upon men's minds than it has today. While this word has no longer any connection with everyday life, in those days it reminded all who heard it of a specific well-known practice. The Greek word *exagorazo,* which we translate by "redeem," when used of human beings, denotes the buying of a slave's freedom. Slaves could actually be bought in the marketplace — thus removing the previous master's right of disposal. It is Satan, the lord of this world, who is the master whose power of disposal is purchased by the death of Jesus. The new Master whose property man becomes through Redemption is, accordingly, Jesus Christ Himself, "our Lord."

Because mankind was redeemed by the death of Jesus Christ, the spiritual foundation of the Church coincides with His death. The Council of Vienne (1311) stated as a doctrine of faith that in the moment when the heart of Jesus was pierced with the lance, the "one immaculate, virgin, holy Mother Church came into being the Bride of Christ."

The grace which has been available for men since the death of Christ and the question of how men can become sharers in the grace of Christ are discussed in the second part of this book.

The hour of Jesus' death is the climax of His mission and of human history:

In His death upon the cross Jesus consummated His Self-renunciation. The suffering and death of Jesus may not be compared with the suffering and death of other men because Jesus is not mere man but both God and man.

In that hour when Jesus offered Himself a sacrifice for men upon the cross, the Redemption of the world was accomplished.

Jesus Christ redeemed men from sin and from the dominion of Satan. He led them back into a life of supernatural fellowship with God, God's love offered again to men, even the very greatest of the gifts which had been lost in paradise through sin.

By the Redemption the condition of the world was altered in a twofold respect:

1. By virtue of the Redemption through the sacrificial death of Jesus Christ it is once more possible for man to enter into the supernatural life of fellowship with God.

2. Sufferings and death, which after the Fall were inflicted as punishment, are now, in imitation of the suffering and death of Jesus Christ the Redeemer, steps on the way to participation in the glory of Jesus Christ in heaven.

Men can share in the graces which Jesus has won through His sacrificial death, by faith in Jesus and love for Jesus, by receiving the holy sacraments, and by taking part in the holy Sacrifice of the Mass.

The Life of the Individual. Jesus suffered unspeakably in body and soul, out of love for men. By this excess of suffering He wishes to touch their hearts, win their love, break through their distrust and coldness, and bring them to repentance, to turn away from their sin into His faithful service.

No matter how many or how great sins you may have committed,

Jesus' greatest grief would be in your failure to repent and your refusal to be moved to repentance by His love.

The Life of the Church. In Holy Week we recall the Passion and Death of Christ the Redeemer. The Church sets before the eyes of the faithful the events in the Passion of Jesus as they happened.

Holy Thursday is dedicated to the institution of the blessed Sacrament and to the memory of the Agony; Good Friday to the Death of Jesus upon the Cross; Holy Saturday anticipates the Mass of the Resurrection which is celebrated (as in olden time) in the night between Saturday and Easter Sunday.

The Church makes a rule that every Christian receive the Blessed Sacrament worthily during the Easter season. All who call themselves Christians ought, during Easter time, to recall the Death of Christ and spiritually celebrate the Resurrection with Him.

16. THE RISEN JESUS, VICTOR OVER SIN AND DEATH

AFTER HIS DEATH our Lord descended into "hell"; that is to say, when His soul had left His body, united with the Godhead, it appeared to the souls of the just who had died in grace and who were waiting for union with God. The souls of the just, already departed, were the first to know the joy of the new age of salvation.

Easter morning came, the dawn of the new order of Salvation. In the Resurrection, the redemptive work of Christ was completed. For this reason the Church sings the Easter Mass with solemn festivity: through His death, Christ our Lord has annihilated death, and through His Resurrection has given life back to us.

Early in the morning, Jesus the Son of God reunited His soul with the body and blood which He had sacrificed for men. There were no witnesses. After this had happened an angel came down from heaven: the earth trembled and the soldiers in front of the sepulcher fell to the ground as though struck by lightning.

The result of the angel's appearance was that the women could approach the sepulcher unhindered. They were the first to whom the angel announced the great message of joy.

When the Sabbath had passed, Mary Magdalen, Mary the mother of James, and Salome bought spices in order to go and anoint him. At a very early hour in the morning on the first day of the week, they set out for the tomb and arrived at sunrise. Now, they had been saying to one another: "Who will roll away for us the stone at the entrance of the tomb?" when, straining their eyes, they saw that the stone had already been rolled away. It certainly was very large.

On entering the tomb, they saw a young man seated at the right, dressed in a white robe; and they were frightened. But he said to them: "Do not be frightened. You are looking for Jesus the Nazarene, the Crucified. He is risen; he is not here. Look, here is the place where they laid him to rest. Go now, and say to his disciples, in particular to Peter: 'He is going to Galilee to await you there; there you are going to see him, just as he has told you.'" (Mt 16:1–7).

So she ran and came to Simon Peter and to the other disciple, whom Jesus loved, and said to them: "They have taken the Lord out of the tomb! We do not know where they have laid him!" Thereupon Peter and the other disciple left the house and set out for the tomb. The two started running together; but the other disciple ran faster than Peter and was the first to reach the tomb. He stooped to look in and saw the linen cloths lying there; but he did not enter. In due time Simon Peter, who had been following him, arrived and went into the tomb. He looked at the cloths lying there, and at the scarf, which had been round his head, not lying with the cloths, but folded up in a separate place. Then the other disciple, who was the first to reach the tomb, also went inside, and because of what he saw, believed. They had not as yet understood the Scripture text which says that he must rise from the dead. The disciples then left for home (Jn 20:2–10).

St. John takes trouble to describe clearly the position and the condition of the cloths which convinced him that Jesus had risen. What John is telling us in this sentence becomes clear if we bear in mind what the same evangelist narrates of the burial of Jesus. The body of Jesus had been wrapped in linen bands, and for this at least sixty-six pounds of spices had been used. The sticky oils had sealed up the bands into a cloth shell which enveloped the body. As with Lazarus, a headcloth had been wound over the head. In a glorified state Jesus had broken through this shell without unrolling the band or the headcloth. John, therefore, concludes his description of the cloths with the words: He believed "because of what he saw."

And then on the evening of Easter Day Jesus revealed Himself to the Apostles as the Risen One. It was not long before the disciples were shouting all over Jerusalem: "The Lord is risen."

For the disciples of Jesus, who were witnesses of the Crucifixion and the Lord's appearances after His Resurrection, Easter was from the very beginning the special feast of the Redemption. The more a Christian lives by the Christian faith, gaining ever deeper insight into it, the more will the Easter festival take on the same significance for him. In every person there is a longing which finds fulfillment only in the faith of Easter, in the knowledge of the Resurrection of Christ and hope in our own resurrection.

The death of Jesus was not the desolate end but the wonderful turning point of His activity:

After His death, the soul of Jesus joined the souls of the departed just, in order to bring them knowledge of the completed Redemption. On the third day after burial Jesus rose from the dead. The resurrection of Jesus was proved to the Apostles by the empty grave and the appearances which Jesus Himself made to them.

In the Resurrection, Jesus raised Himself out of the sealed grave, guarded by enemies, as *victor over Satan and death.* In His own death He conquered death as the ruler over the lives of men and He *gave men thereby a pledge of their own resurrection.* Expressing this idea, St. Paul says: "And if the Spirit of him who raised Jesus from the dead dwells in you, then he who raised Christ Jesus from the dead will also bring to life your mortal bodies because of his Spirit who dwells in you" (Rom 8:11).

The Life of the Individual.   After Easter, the suffering and death of Jesus appeared to the Apostles closely bound up with His Resurrection. The Apostles also acquired a new attitude to suffering and death. They now spoke of suffering and dying for Christ's sake, like men who have discovered a sure method of transforming rubbish into gold and diamonds. Thus they wrote down the following sentences: "But we exult in tribulations also, aware that tribulation produces endurance, and endurance proven virtue, and proven virtue hope" (Rom 5:3–4).

Beloved, do not be startled at the fiery ordeal which befalls you to test you, as though something unusual were happening to you. No, but rejoice to the extent that you share in the sufferings of Christ, so that you may also rejoice and exult when his glory will be revealed (1 Pt 4:12–13).

Consider it genuine joy, my brothers, when you are engulfed by trials of various kinds, since you know that the trying of your faith makes for patience. And let patience accomplish a perfect work, that you may be perfect, flawless, and without shortcoming (Jas 1:2–4).

If we listen to the Word of God, and relate the mystery of suffering in human life to the mystery of Christ's suffering and death, we come to realize that cross and sufferings in the present order of salvation are but messages of God's love contained in black envelopes and we begin to understand why the saints do not merely carry their cross with patience, but seek it eagerly. St. Francis de Sales writes: "Take the cross. From all eternity God's eternal wisdom has seen this cross which He gave you as the most precious gift of His heart. Before He sent it to you, He examined it with His omnipotent eyes, considered it with His divine understanding, tested it with His all-wise kindness, warmed it with loving mercy and weighed it in both of His hands so that it would not be an inch too big or an ounce too heavy. He blessed it with His most holy name, anointed it with His grace and poured out upon it His consolation — and then He looked at you again to see that you were fit to carry it. Then the cross came to you out of heaven as a special greeting, as an alms from the eternal love of your Father. I greet you, O holy cross, my only salvation! In the cross is healing."

The Life of the Church. Because of this the Church celebrates the feast of Easter as the chief feast of the Church's year. Christianity is the only religion on earth whose greatest festival breaks through the bounds of the natural life and is dominated by the thought that there is contained within this life the beginning of a second, higher, and everlasting life.

The significance of the Easter festival as the day of Jesus' victory over Satan and death finds expression in the joyous and spirited verses of the sequence of the Mass of Easter:

> At the Paschal Victim's feet,
> Christians offer praises meet,
> For the sheep the lamb hath bled,
> Sinless in the sinner's stead.
> Christ the Victim undefiled,
> Man to God hath reconciled;
> Whilst in strange and awful strife,
> Met together Death and Life.

Say, O wondering Mary, say,
What thou sawest on the way.
I beheld where Christ had lain,
Empty tomb and angels twain.
I beheld the glory bright,
Of the rising Lord of light.
Christ my hope is risen again:
Now He lives, and lives to reign;
Throned in endless might and power,
Lives and reigns for evermore.
Hail, Eternal Hope on high!
Hail Thou King of victory!
Hail, Thou Prince of life adored!
Help and save us, gracious Lord. Amen.

17. THE ASCENSION OF JESUS INTO HEAVEN: THE INAUGURATION OF HIS KINGDOM

FROM THE RESURRECTION until the Ascension, the Church's life was kept secret, and Jesus revealed Himself only to the men who had been appointed by the Father as witnesses of His Death and Resurrection.

Because this period was not part of the earthly life of our Lord, these days were clouded over by no sadness of farewell.

St. Luke writes:

> Thus, for example, while eating with them, he charged them not to depart from Jerusalem, but to await what the Father had promised. "This you have heard from me," he said, "that while John baptized with water, you shall be baptized with the Holy Spirit not many days hence."
>
> So, when they had come together they asked him, "Lord, will you at this time restore the kingdom to Israel?"
>
> "It is not for you," he answered them, "to know the times or the dates which the Father has fixed by his own authority; but you shall receive power when the Holy Spirit comes upon you, and you shall be my witnesses in Jerusalem and in all Judea and Samaria and even to the very ends of the earth."
>
> After he had said this, he was lifted up before their eyes, and a cloud took him out of their sight. While they were gazing up to the sky as he went, at that moment two men stood beside them in white garments and said, "Men of Galilee, why do you stand looking up to the sky? This Jesus who has been taken up from you will come in the same way as you have seen him going into the sky" (Acts 1:4–11).

When Jesus left the city of Jerusalem with His disciples we may be sure that it was only the disciples who accompanied Him who saw Him. Jesus descended the slope with the disciples, crossed the brook Cedron, and, ascending the Mount of Olives, passed by the garden where He had begun His Passion. From the summit of the Mount of Olives Jesus ascended to His Father.

Jesus' entry into heaven passes human comprehension. As a glorified man, the Son of God entered into heaven. For the first time now, the hosts of angels paid homage to Him in human form.

With His entry into heaven Jesus inaugurated His office as mediator between God the Father and men, in order to apply the grace which He had won by His atoning death to every man who would live upon earth until the end of time.

After the Resurrection from the grave the work of Redemption proceeded in the following way:

On the fortieth day after the Resurrection, Jesus Christ went up into heaven before the eyes of His disciples. Along with Christ there entered into heaven the souls of the just who had departed this life since Adam's death, to be the firstfruits of the Redemption.

Jesus went up into heaven:

1. In order to share, in His humanity, in the glory which is due Him as the Son of God, the Lord and King of all.
2. In order to prepare a place for all of us in heaven.
3. In order to be our advocate with the Father until the hour of His coming again in judgment.

To Christ the King, seated on the right hand of the Father, we owe honor, thanksgiving, love, and service.

The Life of the Individual. The lively awareness that Jesus in heaven is a day-to-day mediator and advocate, interceding for us with His heavenly Father, is of the utmost importance, especially for our understanding of prayer. To go to the celebration of the holy Mass with the idea that in every Mass Christ enters into His Father's presence and shows Him the wounds in His hands and His side, is to penetrate deeply into the prayers which accompany the Mass; it is to become possessed by a spirit which causes us to pray no longer only for ourselves, but for all who are gathered with us for the sacrifice, and to remember all of those who are not present but who require the intercession of Christ the mediator in heaven just as much as ourselves — perhaps more.

The Life of the Church. The belief that Jesus Christ assumed Lordship over the human race and over all things on the day of His Ascension into heaven is as old as the Church itself; but it only received liturgical expression by the introduction of the feast of Christ the King in 1925. This feast was inaugurated to declare solemnly that Jesus Christ even now possesses dominion over every individual person, over all human societies, over all communities, and over all states and nations.

The understanding of the liturgical prayers is made very much easier if we keep in mind the way in which the form of prayer "through Jesus Christ Your Son, our Lord, who with You lives and reigns in all eternity" arose. This formula came into being because of the following two facts:

1. The Apostles and disciples who were witnesses of Christ's Ascension regarded the life of Christ as continuing with the Father in heaven where He continued to be active as their mighty advocate and mediator. 2. At the Last Supper Jesus had expressly instructed the Apostles that on "that day," that is, in the time after His Ascension, they would pray in a new manner, would pray in fact in His name to the Father. He said to them: "It is the real truth when I tell you that, if you make any request of the Father, he will grant it to you in my name. Up to the present you have made no requests in my name. Make them and they will be granted. Thus nothing will be wanting to your joy" (Jn 16:23–24).

In such circumstances the Apostles instinctively created the well-known prayer form and ended prayers to God the Father with the words: "Through Jesus Christ Your Son, our Lord, who with You lives and reigns in all eternity." The expression "Through Jesus Christ" indicates in this case that Jesus is to make His own the requests which the faithful direct to the Father. Prayer thus goes through Jesus Christ to the Father.

18. THE FUTURE JUDGMENT OF MANKIND BY JESUS CHRIST

BEFORE HIS DEATH Jesus looked forward to that far-off day at the end of time when He would return to earth as Lord and Judge, to complete the work which the Father had delegated to Him. Before enemies and friends He solemnly testified that one day He would appear as Judge of the living and the dead.

Before His enemies He declared:

"Serpents! Vipers' brood! How are you to escape being sentenced to the pit of hell! For this reason, mark my words, I am sending to you prophets and wise and learned men. Of these, you will kill and crucify some; others you will flog in your synagogues or pursue from city to city. As a result, all the innocent blood ever shed on earth — beginning with the blood of the innocent Abel to the blood of Zachary, son of Barachias, whom you murdered between the sanctuary and the altar — shall be avenged upon you. Yes, indeed, I tell you, all this bloodshedding must be avenged upon this nation.

> Jerusalem, Jerusalem!
> Murderess of prophets!
> Stoner of the messengers sent to you!
> How often have I been willing
> to gather your children
> as a mother bird gathers her brood
> under her wings!
> But you refused it!

Mark well: you will find your house abandoned — a prey to desolation. Yes, I tell you, you will not see me again till you cry out: 'A blessing on him who comes in the name of the Lord!'" (Mt 23:33–39.)

To His friends the Apostles He said:

"There will be striking phenomena in sun and moon and stars; on the earth anguish will grip the nations, perplexed by the roar and surge of the sea; men will faint away from fright and expectation of what is yet to befall the world; for the foundations of the universe will rock. At last they will see the Son of Man riding upon a cloud with great might and majesty. When these phenomena are well under way, raise your heads and look up, for then your redemption is close at hand."

He also told them a parable: "Look at the fig tree, or any of the trees: the moment they begin to shoot, you need but open your eyes to know that summer is near. Apply this to yourselves: as soon as you see these events in progress, you know that the kingdom of God is at hand. Yes, I assure you, this generation will not pass away before all these events have set in. Heaven and earth will fail; my words will never fail" (Lk 21:25–33).

The coming of the Lord in judgment will be like His ascension into heaven. The disciples had seen Him travel upwards and disappear in a cloud of light. On His return, a cloud of light will again appear and the Lord will descend in a radiance of majesty.

Here is Jesus' own description of the coming judgment.

"When the Son of Man returns in his glory, and escorted by all the angels, he will seat himself on a throne befitting his glory. All the nations will assemble in his presence, and he will part mankind into two groups just as a shepherd parts the sheep from the goats. The sheep he will range at his right, and the goats at his left.

"Then the king will say to those at his right: 'Welcome, favored of my Father! Take possession of the kingdom prepared for you from the beginning of the world. For when I was hungry, you gave me to eat; when I was thirsty, you gave to me drink; when I was a stranger, you took me into your homes; when I was naked, you covered me; when I was sick, you visited me; when I was in prison, you came to see me.' Then the saints will be surprised and say to him: 'Master, when did we see you hungry and feed you? or thirsty and give you to drink? And when did we see you a stranger and take you into our homes? or naked and cover you? When did we see you sick or in prison, and come to visit you?' And in explanation the King will say to them: 'I tell you the plain truth, inasmuch as you did this to one of these least brethren of mine, you did it to me.'

"Next he will say to those at his left: 'Out of my sight, you cursed ones! Off into the everlasting fire prepared for the devil and his ministers! For when I was hungry, you did not give me to eat; when I was thirsty, you did not give me to drink; when I was a stranger, you did not take me into your homes; when naked, you did not cover me; when sick and in prison, you did not visit me.' Then they, in turn, will be surprised and say to him: 'Master, when did we see you hungry or thirsty or a stranger or naked or sick or in prison, and did not minister to your wants?' Then will he hurl back at them this answer: 'I tell you the plain truth: insofar as you failed to render these services to one of those least ones, you also failed to render them to me.' And so the latter will be consigned to everlasting punishment, while the saints will enter into everlasting life" (Mt 25:31–46).

In the discourse of the Last Day Jesus states the rule according to which He will execute judgment: "When you did it to one of the least of my brethren here, you did it to me. When you refused it to one of the least of my brethren here, you refused it to me."

Love of God and love of our neighbor are fundamentally one virtue; they are like the right and left banks of one and the same river. This judgment rule of Jesus is of such a kind that from it no one can exempt himself. Every human being has his "neighbors."

The consummation of the redemptive work of Christ is still to come.

At the end of the world Christ will appear in order to pass judgment on the living and the dead.

Christ will hold judgment upon earth in order to reveal His kingly rule before assembled humanity, and that He may reward the good for their faithfulness in the eyes of all, and punish the wicked in the eyes of all for their unfaithfulness.

A Christian has to regard the time between the Ascension and the end of the world as the growing time of the kingdom of God, the time between sowing and harvest.

The Life of the Individual. Christ's prophecies of the end of the world are distinguished from all non-Christian oracles about the world's decline. The latter think of the end of the world as a running down, a finishing, a death. For the Christian, the end of the world is a beginning, a transfiguration. A new heaven and a new earth come to life.

The Life of the Church. In the time of St. Paul, there spread among the Christians of Thessalonica the conviction that the end of the world was at hand. Many of those who awaited Christ's coming in judgment ceased working and gave themselves up to idleness. Disorder threatened to break out. St. Paul admonished all to return to work and to set aside all fanciful notions (cf. Thes 3:11).

The words of St. Paul hold for Christians of all times. If the Church has the Gospel of the Last Judgment read on the last and the first Sundays of the liturgical year, it is not because she wants to fill the faithful with paralyzing fear, but to spur them on to an active life for Christ. This appears from the Epistle which is appointed to go along with this Gospel. There we read:

"And this do with due regard for the time, for it is now the hour for you to rise from sleep, because now our salvation is nearer than when we came to believe. This night is far advanced; the day is at hand. Let us, therefore, lay aside the deeds prompted by darkness, and put on the armor of light. Let us conduct ourselves becomingly as in the day, not in revelry and drunkenness, not in debauchery and wantonness, not in strife and jealousy. But put on the Lord Jesus Christ, and take no thought for your lower nature to satisfy its lusts" (Rom 13:11–14).

These words of St. Paul present something remarkable: St. Paul wrote the Epistle to the Romans, in which these sentences occur, about A.D. 55, that is, a good twenty years after the death of Christ. The congregation of Roman Christians was in a good condition; there were no special abuses. In spite of this the Apostle thought it not out of place to appeal to the Christians to awake from sleep. Even the baptized man feels tempted every now and again to "sleep a little," and to "let himself slide a little," although the Lord exhorts us so emphatically to be vigilant.

19. THE HOLY SPIRIT WHO LEADS MEN TO CHRIST AND THE FATHER

ON THE EVENING before His Passion, Jesus began to speak about the "helper" whom He wished to send from heaven after His death. He said:

"And I will ask the Father, and he will grant you another Advocate to be with you for all time to come, the Spirit of Truth! The world is incapable of receiving him, because it neither sees him nor knows him. You will know him, because he will make his permanent stay with you and in you" (Jn 14:16–17).

"I have told you all this while I am still lingering in your midst; but the Advocate, the Holy Spirit, whom the Father will send in my name, will teach you everything, and refresh your memory of everything I have told you" (Jn 14:25–26).

"How pitiful that this saying in their Law must needs be fulfilled 'They have hated me without cause!'"
"When the Advocate whom I am going to send you with a mission from the Father — the Spirit of truth, who proceeds from the Father — has come, he will witness in my behalf. And you, too, will witness, because you have been with me from the beginning" (Jn 15:25–27).

"There is still much I might say to you; but you are not strong enough to bear it at present. But when he, the Spirit of Truth, has come, he will conduct you through the whole range of truth. What he will tell does not originate with him; no, he will tell only what he is told. Besides, he will announce to you the future. He is to glorify me, for he will draw upon what is mine and announce it to you. Whatever the Father possesses is mine; that is why I said that he will draw on what is mine and announce it to you" (Jn 16:12–15).

Jesus speaks constantly of the Holy Spirit as a divine Person. The Father will send Him in the name of Jesus. The Holy Spirit is that "other" helper, the one who takes the place of the first helper — Jesus. This "other" helper will then remain with the disciples until Jesus appears in judgment. He will teach the disciples "all things" — all things in the most comprehensive sense: all things which pertain to the preaching of the new order of salvation. This assurance of Jesus implies that the Holy Spirit will give the Apostles understanding of such divine truths as had been beyond their reach during the earthly life of Jesus. To this category belongs insight into the meaning of the suffering and the sacrificial death of Jesus.

Beside this (Jesus promises) the Holy Spirit will call to their mind all that Jesus Himself told them. This recollection will be no mere refreshment of memory: rather, what Jesus told them and what they often understood only imperfectly will now come alive to their understanding in the sense in which Jesus meant it.

The same Holy Spirit, of whom Jesus spoke openly during the last days, had, however, been present since the beginning of the creation.

Under the Old Covenant it was the Holy Spirit who, along with the Father and the Son, had prepared mankind for the appearance of the Redeemer. He had illumined and strengthened the men of God who appeared down the course of the centuries.

The Redeemer was foretold as the one upon whom the gifts of the Holy Spirit should rest. The prophet Isaiah says:

> "The spirit of the Lord shall rest upon him: a spirit of wisdom and of understanding, a spirit of counsel and of strength, a spirit of knowledge and of fear of the Lord, and his delight shall be the fear of the Lord" (Is 11:2).

It was the Holy Spirit who preserved the mother of the Redeemer from original sin and from all actual sin. He was active in the very moment when the Son of God assumed human nature in the Virgin Mary and thus entered the world: "The Holy Spirit will come upon you, and the power of the Most High will overshadow you" (Lk 1:35).

When Jesus began His public ministry of teaching, it was the Holy

Spirit who came down upon Him in the form of a dove. Impelled by the Holy Spirit, after His baptism He went into the wilderness in order to fortify Himself for His mission under the guidance of the Spirit.

When, in the course of His wanderings as a preacher, Jesus returned to the town of Nazareth where He had spent thirty years in seclusion, He reported at the synagogue to preach a sermon. Before His astonished fellow citizens, He explained that He was the One upon whom the Holy Spirit rested. From the Book of the prophet Isaiah He read out the passage:

> "The Spirit of the Lord rests upon me,
> because he has anointed me.
> He has appointed me a messenger
> to bring the Good News to the humble;
> to announce release to captives,
> and recovery of sight to the blind;
> to set the oppressed at liberty;
> to proclaim a year of grace
> ordained by the Lord" (Lk 4:18–19).

And when at last the hour of His going home to His Father arrived, He announced to His disciples that after His departure, the Holy Spirit, who had prepared Him for the work of Redemption and had accompanied His public activity, would descend in person from heaven, sent by Father and Son, to remain forever with the Church.

Accordingly in the Acts of the Apostles, St. Luke represents the whole being and growth of the Church as an activity of the Holy Spirit. He is forever speaking of the Holy Spirit.

It is this conception of the Holy Spirit as the moving power within the Church which dominates the statements in the Creed about the Holy Spirit.

If we look at the Creed in its broad outline we see at the first glance that it is concerned first with God the Father Almighty and His activity as Creator, and then with Jesus Christ His only-begotten Son and His work as Redeemer. Toward the end, however, we get the impression that after a quick glance at the Holy Spirit, we are concerned with the Catholic Church.

Those who first used the Creed, however, saw things in a different light. In the statements: "I believe in the holy Catholic Church, the

Communion of Saints, the forgiveness of sins, the resurrection of the body and the life everlasting," they saw nothing but concise statements about the working of the Holy Spirit within men.

For them the words "the Communion of Saints" did not mean chiefly the saints in heaven, but the community of "holy possessions," the goods of salvation, which belong to all. The early Christians understood the words "the forgiveness of sins" in the sense that the Holy Spirit manifested His activity in the Church in a special way through this power.

At the words "the resurrection of the dead" they thought about those who are to rise, following Christ, the firstfruits, into heaven. Accordingly "life everlasting" signified eternal blessedness in contemplating God in heaven.

These key phrases, which implied the activity of the Holy Spirit, were like banners for the early Christians, which they waved in joy and exultation. In the working and power of the Holy Spirit they had a pledge of victory.

The guidance of the children of God upon earth belongs to the Holy Spirit. "Whoever are led by the Spirit of God, they are the sons of God" (Rom 8:14).

The Holy Spirit is the third Person in the Trinity. He is true God, like the Father and the Son. He proceeds from the Father and the Son together.

"He is to glorify me, for he will draw upon what is mine and announce it to you. Whatever the Father possesses is mine" (Jn 16:14–15).

The words "I believe in the Holy Spirit" are the introduction to the third part of the Creed. The statements, "I believe in the holy Catholic Church, the Communion of Saints, the forgiveness of sins, the resurrection of the body, and the life everlasting" are to be taken as statements about the activity of the Holy Spirit in the world.

The Life of the Individual. By baptism, the Christian enters into a special relation with the three divine Persons: to the Father as the Giver and Lord of life; to the Son as the Redeemer and Guide to the Father; to the Holy Spirit as the inward Enlightener, Strengthener, and Comforter of the soul. These relationships determine a man's whole life. Life, which is the gift of the Father, is sustained by Him at every moment; Jesus Christ the Son is continually active in heaven as the advocate of the redeemed: the Holy Spirit goes on speaking in His own special way within the hearts of men.

The activity of the Holy Spirit is of the utmost importance because the Holy Spirit is the Spirit of love, and it is through His operation that love of God is awakened in men. Something new comes into the person, something of which he was unaware before, and of which, without the operation of the Holy Spirit, he would never become aware. A man begins to see everything in a different way, he sees his relationship to God the Trinity, to his fellowmen, to things in the world, in a different light; everything now fits together in a new unity. Men have become "new creatures."

The Holy Spirit is the Spirit of consolation. The Savior Himself often described him as the Comforter (cf. Jn 14:16; 14:25; 15:26; 16:7). Thus it is His task and gift to comfort men. Today the number of people is very great to whom the word "comfort" suggests something which may be appropriate for children, but which is out of the question for grown men. In truth, it is such who are most in need of the divine solace which they spurn; for insight into human life, without this consolation, leads to despair.

The Life of the Church. It means a heavy and permanent loss to the Christian life if the living relationship to the three divine Persons is forgotten: the relationship to the Father as Creator, the relationship to the Son as the incarnate Redeemer, and the living relationship to the Holy Spirit as the Guide whom Jesus sent down to earth from heaven. Yes, if this slipping back goes far enough, without becoming aware of it, a Catholic can become a man who possesses only as much of Christian doctrine as the Mohammedans call their own.

Just as the little band of disciples in the room at Jerusalem — the hidden Church — prayed for the first coming of the Holy Spirit, so at every Pentecost the Church supplicates anew for the coming of the Holy Spirit:

> Come, Thou Holy Paraclete,
> And from Thy celestial seat
> Send Thy light and brilliancy.

Father of the poor, draw near;
Giver of all gifts, be here;
Come, the soul's true radiancy.

Thou, of comforters the best,
Of the soul the sweetest guest,
Come in toil refreshingly.

Where thou art not, man hath nought;
Every holy deed and thought
Comes from Thy Divinity.

(Tr. John Mason Neale)

20. THE VISIBLE STRUCTURE OF THE CHURCH BUILT BY CHRIST UPON THE FOUNDATION OF THE APOSTLES

LOVE ALWAYS SEEKS the presence of the loved one. With Jesus, the incarnate Son of God, this law operates infinitely more powerfully than with any human love. Jesus spent Himself, longing for union with mankind. He desired to take all men up into His divine life and to form them into a community of which He would be the Head. And so He founded the Church, His *Mystical Body*. This expression signifies that through grace Christ unites the faithful in a real, *visible* unity with Himself, so that it can be determined whether or not a person belongs to the Church, although true spiritual membership in Christ through the Church remains invisible.

The members of a physical, tangible body such as men possess lack any sort of independence. By contrast, the members of the Church, even after their reception into the Mystical Body of Christ, are and remain free personalities. The members of a human society unite in order to reach a particular end. By contrast, the members of the Mystical Body of Christ are not united through some external goal, but inwardly through Jesus Christ the second Person of the Trinity, drawn together into a spiritual unity of life.

During His public ministry Jesus designed the structure of His Church which was to be at once a spiritual community and a visible society.

It was at this time that He went out to the mountainside, and passed the whole night offering prayer to God. And when day dawned, He called His disciples to Him, choosing out twelve of them; these He called His Apostles. Their names were Simon, whom He also called Peter, his brother Andrew, James and John, Philip and Bartholomew, Matthew and Thomas, James the son of Alphaeus, and Simon who is called the Zealot, Jude the brother of James, and Judas Iscariot, the man who turned traitor (cf. Lk 6:12–16).

Jesus called these twelve men His *Shalliach,* His Apostles, that is, His *emissaries,* His *representatives.* At that time the word *Shalliach* had a specific, legal meaning and denoted a man who acted for another, in his name and with full authority. Jesus thereby was describing these selected men as His plenipotentiaries and representatives. That they had been elected with an eye to the future was already recognized to some extent by the men themselves and by all present.

A considerable time passed and then one day Jesus asked these Apostles

"Who do people say the Son of Man is?" "Some say, John the Baptist," they replied; "others say, Elias; still others, Jeremias or some other prophet." "But you," he went on to say, "who do you say I am?" Then Simon Peter spoke up. "You are the Messias, the Son of the Living God." Jesus acquiesced and said to him: "Blessed are you, Simon, son of Jona. It was my Father in heaven that revealed this to you, and not flesh and blood. And I, in turn, say to you: You are Peter, and upon this rock I will build my Church, and the gates of hell shall not prevail against it. I will give you the keys of the kingdom of heaven, and whatever you bind on earth shall be bound in heaven, and whatever you loose on earth shall be loosed in heaven" (Mt 16:13–19).

When Jesus announced the delivery of the keys to Peter, He was pointing ahead to a time when the Church which He founded would still be in existence, but when He would no longer be present as visible Head.

In the promise to Peter, Jesus uses the word "Church." By a *Kachal,* to use the corresponding Aramaic word, is understood a community of a religious kind, whether one is thinking of an assembled community or of a community which meets regularly and hence, even when temporarily separated, still regards itself as a spiritual unity.

In the writings of the New Testament, the word "Church" can have both meanings equally well. In present-day speech, the word "Church" means the community of all the faithful as an enduring society. The faithful of one region today are not called a "Church" strictly, but a parish congregation or a diocese.

From the very beginning, the Church was a work of the love of Jesus for people of every land and time:

When He was upon earth, Jesus not only drew near to each person He met, but with the same love longed to unite with Himself in grace, people of every land and time.

During His *public life* Jesus laid the *external foundations* of the future Church: He gathered believers around Him, chose from among them twelve men as leaders of the future Church, and out of these appointed St. Peter to be primate of the Church.

The twelve chosen ones Jesus designated as His *Apostles,* as His *representatives.* He Himself used the word "Apostle" in the sense of representative when He said: "As the Father has sent me, so I send you" (Jn 20:21, Knox tr.).

Jesus has given to the Apostles as His representatives the *teaching office,* the *priestly office,* and the *pastoral office* — those offices which belonged to Himself as Son of God, the mediator between God and man.

As successors of the Apostles, the bishops are not mere external representatives of the Pope, but regular pastors, appointed by the Lord Himself. The subjection of the faithful to the twofold superiority of the bishops and the Pope leads to no confusion, however, because the bishops not only individually but as a body are subject to the Pope. With him they form the Apostolic College.

The Life of the Individual. It is by faith, an inward teaching of the Holy Spirit, that men discern the true form and nature of the Church. Thus illumined they find their home in the one Church designed by Christ. They do not mistake the faults of individual members of the Church for defects in the Church herself. Ultimately their trust in the Church is trust in Christ's word of promise to His Church.

The Life of the Church. The Church is forever reminding the faithful that they owe their existence to the preaching of the Faith by the Apostles. She commemorates the twelve Apostles in every holy Mass; in the Litany of the Saints she invokes them in turn by name, while only single representatives of the other groups of saints are named. She observes days commemorating the Apostles as feasts of higher rank.

Why did Jesus accept Judas in the number of the Apostles, when He knew in advance that he would betray Him?

In this way, Jesus made His own the Church's bitter experience of the faithlessness of men. The calling of Judas is a warning to all who wish to present themselves as priests in the service of Christ, and for all who have so presented themselves.

Obedience to one's ecclesiastical superiors, more exactly, the obedience of the faithful to their pastors and the pastors' obedience to their bishops, is taken as the measure of the spirit of the Church. In no way, however, should the notion of ecclesiastical obedience be borrowed from secular or political ideas of obedience. There is no better expression of the meaning of obedience in the Church than that of St. Ignatius of Antioch when writing to the church at Smyrna, before his martyrdom in Rome. "All of you, follow the bishop as Jesus Christ did the Father, and the presbyters as apostles; reverence the diaconate as you would the law of God. Let no one arrange church matters apart from the bishop. Only that Eucharist is to be considered valid which takes place under the bishop or him whom he has delegated. Where the bishop appears, there also shall the congregation be, as where Christ is, there is the universal Church. Without the bishop, it is not permissible to baptize or hold an Agape; furthermore, only what he has approved is pleasing to God, and so shall everything which is done be true and reliable. Who honors the bishop will be honored by God; whoever does anything without the bishop's knowledge serves the Devil" (VIII, IX).

21. THE ATONING DEATH OF CHRIST, THE SPIRITUAL FOUNDATION OF THE CHURCH

EZECHIEL, the third major prophet of the Old Covenant, had a vision in which he saw streams of life-giving grace welling up from the side of Christ.

> Then he brought me back to the entrance of the temple, and I saw water flowing out from beneath the threshold of the temple toward the east, for the façade of the temple was toward the east; the water flowed down from the southern side of the temple, south of the altar. He led me outside by the north gate, and around to the outer gate facing the east, where I saw water trickling from the southern side. Then when he had walked off to the east with a measuring cord in his hand, he measured off a thousand cubits and had me wade through the water, which was ankle-deep. He measured off another thousand and once more had me wade through the water, which was now knee-deep. Again he measured off a thousand and had me wade; the water was up to my waist. Once more he measured off a thousand, but there was now a river through which I could not wade; for the water had risen so high it had become a river that could not be crossed except by swimming. He asked me, "Have you seen this, son of man?" Then he brought me to the bank of the river, where he had me sit. Along the bank of the river I saw very many trees on both sides. He said to me, "This water flows into the eastern district down upon the Araba, and empties into the sea, the salt waters, which it makes fresh. Wherever the river flows, every sort of living creature that can multiply shall live, and there shall be abundant fish, for wherever this water comes the sea shall be made fresh. Fishermen shall be standing along it from En-gaddi to En-gallim, spreading their nets there. Its kind of fish shall be like those of the Great Sea, very numerous. Only its marshes and swamps shall not be made fresh; they shall be left for salt. Along both banks of the river, fruit trees of every kind shall grow; their leaves shall not fade, nor their fruit fail. Every month

they shall bear fresh fruit, for they shall be watered by the flow from the sanctuary. Their fruit shall serve for food, and their leaves for medicine" (Ez 47:1–12).

On the Feast of Tabernacles before His Passion, Jesus applied this picture to Himself and declared that He was the Fount of Life. Opportunity to do this occurred at the solemn procession which took place daily during the week of the festival. The priests went down to the Pool of Siloam, filled a golden pitcher with water, and then climbed in procession up to the temple. As soon as they set foot in the temple three blasts — short, long, short — were sounded on the trumpets. From the Court of Women the priests then moved to the Altar of Burnt Offerings. There the water was poured into a basin from which it was spilled onto the Altar of Burnt Offerings.

On the minds of the pilgrims who lived in a land of drought, this procession with the water jug made a deep impression. From this procession the Court of Women derived the name, "the place of refreshing." This name could be truly significant only if this procession was seen as a symbolic proclamation of that spiritual drink, prohesied by Isaiah: "In joy you shall be filled at the fountain of salvation." As the word "salvation" in Hebrew means the same as the name "Jesus," the verse runs: "In joy you shall be filled at the fountain of Jesus" — the name of Jesus is, therefore, mentioned. At this "place of refreshing" Jesus now declared Himself to be the fountain of that living water which awakens and sustains life in the soul.

The evangelist John relates:

> On the last and solemn day of the feast, Jesus stood erect and cried out: "If anyone thirsts, let him come to me and drink. He who believes in me, will, as the Scripture has said, become a fountain out of which streams of living water are flowing forth." He meant by this the Spirit, whom those who believed in him were destined to receive (Jn 7:37–39).

Had the Church been nothing but a human society having in Jesus a purely human founder, then in His death the Apostles would have suffered the most severe blow which could have struck them; they would in fact, have lost their founder. In reality, in the death of Jesus the infinite plenitude of grace, which had entered the world at His Incarnation, for the first time became available for the world in full measure.

With this fact in mind, the evangelist John solemnly testifies to what happened at that time:

> Since it was Preparation Day, the Jews did not wish the corpses to remain on the crosses during the Sabbath, for that Sabbath was a holy day; so they requested Pilate to order that the men's legs should be broken and the bodies removed. Accordingly, the soldiers came and broke the legs both of the one and of the other that were crucified with him. When they came to Jesus, they saw that he was already dead. So they did not break his legs, but one of the soldiers pierced his side with a lance, and immediately there came out blood and water. This statement is the testimony of an eyewitness. His testimony is true, and he knows that he is speaking the truth, so that you, too, may believe. In fact, these incidents took place that the Scripture might be fulfilled: "Not a bone of his shall be broken." And still another Scripture text says: "They will look upon him whom they have pierced" (Jn 19:31–37).

The sacrificial death of Jesus is the source of every good impulse in the world and of all forgiveness. Whenever that mysterious change is wrought within a sinful man; and, converted and repentant, he becomes a new creature bringing forth the fruits of sanctification; whenever in a good man there occurs a sudden outburst of new love, as if hitherto he had not loved God and man at all, always the power comes ultimately from the sacrificial death of Jesus. His words are fulfilled "I, once I have been lifted up from the earth, will draw all men to myself" (Jn 12:32).

For this reason, John perceived in the opening of Jesus' heart a symbolic event. In that hour the inexhaustible fount of grace began to flow from the pierced heart of the Redeemer, and was never to cease flowing until the end of the world. Now men look up to Him whom they pierced.

And so the Church arises from out of the pierced side of the Redeemer.

Reception into the Church results from baptism which fashions a unique spiritual union between Jesus and the baptized person. The newly baptized begins to share in the divine life. It is precisely by His sacrificial death upon the cross that Jesus has made this sharing in divine life possible. The faithful are baptized "into the death of Jesus."

In the death of Jesus, in the piercing of His heart, the spiritual life of the Church originated.

In *His death,* Christ has opened up to the Church, from within Himself, an inexhaustible *Fount of divine life.* All men without exception receive in Him the power of becoming children of God and of binding themselves in spiritual unity with Him, the Head of the human race, within the divine life.

The spiritual union of the individual with the Redeemer Jesus Christ is effected through baptism. Through baptism the individual becomes a member of the Church.

The Life of the Individual. As Jesus offered His life to the Father in sacrificial death, so the individual Christian most resembles Jesus Christ if he sacrifices his life for Christ as a martyr. The special significance for the Church of death by martyrdom does not lie in its showing forth the spiritual strength of the faithful in the most majestic way possible, but lies much deeper. Through the martyrdom of Christians the heart of the Redeemer is, as it were, moved most powerfully to allow new streams of grace to flow over the world.

The Life of the Church. St. Augustine's sentence on the piercing of Jesus' heart shows how alive he was to the fact that the Church began its existence in the death of Christ. He says: "Here the evangelist used a carefully chosen word. He avoids the expression, 'pierced' or 'wounded' or similar turns of phrase, and used the words, 'he opened his side.'

"There, in the Heart of Jesus, it is as if the doors of life have been thrown open, through which gush forth the sacraments of the Church, without which it is impossible to enter true life. The blood was shed for the forgiveness of sins, the water mellows the cup of salvation — it grants at once both cleansing and drink."

Throughout the whole Easter season, the Church sings at the *Asperges:* "I saw water flowing from the right side of the temple, Alleluia, alleluia. O praise the Lord for He is good; for His mercy endureth forever." The words of this hymn take up the opening words of Ezechiel's vision of the fountain which sprang up in the temple and transformed barren land into a land of trees bearing priceless fruit.

Because the Church has been founded spiritually upon the atoning death of Jesus, the conception of the atoning death of Jesus is closely bound up with the Church's understanding of itself. This appears in the ancient Good Friday liturgy. On this day, the day of Jesus' death, the place of the bloodless sacrifice becomes the scene of the historical remembrance of the sacrificial death of Jesus. The holy celebration begins with the reading aloud of the story of our Lord's Passion. Identifying herself with this, the Church steps in spirit beneath the cross upon which the Lord hangs with transfixed heart. She, who lives by the death of Jesus, now begins to make her supplication to the Father whom Christ has reconciled with the world. She speaks as the bride of the Redeemer, as the mother of all men — she marks out, so to speak, channels at the foot of the cross in which the blood of the Redeemer is to flow over the world in all directions and enlarge its flood in her.

The first bidding prayer in the Good Friday liturgy is: "Let us, dearly beloved, pray for the holy Church of God: that our Lord and God would vouchsafe to give her peace and unity, and preserve her throughout the world, subjecting under her principalities and powers; and also grant that, leading a peaceful life, we may glorify God the Father Almighty." — "Almighty and eternal God, who in Christ have revealed Your glory to all nations; preserve the works of Your Mercy; that Your Church, spread abroad over the whole world, may with a steadfast faith persevere in the confession of Your name."

Thereupon the Church looks around and perceives herself in her parts: there follow the petitions "for our most Holy Father, for the bishops, priests, deacons, subdeacons, and for all the holy people of God."

After the Church has prayed for those who live within her society and who are already united to her in Christ's blood and in baptism, she prays for all those not yet numbered among her own, but for whom the blood of Christ has been shed just as truly. The first of these are those on the threshold, the candidates for baptism; next are those who once were within the Church but left her — our separated brethren of today; next she prays for the people of the Jews from whom our Lord was descended after the flesh; and finally for the heathen to whom in Adam the promise of Redemption has also been given.

22. THE SENDING OF THE HOLY SPIRIT, THE BEGINNING OF THE AUTONOMOUS LIFE OF THE CHURCH

AT PENTECOST, the Church which had been called into being on the death of Jesus stepped out of concealment into the light and began its autonomous life and growth by the Holy Spirit.

St. Luke relates:

When the day of Pentecost had come, they were all together in the place. Suddenly there came a sound in the sky, as of a violent wind blowing, and it filled the whole house where they were staying. And there appeared to them tongues like fire which distributed themselves and settled on each one of them. They were all filled with the Holy Spirit and began to speak in other tongues, as the Holy Spirit prompted them to give utterance.

Now there were staying at Jerusalem devout men of every nation under heaven. When this sound was heard, a crowd of them gathered and were bewildered, because each one heard his own language spoken by the apostles. Everybody was amazed and marveled, saying, "Look, are not all those who are speaking Galileans? How then does each of us hear his own native language? Parthians and Medes, and Elamites, and inhabitants of Mesopotamia, Judea and Cappadocia, Pontus and Asia, Phrygia and Pamphylia, Egypt and districts of Libya and Cyrene, and visitors from Rome, Jews and Proselytes, Cretans and Arabians — we hear them declaring in our own languages the wonderful works of God."

They were all amazed and perplexed, saying to one another, "What does this mean?" Others said in mockery, "They are all full of sweet wine."

But Peter, presenting himself with the Eleven, raised his voice and addressed them: "Men of Judea, and all you who reside in Jerusalem, let me inform you of this, and give ear to my words. These men are not drunk, as you suppose, since it is only nine o'clock in the morning. But this is what was foretold by the prophet Joel:

> 'It shall happen in the last days, says God,
> that I will pour forth my Spirit on all mankind;
> And your sons and daughters shall prophesy,
> and your young men shall see visions,
> and your old men shall dream dreams.
> And on my slaves too and my handmaids
> in those days will I pour forth my Spirit,
> and they shall prophesy.
> I will also show wonders in the heavens above
> and signs on the earth below,
> blood and fire and a cloud of smoke . . .'" (Acts 2:1–19).

The Jews liked to make their morning prayer in the temple at the hour of the morning sacrifice. Most probably this custom was followed by the Apostles and disciples of the Lord, and the hundred and twenty believers who were gathered in the upper room. At this same hour a rushing sound like a storm bore down upon them from heaven's height. A blazing fireball appeared and split up into as many tongues of flame as there were disciples present. A tongue of fire settled upon each of them.

The pilgrims in the alleys and streets had likewise heard the roar from the cloudless heavens. They could pick out the house upon which it had descended, and they assembled in front of it, a motley crowd in dress and in speech.

Peter, the chief of the Apostles, came out and was the first to exercise the threefold office of teacher, priest, and shepherd. He exercised the office of teacher; he preached the basic fact of the Christian Faith, the Redemption through Jesus Christ. He exercised the office of shepherd, when they asked what they should do, by instructing them to repent and be baptized in the name of Jesus. He exercised the office of priest by baptizing.

The other Apostles and disciples began likewise to preach and to baptize. All this took place with the support of the Holy Spirit.

Full of amazement, the people who heard realized that each one of them was hearing what was said in the language of his own country; and every civilized country was represented. By the evening of the day of Pentecost the Church already numbered 3000 members.

Jesus sent the Holy Spirit to the Church after His Ascension.

Immediately before the Ascension, Jesus had given the Apostles the commission to exercise the office of teacher, priest, and shepherd in His name; He said to them: "Go and make disciples of all nations and baptize them in the name of the Father, and of the Son, and of the Holy Spirit." But they were only to begin to exercise this office after Jesus had sent the Holy Spirit to them from the Father.

Ten days after the Ascension, on the feast of Pentecost, Jesus and the Father sent the Holy Spirit to the Church. In the Holy Spirit the Spirit of Jesus Christ has returned to the Church and filled it with His life. Through the Holy Spirit the Church teaches and directs men and mediates to them the graces of Redemption.

In the Holy Spirit Jesus unites the faithful with Himself in love and grace. They live from Him, through Him, and in Him. For this reason the Church is called the Mystical Body of Christ.

The *Pope* and the *bishops* rule the Church. The Pope is the primate over the bishops. Pope and bishops teach in the Church by guarding, preaching, and explaining the doctrine of Jesus Christ.

The Holy Spirit, the support sent from Christ, keeps far from the Church all errors in the teaching of faith and morals; and so one says: the Church possesses *the gift of infallibility*.

The gift of infallibility inheres first of all in the Pope and bishops as a college, and in certain circumstances in the Pope alone also. The Pope is, in fact, infallible if, as supreme pastor and teacher, he solemnly decides a matter of faith or morals for the whole Church.

The Life of the Individual. Men must eagerly desire the true food of life, the medicine of the soul. Hence the Church never ceases to exhort her children to pray to the Holy Spirit. The Church is in deadly earnest about her teaching on the relation between grace and freewill in man. If man is incapable in himself of thinking a good thought or of accomplishing a supernatural deed, then his salvation depends upon God's grace. The efficacy of grace in man is, however, the special work of the Holy Spirit. Out of sinners, the Holy Spirit makes saints; out of the weak, heroes and martyrs.

The Life of the Church. "Christ transformed His intention to found an indestructible Church into action, by the promise to Peter, that is, by the institution of the Primacy, or what is the same thing, of the Papacy. Thus, the Church which is built upon Peter and his successors, and that alone, can be the Church of Christ, in itself one and enduring to the end of the ages, precisely through its subjection to a personal, visible head.

"It was by the dispensation of divine Providence that Peter chose Rome to be the seat of his bishopric. And here in Nero's circus — we have indisputable archaeological evidence for this — he died, a martyr for Christ. Beneath the center point of the great dome was and is the place of his grave. His successors, the popes, have continued his mission down to the present day.

"In the line of Roman popes there were many who, like the Prince of the Apostles, set the seal of their blood upon their faithfulness to Him whose visible representatives they were. Many of them were of great sanctity, had great gifts, great knowledge and were men of strong personality. Alongside them there were indeed others whose purely human characteristics corresponded ill with the eminence of their primatial pastoral office. And yet, the most terrible storms which have broken out since the time of the apostle Peter until our own day, have been unable to destroy the Church or make any breach in the divine mission of her supreme head.

"Each pope receives this divine mission at the moment of his acceptance of election; he receives it directly from Christ, and always with the same plenitude of power and the same gift of infallibility. And if one day — and this is pure supposition — the visible Rome should collapse, if the Church of St. Peter, symbol of the one invincible and victorious Catholic Church, were to bury beneath its ruins the historic treasures and the venerable monuments which it contains, even then the Church itself would neither collapse nor split into pieces. Even then Christ's promise to Peter would still remain true and the papacy and the Church founded upon it would still go on existing. And so it is that the eternal Rome in the Christian, supernatural sense, surpasses the historic Rome. The nature and truth of the Christian Rome do not depend upon the historic Rome.

"And therefore, dear sons and daughters, your faith too ought to be unshakable because it has for foundation the rock upon which the

Church is built. Proclaim this faith and carry it amongst your fellowmen and fellow-women, with a clear vision, with deep conviction, and with a courage that is assured of victory. And pray for the Pope, that the Lord who has willed that he be the pastor and bishop of your souls, will enable him to help by his words and example, those over whom he is placed, that with them he may attain everlasting life" (Pope Pius XII).

As we see, Pope Pius XII in this address does not shrink from the assertion that in the long line of popes there are to be found some who were not worthy, from the human point of view, of this great dignity. But the number of popes who suffered death or persecution for the Faith is immeasurably greater.

The times when less worthy or plainly unworthy popes governed the Church coincided with times when the Church fell under the influence of political powers. Such a thing happened first in the tenth, the so-called "dark," century, approximately from 896 to 964; the second time was in Avignon; the third time was during the Renaissance, from about 1457 to 1543. Of the 265 vicars of Christ upon earth we can point to about fourteen men who were personally unworthy to hold this office.

This personal unworthiness has, of course, nothing fundamentally to do with the "infallibility" of the Pope. The popes are "infallible" in doctrine only insofar as they can never err when they make a decision on matters of faith and morals which is binding on all of the faithful.

A solemn doctrinal definition is an independent function of the Pope with the special support of the Holy Spirit. It does not come about directly by theologians examining the question thoroughly, arriving at a solution which all recognize as true, and then putting their findings before the Pope for endorsement. The exercise of infallibility is not dependent on the judgment of scholars.

23. THE MARKS OF THE CHURCH FOUNDED BY CHRIST

IN THE MOMENT when Jesus the Son of God became man, the foundations of the Church were already laid. Further development consisted in Jesus making available for men through His death that divine life which He had in all its fullness. Because there is in Jesus a single divine life, so there can be only one true Church.

In that solemn prayer before His death in which He commended his own to the Father, Jesus Himself indicated the distinctive marks of the Church in which He would continue His own life. With eyes raised to heaven He addressed His Father in these words:

"Holy Father!
Keep them loyal to your name
which you have given me.
May they be one as we are one!
As long as I was with them,
I kept them loyal to your name.
I shielded and sheltered the men
whom you have entrusted to me;
and none of them is lost
except the one who chooses his own doom.
And thus the Scripture was to be fulfilled!
But now I return to you,
and I say this before I leave the world
that they may taste my joy
made perfect within their souls.

"I have delivered to them your message;
and the world hates them,
because they do not belong to the world,
just as I do not.

"I do not pray you
to take them out of the world,

but only to preserve them from its evil influence.
The world finds nothing kin in them,
just as the world finds nothing kin in me.
Consecrate them to the service of the truth.
Your message is truth.

"As you have made me your ambassador to the world,
so I am making them my ambassadors to the world;
and for their sake I consecrate myself,
that they, in turn, may in reality be consecrated.

"However, I do not pray for them alone;
I also pray for those
who through their preaching will believe in me.
All are to be one;
just as you, Father, are in me and I am in you,
so they, too, are to be one in us.
The world must come to believe
that I am your ambassador" (Jn 17:11–21).

These words of Jesus make it evident that His Church is but one Church and is a united Church. Jesus says: "Keep them loyal to your name . . . may they be one as we are one!"

Jesus' Church is a holy Church; Jesus prays: "Consecrate them to the service of the truth."

Jesus' Church is one Church, descended *from the Apostles* and destined *for the whole world;* Jesus says: "As you have made me your ambassador to the world, so I am making them my ambassadors to the world."

That these words of the Lord hold good for the Church in all time appears from the fact that in His prayer Jesus was thinking not merely of the Apostles but of all "who through their preaching will believe in me" (Jn 17:20).

These marks of the Church are already so well known to St. Paul that in his letters he appeals to them when admonishing the faithful to lead a life in God.

The following passages appear in his letters:

There is one body and one Spirit, even as you, from the moment you were called, had the one hope your calling imparted. There is one Lord, one faith, one Baptism, one God and Father of all, who rules all things and pervades all things and sustains all things (Eph 4:4–6). [*The Church is one.*]

Christ loved the Church, and delivered himself for her, that he might sanctify her by cleansing her in the bath of water with the accompanying word, in order to present to himself the Church in all her glory, devoid of blemish or wrinkle or anything of the kind, but that she may be holy and flawless (Eph 5:26–27). [*The Church is holy.*]

Here there is no Gentile, no Jew, no circumcised, no uncircumcised, no barbarian, no Scythian, no slave, no free man, but Christ is everything in each of us (Col 3:11). [*The Church is catholic, that is, it embraces all peoples, all conditions of men.*]

Let me tell you that if even we ourselves or an angel from heaven should proclaim to you a gospel other than we have proclaimed, let him be accursed. I repeat what I have said: if anyone proclaims to you a gospel other than you have received, let him be accursed (Gal 1:8–9). [*The Church is apostolic, that is, its teaching must agree with that of the Apostles.*]

In the Church, Jesus continues His life upon earth. This fact determines the peculiarity of the Church:

Because there is only one Christ there be only one true Church. Following Christ's words, the Church which He founded is one, holy, catholic, and apostolic.

The Catholic Church is one. Everywhere it has the same doctrine, the same sacraments, and only one supreme head.

The Catholic Church is holy. It has a holy doctrine and all the means of making us holy. From it have emerged many saints who have been glorified by God with miracles.

The Catholic Church is universal or catholic. Since the time of Jesus Christ it has existed for all times and for all peoples.

The Catholic Church is apostolic. Its first directors were the Apostles, and the Pope and the bishops are the legitimate successors of the Apostles.

The true Church, founded by Jesus Christ, is thus the Catholic Church.

One becomes a member of the Catholic Church through faith and baptism. Jesus says: "He that believes and is baptized will be saved" (Mk 10:16).

The Life of the Individual. The believing Christian should feel toward the Church as he would to a mother. With this idea St.

Augustine addresses his contemporaries, and us too: "Love the Lord who loves you; come often to your mother who bore you. Consider what this mother has procured for you by uniting the creature with the Creator, by making children of God out of slaves, brothers of Christ out of minions of the Devil. You show yourself grateful for such benefits by offering her the worthy service of your own presence. No man can have God for his Father who disdains to have the Church for mother. This holy and spiritual mother prepares daily, spiritual nourishment with which to enliven, not your bodies, but your souls."

Whoever belongs to the Church, belongs to Christ. He is to be one with Him, holy in Him, and through Him united with all the faithful, and with the Apostles. He ought never to speak evil of the Church; and he must preserve charity toward bad Catholics.

The Life of the Church.   As a tree always remains the same tree, and yet never remains the same for as much as a single year, so too the Church is always the same Church and yet is never the same but grows through the ages of mankind. The words of Pope John XXIII to the Fathers of Vatican II are appropriate here:

> The salient point of this Council is not, therefore, a discussion of one article or another of the fundamental doctrine of the Church which has been repeatedly taught by the Fathers and by ancient and modern theologians, and which is presumed to be well known and familiar to all. For this a Council was not necessary. But from the renewed, serene and tranquil adherence to all the teaching of the Church in its entirety and preciseness . . . the Christian, Catholic and apostolic spirit of the whole world expects a step forward toward a doctrinal penetration and a formation of consciences in faithful and perfect conformity to the authentic doctrine which, however, should be studied and expounded through the methods of research and through the literary forms of modern thought. The substance of the ancient doctrine of the Deposit of Faith is one thing, and the way in which it is presented is another. And it is the latter that must be taken into great consideration, with patience if necessary, everything being measured in the forms and proportions of a magisterium which is predominantly pastoral in character.

24. THE CHURCH, THE PLACE OF SALVATION IN JESUS CHRIST

IN THE PROPHECIES of the Old Testament, the Savior who was to come had already been heralded as the Good Shepherd. In Ezechiel we read: "I will appoint one shepherd over them to pasture them, my servant David, he shall pasture them and be their shepherd" (Ez 34:23).

Such a prophecy brought to the oriental mind a picture of a shepherd who thought only of his flock, who led them from pasture to pasture, who risked his life fighting robbers and wild animals, who tended the sick animals and carried the weak lambs upon his shoulders.

During the Feast of Tabernacles which preceded His Passion, Jesus applied this prophecy to Himself:

"I am the good shepherd. A good shepherd lays down his life to save his sheep. If a hired man, who is not a shepherd and has no sheep of his own, sees the wolf coming, he abandons the sheep and runs away; and the wolf carries them off or scatters them. After all, he is only a hired man and has no interest in the sheep. I am the good shepherd; and I know mine and mine know me, as the Father knows me and I know the Father; and I lay down my life to save the sheep. Still other sheep I claim as my own, which are not of this fold. I must lead them also to pasture, and they will listen to my voice, and there will be one flock, one shepherd. The Father loves me because I lay down my life, and he wills that I should take it back again. No one can rob me of it. No, I lay it down of my own will. I have power to lay it down, and power to take it back again. Such is the charge I have received from my Father" (Jn 10:11–18).

Jesus describes Himself as the Good Shepherd. He declares explicitly that He knows his own and they know Him. With equal explicitness He indicates that He exercises His shepherd's function according to the will of His Father in heaven. Every person who recognizes the true Church for what it is but fails to enter it, and every person who belongs to the true Church, yet leaves it, separates himself from the Good Shepherd.

The believer as a member of the Church has a given, objective, relation to the Church. But even he who does not belong to the Church has some spiritual relation to the Church. Either he is basically disposed to do whatever God commands and is therefore joined to the Church, or he is not so disposed and hence cut off from the Church.

As Jesus said of individual heathens (e.g., the centurion at Capharnaum) that they excelled the Israelites, so today it can happen that non-Catholics put Catholics to shame by their zeal for what is good.

The expression "only sanctifying Church" must not be misunderstood. It is not meant to assert that outside actual membership in the Church nobody, and inside the Church everybody, becomes blessed, i.e., saved; it only maintains that the Catholic Church is the only one which was established by Jesus Christ and possesses all the powers of sanctification. Unless Christ Himself were to become divided it would be impossible for Him to live simultaneously in several Churches.

The Life of the Individual. It is characteristic of a Catholic Christian that he accounts true whatever the Church teaches. A real doubt of the truth of the Church's teaching is thus excluded. We must distinguish, however, between doubt and the desire to grasp clearly this or that truth, or to bring it into harmony with other established facts. Every man struggles, more or less, to reach clarity on individual truths and to discover the connection between them. Questions asked as a result of this do not constitute doubt of truth.

The Church is the divinely established means by which God's truth is made known to man, and she is the appointed channel of man's approach to God. All must abide by the conditions which the Lord Himself has laid down for all who would draw near to Him. And if people observe willingly and carefully the ceremonial prescriptions which pertain to approaching an earthly ruler, it is fitting in a much higher degree that they should carry out the directions which God has laid down for intercourse between Himself and men.

The Life of the Church. By teaching that she alone possesses all the powers of grace for sanctification, the Church most certainly does not say that all Catholics will reach heaven. As the best medicine is useless if not taken according to the doctor's prescription, so the sacraments and the holy Sacrifice of the Mass are useless if the faithful are not intent on their salvation. St. Peter was already warning Christians to make sure their calling in the Church, through good works; and Paul commands them to work for their salvation in fear and trembling (cf. 2 Pt 1:10; Phil 2:12).

The first thing which a Catholic ought to attribute to all Christians is the gift of prayer. Today all Christians still pray one prayer, the *Our Father,* the *Lord's Prayer,* in common. If all Christians would make use of this prayer which they all have in common, in true love for each other, this would contribute greatly toward drawing together spiritually.

All Catholics must take very seriously the command to love their neighbors, applying this command to those of other Christian denomination and indeed to all men. As far as is in their power, they should, with delicacy and prudence, help to break down the legacy of prejudice which still persists. Obviously this is only possible if the Catholic knows the truths of the Catholic Church, not simply by rote from the Catechism, but has grasped them deeply, and is able to speak about them in language suited to the people he meets. He should also learn to *listen,* to seek an understanding of the faith of his separated brethren, to remove, as far as possible, any obstacles to the unity of the Church.

25. THE COMMUNION OF SAINTS: THE PARTICIPATION OF ALL THE FAITHFUL IN THE TREASURES OF SALVATION THROUGH CHRIST

SOCIETIES (BROTHERHOODS) played an important part in life in the Mediterranean lands at the time of the Apostles. Such a society was called a *koinonia*. The basis of such a *koinonia* usually lay in a common occupation and a certain measure of common property. Thus there were, for example, fisher brotherhoods and weaver brotherhoods.

The members of a brotherhood celebrated their own festivals, brought their own sacrifice, and had their own memorial days for deceased members.

The outward forms of these brotherhoods might vary in details from land to land; but they governed the life of the simple people to such an extent that more or less everyone was familiar with them.

In such circumstances it is understandable that St. Paul should make use of this expression when he sought to explain the Church to the heathen. He does this, for example, in the introductory greeting in the First Epistle to the Corinthians, in which he reminds his readers of the riches they owe to the Church through Christ. He writes:

> I give thanks to my God always on your behalf for God's grace which was given you in Christ Jesus, because in every respect you have been enriched in him with every form of eloquence and knowledge. In proportion as the testimony borne to Christ has been well established among you, you lack no gift. Meanwhile you await the appearance of our Lord Jesus Christ. He will keep you steadfast to the end, unimpeachable on the day of our Lord Jesus Christ. God is faithful; it was he who called you into fellowship with his Son, Jesus Christ our Lord (1 Cor 1:4–9).

Here St. Paul quite simply describes the Church as a *"koinonia* in Jesus Christ."

The brotherhoods which the readers already knew from their own lives were formed mostly from the alliance of members with equal rights; these contributed equally to the property of the brotherhood and chose from among themselves their *archon,* their leader and director.

As St. Paul points out, the *great koinonia of the Church* has been founded by a single person, viz., Jesus Christ the Son of God, and has been endowed with an inexhaustible treasure, the possession of divine life, the possession of the sacraments, and the holy Sacrifice of the Mass, the possession of grace and love in the Holy Spirit. As a result, Jesus is the unique Head of this brotherhood; hence it is properly described a *"koinonia* in Jesus Christ."

The truth which the Church transmits to men in the name of Christ is not merely a truth *from above,* a doctrine which is brought into human life, but is also a doctrine *for above,* a teaching which will lead men on high to eternal blessedness.

Again the means of salvation, the heavenly powers of which the Church disposes in the sacraments and in the holy Sacrifice of the Mass, are not merely means of salvation *from above,* but are also heavenly means of salvation and heavenly powers *for above;* they lift man above himself and bestow upon his natural life a second life, a supernatural life in God.

Jesus Himself is the truth who abides in the Church — He is the Word of God given to His people; His Word lives in Scripture and tradition and is dynamically at work in the Church today. The heavenly power, the Life which He gives is never separated from Him as its fountainhead; and yet it creates grace in the members of His Body, giving true individual existence to those men who receive supernatural life. New, independent creatures by grace, the members of the Church are yet one with each other in love, and also one with Christ from whom they can never be separated if they are to have His life in them (cf. Jn 15:4).

This mysterious indwelling of Christ which does not destroy but creates true individuality is the foundation of the Mystical Body of Christ.

Because that is so, the faithful within the Church are not united with one another primarily as man to man, but through Christ, who is the Way, the Truth, and the Life for all.

Because Jesus did not found this society of His own will, but founded it in the Father, St. Paul describes the reception of the faithful into this society as a calling through the Father in heaven. And when Paul speaks thus, he is presenting a thought which permeated all the sermons of Jesus. Jesus is constantly directing His hearers to the Father in heaven, from whom He was sent to lead all men to God as His brethren.

According to the will of Jesus the founder, the members of this society (*koinonia*), as is the case with other societies, have a duty to give help to one another. Indeed this is the supreme law of the *koinonia*. This *koinonia* was founded by Jesus in suffering and death; and therefore all in a certain measure have to make a contribution of sacrifice, of suffering to the common treasure, thus making themselves spiritually like the founder, Jesus Christ. The faithful on earth pray for one another and intercede for the faithful departed. The saints in heaven pray for the faithful on earth and for the faithful departed.

This is what the *Apostles' Creed* means when it speaks of the Communion of Saints, and what we mean when we speak of the spiritual possessions which pertain to all the baptized, in and through Jesus.

The veneration of the saints on earth is based upon this communion of angels and saints in Christ. They are those friends of the pilgrims upon earth who have already gained acceptance into the hosts of the chosen. As a child venerates those objects which its parents used every day, so the Church from earliest times has venerated relics of the saints and uses pictures and statues to remind us of the saints and their virtues. The saints, as the encyclical on the sacred liturgy (*Mediator Dei,* 1943) says, were imitators of Christ; they can serve, therefore, as models for all who, like them, are to follow in the footsteps of Christ. Thus in the course of the Church's year, the Church commemorates not only the life of Christ and of His holy mother but also the saints of every century.

To Mary as the virgin mother of the Redeemer there belongs a special rank among the saints. She is mentioned in the first place in the liturgical prayers of Mass. When Pope Pius XII solemnly declared the corporal Assumption of Mary to be part of the Church's truth, and did so precisely on the feast of All Saints, he thereby presented Mary to the faithful as the Queen of all the saints.

We are inclined to think of veneration of the saints as something which came into the Church and developed only in recent centuries. The record of Polycarp's martyrdom shows that from earliest times the faithful regarded veneration of the saints as part of their religious life. This record concludes: "We pray to Christ as the Son of God; but we love the martyrs, the scholars and imitators of the Lord, on account of their exceptional faithfulness toward their king and teacher."

The Church in Jesus Christ, the Son of God, is represented as a society possessing all graces and being linked to eternity, through Jesus.

The members of the Church upon earth are called the Communion of Saints because believers in Jesus Christ have a share in all the treasures of salvation.

For the *faithful on earth* the Communion of Saints finds expression in their joining together in love to do homage to God in public worship, and in their genuine brotherly love, in sacrifice, in prayer, and in helping one another by good works.

For the *saints in heaven,* the Communion of Saints finds expression in sharing with the faithful on earth and the holy souls in purgatory their merits, and obtaining help from God through their intercession.

The Communion of Saints finds expression for *the holy souls in purgatory* in their being aided by the faithful on earth who offer for them the holy Sacrifice of the Mass, prayers, good works, and indulgences; and by themselves praying to God for the faithful on earth.

The Life of the Individual. A Catholic in the state of sanctifying grace — possessing the three theological virtues, faith, hope, and charity — is perfectly united to the Church.

A Catholic in mortal sin, as long as he keeps faith and hope, remains linked with God and so also with the Church.

If a man has lost faith, then he has lost contact with God and

Christ and also with the Church. But by virtue of the indelible mark which by baptism he bears within him, God will never cease to hold out to him the grace of repentance.

If he persists in resisting this, then indeed it may well happen that he enters into a new and sinister relation to God and the Church; he begins to hate both.

The Life of the Church. The oldest grace at meals shows the lively awareness of primitive Christians that they formed a spiritual society. They could no longer share even common bread without thinking of the marvelous Bread of the Eucharist. This grace, dating from A.D. 100, runs: "As this bread which we break was scattered upon the mountains (as seed corn), so may Your congregation be gathered together from the ends of the earth into Your kingdom; for Yours is the honor and the power through Jesus Christ."

Inscriptions in the catacombs prove that the veneration of the saints is part of the ancient deposit of faith. In the catacomb of St. Sebastian is to be found a series of inscriptions in which the intercession of SS. Peter and Paul is invoked. It runs: "Peter and Paul, pray for the sinner Priamus."

There is also early evidence for the custom of praying for the dead. At the beginning of the fifth century, for example, we have the sublime request of St. Monica, mother of St. Augustine: "Set down this body anywhere, and do not trouble yourselves at all in its care. This alone I ask, that wherever you shall be, you will remember me at the altar of the Lord."

Earlier still there is the inscription on the epitaph of Abercius, Bishop of Hierapolis — about A.D. 200: "Let him who understands and believes this (i.e., the Catholic Faith, symbolically expressed in the epitaph), pray for Abercius."

From the knowledge of the unity of the faithful with Christ — and through Christ with one another — arose prayers commemorating the living and the dead, and petition for the intercession of the saints. These also found their way into the Mass. In the prayer for the intercession of the saints we find today the word "communion" as the translation of the Greek word *koinonia* which originally occupied the same place.

The thought of purgatory arouses fear of venial sin. Prayer for father and mother, brother and sister, for friends and acquaintances, is a bridge spanning the gap between this world and the next. As the years roll on, the greater becomes the number of acquaintances who await us on the far side; there is no better way of making friends with the thought of death than by praying for them constantly. Whoever does this is acting in the spirit of the Church. It is not only in Masses for the dead that the priest remembers the dead. In every Mass the priest remembers and says with arms outstretched: "To these, O Lord, and to all who rest in Christ, grant, we, pray You, a place of refreshment, of light, and of peace. Through the same Christ our Lord."

26. THE POWER OF FORGIVING SINS—TRANSMITTED FROM CHRIST TO THE CHURCH

DURING HIS EARTHLY LIFE, when Jesus saw a man filled with sorrow over his sins, He gave him the assurance that God forgave him. This happened when, for example, four men brought a lame man to Him. The evangelist St. Mark tells us:

> When he returned to Capharnaum some days later, the news spread that he was at home. Then a crowd gathered, so large that even the space about the entrance could hold no more. While he was explaining the message, a group arrived trying to bring a paralytic before him. Four men were carrying him and since they did not succeed in bringing him into his immediate presence, owing to the crowd, they removed the roof over the place where he was, and through an opening let down the mat on which the paralytic was lying. When Jesus saw their faith, he said to the paralytic, "My son, your sins are forgiven you." Now some of the Scribes were in the audience, and they assumed a critical attitude: "How can the man talk in that way?" "Why, he blasphemes!" "Who can forgive sins except God alone!" Jesus at once read their minds and, aware of their inward criticism, said to them: "Why are you in such a critical mood? Which is easier, to say to the paralytic, 'Your sins are forgiven,' or to say, 'Rise; take up your mat and walk'? Now I want you to understand that the Son of Man has power here on earth to forgive sins." He then addressed the paralytic: "I command you: rise; take up your mat, and go home." He rose and, taking up his mat, walked out before the eyes of all (Mk 2:1–12).

Here, in face of the Scribes and Pharisees, his enemies, Jesus ascribed to Himself, with uncompromising clarity, the power of for-

115

giving sins. He did this knowing that afterward His enemies would persecute Him with increased rage.

Out of love for men, at His departure from earth Jesus bestowed upon the Church full power to remit sin, in the sacraments of Baptism, Penance, and Anointing of the Sick. Today proud spirits resent this in the very same way as the Pharisees in their time were infuriated by Jesus' attribution to Himself of the power of forgiving sins, and by His exercising that power.

It was love which compelled the Lord to grant to the Church the authority of absolving from sin. Not to make use of this power of the Church as often as one needs it is to disdain this love.

In His sacrificial death, Jesus has made atonement for all the sins of the world. From this atonement He has acquired the right to lay down the conditions under which individual men are to receive forgiveness.

Jesus Christ has bestowed upon His Church power to forgive sins.
  Only this power could enable it to carry on with the work of the sanctification of all men in His name.
Sins are remitted in the Sacraments of Baptism, Penance, and Anointing of the Sick.

The Life of the Individual.   A longing for forgiveness can fill only the man who sees in sin an insult to God, and who believes in the forgiving kindness of God. The longing for forgiveness arises, therefore, with greater force according as the conception of God becomes more perfect; and trust in His goodness and love, deeper.

A man who no longer believes in God may well feel some kind of remorse; but he cannot long for forgiveness as does a believer. Who is there to forgive him anyway? He cannot forgive himself for his own faults. And it is senseless to approach other men, for they too, all have their own faults.

The Life of the Church.   In early days it was mostly adults who were received into the Church. Hence, the words, "remission of sins" made one think of Baptism more than they do today. In the *Nicene Creed* recited at Mass it is clearly expressed: "I confess one baptism for the remission of sins." The *Apostles' Creed* kept the more common expression, "forgiveness of sins," but this includes implicitly faith in the sacraments of Penance and of the Anointing of the Sick.

27. THE CONSUMMATION OF THE KINGDOM OF GOD: THE RESURRECTION OF THE DEAD

SOUL AND BODY were created by God as a unity. In God's plan they were never to be separated; rather, man was to be removed from the earth by a kind of transformation through which he was assumed into heaven. Through the sin of Adam, the sin of that man in whom, as natural head of the human race, all men were incorporated, death came into the world for him and for all his posterity.

Through the death of Jesus the Son of God, who was not subject to sin and who was able to make infinite satisfaction for the rest of mankind through His death, the meaning of death has been altered. In the grace of Jesus Christ, to every man is given the possibility of living in and with Jesus Christ, and so to make of death a passage to eternal life. Jesus therefore declares:

"It is the truth when I tell you that a time is coming, in fact, it is already here, when the dead will hear the voice of the Son of God, and those who heed it will have life. Just as the Father is the source of life, so, too, has he given the Son the power to be a source of life; and he has authorized him to pass judgment, because he is a son of man. Do not be surprised at this, for a time is coming when all the dead and buried will hear his summons, and out of the grave they will come — those who have lived good lives will rise to live, those whose lives have been ill-spent will be condemned" (Jn 5:25–29).

At the Last Day, men will hear the voice of the Son of God. The souls of the good and the wicked will be reunited with their bodies. Then the soul will achieve a power over the body, quite different from that which it had during earthly life. The beauty of the souls in grace will irradiate the body like a light through glass; similarly, the inner hatefulness of the damned will be manifest in the countenance, the gestures, and the bearing of their bodies.

St. Paul writes of the state of the risen:

The sun has its own degree of splendor, the moon its own, and the stars their own, Yes, star differs from star in splendor.
It is the same with the resurrection of the dead.
What is sown is perishable;
What is raised is imperishable.
What is sown is sordid;
What is raised is glorious.
What is sown is weak;
What is raised is mighty.
The body sown is natural;
The body raised is glorified.
As surely as there is a natural body,
So surely is there a glorified body (1 Cor 15:41–44).

When Jesus says that those who have done good will rise to life, and those who have done evil to damnation, He connects the fact that there is an eternal heaven with the fact that there is an eternal hell.

The judgment on the wicked at the Last Day runs:

"Next he will say to those at his left: 'Out of my sight, you cursed ones! Off into the everlasting fire prepared for the devil and his ministers!'" (Mt 25:41.)

The picture of hell is drawn in most detail by Jesus in the parable of the rich glutton and Lazarus the beggar:

"Once upon a time there was a rich man who dressed in purple and fine linen, and feasted sumptuously day after day. Close by the portal of his mansion there lay a beggar named Lazarus — a mass of sores! And oh, how he would have liked to satisfy his hunger with the mere refuse from the rich man's table! Not only that: even the prowling dogs would come and lick his sores. Eventually the beggar died and was carried by the angels into Abraham's bosom. The rich man also died and was buried. Finding himself in extreme torments in hades, he raised his eyes and saw at a distance Abraham with Lazarus in his lap. So he called out: 'Father Abraham, take pity on me and send Lazarus to dip the tip of his finger in water and cool off my tongue; I am in agony in this flame.' 'But remember, my son,' replied Abraham, 'that you received all you cared for during your lifetime, while Lazarus, for his part, was in misery. At present, he is here in bliss while you are in agony. And in addition to all this, a deep chasm is once for all fixed between us and you, so that no one who might wish to cross from here to you can do so, nor can any that are there come over to us' " (Lk 16:19–26).

The way in which Jesus speaks of hell is most telling. Almost without exception Jesus speaks of hell, the place of the abandoned by God and of despair, in such a way as to mention heaven at the same time, the place of eternal and blessed vision of God. Man, of his own free will, can choose either alternative for God's grace, indispensable for gaining heaven, will never be withheld. Because Jesus wishes to make men aware of the fact that the choice between heaven and hell lies in their own hands, He is equally happy to present the kingdom of heaven under the image of an invitation to a wedding; one may accept or decline the invitation — if an invited guest declines the invitation, then it is not the host who excludes him from his share of the wedding. He excludes himself by his own act.

The knowledge of what an eternal heaven and hell meant to men exercised an immense influence upon the thought of Jesus. Jesus' spiritual vision was never diverted from these two facts whenever He spoke of eternal life. This explains why Jesus never came to speak with the same clarity of purgatory and of the purification by temporal punishment for sins which the soul must still undergo after death. But the conviction that there was such a place of purification was already common at the time. We read in the Second Book of Maccabees:

> And making a gathering, he sent twelve thousand drachmas of silver to Jerusalem for sacrifice to be offered for the sins of the dead, thinking well and religiously concerning the resurrection. (For if he had not hoped that they that were slain should rise again, it would have seemed superfluous and vain to pray for the dead.) And because he considered that they who had fallen asleep with godliness, had great grace laid up for them (2 Mc 12:43–45).

Judas Maccabaeus was convinced, as the context shows, that Jewish warriors who had taken heathen dedicated offerings were not worthy of damnation; they had, however, placed themselves into a condition in which they could not have been taken up into heaven as resurrected beings. On this assumption he had a collection made among the soldiers which would be presented as an offering of atonement in the temple at Jerusalem for his fallen comrades, so that they would be freed from their guilt.

The collection of money from the common soldiers, and the presentation of it in Jerusalem, could only have been possible in this form, if the common soldiers and the priests in Jerusalem as well as Judas Maccabaeus, were convinced that the dead could be helped by sacrifice.

It is clear that the purification which the souls undergo in the place of purgation is something intensely painful; but it remains a mystery to us.

In the light of God, in which a man sees himself placed after death, he is immediately filled with immeasurable longing for union with God: at the same time he knows that he cannot appear before God until he is freed of all imperfection. Hence man himself, from love of God, desires ardently for purification in the fire of purgatory; and it is the love of God which sends man into purgatory in order to make him fit for heaven.

The earthly history of mankind comes to an end with the Day of Judgment.

At the Last Day all the dead will arise, and God will refashion the bodies of men.

Jesus speaks of heaven and hell simultaneously, in order to make men aware that the decision about their eternal fate lies in their own hands.

Into purgatory go those who are in a state of grace but who have still sins to expiate.

St. Augustine says of the elect: "We will rest and behold; we will behold and love; we will love and praise. Behold, that will be at the end without end!"

The Life of the Individual.   In a hundred years we will no longer matter to the world, nor the world to us. But it will certainly matter to us in eternity how we lived in the world, and how we died.

The man who knows this law of faith and lives by it, will be progressively filled with spiritual momentum. He could be compared to a man doing well in business. Jesus Himself alludes to such a mood when He says: "Be joyful — leap for joy; a rich reward awaits you in heaven" (Mt 5:12).

The Life of the Church. Because the Church sees in the body of the believer a mysterious grain of corn which one day will awake into a new life, she lays every corpse in the lap of the earth with prayer. This is one reason why the Church forbids cremation for the faithful as something which does not do sufficient honor to the human body.

28. THE ENTRY OF THE BLESSED INTO HEAVEN: THE CONSUMMATION OF THE KINGDOM

THE LIFE OF ST. JOHN differs from the lives of the rest of the Apostles. He was not martyred and he outlived the other Apostles by a generation. He died about the year A.D. 100, and by then the Faith had spread all around the Mediterranean. Heathendom had already acknowledged that the Church was a spiritual power whose very existence endangered the spirit of this world. Under the Emperor Nero — that is about a generation after the death of Jesus — the first persecution instigated by the Roman state itself broke out against the Church. Under the Emperor Domitian the battle flared up again. This time the evangelist John was apprehended and banished to the Isle of Patmos.

Here in solitude St. John had a series of visions about the fate of the Church: the Church is and remains the kingdom of God on earth, ever struggling but never annihilated. A day will come, however, when the struggle is over, and God is victorious; when the host of the elect, awakened from death, enter into heaven and assemble around Christ the Lord who sits enthroned at the right hand of the Father. Then the kingdom of God shall be complete — that kingdom which began with the coming of Jesus into the world, and even then carried within itself the guarantee of victory.

In majestic imagery the Apostle saw the far-off day when the battle for the kingdom of God would be over:

> The seventh angel sounded his trumpet. Then there were loud voices in heaven saying: "The reign over this world has passed to

our Lord and to his Christ, and he will reign for ever and ever."
The twenty-four elders who were seated on their thrones before
God prostrated themselves and worshiped God. "We give you
thanks, O Lord God Almighty," they said, "whose name is 'He is'
and 'He was,' because you have taken possession of your great
power and have begun to reign. The nations had aroused themselves to anger. Then the day of your anger came, the time to judge
the dead and to reward your servants — the prophets, the saints,
and those who revere your name, little or great. The time has come
to destroy the destroyers of the earth" (Ap 11:15–18).

I saw a new heaven and a new earth, for the first heaven and the
first earth had passed away, and the sea was no more. I also saw
the holy city, New Jerusalem, coming down out of heaven from
God, prepared as a bride adorned for her husband. I heard a loud
voice from the throne say,
>"How wonderful! God's dwelling place is among men;
>   he shall make his home among them.
>They shall be his people,
>   and God himself shall abide in their midst.
>He shall wipe away every tear from their eyes.
>No longer will there be death.
>No longer will there be mourning
>   or cry of anguish or pain,
>Because the former things have passed away."

He who was seated on the throne said, "See I make all things
new." Then he added, "Write, because these words are trustworthy
and true." He said to me,
>"It is done. I am the Alpha and the Omega,
>   the beginning and the end.
>To him who thirsts I will give the water of life
>   free of charge from the fountain.

>He who is victorious shall possess these blessings,
>   and I will be his God, and he shall be my son.
>But as for the cowardly, unfaithful, and abominable peoples,
>   the murderers, immoral persons, and sorcerers,
>   the idolaters and liars,
>   their portion shall be in the lake
>   that burns with fire and brimstone.
>This is the second death" (Ap 21:1–8).

St. Paul says of the days of the consummation:

Then the end, when he will hand the kingdom over to his God and Father once he has reduced to nothing every other principality and every other authority and power. He must indeed exercise royal authority, "until he has put all his enemies under his feet." The last enemy to be destroyed will be death, because "he put all things under his feet." But when it is said, "he put all things under his feet," it is evident that he who subjected them is to be excepted. Once everything has been brought into subjection to him, then the Son himself, in order that God may be everything to everyone, will be brought into subjection to the Father who subjected everything to him, in order that God may be everything to everyone and everything (1 Cor 15:24–28).

The end of the world is not the end of all things:

The end of the world does not mean destruction, but a transition to a new existence. "God will make a new heaven and a new earth" (cf. Ap 21:1; 2 Pt 3:13).

The Life of the Individual. "Consider the four last things: death, judgment, hell, heaven — and you will not sin forever." These words are worth pondering. They mean: think on the *four* last things; they do not mean: think *only* on death, *only* on judgment, *only* on hell, *only* on heaven, but: think on these four things as a unity. By the four things together one is made conscious that life is something which cannot be repeated, and that in this life one may not avoid deciding for or against God.

The Life of the Church. In the Preface of the Mass of the feast of Christ the King, the Church draws attention to the consummation of the kingdom of God which occurs at the end of the world.

"You have anointed Your Son, our Lord Jesus Christ, the eternal High Priest and King of all things, with the oil of gladness; that, offering Himself on the Altar of the Cross as an immaculate host and peace offering, He might complete the mysteries of man's redemption; and all creation being made subject to His dominion, He might deliver into the hands of Your unbounded Majesty an eternal and all-enfolding kingdom, a kingdom of truth and life, a kingdom of holiness and grace, a kingdom of justice, love and peace."

THE NEW COVENANT BETWEEN THE BLESSED TRINITY AND MAN, ESTABLISHED THROUGH JESUS CHRIST WITHIN THE CHURCH, THE MOTHER OF ALL THE FAITHFUL

BASIC INTRODUCTION

MAN SHARES AGAIN IN THE DIVINE LIFE THROUGH THE GRACE OF JESUS CHRIST

Blessed be the God and Father of our Lord Jesus Christ, who in Christ has blessed us with every manner of spiritual blessing in the heavenly realm. These blessings correspond to his choice of us in Christ before the foundation of the world, that we should be holy and without blemish in his sight. Out of love he predestined us for himself to become through Jesus Christ his adopted children, conformably to the good pleasure of his will, to the praise of his resplendent grace, with which he has adorned us in his beloved Son.

In him we have our redemption through his blood, the remission of our transgressions, in keeping with the riches of his grace (Eph 1:3–7).

1. SANCTIFYING GRACE: MAN SHARES IN DIVINE LIFE

IT OFTEN HAPPENS that we experience things which we do not understand until long afterward. For example, the child turns to its mother and father, full of trust, before it understands the parent-child relationship.

Something similar applies to human history as a whole. Adam and Eve went through a terrible experience. In a way quite different from what they expected, they learned to distinguish between good and evil. But it was only ever so slowly, under the influence of divine guidance, that man came to a deeper understanding of that which had been lost in paradise, and which was to be regained by redemption in Jesus Christ — participation in the divine life, the grace of inward sanctification.

Under the old Covenant, grace was portrayed now as mercy, now as kindness toward men. In the new Covenant, Jesus the Son of God Himself brought men knowledge of grace, that spiritual, mysterious union with God.

In the Gospels, it is true, there is no discourse of Jesus which could be called a "Discourse on the Doctrine of Grace." Grace is in fact something which takes hold of the whole man; and therefore it is impossible to pin down in a single statement all that grace is and means. Jesus' practice was to unfold the mystery of grace to men in a series of statements and stories.

1. Right at the start of His public ministry, Jesus stated clearly the relation of grace to human nature; and He described grace as something above nature — something supernatural. St. John the Evangelist writes:

A member of the Pharisaical party, Nicodemus by name, a leader in the Jewish community, came to him one night, and said to him:

"Rabbi, we know that you have a mission from God to teach. Surely, no one can give such striking proofs of his claims as you are giving, unless God is with him." Jesus seized the opportunity and said to him: "I must be frank with you: if one is not born anew, he cannot see the kingdom of God." "But how," replied Nicodemus, "can a man be born in his old age? Can he really enter his mother's womb a second time and have another birth?" Jesus answered: "I am telling you the plain truth: unless a man is born of water and the Spirit, he cannot enter the kingdom of God! What is born of the flesh is flesh, and what is born of the Spirit is spirit. Do not be perplexed because I said to you: you must all be born anew" (Jn 3:1–7).

Since Nicodemus was a learned man, to him the Lord made deep statements about the new life in God. Jesus spoke of a rebirth which brought about a return to that wondrous condition in which God had created Adam and Eve; a rebirth by the Holy Spirit, resulting in participation in the divine life. Jesus portrayed grace as something which life is incapable of supplying for itself, but which it can receive — *a supernatural gift.* (The words of Jesus on this occasion will appear again in the section on the sacrament of Baptism.)

2. On another occasion the Lord refers to the spiritual relation which unites God and man in faith, love, and grace. St. Matthew relates:

He was still speaking to the crowds when who should be waiting outside but his mother and his brothers, desiring to speak to him. "Please," someone said to him, "your mother and your brothers are waiting outside, wishing to speak to you." But he protested and said to the messenger: "Who is my mother? And who are my brothers?" Then, with a wave of his hand toward his disciples, he said: "Look! Here are my mother and my brothers. Yes, anyone that does the will of my Father in heaven is brother or sister or mother to me" (Mt 12:46–50).

Grace, therefore, according to our Lord's own statements, signifies a union with the Lord Himself, the closeness of which cannot be compared with the bonds of natural love.

3. On a third occasion the Lord declared that grace unites man with God his Creator in such a way that his life is taken up into the life of God. He said:

"I am the real vine, and my Father is the vinedresser. He prunes away any branch of mine that bears no fruit, and cleans any branch that does bear fruit, that it may bear yet more abundant fruit. By now you are clean, thanks to the lessons I have given you. Remain united with me, and I will remain united with you. A branch can bear no fruit of itself, that is, when it is not united with the vine; no more can you, if you do not remain united with me. I am the vine, you are the branches. One bears abundant fruit only when he and I are mutually united; severed from me, you can do nothing. If one does not remain united with me, he is simply thrown away like a branch, and dries up. Such branches are gathered and thrown into the fire to be burned. As long as you remain united with me, and my teachings remain your rule of life, you may ask for anything you wish, and you shall have it. This is what glorifies my Father — your bearing abundant fruit and thus proving yourselves my disciples" (Jn 15:1–8).

According to this pronouncement of Jesus, man is drawn into the divine life and has part in it as the branch of the vine has part in the life of the vinestock.

4. In these statements about grace, attention has been focused on the individual. It is, therefore, no accident that these three discourses of Jesus contain sentences beginning with "anyone" or "one" or their equivalent. "If one is not born anew . . ." "Anyone that does the will . . ." "Whoever lives on in me . . ."

But there is a whole series of sayings about grace, in our Lord's preaching, in which men in a state of grace are thought of collectively as a unity in Christ. To these sayings belong all those discourses in which Jesus speaks of the kingdom of heaven, of the kingdom of God, of the Church which He intends to found.

For instance, we read in St. Luke:

On hearing this, one of the fellow guests said to him: "O what bliss it must be for anyone to feast in the kingdom of God!"
He replied: "Once upon a time, a man planned giving a great supper and sent out many invitations. About the time set for the supper he sent his servant to give notice to those invited: 'Come; everything is now ready.' Then all alike proceeded to beg off. The first said to him: 'I have bought a farm, and I must of necessity go and inspect it. I beg you, consider me excused.' Another said: 'I have bought five teams of oxen; and I am just going to try them out. I beg you, consider me excused.' Still another said: 'I just got

married, and for that reason I cannot come.' When the servant returned, he reported these excuses to his master. The head of the house flew into a rage. 'Go out quickly,' he said to his servant, 'into the streets and lanes of the city, and bring in here the poor and crippled and blind and lame.' Again the servant reported: 'Master, your order has been carried out, and there is still room for more.' The master then said to the servant: 'Go out on the highways and among the hedges, and compel people to come in. My house must be filled to capacity.' I tell you, therefore, not one of those originally invited will taste my supper" (Lk 14:15–24).

In this parable, Jesus is no longer concerned with the attachment of the individual to God, through grace, but with the community of all individuals in God. According to the parable, all of those who share the meal represent a community.

When the Apostles began preaching the Faith, following the Lord's example, they stressed now one, now another aspect of grace. St. Peter, for example, described grace as participation in the divine nature. St. John the Evangelist calls grace "a being from God and in God." According to the Apocalypse, with grace every person receives a new name, something which is "his very own." St. Paul speaks of men in grace as "living stones," built together into a living temple upon the Foundation Stone which is Christ.

In the years immediately following Christ's Ascension, the word "grace" took a prominent place in Christian thought. This is shown by the following detail. The heathen Greeks and Romans always prefaced their letters with a wish for health and well-being, and expressed this wish by the word *salus*. In place of this word meaning health and earthly well-being, Christians began to use the word *gratia* — "grace." The first thing they wished one another, in good times and bad, in prison, in captivity, in forced labor camps, was the grace of Christ.

This is the tenor of the Epistle of St. Paul to the Romans when he writes: "To all God's beloved, saints by vocation, at Rome, grace be to you and peace from God our Father and the Lord Jesus Christ" (Rom 1:7). Both letters to the Corinthians begin with the words: "Grace be to you and peace from God our Father and the Lord Jesus Christ" (1 Cor 1:3; 2 Cor 1:2). Like the Apostle St. Paul, St. Peter, the primate of the Church, also begins his first letter with the wish: "Grace and peace be yours in abundance" (1 Pt 1:2). In his second letter he replaces this with the expanded sentence: "Grace and peace be yours in a measure ever increasing in proportion to your deep knowledge of our Lord" (2 Pt 1:2).

Every man is called by God to behold Him one day in grace. In respect of this objective, all men are the same, without distinction of race or time.

In His love, God has destined men for a blessedness which surpasses all natural happiness. He has decreed that they should be able to look upon Him for all eternity. This vision of God can only be gained after a spiritual change and the exaltation of man, effected by God. This is sanctifying grace.

Sanctifying grace brings about a mysterious change in man's being:

1. Through sanctifying grace a person wins a share in the divine life, is born of God, and so receives something which transcends nature. Therefore sanctifying grace is called a *super-natural gift*.

2. Through sanctifying grace, God in Christ enters into a union with man, which surpasses all other bonds of love. Man draws near to God in a way which exceeds the bounds of nature and which thus satisfies the longing of the creature to rest in His Creator in a way beyond all imagining.

3. Through grace and in the moment when he receives it, a man becomes a living member of the Mystical Body, that is, of the Church.

Man's union with God becomes broken by mortal sin. Jesus says, "If one does not remain united with me, he is simply thrown away like a branch, and dries up" (Jn 15:6).

A man can win back sanctifying grace after mortal sin by perfect contrition joined with the resolve to confess later, and by a contrite confession. For the remission of sin in confession, imperfect contrition is sufficient.

The Life of the Individual. A proper notion of grace is the best basis for a right understanding of the Church as Christ's foundation, and of the relation of the individual believer to it. According to Christ's teaching, man can neither do anything on his own which will secure sanctifying grace, nor can he, once his being had been permeated by this grace, keep it by his own power. Whoever is truly aware of this will instinctively want to receive the sacraments and to assist at the holy Sacrifice of the Mass; and will see the Church as the community of the faithful who are united in Christ. He will not be deceived by the notion that reception of the sacraments and assistance at Mass are purely optional matters, and that the really important thing is to lead a respectable life.

The Life of the Church. Sanctifying grace is conferred in the sacrament of Baptism. The symbolic actions which accompany the administration of Baptism, the giving of the lighted candle and the baptismal robe, take us back to the first ages of Christianity. At that time Baptism was administered, as a rule, to adult heathens who had come to believe in Christ.

Handing over the white robe, the priest said: "Accept this white garment, and bring it unspotted before the Judgment Seat of God, our Lord Jesus Christ, so that you may attain to everlasting life."

Giving the lighted candle he said: "Take this burning light and preserve your baptism without spot. Keep the laws of God, so that, when the Lord comes to the marriage feast, you may, with all the saints, be able to hasten toward Him in the halls of heaven and live forever."

The giving of the white robe and the lighted candle form a single symbolic action. By the giving of the lighted candle the death of the believer is compared to a summons to a marriage feast; and thus the white robe which is mentioned earlier must signify not just any white dress, but the marriage garment. In this way the sacrament of Baptism, which confers sanctifying grace, is described as a marriage with God. This "bridal love" is to unfold itself in this life and find completion in the next.

2. GOD'S COOPERATION WITH MAN: ACTUAL GRACE

SANCTIFYING GRACE brings participation in the divine life: it enables men to perform supernatural acts.

Just as human love is always proving itself by fresh gifts, so in an even higher degree God's love demonstrates itself by continually influencing men in a special way. This influence of God upon men who are already in a state of grace is called *actual grace*.

Such actual grace is received even by men whose lives have not as yet been supernaturalized by sanctifying grace, but whom God intends to raise up out of sin and draw to Himself.

How God's grace cooperates with man's free-will without robbing him of freedom is a problem which remains insoluble for human thinking. In what follows a graded sequence of reactions will be adduced, reactions which admittedly do not explain the mystery, but which lead up to the actual process.

If an apple falls to the ground, one inert object acts upon another. If a man shakes an apple from the tree, a rational being acts upon an inert thing. If one man intimidates another by threats, one rational being is acting upon another. But a threat represents something which does not touch the real spirit of a man.

It is totally different when one man influences another through constraining love, so that he is led to do, of his own accord, something which is in accord with his nature and circumstances. It is with this sort of influence that we can compare the working of the grace of God. Its starting point is the idea that a man should unfold, from within himself, all the good of which he, and only he, is capable.

If a man responds eagerly to grace, it brings in its powerful train one good work after another. Of this St. Paul bears witness when he writes to the Corinthians:

Are they ministers of Christ? I — to speak like a man out of his mind — surpass them by reason of fatiguing labors more abundant, imprisonments more frequent, lashings innumerable, many threats of death. From the Jews five times I received forty lashes less one. Three times I was scourged, once I was stoned, three times I suffered shipwreck; a night and a day I was adrift on the high sea; in frequent journeys on foot, in perils from floods, in perils from robbers, in perils from my own nation, in perils from the Gentiles, in perils in the city, in perils in the wilderness, in perils on the sea, in perils from false brothers, in fatigue and hardship, in many sleepless nights, in hunger and thirst, in fastings, often in cold and nakedness. Apart from these things, there is my daily pressing anxiety, my solicitude for all the congregations! (2 Cor 11:23–28.)

And, to the same Corinthians, St. Paul explains:

By God's grace I am what I am, and the grace which entered me was not fruitless. On the contrary I have worn myself out in toil more than any of them. No, not I but the grace of God working with me (1 Cor 15:10).

What St. Paul says about himself applies to everyone; it is not a man himself who does good, but the grace of God working with him.

But man is able to exclude the mysterious working of God from his soul, to reject the grace of God. Our Lord Himself speaks very plainly of this in His challenge to Jerusalem:

"Jerusalem, Jerusalem!
Murderess of prophets!
Stoner of the messengers sent to you!
How often have I been willing
to gather your children
as a mother bird gathers her brood
under her wings!
But you refused it!

Mark well: you will find your house abandoned — a prey to desolation" (Mt 23:37–38).

Christ's saying "You refused it" applies to everyone who rejects the actual grace of God.

In the parable of the talents, Jesus explains how a man fares when he cooperates with grace and so is assured of a rich reward from God; and how by declining grace he cuts himself off from God and so delivers himself over to misery.

"Furthermore: imagine a man who, before going abroad, sent for his officials and entrusted to them his money. To one he gave five talents, to another two, and to a third just one — to each the amount proportioned to his individual ability. He then went abroad. At once the recipient of the five talents went to invest them in enterprise and made another five. In like manner, the recipient of the two talents made another two. But the recipient of the one talent went away to dig a hole in the ground and buried his master's money. After a long delay the master of those officials returned and settled accounts with them. So the recipient of the five talents came forward and presented five additional talents. 'Master,' he said, 'you trusted me with five talents; look, I made another five.' 'Well done, my good and faithful servant,' the master said to him; 'you were faithful in managing something small; I will now put you in charge of something great: share to the full your master's happiness.' When the recipient of the two talents came, he said, in turn: 'Master, you trusted me with two talents; look, I made another two.' 'Well done, my good and faithful servant,' his master said to him; 'you were faithful in managing something small; I will now put you in charge of something great: share to the full your master's happiness.' Finally the recipient of the one talent came before him and said: 'Master, I know you are a hard taskmaster; you reap where you have not sown, and you store away what you have not winnowed. So I shrank from doing anything at all and went to bury your talent in the ground. Here you have your capital back again.' But his master had an answer for him: 'You lazy, good-for-nothing fellow!' he said to him; 'you knew that I reap where I have not sown, and store away what I have not winnowed! Then you ought to have put my money in the bank, and on my return I might at least have recovered my capital plus the interest. Therefore take the talent away from him and give it to the one who has the ten talents. Every man who already has will receive yet more till he abounds in wealth, while the man who does not have will lose even what he has. And as for that unprofitable official, throw him into the darkness outside.' There it is that weeping and gnashing of teeth will really be heard" (Mt 25:14–30).

Each individual has his own appointed place in God's plan. This is as true of the king as of the beggar, as true of one who dies in infancy as of him who lives to be a hundred. The task which God has allotted to the individual is a secret; but it is always adapted in the closest possible way to the circumstances of his life.

Every man, therefore, must come to see what it is that he has to do here and now, and ought not to fuss about what may be years hence. Of this, Pascal says: "The present is the only time which truly belongs to us and which we must use according to the will of God. Our minds must be concerned above all with that. The world, however, is so restless that it scarcely ever thinks of present existence and of the moment in which it happens to be living, but thinks only of that in which it shall live. Thus men are always living for the future and never for the present. Our Lord never intended that our prospect should extend farther than the day in which we are. We must respect this limit for the sake of our salvation and our peace. These Christian precepts are indeed full of comfort — much more, I maintain, than the wisdom of the world."

As human love keeps on giving to the beloved new tokens of love, so God continues to influence men according to their condition at the moment. This influence is called actual or supporting grace.

Through *actual grace* God affects man directly and in a supernatural manner, illuminating his mind and strengthening his will, so that he does good and avoids evil. Without actual grace there can be no renunciation of sin and no perseverance and growth in goodness. Actual grace has the following attributes:

1. In grace man cooperates with God in such a way that the good action he does is genuinely both an act of grace and an act of the man's free choice, and thus merits a supernatural reward.
2. Every good action done with the help of grace increases participation in divine life and adds to the corporate vitality of the Mystical Body of Christ, the Church.

God grants to all men sufficient help to allow them to be sanctified. "God our Savior . . . wills that all men be saved and come to the knowledge of the truth" (1 Tm 2:4). As they cannot arrive at truth without abundant grace, it is implied that it is God's will to give an abundance of grace. But the measure in which God apportions effective, actual grace to each individual is a mystery of His love.

The Life of the Individual. A man responds to God's desire for his love by directing all his doings at all times to God with a pure heart, that is, by arousing a "right intention." This is St. Paul's meaning when he says: "Whatever you do or say, let it always be in the name of the Lord Jesus, while you give thanks to God the Father through him" (Col 3:17).

A right intention can be aroused in a general way. For example: "In the name of God!" "All for the glory of God!" "All from love of God!" But it can also be aroused with reference to specific mysteries of faith. Thus, for example, one can take up some work or some suffering, thinking of the Blessed Trinity, of the Passion of Christ, or of the Sacred Heart of Jesus.

Anyone who daily adopts a right intention knows in the depths of his heart that nothing he does is in vain. On the other hand, a man who during work loses sight of God is secretly aware that in the end his work will be of little worth.

How right is the emphasis of Pope Pius XII in an address delivered on April 26, 1950: "For the Christian, work is a kind of worship. Never let it become for you, therefore, something which you avoid; and as little let it become an end in itself or an idol whose slave mankind becomes. In its monotony and because, according to the sentence of God in paradise, it has become something difficult and burdensome, work remains for you one of the most important means of sanctification and one of the most effective means of submitting yourself to the will of God and of meriting heaven."

The Life of the Church. In our redemption by Jesus Christ, the love of God the Father breaks through, flooding the earth in a blaze of light. The relationship between man and God is transformed. Prayer receives a new form. The holy sacraments, new and hitherto unheard-of sacred transactions, begin to penetrate life and ennoble it.

A new sacrifice replaces that of the Old Covenant, a sacrifice wherein Christ with the Church and in the Church approaches the heavenly Father. The baptized person lives but no longer on his own — Christ lives in him, and in Christ he is united with all the other members of the Church.

EXPOSITION IN DETAIL

MAN'S COMMUNION WITH THE TRINITY:
BY PRAYER, IN THE SACRAMENTS, AND
IN THE SACRIFICE OF THE NEW COVENANT

Let us hold fast to the faith we profess. We do not have a high priest incapable of sympathizing with our weaknesses. He has experienced them all, just as we, yet without sinning. Let us, therefore, confidently draw near to God's throne, the source of grace, that we may obtain mercy and find grace to aid us when we need it (Heb 4:14–16).

3. BEFORE THE APPEARANCE OF THE REDEEMER. PRAYER TO GOD THE ONE AND ONLY

PEOPLE OF ALL AGES and places have known prayer. Babylonians and Assyrians, Egyptians and Greeks, Romans and Teutons — all have prayed.

The content of their prayers was dictated by the conceptions which the worshipers had of God. People who believed in many gods had to distribute their prayers among these.

Before Christ, the people of Israel were the only civilized nation who prayed to the one, true God. This people possessed, moreover, the most spiritual and beautiful prayers. Neighboring peoples who surpassed them in knowledge, wealth, and power, could not compete with them in prayer.

Among the books of the Old Testament there is one composed of nothing but prayers and pious songs — the Book of Psalms. Even today its prayers and hymns — 150 in number — form the basis of many parts of the Mass and of the daily, official prayer of the clergy. They are known and loved by all Jews and Christians.

In the Scriptures of the old Covenant there occur many declarations about God which retain their validity to this day.

Here are some examples:

He who serves God willingly is heard; his petition reaches the heavens. The prayer of the lowly pierces the clouds; it does not rest till it reaches its goal, nor will it withdraw till the Most High responds, judges justly and affirms the right (Sir 35:15–18).

Bless God at all times, and desire of him to direct your ways and that all your counsels may abide in him (Jb 4:20).

The great man of prayer of the Old Covenant was Moses, the liberator of the people of Israel. When the Lord God was moved to anger by the faithless people, Moses appeased Him in prayer and thus displayed his leadership precisely by prayer:

With that, the Lord said to Moses, "Go down at once to your people, whom you brought out of the land of Egypt, for they have become depraved. They have soon turned aside from the way I pointed out to them, making for themselves a molten calf and worshiping it, sacrificing to it and crying out, 'This is your God, O Israel, who brought you out of the land of Egypt!' I see how stiffnecked this people is," continued the Lord to Moses. "Let me alone, then, that my wrath may blaze up against them to consume them. Then I will make of you a great nation."

But Moses implored the Lord, his God, saying, "Why, O Lord, should your wrath blaze up against your own people, whom you brought out of the land of Egypt with such great power and with so strong a hand? Why should the Egyptians say, 'With evil intent he brought them out, that he might kill them in the mountains and exterminate them from the face of the earth'? Let your blazing wrath die down; relent in punishing your people. Remember your servants Abraham, Isaac and Israel, and how you swore to them by your own self, saying, 'I will make your descendants as numerous as the stars in the sky; and all this land that I promised, I will give your descendants as their perpetual heritage.'" So the Lord relented in the punishment he had threatened to inflict on his people (Ex 32:7–14).

This narrative makes three things plain.

What was enacted here in a visible event is repeated in an unseen way every time a person turns to prayer: he speaks with God.

Just as Moses did not hesitate to pray for those committed to his care, so everyone is able to intercede for his fellowmen.

Moses, as leader of the chosen people, was a type of Christ, the head and the leader of mankind; his prayer on behalf of the children of Israel heralded the coming of a Savior who, as the Son of God made man, and interceding not merely for Israel but for the whole of mankind, would reconcile God and man.

"What is the use of prayer?" Only think what prayer is and this question is answered, for objections to prayer can only be made by those with no belief in a personal God.

In prayer, man turns to God in thought or in words.

Because it is to God that man turns in prayer, the degree of knowledge of God exercises a profound influence on prayer.

The prayer of Israel was distinguished from the prayer of other civilized nations by being addressed to the one true God who had revealed Himself as Creator of heaven and earth.

The Life of the Individual. The philosopher Feuerbach, a man full of zeal for unbelief, said this: "The deepest thing in religion is revealed by the simplest activity of religion — prayer."

Investigations during recent decades have brought to light prayers belonging to ancient civilizations, notably Egyptian. Among the annals of Egypt we find, for example, the following:

"I, Demetrius, have come to the great Goddess Isis, praying for my parents, my brothers and sisters and friends by name" (temple inscription). "All my prayer and my care is that no evil befall you and that you will be in excellent health" (from a father's letter to a son). "I remember you in prayer before the gods who are honored in this place" (from the letter of a soldier to his sister).

In modern times also many prayers are known, belonging to surviving primitive peoples whose religious customs and outlook have remained unchanged for thousands of years. It now appears that the prayer of primitive peoples is much closer to the prayer of revealed religion than is the prayer of ancient civilizations. Among these primitive prayers we find many whose expression of trust and of childlike dependence on God is reminiscent of the Psalms.

Characteristic of the prayers of these peoples is the invocation with which they begin. "O Thou great Spirit above!" is the opening, for example, of a prayer of the Delaware Indians; "O Lord on high," of the Navaho Indians; "Our Father of chiefs," of the Hottentots.

The Life of the Church. Places of prayer can be likened to electric generators. Streams of energy flow out from these and are transformed into all manner of activity. They give light, turn wheels, heat cold buildings. But if one unacquainted with modern inventions were to judge these machines according to his own ignorance, he would consider it profitless for man to harness rushing water into pipes. In the same way, a man who has no relationship to God might regard prayer as a waste of time or as idleness combined with pride.

4. PRAYER SINCE CHRIST'S ASCENSION INTO HEAVEN. THE MEDIATION OF JESUS CHRIST

WHENEVER A CHANGE OCCURS in knowledge of God and in the relation with God, prayer and sacrifice likewise alter. Thus, with the inauguration of the new Covenant, prayer and sacrifice reached spiritual fulfillment. Jesus Himself had foretold the great change which was to be inaugurated under the new Covenant. This took place in His talk with the Samaritan woman at Jacob's Well. St. John narrates:

"I see, sir," the woman said to him, "you are a prophet! Our fathers worshiped on this mountain, and your people say that Jerusalem is the place for worshiping." "Take my word for it, madam," Jesus replied, "a time is coming when you will worship the Father neither on this mountain nor in Jerusalem. You worship what you do not know; we worship what we do know. Salvation comes from the Jews. And yet a time is coming, in fact, it is now here, when true worshipers will worship the Father in spirit and in truth. Such are the worshipers the Father demands. God is Spirit, and his worshipers must worship in spirit and in truth." "I know very well," the woman said, "that the Messias" — the Christ, as he is called — "is to come and, when he comes, will tell us everything." Jesus then said to her: "I am he — I who now speak to you" (Jn 4:19–26).

In this context, by "worship" we are to understand the total intercourse of man with God; all aspects of prayer; prayer of adoration, of praise, of thanksgiving, of expiation and supplication, and in particular the actual activity of worship — the sacrifice.

Jesus explains therefore: the time is now come when Jerusalem is to lose its special importance as the place where the true God is worshiped. From now on men will worship God "in spirit," i.e., with more perfect knowledge of God. From now on men will likewise worship God "in truth"; they will be able to approach God in a much more perfect way than before.

This new knowledge of God was to be received from Jesus, the Son of God, who reposed in the bosom of the Father; and the new way to God was to be opened up for them through the mediation of Christ who returned to the Father to make intercession for men as long as they required it.

One day the disciples asked Jesus to teach them a prayer. He taught them: "Our Father who art in heaven. . . ." The *Our Father* is literally *the* prayer in the Spirit and name of Jesus.

Conscious that His ascension into heaven would open up a new life of prayer for men, during the Last Supper Jesus said:

> "That will be the time when you ask me no more questions. It is the real truth when I tell you that, if you make any request of the Father, he will grant it to you in my name. Up to the present you made no requests in my name. Make them, and they will be granted. Thus nothing will be wanting to your joy.
>
> "Thus far I have spoken to you in figures. A time is coming when I no longer speak to you in figures, but tell you about the Father in plain language. That will be the time when you make requests in my name; and I do not tell you that I shall then petition the Father in your behalf. Of his own accord the Father loves you dearly, because you are settled in your love for me and in your conviction that I come from the Father" (Jn 16:23–27).

"A time is coming" is to be understood as that time when the Lord will have left the disciples, ascended into heaven, and sent down the Holy Spirit.

Through union with Christ under the new Covenant the prayer of the faithful for one another and, in particular, the intercession of the saints in heaven, increases in significance. An order of prayer of the second degree is established.

First, the faithful call in intercession upon the most blessed Virgin Mary, the mother of Jesus, who by her voluntary acceptance of the motherhood of the Redeemer has become the mother of all. The most perfect supplication to Mary is the *Hail Mary*.

Alongside Mary, the mother of God, are St. Joseph, our Lord's foster father, the Apostles and martyrs, and the rest of the saints, whose intercession is also asked. It is an ancient custom to give a saint's name to every child at baptism and to put the child under his special protection.

He counts himself fortunate who is able to pray as a Christian.

Prayer under the New Law is superior to that under the Old in that it is addressed to God the Trinity and is constantly supported by Jesus Christ the Mediator between the Father and mankind.

The most perfect prayer in the Spirit and name of Jesus is the *Our Father,* also known as the *Lord's Prayer.*

The most perfect supplication to the Mother of God is the *Hail Mary.*

The liturgical prayer of the Church is addressed to God the Father in heaven "through our Lord Jesus Christ, His Son, who lives and reigns with Him in the unity of the Holy Spirit, God for ever and ever." This phraseology derives from the Holy Scripture of the new Covenant; it is already in use with St. Paul as the normative pattern of such prayer — as in his "Give thanks to God the Father through Jesus Christ" (Col 3:17).

The Life of the Individual.   We should practice prayer as zealously as an athlete keeps in training. Without the sustained effort of our cooperation, which is prayer, we cannot win the prize which is eternal life.

Shortly before his death a notable professor of philosophy said: "And now, if you were to ask me before I go for good, if I know of a magic key to unlock the ultimate door to wisdom, I would answer without hesitation. The magic key is not thought, as you might expect a philosopher to say, but is prayer. Only praying souls receive the great things of existence: and praying is best learned through suffering. . . ."

Where do we stand in respect to this?

Do we pray? Do we pray as a Christian? Do we pray so that in some way or other we are conscious that our prayer is quite different from what it would have been had Christ not become man, had not died for us, and did not act for us now as Mediator with the Father? He who has lost all sense of this kind of prayer which proceeds from specifically Christian truths prays like a Mohammedan, for he too believes in a personal God in heaven.

The Life of the Church.   The account of the martyrdom of St.

Polycarp, Bishop of Smyrna (A.D. 156), shows how the faithful in early Christian times turned to God the Father through Jesus Christ in their private prayers. Before his death the bishop prayed: "I praise, honor and glorify You, through the eternal High Priest Your beloved Son, through whom be glory to You with Him and the Holy Spirit, now and for evermore. Amen." (The beginning of this prayer corresponds to a section of the *Gloria.*)

At prayer men have always adopted an exterior attitude which corresponds with the attitude in which they approach their ruler. In olden times, when presenting their requests, men bowed before the ruler; and in cases of special need, they prostrated themselves completely on the ground before him with arms outstretched.

The Greeks used the word *hiketes,* and the Romans the word *supplex* to denote one who threw himself down in supplication. The word *supplex* appears also in ancient petitions of the Church. We find there phrases like, "Prostrate before You, O God!" This expression — so strange to us today — has a history which takes us right back to the time of Christ.

Much more important in the eyes of the Church than the exterior attitude of prayer is a right inward disposition in the faithful at prayer. This concern for a right inward disposition provides the key to many of the petitions in the Holy Mass. Thus, for example, we have the collect for the ninth Sunday after Pentecost. "Let the ears of Your mercy, O Lord, be open to the prayers of Your supplicants: and that You may grant them what they desire, make them ask the things that are pleasing to You."

5. WHAT JESUS DEMANDS OF HIS PEOPLE AT PRAYER: HUMILITY AND TRUST

IN PRAYER, man turns in word or in thought to God. A good prayer must, therefore, be in keeping with the relation in which man stands to God. Full of humility, the worshiper must approach God as the One who is exalted above all things. And he must have unshakable trust in Him as the All-Sufficient and All-Merciful.

The Lord used parables to impress this upon His disciples. He sought to remove from their hearts the pride which destroys, and the lack of trust which cripples prayer.

In order to teach that humility is the fundamental prerequisite of a good prayer, Jesus told this parable.

"Once upon a time, two men went up to the temple to pray, the one a Pharisee, the other a tax collector. The Pharisee stood conspicuously apart and soliloquized this prayer: 'O God, I thank you that I am not like the rest of men — robbers, rogues, adulterers — or like that tax collector over there. I fast twice a week; I pay a tax of ten per cent on every item of my income.' The tax collector, on the contrary, kept in the background and would not so much as raise his eyes to heaven, but struck his breast and said: 'O God, have mercy on me the sinner.' I assure you, this man went down to his home acquitted of all guilt; not so the other. Everyone who exalts himself shall be humbled, and he who humbles himself shall be exalted" (Lk 18:10–14).

In two more parables Jesus showed how a good prayer requires trust and persistence. In the one Jesus describes a midnight disturbance by a neighbor who wants to borrow bread; in the other, He describes a very aggressive widow.

In the old Palestinian houses everyone slept in one room. If someone knocked at the door in the middle of the night and the father arose, immediately all the children would put their heads out of the

147

bedclothes and begin to shout. We must imagine ourselves in this situation when we read the parable in which Jesus demands perseverance in prayer:

"Suppose," he also said to them, "some one of you has a friend and goes to him at midnight and says to him: 'Friend, lend me three loaves of bread; a friend of mine has just turned in from the road to visit me and I do not have a thing to set before him': shall then the man inside remonstrate and say: 'Do not pester me; at this late hour the door is barred; my little ones are in bed with me; I cannot get up and accommodate you'? I tell you, he may not get up and accommodate him just because he is his friend, but he will certainly get up for shame's sake and give him all he asks for.

"That is why I say to you: ask, and you will receive; seek, and you will find; knock, and you will gain admission. In fact, only he who asks receives; only he who seeks finds; only he who knocks will gain admission" (Lk 11:5–10).

The second parable in which Jesus exhorts to perseverance in prayer is among the most remarkable which the Gospels have given to us:

"Once upon a time," he said, "there was a judge in a town somewhere who did not fear God and had no regard for man. In the same town, there lived a widow who used to come to him and say: 'See that justice is done me! Rid me of my persecutor!' For a time he refused; but later he said to himself: 'I do not fear God and have no regard for man; but, at any rate, since this widow is pestering me, I will see that justice is done her. I am afraid she may finally come and beat me black and blue.'" The Master then added: "Listen to what the dishonest judge says! And God will not see full justice done to his faithful who cry to him day and night? Will he really delay acting in their behalf? I tell you, he will see that justice is done them with all speed! But, when the Son of Man returns, will he find the necessary faith on earth?" (Lk 18:2–8.)

Upon His own people who are children of the heavenly Father and His brethren, Christ makes the following demands:

Their prayer must be made in humility, with perseverance and trust. We arrive at this kind of prayer if we keep the love of God always in mind and remember the decisive importance of prayer as a means of salvation. Then we will pray regularly, and thus, sooner or later, will learn to pray really well.

The Life of the Individual.   St. Alphonsus of Liguori writes: "Anyone who prays is bound to become holy: anyone who does not pray is bound to be lost. All the saints (apart from infants) have got to heaven solely by prayer: all the damned are in hell simply because they did not pray. Had they practiced prayer, they would not have been lost. Therefore, in all eternity these miserable creatures will be moved to the bitterest despair by this very thought — that they could so easily have become holy. They had only to ask God for the necessary graces; but for them now, the time for prayer is past."

The Life of the Church.   The Church never tires of repeatedly exhorting the faithful to pray. To certain prayers which she considers specially good and which she wishes should be used extensively, she attaches indulgences. Most of these prayers are very short so that they can be used frequently as ejaculatory prayers, thus enabling us to obey our Savior's admonition to "persevere in prayer and not lose heart" (Lk 18:1).

The saying is common: "A short good prayer is better than a long bad one." But some people, acting on this saying, diminish their prayer year by year, until, in the name of that stress on quality on account of which they shorten it, their prayer finally ceases altogether. Is there any truth at all in the above saying? The following passage from St. Augustine gives the answer.

"From those worldly affairs, which do much to weaken our yearning for God, we must recall our spirit to *set hours of prayer,* in order to spur ourselves on to greater fervor, so that our weakened yearning does not die altogether, and the fire, which we ought more often to kindle, does not go out. . . .

"In such circumstances it is worth insisting that *considerable time should be set aside for prayer,* as long as other duties are not neglected. But all other activities ought to be elevated into prayer by that yearning for God which I already mentioned. Long prayer need not be — as many suppose — wordy prayer. Much speaking is not, however, the same thing as protracted devotion. It is reported of our Lord Himself that He spent whole nights and frequent long periods in prayer. Is this not an example to us from Him who on earth was our mighty intercessor and who now hears our prayers forever beside the Father?"

6. THE *OUR FATHER:* THE PRAYER IN THE NAME AND IN THE SPIRIT OF JESUS

WHILE THEY WERE LIVING with our Lord the Apostles often saw Him spend long periods — even whole nights — in prayer. Every time He returned to them after a night of prayer, there was in His countenance, in His whole bearing, something which aroused longing in them to be able to pray as He did.

> Once he was somewhere engaged in praying. When he had finished, one of his disciples said to him: "Lord, teach us how to pray, just as John taught his disciples."
> He said to them: "When you pray, say as follows:
> 'Father, may you be known and glorified;
> may your kingdom be established;
> give us day after day our daily bread;
> and forgive us our sins,
> for we also forgive everyone indebted to us;
> and do not expose us to temptation.'"
>
> (Lk 11:1–4; cf. Mt 6:9–13)

In His answer to the disciples' request to be taught how to pray, Jesus deliberately distinguishes between His own prayer and theirs. He said: "When *you* pray, say." No other person could ever pray as He did. His manner of praying was a personal mystery connected with the mystery of His divine Sonship.

The prayer which Jesus commanded His disciples to pray is, in a unique way, a prayer in the name of Jesus. What other prayer could be so truly in the name of Jesus as this one which He composed and taught?

Furthermore, the *Our Father* is a prayer in the Spirit of Jesus;

150

a prayer in which each for all and all for each and all together ask the heavenly Father to supply both spiritual and temporal needs.

The *Our Father* contains an address to God and two parts, each having three petitions. Each petition has its own keyword.

The address is: Our Father, who art in heaven.

The three petitions of the first part with their keywords are:

Hallowed be thy name　　Key word: the *name of God*, the Father
Thy kingdom come　　　Key word: the *kingdom of God*, the Father
Thy will be done on
earth as it is in
heaven　　　　　　　Key word: the *will of God*, the Father

The three petitions of the second part with their keywords are:

Give us this day our daily bread　　Key word: *Our bread*
Forgive us our trespasses as we forgive
those who trespass against us　　Key word: *Our trespasses*
Lead us not into temptation but de-
liver us from evil　　　　　　Key word: *Our temptations*

Looking more carefully at those keywords we see that they are all words which have great significance in our Lord's sermons. The *Our Father* embodies the chief points of our Lord's teaching in prayer form; and so there is no better commentary on the *Lord's Prayer* than what can be constructed out of our Lord's sayings on sanctifying the name of God; on the coming of the kingdom of God; on doing the will of God; on the sorrows of daily life; on repentance and forgiveness and temptation.

God's name is hallowed if the number of men increases who worship and honor the true God and if the zeal of these men for the recognition of the majesty of God keeps on growing.

God's kingdom comes to us when men carry out their occupation in conformity with the laws of God, and do it for love of God.

The will of God the Father is done on earth as in heaven when men submit to Him in love and joy.

In the words, "Give us this day our daily bread," we ask God that the good things of this world may be so distributed that all may have wherewith to live.

In the words, "Forgive us our trespasses as we forgive those who trespass against us," we ask God to keep on forgiving us, and we declare our own readiness to continue forgiving our fellowmen likewise.

In the words, "Lead us not into temptation, but deliver us from evil," we ask God never to abandon us to temptation but to keep us from consenting to evil.

The word "Amen" means: so let it be.

Judging by its contents the *Our Father* is not a prayer of petition in the commonly accepted sense. In the first three petitions we are not asking for any kind of spiritual goods which apply first and foremost to man. In particular, the first petition — the wish that God's name be hallowed — is equivalent in oriental speech to praising God.

The *Our Father* is the prayer in the name and Spirit of Jesus.

Jesus Christ Himself taught the *Our Father* and commanded us to use it. Being made brethren of Jesus by Baptism, in this prayer we address the heavenly Father as our own Father.

The *Our Father* is the prayer proper to the children of God. It is composed of an address and two parts each containing three petitions.

The three petitions of the first half are concerned directly with the glory of God; the three in the second, indirectly with the glory of God.

The keywords of the first half of the *Our Father* are:

The name of God
the kingdom of God
the will of God

The keywords of the second half of the *Our Father* are:

Our daily bread
our trespasses
our temptations

The Life of the Individual. Cardinal Newman once said, "In its commencement religion is necessarily almost a task and a formal service." To him that was neither a misfortune nor an error. Error and misfortune begin, as he says, only when we do not let this service form us and become the expression of our own spiritual life. This applies above all to the *Lord's Prayer.*

The *Our Father* unfolds itself of its own accord in our heart, if we are conscious, every time we pray, of what is happening. As often as we pray it we are saying that prayer which Jesus Himself commanded His people to address to His Father in heaven. And at the time when He did this, He had in mind the fact that when we would be praying, He would be standing before His Father's throne, taking up our prayer into His own, and placing it before the Father in union with His own.

It is certain that we shall never fathom the ultimate depths of the *Our Father;* in the end we are still like children who present petitions to the Father in heaven, which have been composed for us by the Son of God Himself. This does not at all mean that the *Our Father,* the *Lord's Prayer,* which is the deepest of all prayers, is the very prayer which men pray with least thought. If we impress on our minds the six keywords, it is relatively easy to keep the petitions filled with substance.

Every recited prayer takes life from the inner mental attitude of the one who prays. The attitude which we as Christians should have or should aim at having with regard to the *Our Father* is expressed by St. Cyprian in the introduction to his study of this prayer. "He had already foretold that the hour was coming when the true worshipers would adore the Father in spirit and truth. He fulfilled His prophecy; and we who have received the spirit and truth through His work of sanctification, may also pray in spirit and truth through His instruction. What could be more spiritual than the prayer of Christ who sent us the Holy Spirit? What prayer could have more of truth in it than that which came from the Son who is the Truth of the Father's utterance?

"Dear friends, let us pray as God has shown us. To make our requests of Him in His own words, to rise to His hearing with the petition of Christ — this is to pray as a friend and intimate. When we pray, may the Father recognize the words of the Son; may He who dwells in our hearts be also in our voice. We have an Advocate for our sins with the Father; when we seek pardon, let us speak in His words. He has promised: 'Whatever you ask the Father in my name, he will give it to you.' How much more effectively will we obtain what we ask in Christ's name if we seek with His prayer?

"But our prayer must be under rule: it should be quiet and modest.

Remember: we stand in the sight of God; our manner of speech and bodily bearing must be pleasing to Him. The brazen man makes a din in prayer; the modest man controls himself.

"And when we meet our brothers to celebrate divine sacrifices with God's priest, let us be modest and disciplined. There should be no indiscriminate confused airing of prayers, no restless talkative parading of petition but a quiet offering of it to God."

A deeper grasp of the *Our Father* can be gained by saying it slowly, meditating on each word. The same end is achieved by repeating the *Our Father* several times over as one member of a congregation. This is no "vain repetition" in the sense which our Lord condemned. In this very manner the Savior Himself had prayed for three hours on the Mount of Olives, repeating the same request, always in the same words: "My Father, if it is possible, let this cup be spared me" (Mt 26:38–46).

The Life of the Church.   The *Our Father* is a private prayer when one uses it alone; a public prayer when used along with others in church; and it is a liturgical prayer when used in the celebration of holy Mass.

The words by which the *Our Father* is introduced in the Mass show us with what reverence the Church regards this prayer which Jesus Himself taught. "Instructed by Your precepts, and following Your divine institution, we are bold to say: *Our Father . . .*"

There is evidence that from the earliest times Christians said the *Our Father* thrice in the day.

7. THE *HAIL MARY:* ASKING FOR MARY'S INTERCESSION WITH HER SON

THE EFFICACY of any intercession depends upon two things. The intercessor must love him for whom he intercedes and must have influence with the person with whom he intercedes.

From this we see that the intercession of the mother of God has unique rank. At God's behest, Mary accepted motherhood of Jesus for the sake of the children of Adam, with unconditional and loving devotion; hence the prayers which Mary addresses to Jesus Christ arise out of a heart which overflows with love for men.

The unique effectiveness of Mary's prayers derives from her motherhood of Jesus, the Son of God. Her words are indeed the words of that mother who received Jesus, the Son of God, into her virgin womb, nursed Him as an infant, was with Him throughout those quiet years at Nazareth, and finally suffered in love beneath the cross with Him as He offered Himself, an atoning sacrifice for men.

The Church's usual intercession to Mary is:

> Hail Mary, full of grace, the Lord is with thee: blessed art thou among women and blessed is the fruit of thy womb, Jesus. Holy Mary, Mother of God, pray for us sinners, now and at the hour of our death. Amen.

The angelic salutation: "Hail Mary, full of grace, the Lord is with thee," and Elizabeth's words to her favored relative: "Blessed art thou among women and blessed is the fruit of thy womb," are already to be found in the old Mass for the fourth Sunday in Advent which, as the last Sunday before the festival of Christ's birth, was kept as a Marian Sunday, the Offertory psalm being joined with a greeting in homage to the Virgin. To these two sentences which formed this greeting was added later the prayer of intercession which runs: "Holy

Mary, Mother of God, pray for us sinners, now and at the hour of our death. Amen."

Beginning, as it does, with a greeting, the *Hail Mary* is specially suited to repetition.

In the *Angelus,* the angel's greeting to Mary is repeated thrice and each time the *Hail Mary* is preceded by a verse, giving us the following prayer:

> The angel of the Lord declared unto Mary:
> And she conceived of the Holy Spirit. *Hail Mary,* etc.
> Behold the handmaid of the Lord:
> Be it done unto me according to Thy word. *Hail Mary,* etc.
> And the Word was made flesh:
> And dwelt among us. *Hail Mary,* etc.

The first verse alludes to the mystery of the Incarnation as a whole; then follow two verses, one of which reminds us of Mary and the other of Jesus the Redeemer.

Of Mary we are told that she said, "Behold the handmaid of the Lord, be it done unto me according to Thy word."

Of Jesus we learn: "And the Word was made flesh and dwelt among us." By the "Word" we must understand Jesus the Son of God. St. John describes Him thus in the prologue to his Gospel. "Flesh" refers to the human, passible, mortal nature of Jesus. In the same sense Jesus Himself says to Peter: "It was my Father in heaven that revealed this to you, and not flesh and blood," i.e., "It is not your own weak human understanding which has taught you this, but God in heaven has enlightened you."

As a repetitive prayer, the *Hail Mary* forms the basic vocal prayer in honor of Mary. The repetition of this prayer, interspersed with the *Lord's Prayer,* is called the *Rosary.* In the *Rosary* we implore the intercession of Mary the mother with Jesus the Redeemer, and as we do this we inwardly meditate on those events in the life of Jesus in which His life and His mother's are bound together in unity. These events are called "mysteries."

The mysteries of the life of Jesus to which the worshiper should direct his mind during the *Rosary* fall into three groups of five each: the *Joyful Mysteries;* the *Sorrowful Mysteries;* and the *Glorious Mysteries.*

The fifteen mysteries of the *Rosary* are:

The Annunciation
The Visitation
The Nativity
The Presentation in the Temple
The Finding in the Temple

The Agony in the Garden
The Scourging at the Pillar
The Crowning With Thorns
Jesus Carries His Cross
Jesus Dies Upon the Cross

The Resurrection
Ascension
The Descent of the Holy Spirit Upon the Apostles
The Assumption of the Virgin Mary Into Heaven
The Crowning of the Virgin Mary as Queen of Heaven.

Among prayers not addressed directly to God the Trinity, to the Father, to Christ, or to the Holy Spirit, prayers to Mary the mother of the Redeemer take first place.

The *Angelic Salutation* (*Angelus*) is said thrice daily according to ancient custom, as thanksgiving for Christ's Incarnation, and, following the angel's example, in honor of Mary the Lord's mother. The *Rosary* consists of the repetition of the two most perfect prayers, the *Our Father* and the *Hail Mary*. The mysteries set before the worshiper's eyes the principal events in the life of Jesus and His mother. As the encyclical *Mediator Dei* tells us, among devotions in honor of Mary, the *Rosary* takes first place.

The Life of the Individual. The *Rosary* is in no sense a substitute for liturgical prayer: it meets another equally important need of devotional life.

The *Rosary* is not merely a prayer for simple folk: it rises and falls according to the mind of the worshiper. Like any other prayer, it can be performed in such a way that it becomes no true prayer at all. On the other hand it can equally well become a prayer of the highest contemplation.

The Church urges priests to recite the *Rosary* every day, and desires that the faithful do likewise.

In his encyclical on the sacred liturgy (*Mediator Dei*), Pope Pius XII had this to say about veneration of Mary, the Mother of God:

> Among the holy citizens of heaven the Virgin Mother of God receives honor of a special kind. By reason of her God-given function, her life is most closely interwoven with the mysteries of Jesus Christ; and assuredly no one better or more closely followed in the footsteps of the Word Incarnate, no one enjoys greater favor or influence with the Sacred Heart of the Son of God, and through It with the heavenly Father. She is holier than Cherubim and Seraphim and enjoys greater glory than all the heavenly citizens, because she is "full of Grace," because she is the Mother of God, and because by her blessed child-bearing she gave us the Redeemer. She is "Mother of mercy, our life, our sweetness and our hope," and therefore let us all cry to her "mourning and weeping in this vale of tears," and with confidence commit ourselves entirely to her patronage. She became our mother while the divine Redeemer was offering the sacrifice of Himself; and therefore, by this title too, we are her children. She teaches us all virtues; she gives us her Son and, with Him, all the helps we need; for God "has willed us to have everything through Mary."

The Life of the Church. Between 1883 and 1898, Pope Leo XIII produced a series of encyclicals, all of which were concerned with the revival of devotion of the *Rosary*. In the encyclical of 1898 he ordained that the feast of the Holy Rosary be made a feast of the second class, and that the invocation "Queen of the Holy Rosary" be added to the *Litany of Loretto*.

In 1943 Pius XII solemnly consecrated the Church and mankind to the Immaculate Heart of Mary. The dedicatory prayer begins with the invocation of Mary as "Queen of the Holy Rosary" and ends with the words: "May she, the most holy mother of all of the members of Christ, now radiant in body and soul in the glory of heaven and reigning there on high with her Son, constantly entreat this Son of hers to pour down rich unfailing streams of grace from the exalted Head upon every member of the Mystical Body." By speaking thus at once of the devotion of the *Rosary* and of the Immaculate Heart of Mary, the Pope portrayed the *Rosary* as a devotion which includes veneration of the heart of Mary.

In the dogmatic definition of the doctrine of the bodily assumption of Mary into heaven, Pope Pius XII points out that the two last mysteries of the *Rosary* are evidence of age-old universal belief in Mary's Assumption. All fifteen decades of the *Rosary* show Mary as nothing less than "the companion of Jesus," the divine Redeemer, as He fulfills His work of salvation, from the first moment of the Incarnation until the consummation in the now effective dispensation of grace.

8. JESUS AT PRAYER: THE MODEL OF PRAYER FOR HIS PEOPLE

THERE ARE PEOPLE who say their morning and evening prayers in solitude. If they were invited on some occasion to say the *Rosary* along with others they would decline, explaining that it is said in Scripture that we should pray in the privacy of our own room. There are others again who gladly join in the *Rosary* but who, day in, day out, never once pray in private. And then there are people who like to join in the prayer of a public Mass, but who consider the *Rosary* and the litanies outmoded.

However they may differ in detail, all of these people labor under the same delusion. They forget that man has a duty to pray in various respects, and that these different duties cannot be substituted one for the other.

1. Man as an individual is bound to pray. It is this prayer which our Lord intends should be carried out in secret.

2. Man as a member of the family and of the community is bound to pray. For the sake of this membership he ought not to dissociate himself from public devotions. "Where two or three are assembled in my name, there I am in the midst of them," says the Savior (Mt 18:20).

3. Man is bound to assist on Sunday at the holy Sacrifice of the Mass. He participates best in the celebration if he can follow the liturgical prayers.

For every type of prayer, Jesus gives us an example.

Jesus prayed alone:

> Very early the next morning — it was still dark — he rose, left the house, and went to an out-of-the-way place; and there he prayed. But Simon and his companions started in pursuit of him, and, when they found him said to him: "All seek you" (Mk 1:35–37).

Jesus took part in the prayer of the community. All the evangelists describe in almost identical words how, at the miracle of the loaves, Jesus said the grace before meals.

Then he took the five loaves and the two fish into his hands, and, looking up to heaven, said grace over them, and broke them into portions which he gave to the disciples to serve to the crowd. All ate, and everyone had a plentiful meal (Lk 9:16).

Then, taking the loaves and the two fish into his hands, he looked up to heaven and, after saying grace, broke the loaves into portions, which he gave to his disciples to serve to the people (Mk 6:41).

He then ordered the crowds to recline on the grass, took the five loaves and the two fish into his hands, looked up to heaven, and, after saying grace, broke the loaves into portions, which he gave to his disciples. The disciples then passed them out to the crowds (Mt 14:19).

Jesus then took the loaves into his hands and, after saying grace, had the loaves as well as pieces of fish distributed among the people reclining about the ground. Everyone got as much as he wanted (Jn 6:11).

Jesus greatly honored the celebration of the liturgy. St. Mark tells us:

On the first day of the feast of the Unleavened Bread, when it was customary to sacrifice the paschal lamb, his disciples said to him: "Where do you want us to go and get things ready for you to eat the paschal supper?" So he sent two of his disciples with these instructions: "Go into the city and you will meet a man carrying a pitcher of water; follow him, and where he enters, say to the owner of the house: 'The Rabbi says: Where is my dining room, where I may eat the paschal supper with my disciples?' He will then show you a room upstairs, spacious, furnished, and ready for use; and there get things ready for us." The disciples went and came into the city, and when they found things as he had told them, they prepared the paschal supper (Mk 14:12–16).

As these passages show, Jesus gave us an example that we should, first of all, pray as individuals, then as members of the family, and finally as members of the community of the Church.

Included in public prayers are processions. When these are carried out in a devout spirit, they increase the fervor of the prayer of the participants and the onlookers.

The same holds of pilgrimages. Many a time, in days of distress, people have been sustained and strengthened by making pilgrimages to time-honored places of grace.

Jesus has given His people an example of how, in various respects, prayer is to be made part of their lives:

Following the model of Christ, it is a characteristic of the prayer life of a Catholic Christian, that he *pray alone;* that he pray *in the family and along with the community;* and that he pray to God *in the liturgical sacrificial community* of the Church. The most important common prayer is the grace before and after meals. The family which prays together stays together. And the family which ceases from common prayer loses its united inner life before God.

The Life of the Individual. There are believers who consider themselves to be good Christians, who yet affirm that they have no time for prayer.

There are others who have firmly bound themselves to some rule of prayer, yet seize any sort of excuse for freeing themselves from it.

And there are still others who keep their rule of prayer as far as is in their own power, but welcome all legitimate obstruction of their rule caused by others as if this were a blessed deliverance.

Finally there are those who pray regularly every day amid all the duties which make up the daily round; but none do they perform with such haste as their daily prayer.

What a contrast this is to Jesus' words that men should pray continually and never give up (cf. Lk 18:1).

The Life of the Church. The Church leaves everyone free to choose his own prayers. She demands, however, that all printed prayer books must be presented for examination. Prayers used publicly in church must, furthermore, be approved either by the Pope or the diocesan bishop.

The Church's principles governing the education of the faithful in prayer are contained in the following words of Pius XI:

One can only be amazed at the broad-mindedness of the Church in her conception of prayer.

With tender sympathy for the weakness of frail human beings, she permits even such forms of prayer as are, indeed, quite defective and imperfect. Her idea is: at least pray like this if you do not know how to pray better; the main thing in the end is to pray at all costs.

If, however, one considers the question of how the Church herself assesses the various kinds of prayer, then one must take liturgical prayer as the standard.

The following basic principles for education in prayer arise out of this attitude of the Church. It is not fitting that anyone should suppress or abolish any modes of prayer which the Church herself still permits to continue: the goal should be rather to lead the faithful gradually to a more perfect manner of prayer and to teach them to pray as the Church prays. The liturgy is a thing of extraordinary significance: It is the most important organ of the Church's teaching office. One must see in the liturgy not the scholastic wisdom of this or that man, but the instructing wisdom of the Church herself.

9. THE SACRAMENTS: MAN'S COMPANIONS ALONG THE ROAD OF LIFE

WHEN A HUMAN BEING is born, Christ offers to supplement natural life with supernatural life, the life of grace, through Baptism. The child is united to God by the grace of sanctification.

When man matures, Christ takes him, through Confirmation, into the ranks of those who shall confess Him before the world.

If anyone should lose kinship with God by grave sin, Christ offers him back the grace of reconciliation, on condition that he repent of his sin. This is done through the sacrament of Penance.

All life requires its appropriate nourishment. Divine life requires a divine food and this is provided by the Holy Eucharist.

If a man is seriously ill, Jesus comes with a special grace to purify and strengthen his spirit. This is conferred through the Anointing of the Sick.

These are the five sacraments by which Christ accompanies the individual on his way through life.

In human life, there are, however, two decisions which affect not only those who make them but society as a whole.

When a man obeys the call of God and dedicates his life completely to Him in the sacramental state, Jesus gives him divine authority and power. This is done by the Sacrament of Holy Orders.

When two believing people take one another for life in married love, Jesus Himself raises their promise to the dignity of a holy contract and promises His support throughout their lives. This is accomplished through the sacrament of Matrimony.

Baptism, Confirmation, and Holy Orders fix the spiritual relationship of the human being to Christ in the Church. Through Baptism a man is received as a child of God into the living society of Christ and the Church; by Confirmation the baptized is elevated, within this society, to the level at which each member must accept responsibility for himself and for others; through Holy Orders the person ordained is raised to membership of that group where individual personality recedes and action in Christ's name characterizes their entire vocation.

These three sacraments, which bring a person into a special relationship with Christ, impress his soul with a particular character. The soul of the baptized is distinguishable from the soul of the unbaptized; the soul of the confirmed from the unconfirmed; the soul of the priest from the soul of him who is not ordained. These indelible characters are marks of honor for the blessed in heaven: for the damned in hell they are signs which reveal the degree of their faithlessness.

Within the Church Christ continues His influence upon men through the seven sacraments.

The sacraments are visible signs through which we receive from Christ the spiritual graces which they indicate.

In the sacraments Christ gives us a *divine guarantee* that He Himself comes to us with His grace under specific visible signs.

In the sacraments we encounter the Lord, who acts through them to touch men personally.

Christ instituted seven sacraments: Baptism, Confirmation, the Holy Eucharist, Penance, the Anointing of the Sick, Holy Orders, Matrimony.

Through Christ, the sacraments bring to life or strengthen the divine life in the soul and supply grace with special support. Three of the sacraments, Baptism, Confirmation and Holy Orders, imprint an indelible character upon the soul.

The sacraments receive their power from Christ who instituted them. St. Augustine says: "It is Christ who baptizes." Similarly it is true to say that it is Christ who confirms; Christ who absolves from sin; Christ who offers Himself as the Food of souls in Holy Communion; Christ who strengthens the sick; Christ who in Holy Orders consecrates His priests; Christ who accepts the marriage vows of the bridal couple.

The Life of the Individual. The sacraments correspond to a deep need in man. It is in man's nature to look for sacred signs and actions through which he can make contact with God. This constitutes an advantage and also a danger: an advantage in that even a child can already grasp, to some extent, what is meant by a sacrament; a danger, in that the faithful so easily forget what a miracle of grace the sacraments are.

The Apostles had already made a sharp distinction between the sacraments and magic practices. Their repulsion of Simon Magus in Samaria, who wanted to buy the power of administering sacramental grace, shows this (cf. Acts 8:18). The sacraments have their power directly from God; but one condition on the part of man is absolutely required — the opening of the heart to receive the grace of God. At Baptism, the opening of the heart is in the desire to be a member of the Church; at Confirmation in readiness to stand up for Christ before the world; at Penance, in turning away from sin; on receiving Holy Communion, in the desire to be strengthened by Christ; in marriage, in making the marriage vows before God; at Holy Orders, in unconditional, personal self-offering to God; and at the Anointing of the Sick, in a final renunciation of sin and evil inclinations of the heart.

The Life of the Church. In all seven sacraments Jesus is applying the graces of His sacrificial death to men, under specific signs. Just as the Lord died upon the cross, a substitute for men, so now He Himself represents men before the Father's throne in heaven and all the while arranges for the graces, which as the Lamb of God He won for men, to be distributed upon earth by substitutes.

The manner in which the grace of God reaches people is not the same in all of the sacraments. In six sacraments — Baptism, Confirmation, Penance, the Anointing of the Sick, Holy Orders, and Marriage — Christ is active while the priest as His representative performs appointed signs which indicate the inward grace. But in the Blessed Sacrament Christ acts not merely momentarily and inwardly: He reveals Himself under visible signs. In the celebration of the Sacrifice of holy Mass, the Lamb who was slain and who now stands before the throne of God in heaven, is present upon the altar under the appearances of bread and wine as a sacramental victim. Following the celebration of the sacrifice the Lord gives Himself to the faithful, joined to Him by grace, so that He may live in them and they in Him.

Because the Holy Eucharist as the bloodless sacrifice of the New Covenant, and as Holy Communion, ranks high above the other sacraments, it will be treated on its own after the other sacraments.

10. BAPTISM: THE SACRAMENT OF NEW BIRTH

THE MOMENT a child is born, Christ's love grants him a second life — that life by which he is raised to the status of a child of God and an heir of heaven. The love of God desires to dwell in the child, taking first place there.

Jesus discoursed on the significance of Baptism within the new scheme of salvation to Nicodemus the leader who came to visit Him by night. St. John relates:

> Jesus answered: "I am telling you the plain truth: unless a man is born of water and the Spirit, he cannot enter the kingdom of God! What is born of the flesh is flesh, and what is born of the Spirit is spirit. Do not be perplexed because I said to you: you must all be born anew. The breeze blows at will, and you can hear its sound; but you do not know where it comes from or whither it goes. Something like this takes place in everyone born of the Spirit." Nicodemus demurred. "How," he said to him, "are such things possible?" "You are the teacher of Israel," Jesus answered him, "and do not understand things like this! I tell you the plain truth: we speak what we know, and testify to what we have seen; but you all refuse to accept our testimony! If I have told you of earthly things and you refuse to believe, how will you believe if I tell you of heavenly things!" (Jn 3:5–12.)

Speaking to Nicodemus, Jesus describes Baptism as a new birth by water and the Holy Spirit. Jesus' saying presupposes the ancient custom of baptism by immersion in water. The person being baptized is immersed in water; he remains for a short time in the water, as in some mysterious womb of life, and it is the Holy Spirit Himself who thereupon fills the soul with new life. At Baptism, the water becomes a symbol of the redeeming blood of Jesus. St. Paul addresses the Romans in this sense: "Do you not know that all of us who have been baptized into union with Christ Jesus have been baptized into union with his death?" (Rom 6:3.)

168

Before His Ascension into Heaven, Jesus commanded His Apostles: "Go, therefore, and make all nations your disciples: baptize them in the name of the Father, and of the Son, and of the Holy Spirit" (Mt 28:19).

The outward sign of the sacrament of Baptism is the pouring of water. As this is done, Christ purifies man inwardly from all stains and imparts to him the life of grace. Simultaneously, his soul is imprinted with an indelible character.

The importance attached to Baptism is shown very beautifully in the address which was given in early days by the bishop. He explained: "The Sacrament of Baptism which you are about to receive expresses in its ceremonies the hope of resurrection; the sinner descends into the water, and the just man rises up out of its floods. That which gives us life is accepted. Through the grace of Christ you are born, not of the will of the flesh, but by the power of the Holy Spirit.

"The true soldiers of Jesus Christ experience always the invincible power of the weapon of faith against all the snares of the Adversary. May the evil Spirit, who never ceases from leading men into temptation, always find you armed with this profession, so that you vanquish this Adversary whom now you renounce; and so that the grace of God to whom now you pledge your troth keep you to the end unharmed and unspotted.

"And so, through Him who has absolved your sins, you will attain to the glory of the resurrection."

The significance of Baptism and the vocation inherent in it has never changed in the least since these far-off days. And therefore the words just quoted still hold good today.

Baptism is the sacrament of new birth into participation in the life of God.

The performance of Baptism was commanded by Jesus in the words: "Go therefore, and make all nations your disciples: baptize them in the name of the Father, and of the Son, and of the Holy Spirit" (Mt 28:19).

The *visible action* at Baptism is as follows. The one baptizing pours water upon the baptized, saying, as he does: "I baptize you in the name of the Father and of the Son and of the Holy Spirit." By this, the baptized is *inwardly* freed from original sin, from all actual sins committed before Baptism and from the punishment due to them: and he is born to a new life in the grace of Christ, filled with gifts of the Holy Spirit and incorporated as a member in the society of the Church. Christ impresses a corresponding indelible seal upon the soul of the baptized, marking him as a Christian.

Reception of the sacrament of Baptism brings the guarantee that Christ has freed the baptized from original sin and from all sins committed before baptism, has made him a child of God, and as God's child has provided him with a special characteristic mark, and has thus presented him to His Father as His child and taken him into His Church.

The Life of the Individual. Sometimes it is said that children ought not to be baptized until they are able to answer for themselves. That would be the same as saying that one ought not to attribute the parents' nationality to children at birth, but should wait until they are old enough to choose a nationality for themselves. A child, from the first moment of its life, belongs in a much higher sense to Christ the Redeemer than to its parents or to the State. For this reason it can with full justification be baptized as soon as it is born.

In the sight of God, all human distinctions fade into insignificance before the distinction between those who are baptized and those who are not.

The Life of the Church. It is an ancient custom in the Church to provide every child with the support of two godparents. Should the parents die, or should there be other reason, these must insure that the child is instructed and brought up in the Faith.

In the early days of the Church, the number of adults baptized was much greater than that of infants. Baptism was preceded, therefore, by long and careful preparation. The candidate was led in stages to the baptismal font. Today the sacred actions, which in those days were spread over a period of time, are drawn together.

The office of godparent ought not be regarded as fulfilled merely by the giving of presents at Christmas and on birthdays. The godparent must always remember that he stands in a spiritual relation to the child.

11. CONFIRMATION: THE SACRAMENT OF INDIVIDUAL RESPONSIBILITY

CHILDREN GROW UP very quickly and it is not long before they can judge between good and evil, thus becoming responsible for their actions. As their insight increases, so also do the temptations and attractions of the world.

For this reason, Jesus binds to Himself with new bonds of grace the baptized children who are now growing up. The boys are to become happy and self-reliant young men; the girls, docile, resolute, and faithful young women.

Scripture shows that Confirmation is a sacrament distinct from Baptism:

> Now when the apostles in Jerusalem heard that Samaria had accepted the word of God, they sent Peter and John to them. On their arrival they prayed for the Samaritans, that they might receive the Holy Spirit. As yet he had not come on any of them, because they had only been baptized in the name of the Lord Jesus. Then Peter and John laid their hands on them, and they received the Holy Spirit. When Simon saw that the Holy Spirit was imparted through the laying on of the apostles' hands, he offered them money, saying, "Give me also this power, so that anyone on whom I lay my hands may receive the Holy Spirit."
>
> But Peter said to him, "May your money go to destruction with you, because you thought that the gift of God could be purchased with money. You have no part or lot in this matter, for your heart is not right with God" (Acts 8:14–21).

This account makes it quite clear that this laying on of the hands accompanied by prayer took place only after Baptism, and that it caused the Holy Spirit to descend upon those whom the Apostles thus confirmed.

171

Since Peter and John themselves went specially to Samaria to confirm, obviously the deacon Philip did not possess authority to perform the laying on of hands.

The outward sign of Confirmation is anointing and the laying on of hands. This symbol had great meaning for the Christians of old because at that time people used to anoint their bodies with oil to give strength. Confirmation gave the person confirmed a new status among the faithful, the status of one who has to answer for himself and consequently for Christ and His Church. It is the sacrament of Christian courage — moral courage as well as physical courage.

The sacrament of Confirmation often fails to have its full effect because the confirmed forget all about it. Every time we have to decide for or against Christ, we should call upon the Holy Spirit for grace, appealing to this sacrament.

Confirmation is the sacrament of entry into Christian individual responsibility.

That Confirmation is a sacrament is proved by the account in Scripture of how Peter and John traveled specially to Samaria to lay hands on those faithful whom the deacon Philip had baptized.

The *visible action* in Confirmation is this: the bishop prays over all of the candidates; he lays his hands upon each one individually and with the oil of chrism signs a cross on his forehead, saying as he does: "I sign thee with the sign of the cross and I confirm thee with the chrism of salvation, in the name of the Father and of the Son and of the Holy Spirit." He gives each candidate a slap on the cheek.

When the sacrament of Confirmation is received, a *divine guarantee* is given that Jesus Christ will strengthen the candidate with the power of the Holy Spirit for the life of an individually responsible Christian. The person confirmed receives a characteristic mark — the sign of the soldier of Christ.

As a rule, the sacrament of Confirmation is administered by the bishop. In very recent times priests have been permitted to administer Confirmation in certain prescribed circumstances.

The Life of the Individual. If you have been confirmed you share responsibility for your deeds as one called to share in the kingdom of

God. In every situation of life turn, therefore, to the Holy Spirit whose support has been guaranteed you by the Lord in this sacrament.

The difference between the unconfirmed and the confirmed is that between children who act under the direct supervision of their parents, and grownup sons and daughters who play their part for the weal or woe of the family on their own initiative. Everyone who is confirmed is called to labor with Christ in the Church. This saying of St. John Chrysostom applies to the confirmed: "How can that soul be saved which only desires its own salvation?"

The good Christian of today must become "of age." A Christian who is of age is characterized not merely by religious knowledge learned by rote, but by having applied his knowledge to the affairs of life in which he and his fellowmen are living. He *sees, judges,* and *acts* according to the principles supplied by his Faith.

The adult Christian requires increased power of action and greater readiness to make sacrifices. If these are not forthcoming then increased knowledge merely leads to empty talk.

The life of an adult Christian cannot be led on a person's own strength but only in the power of the Holy Spirit. A confirmed person can seek this power at any time by invoking the Sacrament of Confirmation. This practice should become a habit.

There is a real danger today that so-called broad-mindedness, which is in fact an abandonment of solid Christian principle and morality, be mistaken for Christian maturity. True charity, true ecumenism, demands maturity, strength, courage.

The Life of the Church. The Church desires that the external customs associated with the sacrament of Confirmation should be in keeping with the sacred action. The sponsors should see to it that the child can look back all his life with joy to the day of his Confirmation. The entertainment which they provide for him should not be of a kind which will disturb or destroy the sacred mood of the preceding solemnity.

12. THE SACRAMENT OF PENANCE: THE SACRAMENT WHICH RENEWS RECONCILIATION IN THE ATONING BLOOD OF CHRIST

THROUGH HIS DEATH on the Cross Christ made atonement to His Father in heaven for all the sins of men. Possessing judicial power to dispose of sins, He could lay down the conditions under which they were to be forgiven.

Christ has decreed that on being reconciled through Baptism a man has all of his sins absolved.

But should a man commit serious sin after Baptism, a breach is made in the pact of fidelity which had been affected, and a separation from the life of the Church follows. Christ has ordained, therefore, that in this case the sinner has not merely to repent privately of his sins but has to confess them to a priest as His representative, and in this way to repair the breach of faith as far as possible and to restore membership in the Church's life through an exterior act. Accordingly, Christ has bound every priest to absolve from sin every sinner who truly repents of his sins, and to withhold absolution from any who do not repent. This direction was given to the Apostles on the evening of the day of the Resurrection.

St. John the Evangelist relates:

> Late in the evening that same day — the first day of the week — although the doors of the place where the disciples had gathered were bolted for fear of the Jews, Jesus came and stood before them, and said: "Peace be to you!" With that, he let them see his hands and his side. The disciples were delighted to see the Lord. Then Jesus said to them again: "Peace be to you! As the Father has made me his ambassador, so I am making you my ambassadors." With this, he breathed on them and said: "Receive the Holy Spirit. Whenever you remit anyone's sins, they are remitted; when you retain anyone's sins, they are retained" (Jn 20:19–23).

During the preceding years, Jesus had prepared the disciples for this hour when He would leave to them the power of forgiving sins by His own authority. In contrast to the Pharisees in particular, He had shown that this authority was His prerogative as the Son of Man. And now after the completion of His saving work, He handed on the exercise of this authority to the Apostles.

The Apostles, not having the Lord's omniscience, could only make use of the power to remit sins under the condition that the faithful tell the sins they have committed, with the intention of gaining remission.

The sacrament of Penance thus consists in the contrite self-accusation of the sinner before the priest so that he may obtain forgiveness through the merits of Christ.

In the parable of the Prodigal Son the Savior gave a magnificent portrayal of that inner repentance which is the prerequisite of a good confession:

"Once upon a time," he said, "a man had two sons. One day the younger of them said to his father: 'Father, give me the part of the property that falls to my share.' So he divided his property between them. Not many days later, the younger son cashed everything and went off to a far-off country, where he squandered his money by licentious living. When he had spent everything, a terrible famine swept over that country and he faced starvation. So he went to throw himself on the mercy of a citizen of that region, who sent him to his farm to tend pigs. And oh, how heartily he would have feasted on the pods on which the pigs were feeding! But no one would give them to him. At last he came to his senses. 'How many of my father's hired men,' he said, 'have food enough and to spare, while I am here perishing with hunger! I will quit this place and go to meet my father. Father, I will say to him, I have sinned against heaven, and you know that I am no longer fit to be considered your son. Treat me as one of your hired help.' So he quit the place and went to meet his father.

"He was still a good way off when his father caught sight of him and, stirred to pity, ran and threw his arms round his neck and kissed him affectionately.

"The son then said to him: 'Father, I have sinned against heaven and before you, and you know that I am no longer fit to be considered your son.' But the father said to his slaves: 'Quick; bring out the finest robe and put it on him; then put a ring on his hand and sandals on his feet; also get the fatted calf and kill it; let us feast and celebrate. This son of mine was dead and has come back to life again, was lost and has been found again.' And so they gave themselves up to celebrating" (Lk 15:11–24).

In this parable of Jesus the separate parts of the sacrament of Penance are contained as parts of the story:

1. The penitent looks into his own soul; like the prodigal son, he considers the situation in which he finds himself.
2. The penitent alters his attitude to sin: like the prodigal son, he goes back on his actions — he repents.
3. The penitent takes up a definite attitude for the future: like the prodigal son, he makes a firm resolution of amendment.
4. The penitent, like the prodigal son, confesses his sins to his father.
5. The penitent, like the prodigal son, is ready to make amends.

The sacrament of Penance is the tribunal of divine mercy. Here it depends not on the judge but on the accused whether acquital results or not. Whoever repents of his sins for the sake of God and His holiness is cleansed in the blood of Christ: "Though your sins be like scarlet, they may become white as snow" (Is 1:18).

Penance is the sacrament of reconciliation with God through the atoning blood of Christ.

The sacrament of Penance consists in a contrite self-accusation of the sinner before the priest, so that he may obtain forgiveness through the merits of Christ. The sacrament of Penance is the *tribunal of the grace of Jesus Christ.*

Jesus Christ instituted the sacrament of Penance in the words: "Receive the Holy Spirit. Whenever you remit anyone's sins, they are remitted; when you retain anyone's sins, they are retained" (Jn 20: 21–23).

Because, through mortal sin, the baptized person has destroyed perfect union with both God and the Church, he must confess his sins contritely to God and before the Church.

The *outward action* in Penance is as follows:

1. The believer contritely confesses his sins to the priest in order to receive absolution from him.

2. The priest says to the penitent: "I absolve thee of thy sins, in the name of the Father and of the Son and of the Holy Spirit." On receiving the sacrament of Penance a *guarantee* is given that Jesus, who made atonement on the cross for the sins of mankind, absolves the penitent from all of the sins which he has confessed contritely.

The Life of the Individual. Many think confession a burden too heavy for man to bear. Goethe, a deep thinker yet not a Catholic, thought differently. "In former days," he said, "the burden on a man's conscience was lifted by absolution, but now everyone must carry along his burdened conscience and so loses the power of making peace again with himself. Auricular confession ought never to have been taken away from men."

Others bring against confession the very opposite objection that it is too easy. By assuring the erring one that he will be unpunished, they argue, it encourages a careless way of life. In St. Augustine's time the Church was already bearing this reproach, and his reply can still be ours. "True," he said, "it is conceivable that many men, in view of forgiveness, avoid sin too little. But it is certain that were there no Confession a far greater number of people would, as a result, throw themselves into the arms of sin because they despaired of the possibility of forgiveness. So that men will not despair, the Lord has instituted Penance. And so that, in spite of the possibility of forgiveness, men will not lead careless lives, there is no avoiding the day of death which comes to all."

The Life of the Church. The Church desires that the faithful, even when in a state of grace, should make frequent use of the sacrament of Penance. Pope Pius XII in the encyclical *Mystici Corporis Christi* expressly described so-called *confession of devotion* as an outstanding means of sanctification.

"We highly recommend the pious practice of frequent confession, introduced by the Church under the guidance of the Holy Spirit; for by this means we grow in a true knowledge of ourselves and in Christian humility, bad habits are uprooted, spiritual negligence and apathy are prevented, the conscience is purified and the will strengthened, salutary spiritual direction is obtained, and grace is increased by the efficacy of the sacrament itself."

13. THE FIVE PARTS OF THE SACRAMENT OF PENANCE: EXAMINATION OF CONSCIENCE; REPENTANCE; PURPOSE OF AMENDMENT; CONFESSION; SATISFACTION

1. EXAMINATION OF CONSCIENCE

THE PRODIGAL SON'S return began by his thinking over his misdeeds. The inward desire of the penitent to be reconciled with God drives him to examine his conscience.

No man likes looking into his own soul, and all require the help of the Holy Spirit if they are to acknowledge their sins frankly.

To insure a proper examination of conscience we may have to measure ourselves against a list of sins such as is found in some devotional books. Such a practice may not be suitable, and we should ask our confessor to advise us about the best way to make a good confession. With grave sins, the number of times committed must be told; the circumstances which alter the gravity of a sin must also be made known.

We should also state when we last went to confession and consider whether that confession was a good one.

The best assurance of a good examination of conscience before confession is daily examination of conscience in the evening. This need not be a lengthy business but should never be omitted.

Not a few give up daily examination of conscience because they grow sick of it. Very often this results from failing to distinguish between the daily examination and that which is performed in preparation for confession. Daily examination of conscience should be carried out with the main idea of helping us to know how we stand in general.

Here are a few questions which experience has proved useful to many.

1. *What sins have I committed today?*

   If we have been guilty of serious faults then what circumstances led to these sins and what should we do to avoid them in the future?

2. *What has been my dominant mood today?*

   If we have been in good humor, we should thank God. If we have been ill-tempered we should try to discern the causes (overwork, physical upset, conflict with superiors, with fellow workers or with subordinates).

3. *How well have I discharged the duties of my station in life?*

   We should note specific faults such as touchiness, carelessness, hurry, or lethargy.

4. *How have I treated people whom I do not like?*

Examination of conscience must always begin with prayer and end with repentance for sins.

2. REPENTANCE

Repentance is a decision of the will. The will adopts toward sins an attitude which corresponds to God's judgment upon sin. When he commits a sin, a man says in effect: "I will do this and I will have this, even if I should lose the love of God by it." With repentance, a man is taking up a new attitude to what he has done and says: "For the sake of absolutely nothing I have rejected God's love. I wish I had never done it."

In this way he cuts loose from the bonds of sin. Jesus Himself describes repentance as *metanoia* — a spiritual turning around.

If the sinner is sorry for his sin out of love of God, his contrition is said to be perfect. If the sinner repents of his sin out of fear, thinking that he will lose heaven and earn the punishment of hell, his contrition is said to be imperfect (attrition). Attrition suffices for reception of the sacrament of Penance.

Contrition decides the value of a confession. The person who is sorry for his sins will as a rule make a good confession, a serious resolve of amendment, and will gladly accept his penance.

It is good when seeking to arouse contrition to picture the Savior upon the cross.

3. Purpose of Amendment

A man who is truly sorry for his sins must make a start spiritually. He must determine to avoid serious sin and the voluntary occasions of sin, to make up for any harm done and to do everything which will insure that he does not fall again into sin. This purpose of amendment is located in the will, not in the emotions. Thus Jesus says: "Not everyone that says to me, 'Master, Master,' will enter the kingdom of heaven, but only he that does the will of my Father who is in heaven" (Mt 7:21).

A person who is unable to avoid the occasion of sin must fortify himself against falling into sin by increased prayer and fervent reception of the sacraments.

4. Confession

Remission of sins is effected in confession in the form of an acquittal announced in response to a self-accusation. Consequently, the penitent must himself make his sins — i.e., his mortal sins — known to the priest.

Confession of sins was not something which the Church had to introduce as completely new. Holy Scripture recounts how the people who came to John for Baptism confessed their sins, and the Dead Sea Scrolls show that this was a practice among the community at Qumran. The presentation of certain sacrifices was associated with this to show that he who presented them had already admitted his transgressions. When Jesus said to the Apostles, "Whose sins you shall forgive, they are forgiven them; and whose sins you shall retain, they are retained," the Apostles inevitably assumed that the faithful would come to them and confess their sins in the same way as the repentant Israelites had done to the Baptist.

From the beginning the Church has made use of the authority to forgive sins. The outward forms in which this authority has been exercised have changed with the passage of time; and these have matured with the experience of the Church.

In early Christian times certain grave sins had to be confessed publicly and expiated. But we have evidence, as in St. Cyprian (d. 258), that even at an early date confession was concerned with secret sins of thought. In his treatise *On the Fallen* — i.e., those Christians who had apostatized during the persecution — St. Cyprian refers to the confession of sins of thought: "How these Christians distinguish themselves by faith and holy fear who indeed have not sacrificed to idols nor made any appearance of sacrificing, who even if the thought crossed their minds, confessed their guilt with pain and honesty of heart to the priests of God and so won peace of conscience!"

St. Athanasius (295–379) wrote: "Just as it is from a priest that a man receives Baptism and is enlightened by the grace of the Holy Spirit, so it is through a priest that the contrite man who confesses his guilt receives forgiveness in the love of Christ."

St. Ambrose (d. 379) wrote: "The sinner confesses his sins not merely in general — no, he counts them up and accuses himself of them; for he does not wish to disguise his transgression." The assertion that the Church invented confession is untrue. The Church has merely issued regulations as to how and when the sacrament of Penance is to be received.

Public confession, which formerly was demanded of the faithful who had committed certain sins, was followed by a public penance. As public confession fell into disuse, so public penance was discontinued.

In confession, all grave sins and all the material circumstances affecting their gravity must be made known. If a grave sin is forgotten it must be confessed at the next confession. If a grave sin is concealed or told in such a way as to appear unimportant the confession is invalid. At the next confession this fact would have to be disclosed and the whole content of the previous invalid confession confessed again.

5. SATISFACTION

The sacrament of Penance is Christ's Easter present to His people. Sins can be forgiven because Christ died on the cross and rose victoriously as the conqueror of sin on Easter. At confession the sinful Christian is washed in the blood of the Lamb of God, in the blood of his Lord.

Every sin is at once an offense against God and against the Church. As part of confession, therefore, the Church imposes a penance upon the sinner, and in addition requires that he repent of his sin through contrition before God. He should accept this penance first, as an imposition of the Church; and then as a means of uniting him with Christ who took upon Himself the supreme penance of atonement.

Because He suffered so much for us, our unity which Christ demands that we should not remain utterly lacking in reparation and satisfaction. St. Paul says, "What is lacking to the sufferings of Christ I supply in my flesh for the benefit of his body, which is the Church" (Col 1:24).

The penances which the faithful ordinarily receive today are indeed so slight that there could be no question of any further mitigation of penance.

During the past few decades a movement has been growing which seeks to encourage the making of reparation to God for our own sins and for the sins of others. This movement took its origin in the apparitions of the Sacred Heart of Jesus to St. Margaret Mary Alacoque which gave rise to the First Friday Devotions in honor of the Sacred Heart. Pope Pius XI drew attention to the duty of the faithful to make reparation to Jesus for their own sins and those of others in the encyclical on the introduction of the feast of Christ the King; and then in 1928, expanded the theme of reparation due to the Sacred Heart of Jesus.

The sacrament of Penance is the tribunal of Christ's grace.

Five parts make up the total action required for the reception of the sacrament: (1) examination of conscience; (2) contrition; (3) firm purpose of amendment; (4) confession; (5) satisfaction.

The examination of conscience consists in preparing with the help of the Holy Spirit for self-accusation before the priest as the representative of Jesus Christ. The examination must take account at least of all grave sins committed since the last confession. It is recommended that we should extend this to venial sins also.

Contrition consists in the sinner's turning to God, inwardly renouncing his sins and hoping for forgiveness for the sake of the passion and death of Christ.

If the sinner repents of his sin from love of God, his contrition is *perfect*. Perfect contrition has the power of instantly canceling sin, but the duty to confess sins remains.

Imperfect contrition or *attrition* is repentance motivated by fear of divine punishment. This is sufficient to allow the merits of Christ to operate through the sacrament of Penance.

True contrition, whether perfect or imperfect, is always allied to a *firm purpose* never to sin in the future and to avoid the occasions of sin. If these occasions cannot be avoided, the penitent must determine to strengthen himself in the struggle against sin by prayer and frequent reception of the sacraments.

The sin of a baptized person is a breach of fidelity with Christ and the Church. Therefore Christ has given the sacrament of Penance such a form that the sinner seeks the forgiveness of God through the Church. Confession is a way to Christ, the physician of all souls. "The sick have need of a physician, not the healthy. It is my mission to call sinners" (Lk 5:31). *Because every mortal* sin causes separation from God, every mortal sin and the circumstances which affect its gravity must be confessed.

Confession derives its reconciling power from the passion and death of Christ.

The canceling of sins in confession is effected by the priest, as representative of Christ, saying: "I absolve thee of thy sins in the name of the Father and of the Son and of the Holy Spirit, Amen."

The priest imposes a penance upon the penitent so that he may resemble the atoning Savior. For the sake of Christ God accepts this penitential act. But besides the prescribed penance, the faithful should do further acts of penance and reparation. This can be done by leading a Christian life, by prayer, fasting, and almsgiving, and especially by patiently bearing the cross of suffering.

The faithful ought to confess often so that they preserve the spirit of penitence and are able to struggle effectively against their faults.

The Life of the Individual. St. Augustine prescribes this rule of life: "Should you desire to become other than you are, always be dissatisfied with your present state; for wherever you pause, there you will stay. And as soon as you say: I have done enough, you are lost." There is no better way of following this rule of life than by frequent confession.

The Life of the Church.   Many say to themselves: If only my confessions bore more fruit in improving my life, then I would gladly confess more often! But all the old sins are still there.

The answer to this is: Every valid confession is a great gain. It cancels sin. Besides this, no one who confesses regularly knows what state he would have been in had he given this up. Along with the old faults there might have been many new and worse ones.

We may only recognize the blessing of regular confession when we reach an age from which we can look back over our life as a story which has reached some kind of a conclusion.

It is well known that venial sins are expiated through good works. Why then should people who have committed nothing but venial sins confess frequently? Are not good works equivalent to the confession of devotion? This opinion is wrong. Confession of devotion has a special effect which belongs to no good works. In confession we appear before Christ Himself in order to beg forgiveness of sins. Confession makes possible for us the assurance of forgiveness for specific sins; on the other hand, specific good works do not make possible the cancelation of specific venial sins.

14. INDULGENCES: REMISSION BY THE CHURCH OF TEMPORAL PUNISHMENT DUE TO SINS

ALL RULERS claim the right and power of granting amnesties and reprieves to their subjects.

Right of government belongs to the supreme head of the Church also. It is implied in our Lord's words to Peter: "You are Peter, and upon this rock I will build my Church, and the gates of hell shall not prevail against it. I will give you the keys of the kingdom of heaven, and whatever you bind on earth shall be bound in heaven, and whatever you loose on earth shall be loosed in heaven" (Mt 16:18–19).

The Church's power to rule is exercised by the Pope as vicar of Christ when he remits in part (partial indulgence) or in full (plenary indulgence) the temporal punishments which are still demanded in expiation of sin. But the sins must first have been forgiven. An indulgence can never forgive or cancel sin. The repealing of such temporal punishment due to sins flows from Christ's love for His people and is possible through the superabundance of the merits of Christ and of His saints.

The Church grants the faithful countless opportunities of gaining indulgences for themselves and for the faithful departed in purgatory.

The Church attaches partial indulgences to certain prayers. Among these are the following.

1. "Jesus, my God, I love Thee above all things."
2. "Sweetest Jesus, be not to me a Judge, but a Savior."
3. "O Sacrament most holy, O sacrament divine, all praise and all thanksgiving be every moment thine."
4. "O sweetest heart of Jesus, I implore, that I may ever love Thee more and more."
5. "My Jesus, mercy."
6. "Jesus and Mary."
7. "O Mary conceived without sin, pray for us who have recourse to Thee."

8. "Jesus, Mary, Joseph, I give you my heart and my soul.
"Jesus, Mary, Joseph, assist me in my last agony.
"Jesus, Mary, Joseph, may I breathe forth my soul in peace with you."

Apart from the satisfaction made through the acceptance of a penance in the sacrament of Penance, the Church can remit the temporal punishment due to sin in another way — by indulgences.

The right of the Church to grant to the faithful remission of temporal punishment of sins which have already been forgiven is implied in Jesus' saying to Peter: "I will give you the keys of the kingdom of heaven, and whatever you bind on earth shall be bound in heaven, and whatever you loose on earth shall be loosed in heaven" (Mt 16:19).

The Life of the Individual. If anyone knew in advance that he was going to be taken prisoner but that he could do something now to reduce the time of that captivity, he certainly would do it.

If a man had friends far away who were in great distress and if he had a reliable means of sending them help, he would feel bound to make use of it. If he did not, we would not think much of his love for his friends. How many of us forget to gain indulgences for our friends and relatives in purgatory?

The Life of the Church. The Christian quality of any age is revealed by the regard it has for indulgences.

A sort of accountancy is a characteristic of the religious life of an age which sets great store by indulgences. Thus in the Middle Ages it sometimes came about that the importance of indulgences was obtruded to such a degree that it no longer corresponded to the teaching of the Church. On the other hand there are people who would like to sever from religious life anything the least resembling calculation. To them, mechanical regularity constitutes an attack upon the freedom of love. Such a point of view is just as dangerous as an excess of calculation. The doctrine of indulgences is founded upon the mercy and the justice of God and upon the doctrine of the vicarious satisfaction of Jesus Christ for all the sins of the world, and upon the doctrine of the Communion of Saints by virtue of which the faithful on earth can come to the assistance of the holy souls in purgatory.

15. THE ANOINTING OF THE SICK: CHRIST BESIDE THE SICK

WHEN A MAN IS SICK he is visited by Christ, who knows that the worst part of sickness is despondency, and that the ultimate cause of despondency is often sin or its aftermath. He comes in the sacrament of the Anointing of the Sick, to bring courage and strength to the sick person, for his journey into the kingdom of his Father: or He gives him strength to return from sickness into the life of this world. The Apostle St. James writes of the anointing of the sick:

"Is anyone of you sick? He should call in the presbyters of the Church, and have them pray over him, while they anoint him with oil in the name of the Lord. That prayer, said with faith, will save the sick person, and the Lord will restore him to health. If he has committed sins, they will be forgiven him" (Jas 5:14–15).

The sacrament of the Anointing of the Sick has power to effect the same change as that which Jesus brought about in His earthly life. This sacrament is nothing less than a visit by Jesus to one of His friends who lies sick.

Walking upon the earth, Jesus said now to this one, now to the other: "Your sins are forgiven," and all guilt departed from the one addressed. In like manner through the sacrament of the Anointing of the Sick the Lord forgives the sins of those who are truly sorry, even if they cannot recall those sins and are in no state to make confession of them.

The Anointing of the Sick is the sacramental visit of Christ to the seriously sick.

The Anointing of the Sick is a sacrament, as the words of the Epistle of James show. Here the Anointing of the Sick is described as an anointing, performed by the priests following the command of Christ, and having a specific spiritual effect (cf. Jas 5:4).

187

The *visible action* in the sacrament of the Anointing of the Sick is this. The priest prays over the sick person and anoints him with holy oil on his senses, saying the words: "By this holy unction and by His tender mercy may the Lord forgive you whatever sins you have committed by sight, hearing, smell, touch and talking."

It is peculiar to the Anointing of the Sick that to be able to receive it a person must be suffering from a serious illness. Then a Christian doctor must tell the sick person or his relatives that the situation is serious. The Anointing of the Sick can be repeated.

The Life of the Individual.   Although the Anointing of the Sick can be administered when the sick person is unconscious, it is much better if a priest be called before this stage. Relatives are seriously lacking in love if they call the priest to a sick person only after he is unconscious.

The Life of the Church.   A difference in the form of administering this sacrament arose at an early date between the East and the West. In the East the sacrament is administered by three or seven priests; in the West one priest administers it by himself.

16. THE SACRAMENT OF MARRIAGE: THE CONSECRATION OF PARENTHOOD

BEFORE THE FALL in paradise, at the very moment of natural conception, a child would have received supernatural life — the life of grace.

In our present state, supernatural life is imparted through Baptism. The sacrament of Marriage is meant to equip the married couple to love one another as spouses in God, and in this love to bring up their children for God. And so Holy Scripture tells us:

> Husbands, love your wives, just as Christ loved the Church, and delivered himself for her, that he might sanctify her by cleansing her in the bath of water with the accompanying word, in order to present to himself the Church in all her glory, devoid of blemish or wrinkle or anything of the kind, but that she may be holy and flawless. Even so ought husbands to love their wives as their own bodies. He who loves his wife, loves himself. Now no one ever hates his own flesh; on the contrary, he nourishes and cherishes it, as Christ does the Church, because we are members of his Body.
> "For this cause a man shall leave his father and mother,
> and cling to his wife;
> and the two shall become one flesh."
> This is a great mystery — I mean in regard to Christ and the Church. Meanwhile, let each of you love his wife just as he loves himself, and let the wife reverence her husband (Eph 5:25–33).

In the sacrament of Marriage the whole world of marriage with its alternations of sorrow and joy, of laughing and weeping, of understanding and misunderstanding, is elevated and becomes a copy of the love between Jesus and the Church, and so also to be a constantly flowing fountain of supernatural love. Christ Himself takes married

189

love up into His grace in order to guard it against the dangers which threaten it. Christ turns the marriage vows into a contract before God. The evangelist Mark tells us:

> Leaving that country for good, he set out for the province of Judea by the Transjordanian route. And again people flocked to him, and again, as was his wont, he instructed them.
>
> One day the Pharisees approached and, with a view to sounding him out, laid this case before him: "Is it right for a husband to divorce his wife?" He answered by asking them: "What ruling has Moses given you?" They replied: "Moses gave permission to write a bill of separation and thus effect a divorce." "It was with an eye to your hardness of heart," Jesus said to them, "that Moses drew up this ruling for you. At the beginning of creation God made human beings male and female; and for this reason a man must leave his father and his mother, and the two are to become one, so that they are no longer two persons but one. Consequently, what God has yoked together man may not separate."
>
> After coming indoors, the disciples asked him still further about the matter. "Whoever," he said to them, "divorces his wife and marries another commits adultery in regard to the former; and if a wife divorces her husband and marries another, she commits adultery" (Mk 10:1–12).

Christ stressed the fact that God created man in two sexes — man and woman — and that in God's ordinance marriage is indissoluble. The breaking of marital fidelity between man and wife He called a hardness of heart, a lack of love for God.

The sacrament of Marriage can only be received legitimately and validly by those who accept the appropriate conditions of marriage contract.

A marriage is illicit and intrinsically invalid if, for example, the couple are blood relations (up to and including the third degree) or relations by marriage (up to and including the second degree); if one of the pair has received major orders or made solemn religious profession; if one party is Catholic and the other is unbaptized; if one of the pair has already contracted a valid marriage.

A marriage is illicit, but intrinsically valid, if one of the pair belongs to an atheistic society; or if both are baptized Christians but one party belongs to a non-Catholic Church (a mixed marriage).

The sacrament of Marriage is the sacrament which consecrates parenthood and so the family; the Church must therefore discourage marriages in which one party, although Christian, is not Catholic. In such a case the education of the children is made difficult.

Furthermore, it has also to be taken into account that non-Catholics often consider divorce permissible or at least will indulge in it without bothering about the situation in which they will leave their Catholic partner.

Thus the Church permits a mixed marriage only if there are good reasons for it, and demands also a guarantee that all children will be brought up as Catholics and that the Catholic party will not be obstructed in the practice of his religion.

Because marriage was ordained by God for the sake of children, it is contrary to God's law for the marriage act to be performed in such a way that conception is obstructed. The word "contraception" is a thoroughly un-Christian word. Married people are free, however, to limit intercourse to those days when conception is unlikely to take place.

The sacrament of marriage is the sacrament which consecrates parenthood.

According to Christ's words marriage consist in the indissoluble life-long partnership of a man and woman. This law was expressed by Jesus in this statement: "What God has yoked together, man may not separate" (Mk 10:9).

As a sacrifice of the New Covenant, marriage is an image of the indissoluble and grace-giving union of Jesus with the Church.

The *visible action* in the sacrament of Marriage is this: the bridal couple promise before the priest and two witnesses to live as man and wife in married fidelity until death. The priest gives them the Church's blessing. Through Christ the following *spiritual* effect results:

1. Christ raises the vows of both partners to the dignity of an indissoluble and grace-filled copy of His own bond of love for the Church.

2. Christ increases sanctifying grace in the couple and supports them with the help of God in the faithful discharge of the duties of the married state until the end of their lives.

Along with the sacrament of Marriage *divine guarantee* is given that

Christ elevates the natural love of the married couple to be a replica
of His own love of the Church.

There are *impediments to marriage* which render a marriage *illicit*
but not *invalid,* and impediments which render it both *illicit* and
invalid. The Catholic Church permits a mixed marriage only for
grave reasons and then only if the couple promise:

1. That all children will be baptized and brought up Catholics,
2. That the Catholic partner and the children will not be obstructed
   in the practice of their religion,
3. That the religious solemnization of the marriage takes place only
   in the Catholic church.

Deliberate prevention of conception is against God's design for married
union and is therefore never permissible. Married people are free
to use the sterile period if there is grave reason. In his encyclical
on marriage, Pius XI expressly declared that married people do
not sin against nature who make a right use of this, although, as a
result of the natural conditions provided by the sterile period, this
action does not give rise to new life.

The solemn celebration of marriages may not take place from the first
Sunday in Advent until Christmas, nor from Ash Wednesday until
Easter.

The Life of the Individual. At the time when the Christian Faith
was spreading throughout the Roman provinces, the natural reverence
for the family which had originally characterized the Roman people,
had long since disappeared. But through the power of the Faith new
generations arose who in faith regarded marriage as something holy.
Tertullian, who died between A.D. 220 and 240 writes thus:

> Where am I to find words to describe the felicity of that marriage
> which is celebrated before the Church, confirmed with the Holy
> Sacrifice, sealed with blessing, proclaimed by the angels and ac-
> counted dear to the Father? What a noble team are a believing
> couple, who follow one hope and one end of desire in a united
> manner of life according to one manner of service. Both pray
> together, kneel together, and celebrate the same festival days.
> They mutually instruct, exhort and bear with one another. They
> are together in God's house and at the Lord's table. They stand
> together in oppression and persecution, and in happy days. Neither

has secrets from the other, neither avoids the other or is a burden to him. Gladly they visit the sick and assist the needy. They give alms cheerfully and readily, and sacrifices are accepted without fuss or vexation; the daily practice of their religion is never hindered. The Sign of the Cross is not made furtively, holy salutations are not pronounced in fear, and they bless not in thought alone. Both their voices utter psalms and hymns and they seek to outstrip one another in singing the Lord's praise. Seeing and hearing such people is a joy to Christ. To those He grants His peace.

The Life of the Church. The form of marriage is now uniform everywhere. The prescriptions fall under four heads.

1. First it must be ascertained in advance that the couple are free to contract a valid marriage.
2. The faithful must avoid contracting a marriage which they know in advance will be a great burden and beset with spiritual dangers.
3. Assurances must be procured that the contract is not liable to be disputed later.
4. The marriage must be solemnized before a priest and two witnesses.

These prescriptions serve both to promote the common good and also to protect those who marry from subsequent disruption of the marriage.

If the Church presents as revealed truth that marriage is a life-long, indissoluble union of man and wife, this is only what nature herself seems to indicate. Whenever a normal young man falls in love with a girl, his deepest feelings are expressed in the words: "I love you alone forever!" In the finest love poems of all peoples this is the constant refrain!

Many people think the Church has followed the example of secular legal practice in her rules governing the solemnizing of marriage. The truth is that marriage is a sacrament, and even in the earliest times it was contracted before a priest — before the bishop in fact. In the letters of St. Ignatius, Bishop of Antioch, who was dragged to Rome from Syria in A.D. 110 and martyred under the Emperor Trajan, we find this: "It is proper that the bridegroom and bride take one another in marriage with the consent of the bishop so that their marriage accords with the will of God and not sensual desire. Let everything be done to the glory of God."

We even have a Preface for marriage, coming down from ancient times. It contains the following paragraph: "Almighty and eternal God, You have fashioned the vow of marriage with the sweet yoke of concord and the indissoluble bond of peace so that by holy marriages Your children shall be multiplied, whom You desire to have for Your saints. For Your fatherly care and Your grace bestow two things together: that which brings growth and beauty to the world through procreation is to be changed through new birth into the growth of the Church."

17. SELF-DISCIPLINE: THE INDISPENSABLE PREPARATION FOR MARRIAGE

MARRIAGE IS FOUNDED upon love, and love is founded upon thoughtfulness. Married people come to know and feel each other's weaknesses and can only preserve mutual love if they have learned always to consider the other first, to make sacrifices, to exercise restraint, and to practice meekness.

The preparation for marriage consists, much more than people think, in self-discipline. The first school for marital love is love for father and mother; the second is love for brothers and sisters. The better a young person acquits himself in these schools, the better is his prospect of a happy married life.

It is important also that young people do not count every attraction as true love and that they do not play with love. He who trifles with love will find his own love made light of. Suspicion in marriage only too often has its real roots in that easy-going philandering to which a person yielded before marriage.

One of life's most powerful illusions is that sexual love can bring happiness apart from God — even in defiance of God. But sexual love is not capable of doing this.

It is this false idea about a happiness which getting married will bring entirely of itself that is responsible in many cases for the disillusionment young people experience after a brief honeymoon. Along comes the first marriage quarrel and with it the hour when married love must prove itself. It will be the better able to do so if the couple have learned before marriage to consider others and to make sacrifices for others.

The basis for a happy marriage is found in reciprocal self-discipline and in mature Christian convictions.

The most important thing in preparation for marriage is self-discipline in sacrificial love. The first school for this is the relationship to father and mother, and to brothers and sisters.

It is part of preparation also that the young man should be well trained for a definite job and that the young woman should be instructed and have practice in all things connected with house-keeping and the upbringing of children.

The Life of the Individual. He who wishes to marry must have learned self-mastery. If you want to judge whether you have learned this or not, ask yourself these questions:

Can you bury, and leave buried, the past — not merely your own?

Can you forgive?

Can you bear misfortune with equanimity?

Can you remain serene and goodnatured when there is much to do?

Can you keep your temper even under provocation?

Can you refrain from having the last word?

Are you patient with children?

Can you bear ingratitude?

Not only must the individual prepare positively for marriage: he must also resist those many influences in the time before marriage which make for its destruction. Among those influences are to be numbered those novels which represent life as though sensual love could and must make men completely happy, and that if people do not find it so, they can always have a divorce. Films which portray this idea are even more pernicious. There is something uncanny about the way in which voluptuous images can be stored in the imagination: they become, as it were, inhabitants of the soul and erupt into consciousness at those very moments when they can do most harm.

The Life of the Church. Of preparation for marriage Pope Leo XIII says, in his encyclical on marriage, that many a misfortune and separation would never arise, "if men and women entered into the married state with proper dispositions, not influenced by passion, but entertaining right ideas of the duties of marriage and of its noble purpose; neither would they prepare for marriage by a series of sins drawing down upon them the wrath of God.

"To sum up all in a few words, there would be a calm and quiet constancy in marriage if married people would gather strength and life from the virtue of religion alone, which imparts to us resolution and fortitude; for religion would enable them to bear tranquilly and even gladly the trials of their state, such as, for instance, the faults that they discover in one another, the difference of temper and character, the weight of a mother's cares, the wearing anxiety about the education of children, reverses of fortune, and the sorrows of life."

18. THE SACRAMENTALS: THE INCORPORATION OF NATURE IN THE BLESSING OF REDEMPTION

WHEN ORIGINAL SIN severed the union between God and man, material things acquired a fateful power over man's nature. They gained power to lure him away from God, and to produce the illusion that in them he could find comfort, security, and happiness.

St. Paul says, therefore, that even inanimate things stand in their own fashion under the law of sin, and yearn for the day when they will be led back into the assured service of God. He points out that the redemption of man, it is true, begins in this world, but it will not be complete, and the things of this world will not be fully wrenched away from the influence of sin until the end of the world. In the Epistle to the Romans we read:

> All creation awaits with eager longing the manifestation of the sons of God. For creation was made subject to vanity not by its own choice but by the will of him who made it subject, yet with the hope that creation itself would be delivered from its slavery to corruption, to enjoy the freedom that comes with the glory of the children of God. For we know that all creation groans and travails in pain until now.
>
> And not only that, but we ourselves who have the Holy Spirit as first fruits — we ourselves groan within ourselves, waiting for the adoption as sons, the redemption of our body. As yet, our salvation is only a matter of hope. Now there is no hope when the object which had been hoped for is seen. How can a man hope really for what he sees? (Rom 8:19–24).

To consecrate material things to the service of Christ, the Church from earliest times has made use of sacramentals.

Sacramentals represent prayers which are related to particular times, places, or things and are often accompanied by symbolic actions. Objects over which special prayers of blessing have been said are also known as sacramentals.

1. The Church, following the example of Jesus, employs exorcisms; that is, by prayer she orders Satan to withdraw and depart from people and things. Exorcisms very often introduce or accompany blessings as, for example, in the administering of Baptism.

2. The Church blesses, i.e., she performs special prayers invoking God's blessing upon certain people, places, or things. Most important in this category are Benediction of the Blessed Sacrament, the blessing at the conclusion of Mass, the blessing of the sick, the nuptial blessing, and the blessing of mothers. Places which are important to men for living or working are blessed — dwelling houses, farms, and fields.

Fruit and salt are blessed. Since time immemorial animals too have been blessed. The machines which serve men are blessed, and the means of transport: ships, cars, and aircraft.

3. The Church consecrates. If a person, a place, or a thing is set apart from common use for the service of God it is solemnly consecrated with prayer by the Church. In this sense we speak of the blessing of an abbot and of consecration to religious life by solemn clothing. Holy Orders is not a consecration in this sense but it is a sacrament.

Churches, chapels, altars, and cemeteries are consecrated.

So are the following: church vessels and vestments, bells, baptismal water, holy water, rosary beads, crosses, medals, and candles.

The essential needs of man's life are always the same; and so Jesus Himself was able to institute the seven sacraments which are the same for every place and time. But, without prophesying about technical progress, Jesus could not give the Church express authority for particular blessings such as the blessing of aircraft and cars.

The mode of operation of sacramentals is thus different from that of the sacraments. The sacraments have a precise and particular effect as often as they are received worthily, and this effect never fails. It is Christ Himself who is mysteriously at work in the sacraments. The effect of sacramentals, on the other hand, issues through the intercession of the Church with God. The effect of sacramentals is not precisely defined as is that of the sacraments and is not infallibly assured as in the worthy reception of the sacraments. The prayers associated with the sacramentals are intended to strengthen the faith and trust of those who unite themselves with the intercession of the Church in order to receive the blessings of God.

But just as in Jesus' time there were people who would have preferred a fresh multiplication of loaves to the gift of bread for the soul, so, today, many unconsciously cherish the wish that the sacramentals might assist natural life as infallibly as the sacraments do the spiritual life. This is superstition and magic.

From time to time men may think that with the advance of technology this or that blessing becomes superfluous. For example, when insurance against hail and loss of cattle became common there were people who said that now the time for blessing of fields and weather was past. Such people had only a very superficial idea of what blessing really is. Today when everything is, so to speak, insured, we can use blessings just as well as in days past.

The most commonly used sacramental is undoubtedly holy water. By the use of holy water the Church makes all the faithful capable of applying the Church's blessings to themselves as often as they please. On blessing the water the priest prays that through the power of the blessed water God shall restrict the power of Satan, drive away illness and calamity and protect or restore health of body and soul.

Through the sacramentals the Church incorporates nature in the blessing of Redemption:

The Church employs *exorcisms* in order to repel the influence of Satan.

The Church *blesses* in order to call down God's blessing upon people, places, and things, thus desiring to mitigate the burden of original sin which lies upon creatures.

The Church *consecrates* in order to dedicate exclusively to God's service certain people, places, and things.

The Life of the Individual. In the education of children Christian customs are an immense help. By them the children themselves can "do something." Christian customs based upon the sacramentals possess an educative value which nothing else can replace. Clearly, blessings and consecrations are lower in rank than the sacraments and the

Sacrifice of the Mass, but they contain great possibilities of penetrating people's lives at every point. The sacraments and Holy Mass bring people together into the Church; by contrast, in the sacramentals the Church comes to families in their own homes. Few things make such an impression upon a child as the practice of Christian customs along with parents and brothers and sisters. Man cannot go on living indefinitely without some sort of sign in which he has promise of happiness and protection.

The Life of the Church. Under the Old Covenant even the highest transactions of worship, the temple sacrifices, had the character of sacramentals, i.e., they dispensed the grace which they signified, not by and in themselves infallibly, but only by virtue of the intercession of the priest and the devout attitude of the recipients; and all took place with reference to the merits of Jesus Christ, the coming Redeemer.

Under the New Covenant the sacramentals are auxiliaries. Above the sacramentals are the sacraments, and at the summit of the sacraments is the holy Sacrifice of the Mass.

19. HOLY ORDERS: SOLEMN DEDICATION AS A REPRESENTATIVE OF CHRIST

SHORTLY AFTER the beginning of His public ministry Jesus chose twelve men whom He called apostles — i.e. *sent men.* This name indicated that one day they were to act as His representatives. Jesus introduced these Apostles step by step into the three offices which He Himself possessed: the *teaching office,* the *priestly office,* and the *pastoral office.*

To begin with He sent them out to proclaim the glad tidings of the kingdom of God, giving them the following instructions.

"Whatever house you enter, the first thing you say must be: 'A blessing on this household.' If there is a soul in it responsive to a blessing, your blessing will alight on him; if not, it will return to you. Make your headquarters in just that house, and eat and drink whatever they have to offer. After all, the laborer is entitled to his wages. Do not be constantly shifting from house to house. Whatever town you enter, if the people make you welcome, eat what is set before you; take care of the sick in the place; and speak to the inhabitants on this theme: 'The kingdom of God has finally come to you.' But if, in any town you enter, the people do not make you welcome, go out into the streets and say: 'Even the dust of your town that sticks to our feet we are wiping off for you to keep. Nonetheless, be sure of one thing: The kingdom of God has finally come.' I tell you, on that Day it will go less hard with Sodom than with that town.

"Unhappy Corozain. Unhappy Bethsaida; If the wonders done in your midst had been done in Tyre and Sidon, they would long ago have repented in sackcloth and ashes. At all events, at the judgment it will go less hard with Tyre and Sidon than with you. And you, Capharnaum, do you expect to soar as high as heaven? As deep as hell shall you sink! He who listens to you listens to me, and he who despises you despises me; but whoever despises me despises him whose ambassador I am" (Lk 10:5–16).

And then, during the Last Supper, Jesus conferred upon the Apostles the power of celebrating the Sacrifice of the New Covenant by commanding them, "Do this in remembrance of me" (1 Cor 11:24).

Before ascending into heaven Jesus finally summarized the priestly task of the Apostles in the solemn command: "Go, therefore, and make all nations your disciples: baptize them in the name of the Father and of the Son and of the Holy Spirit, and teach them to observe all the commandments I have given you" (Mt 28:19).

In the priesthood of the New Covenant the prophecy of Isaiah was fulfilled. This prophet had already foretold the time when not the sons of Levi alone would be priests, but God would take priests for Himself out of all nations and peoples (cf. Is 66:21).

Priests have a duty to preach true doctrine and to hold the faithful to a life which accords with this doctrine. The faithful have a duty to pay heed to their words and to submit to their leadership.

By Holy Orders weak men are empowered to offer the Eucharistic Banquet and forgive sins.

The priest is Christ's representative. This constitutes his spiritual greatness. He possesses a power above all human powers. For this very reason he counts the world as nothing. And yet he is no philosopher, no scholar, no statesman, and no scientist. Whoever measures the dignity of the priest by such standards makes him a priest according to the ideas of the ancient Greeks and Romans.

The priest is bound to preserve the seal of confession in all circumstances. St. John of Nepomuk is not the only priest, but only the best known, who gave his life to fulfill this duty. The preservation of the seal of confession is likewise binding on any who, through their own fault or not, learn anything about another person's confession.

Holy Orders is the sacrament which dedicates mortal men to be representatives of Christ.

Holy Orders is a sacrament because Christ imparted priestly powers to the Apostles and the Apostles handed these on to others through the laying on of hands.

The *visible action* in the sacrament of Holy Orders consists in the following. The bishop prays over all the deacons who are to be ordained and lays his hands upon each of them. He dresses each one in the Mass vestments, and anoints his hands saying, "Be pleased, O Lord, to consecrate and hallow these hands by this anointing, and our blessing. That whatsoever they bless may be blessed, and whatsoever they consecrate may be consecrated and hallowed." He holds out to each deacon the paten with the host and the chalice with wine, saying, "Receive the power to offer Sacrifice to God, and to celebrate Mass, both for the living and the dead." After Holy Communion he again lays his hands upon the deacons and says, "Receive the Holy Spirit; whose sins you shall forgive, they are forgiven them: and whose sins you shall retain, they are retained." The actual ordination as priests is accomplished with the first prayer over the ordinands which is associated with the Preface.

Ordination to the priesthood is preceded by the exterior steps and interior preparation of the so-called minor orders — porter, reader, exorcist, acolyte. Just as the various ceremonies surrounding Baptism, once performed over a period of time, are now united in a single action, so it happens that today the minor orders are conferred within a short space of time.

Holy Orders produces the following *interior* effects:

1. Jesus Christ imparts to the person ordained a priestly power.
2. Jesus Christ increases sanctifying grace in him who is ordained and furnishes him with the help of grace to live and act as a good priest.
3. Jesus Christ seals the soul of the priest with an indelible sign of priesthood.

When the sacrament of Holy Orders is conferred a *divine guarantee* is given that Jesus conveys to the ordained the authority to practice the teaching, the priestly, and the pastoral offices in His name.

The Life of the Individual. The faithful are to see in priests the ambassadors of God and should distinguish between their human weaknesses and their office. They should pray for priests and so support them in their work. Many a priest has fallen because none of those entrusted to his care was praying for him. The contributions which we are required to give to the Church should not be given out of compulsion, but should be given with the intention of preserving well-ordered religious conditions and of supporting the priests and the priesthood.

The priest who is primarily responsible for any of the faithful is the priest of the parish to which they belong; and the faithful on their part must accept their responsibilities toward him.

The Life of the Church. From earliest times the Church has paid special attention to young men who have a mind to dedicate themselves to the priesthood. They should be men of knowledge and piety. To look after minor and major seminaries for priests is one of the most important tasks of a bishop.

Those who support students preparing for the priesthood perform a work specially pleasing to God. Pope Pius XII urged that special societies for fostering vocations to the priesthood and assisting in the education of candidates for the priesthood be formed in every diocese.

20. SACRIFICE UNDER THE OLD COVENANT; SUBLIME YET LIMITED

MAN HAS TWO DUTIES to God: the duty to keep God's laws and the duty to recognize God as Giver of life and to pay Him homage. To present sacrifices is, as the Council of Trent says, the essential behavior of a religious man.

Through the Fall man lost exact knowledge of the moral law. Under the Old Covenant, therefore, God gave the Ten Commandments. Similarly, men lacked knowledge of the law of sacrifice, and for this reason God established a sacrificial ordinance for the people of Israel. This was as much part of revelation as the Ten Commandments.

The sacrificial system of the Old Covenant embraced blood sacrifices, or victims, and bloodless sacrifices, or food offerings. Blood sacrifices had the preeminence because through these sacrifices man could pay homage to God as Lord of life in a particularly expressive way through shedding of blood. This marked emphasis on the symbolic significance of the blood of sacrifice is peculiar to the people of Israel. The blood here is above all a symbol of life. Concerning this we read in Leviticus:

> Since the life of a living body is in its blood, I have made you put it on the altar, so that atonement may thereby be made for your own lives, because it is the blood, as the seat of life, that makes atonement. That is why I have told the Israelites: No one among you, not even a resident alien, may partake of blood (Lev 17:11–12).

The significance attached to the sacrificial offering of blood to God

206

is shown by the way it is done. During the sacrifices, which were offered on behalf of the whole congregation, the priest had to sprinkle blood on the curtain of the Holy of Holies. During the solemn sacrifice of atonement on the Day of Atonement the high priest himself had to carry the blood of the sacrifice into the Holy of Holies and sprinkle it over the Ark of the Covenant.

St. Paul describes the superiority of the blood-sacrifice over the food offerings in the following sentence: "The law would have all things purified with blood; unless blood is shed there is no remission" (Heb 9:22). He saw in this fact — as we shall develop later — a specific prophecy of the blood-sacrificial death of Jesus Christ on the cross. This fact forms the basis of the Epistle of Hebrews.

The sacrifice of the Old Covenant represented something provisional. The prophets indicated that this sacrificial system would one day be succeeded by a new, better, and permanent ordinance. More precisely, they foretold both a unique blood sacrifice, which would annul the sin of the people, and also a recurrent food offering.

The prophet known as Second Isaiah speaks of the blood sacrifice of atonement to come, alluding to the atoning death of the Servant of God.

> Yet it was our infirmities that he bore, our sufferings that he endured, while we thought of him as stricken, as one smitten by God and afflicted. But he was pierced for our offenses, crushed for our sins; upon him was the chastisement that makes us whole, by his stripes we were healed. We had all gone astray like sheep, each following his own way; but the Lord laid upon him the guilt of us all (Is 53:4–6).

The sacrifice of the life of the Servant of God represents a sacrifice which can be offered only once, but which nevertheless embraces all ages in its effects.

The food offering pertaining to the New Covenant is foretold by the prophet Malachiah in these words.

> I have no pleasure in you, says the Lord of hosts; neither will I accept any sacrifice from your hands, for from the rising of the sun, even to its setting, my name is great among the nations; and everywhere they bring sacrifice to my name, and a pure offering; for great is my name among the nations, says the Lord of hosts (Mal 1:10–11).

According to the prophecy of Malachiah this sacrifice, in contrast to the old sacrifices of Israel, will be offered not only in the temple at Jerusalem, but from sunrise until sunset, i.e., in every land beneath the sun. This fact is attested by the use of the word *goyim* in the prophecy. This word always denotes the heathen peoples, not Israel. The word used here for sacrifice is *mincha* which always denotes the food offering.

The temple at Jerusalem and the temples of the Egyptians, the Greeks, and the Romans resemble one another in outward appearance, as did the external executions of their services of sacrifice, for even the sacrifices of the heathen have their ultimate origin in man's spiritual disposition. Thus their earlier sacrificial services provided both Jews and heathens with a way of approach to the once-for-all, unique sacrifice of Jesus upon the cross.

As far back as the history of man can be traced, we find indications that men have offered sacrifice.

Offering sacrifice is part of man's nature — its highest aspect, indeed. Corresponding to this, God instituted a sacrificial ordinance both for the Old and the New Covenants.

Through the offering of a sacrifice, homage is paid to God the Lord as Giver and Sustainer of life. As soon as men start believing in a multiplicity of gods, they have to sacrifice to all of them; and thereupon sacrifice loses its character of adoration.

The blood sacrifice of the Old Covenant had preeminence over the food offering because it prefigured most clearly the coming blood sacrifice of atonement by Jesus Christ upon the cross.

The Life of the Individual. People who have lost the sense of the sovereignty of God often see sacrifice as something exaggerated or primitive — meaningless today. But, as the Council of Trent explains, sacrifice is something primitive in quite another sense, viz., in the sense that it pertains to man's nature and to those religious activities which are unchangeable.

That service of God which man fulfills through adoration is certainly of quite another kind than that which he renders through observance of the Commandments of God. How different, for example, is the Christian life of a devout peasant from that of a civil servant or a priest in its outward activities. But for all of these, the religious acts by which they worship God are the same — prayer and sacrifice. Sacrifice, especially, represents a religious activity which remains essentially the same for all. Whoever stands aloof from the sacrifice separates himself from the community of those who worship God.

The Life of the Church. We must guard against casting a romantic aura around ancient sacrifices which are no longer known to us first-hand. Even the external arrangements to be found at the temple in Jerusalem were quite matter of fact. From the altar of burnt offering and from the place where animals were sacrificed a special channel led away to the east into the Cedron valley. This provided such a vast quantity of offal outside the temple walls every day that it was sold for dung. The smoke which rose from the burning animals was discolored and greasy and in consequence the soot which descended on the nearby walls was glutinous and sticky. The walls which still stand in the temple precincts at Pompeii are blackened as though the whole building had been roasted in sacrifice. In a calm, this sticky smoke hovered in the air. The first lines of Sophocles' play *Oepidus Rex* tell of how the whole city is filled with the smoldering smoke of the sacrifices which are being offered to the gods in the time of distress. The sizzling of the fat in the fire and the upsurge of smoke could have been edifying only to those who saw in sacrifice a religious transaction.

It is no accident that the Christians of the first century looked at the blood sacrifices of Jews and heathens and, from purely external and sensible considerations, contrasted the holy Sacrifice of the Mass as a sacrifice of a higher sort. St. Cyprian, Bishop of Carthage, speaks twice in his famous pastoral letter at the conclusion of the Decian persecution of the "disgusting, stinking smoke" of heathen sacrifice, which had, for him, a symbolic significance. And upon educated heathens, even if they did not become Christians, in these circumstances the celebration of holy Mass made a deep impression. It is certainly striking to find a heathen philosopher like Maximus of Tyre recommending spiritual rather than blood sacrifices and thus using the same sort of language as St. Paul.

21. THE SACRIFICE OF THE NEW COVENANT, PERFECTED BY CHRIST, IS MADE KNOWN

ARRANGING THE SERMONS of our Lord according to subject matter, we come upon a mysterious gap. In His expositions the Lord never touches on the sacrificial ordinance of the Old Covenant to clarify it spiritually. In a special way this silence of our Lord has a prophetic character. The sacrificial ordinance of the Old Covenant was to be replaced at His death by another "sacrificial ordinance of the new and eternal Covenant."

Jesus refrained from declaring this new sacrifice openly to the Jews because they would then have silenced Him at once; but He proclaimed it at the climax of His ministry by a symbolic miracle — the miracle of the loaves and fishes.

> Some time later Jesus went across the Sea of Galilee, that is, the Lake of Tiberias. A great crowd followed him, because they were witnesses of the miracles which he used to perform on the sick. After going up the mountainside, Jesus seated himself there, surrounded by his disciples. The Passover, the feast of the Jews, was near at hand.
>
> Lifting up his eyes and noticing that a crowd of people were coming to meet him, Jesus said to Philip: "Where shall we buy bread enough for these people to have a meal?" He said this by way of testing him, for he knew his own mind as to what he intended to do. "Bread for two hundred denarii," Philip answered him, "is not enough for each of them to get even a little." Then one of his disciples, Andrew, the brother of Simon Peter, said to him: "There is a lad here who has five barley loaves and two fish; but what is that for so many!" "Make the people recline on the ground," Jesus said. There was much grass in the place. So they reclined, the men numbering about five thousand.

Jesus then took the loaves into his hands and, after saying grace, had the loaves as well as pieces of fish distributed among the people reclining about the ground. Everyone got as much as he wanted. When all had had their fill, he said to his disciples: "Gather up the pieces that are left over; nothing must be wasted." They gathered them up, therefore, after they had finished their meal, and filled twelve baskets with the remnants of the five barley loaves.

When the people realized what miracle he had performed, they said: "This is really the Prophet who is to come into the world!" Jesus, accordingly, knowing that they intended to come and carry him off to make him king, withdrew, all by himself, still deeper into the mountainous region (Jn 6:1–15).

The next day, in the synagogue at Capharnaum, Jesus commented on the symbolic meaning of this miracle:

"I am the bread of life. Your fathers ate the manna in the desert, and they died. The bread which I speak of, which comes down from heaven, is such that no one who eats of it will ever die. I am the living bread that has come down from heaven. If one eats of this bread, he will live forever; and, furthermore, the bread which I shall give is my flesh given for the life of the world."

The Jews then had a violent discussion among themselves. "How," they argued, "can this man give us his flesh to eat?"

Resuming, therefore, Jesus said to them: "What I tell you is the plain truth: unless you eat the flesh of the Son of Man and drink his blood, you have no life in you. He who eats my flesh and drinks my blood is in possession of eternal life; and I will raise him from the dead on the last day; for my flesh is real food, and my blood is real drink. He who eats my flesh and drinks my blood is united with me, and I am united with him. As the living Father has appointed me his ambassador, and I live because of the Father, so, too, he who eats me will have life because of me. This is the bread that has come down from heaven. It is not what your fathers ate; they ate and died. He who eats this bread will live forever."

This discourse he delivered in an instruction at a synagogue service in Capharnaum. The result was that many of his disciples among the hearers said: "Such language is hard to bear; who can listen to it!" But Jesus, inwardly aware that his disciples were grumbling on this account, said to them: "Does this make you waver in your faith? Suppose, then, you see the Son of Man ascend to where he was before? The spirit is the life-giving thing; the flesh as such is worthless. The words I have spoken to you are spirit and, therefore, life. The trouble is, there are some among you that have no faith."

Jesus knew, of course, from the outset, who those were that had no faith, and, in particular, which of them was to betray him. So he continued: "This is what I meant when I said to you: 'No one can come to me unless he has received the gift from the Father.'"

Thereupon many of his disciples went back to their old life and would no longer associate with him. Jesus then said to the Twelve: "Are you, too, minded to go away?" Simon Peter spoke up. "Master," he said to him, "to whom shall we go? You have a message of eternal life; we firmly believe and are fully convinced that you are the Holy One of God!" Jesus interposed. "I personally chose you, the Twelve, did I not? And yet, one of you is a devil!" (Jn 6:48–70.)

Not all of the questioners who addressed Jesus at Capharnaum were called to be His priests. Thus the address of Jesus interprets the miracle of the multiplication of the loaves only with reference to those features which impinge upon the life of the ordinary members of the future sacrificing community.

Accordingly, Jesus announced to those who addressed Him that the miracle of the loaves was not done for its own sake but as a sign in preparation for that miraculous bread which contained life and which could unite the soul to God.

The inner tension of the ensuing dialogue is created by the questioners' seeking in a friendly but persistent way to wrest from the Lord a promise to repeat the miracle of the loaves. But in His replies Jesus gives them to understand, with increasing clarity and firmness, that it is not the miracle, but the truth He proclaims, which alone is important and great.

In the course of His address Jesus adverts specially to one circumstance. The time when He will give His disciples His flesh to eat and His blood to drink is still far off. Between the present and that time there lies a mysterious event. His body first of all will be brought to a new condition in which it can become food for the life of the world. Jesus draws attention to this transformation in the words, "I am the living bread that has come down from heaven" (Jn 6:51).

At the conclusion of the discourse Jesus exhorts his hearers to suspend judgment upon the question as to how He will be able to give His flesh to eat and His blood to drink. It will be time to judge this when the Son of Man has ascended into heaven whence He came.

Jesus clothes this allusion in the words, "Does this make you waver in your faith? Suppose, then, you see the Son of Man ascend to where he was before?" (Jn 6:62–63).

By these two sentences Jesus is explaining that this marvelous nourishment will only be made possible through His death. Through His death He will reach a condition in which that can be realized which at the moment appears an impossibility.

In the solemn announcement of the sacrificial ordinance of the New Covenant, to which belong both the miracle of the loaves and the subsequent discourse, Jesus spoke in detail of a recurrent bloodless sacrifice with a sacrificial meal; and He indicated at the same time that this bloodless sacrifice had as its prerequisite a single blood sacrifice.

The Divine Author of the New Covenant is Jesus Christ Himself. He prepared the Apostles in advance for the introduction of a new sacrificial ordinance.

In the miracle of the loaves and in the subsequent discourse Jesus Christ made known the character of the new sacrificial ordinance. The sacrificial ordinance of the New Covenant — according to our Lord's words — consists of a *single blood sacrifice* which He Himself makes, and a *repeatable bloodless sacrifice* with a sacrificial meal which *forms a unity with the once-offered blood sacrifice.*

The Life of the Individual. In the public life of Jesus the miracle of the loaves is both a climax and a turning point. It is a climax because by it Jesus drew more people to Him than at any other time; a turning point because it made plain who would allow themselves to be led on to faithful expectation of that other Bread, and who would not.

The same sort of thing is repeated in life. Many people look upon the Church as the producer of well-being, withdrawing from her as soon as she fails to fulfill their worldly expectations.

In the discourse following the multiplication of the loaves Jesus was addressing all who in future ages would ask about the meaning of this miracle of the multiplication of the loaves. The words of Jesus are addressed to us.

The Life of the Church. In the same unconditional way as Jesus asked it of the disciples, the Church demands of the faithful belief in the Real Presence of Jesus. The documents and writings of the centuries prove this belief to be part of the inheritance of the Church.

An old Mass prayer, added to a letter of Pope Clement (d. c. 100), reads: "Having received the precious Body and Blood of Christ, let us give thanks."

Justin Martyr (d. c. 167) says: "As Christ Himself said of the bread, 'This is my body,' who then dare doubt it? And as He Himself assured us, 'This is my blood,' who wants to doubt and say that it is not His blood?"

St. Augustine (d. 430) says: "The bread which you see upon the altar is the body of Christ: what is in the chalice is the blood of Christ."

For the Christian, the Eucharist is the liturgical act *par excellence.* Christ, with His members, offers Himself to the Father in a banquet, a love feast. It is to be *celebrated,* i.e., enacted with joy and faith by the community of the faithful. It is *the* sign of unity.

22. THE LAST SUPPER: THE SACRIFICE OF THE NEW COVENANT IS INSTITUTED

JESUS OUR LORD went to meet death, fully conscious that it was coming. His actions and words became transfused with something of that glory which had been His before He entered the world. The evangelists describe the Last Supper in restrained detail.

St. Luke relates:

At last the day of the Unleavened Bread arrived, and the paschal lamb had to be sacrificed. So Jesus sent Peter and John on an errand, with this instruction: "Go to prepare the paschal supper for us to eat." "Where," they asked him, "do you want us to make preparations?" "Listen," he replied; "on entering the city, you will meet a man carrying a pitcher of water; follow him into the house he enters, and say to the proprietor of the house: 'The Rabbi asks, Where is the dining room in which I can eat the paschal supper with my disciples?' He will show you a room upstairs which is spacious and well furnished. There get things ready." They went and found everything as he had told them, and prepared the paschal supper.

When the hour had come, he took his place on a couch, and so did the apostles. "It has been my heart's desire," he said to them, "to eat this paschal supper with you before I suffer. I tell you, I shall not eat it again till it is fulfilled in the kingdom of God." And after receiving a cup and saying grace, he said: "Take this, and divide it among you. I tell you, I shall not again drink of the produce of the vine till the kingdom of God is set up."

He also took bread into his hands and, after saying grace, broke it into portions, which he gave to them with these words: "This is my body, which is about to be given for your sake. Do this as my memorial." He did the same with the cup when supper was over, and said: "This cup is the new covenant sealed by my blood, which is about to be shed for your sake" (Lk 22:7–20).

During the Last Supper the Lord determined of His own accord that His Passion should begin. First, He dismissed Judas from the circle of the Apostles after a last warning. At the same time, dedicating Himself to a sacrificial death, He solemnly carried out the presentation of the food offering with the sacrificial meal in which the sacrifice of the cross was to be perpetuated for all time, and gave the Apostles authority and instruction to repeat what He had done.

These two most sacred acts of Jesus, accomplished in the same hour, in a single happening as it were, are summed up in the words of Pius XII's encyclical on the liturgy: "Christ our Lord, 'priest for ever according to the order of Melchisedech,' 'loved his own that were in the world': and accordingly 'at the Last Supper, on the night on which He was being betrayed,' He willed to leave to His beloved Bride the Church a visible sacrifice such as the nature of man requires; one by which the bloody sacrifice that was to be enacted once upon the Cross should be represented and its memory remain until the end of the world, and its salutary power be applied for the remission of the sins that are daily committed by us. . . . He therefore offered His body and blood to God the Father under the appearances of bread and wine, and under the symbols of the same delivered them to be taken by the Apostles, whom He at that moment was making priests of the New Testament; and to them and to their successors in the priesthood He gave commandment to offer."

The Apostles had been prepared for the institution of a bloodless sacrifice, which would incorporate the re-presentation of the blood sacrifice on the cross, by the miracle of the loaves and its attendant discourse at Capharnaum. But because at that time they had no real insight into the meaning of the death of Jesus, they missed the full import of Jesus' declaration. Only when they began to understand, by the illumination of the Holy Spirit, how Jesus would expiate the sins of the world by His sacrificial death and restore the honor of God, did they begin to see what a treasure the Lord had bequeathed to His Church in the holy Sacrifice of the Mass. And so from the very beginning, the holy Sacrifice of the Mass became the acme of all worship of God.

Christ settled the sacrificial ordinance of the New Covenant on the evening before His passion and death and thus it acquired the nature of a testament of the love of Christ for His people whom He was leaving behind in the world.

The sacrificial ordinance of the New Covenant was founded by Jesus Christ.

Jesus Christ founded the sacrificial ordinance of the New Covenant by presenting Himself for mankind upon the cross a *once-for-all blood* sacrifice to the heavenly Father, and by giving to the Church authority *to re-present repeatedly* this blood offering *until the end of time and thus to enable the faithful to participate in the grace of the sacrifice of the cross.*

The Last Supper has a twofold meaning in the new sacrificial order. In this hour Jesus prepared Himself for the blood sacrifice of the cross and at the same time instituted the bloodless food offering of the New Covenant.

The Life of the Individual. In the Epistle to Hebrews St. Paul the Apostle contrasts the essence of the Old Covenant with that of the New:

> You have not come to a mountain that may be touched, to a flaming fire, to black clouds and a thunderstorm and a whirlwind, to a resounding trumpet and to a voice so speaking that those who heard it begged that it speak no further word to them. Why? Because they could not stand the order given, "If even a beast touches the mountain, it is to be stoned." The spectacle was indeed so terrifying that Moses said, "I am overcome with fear and trembling." But you have come to Mount Sion, to the city of the living God, the heavenly Jerusalem, to countless angels, to the festive gathering and assembly of the first-born who are enrolled in heaven, to God, the judge of all men, to the spirits of just men made perfect, to Jesus the Mediator of the new covenant, to the sprinkling blood that speaks more eloquently than Abel's (Heb 12:18–24).

The Life of the Church. The Church commemorates the institution of Mass and the Blessed Sacrament first of all on Maundy Thursday, the day on which our Savior celebrated the Last Supper with His disciples. But the Church also commemorates this institution of Jesus on a special feast day called Corpus Christi, which falls each year during the second week after Pentecost. The Church selects this time for the celebration of this feast because it was in the days after the descent of the Holy Spirit, i.e., after Pentecost, that the Apostles, following Christ's command, began to offer the holy Sacrifice of the Mass.

Looking back to the sacrifice of the Old Covenant, the Church addresses the following prayer to God the Father in the course of the holy Mass: "Look with favorable and gracious countenance (upon this oblation) and accept them, as You accepted the gifts of Your just servant Abel, and the sacrifice of our Patriarch Abraham, and that which Your high priest Melchisedech offered to You, a holy Sacrifice, an unspotted victim."

In the minds of the Apostles who were eyewitnesses at the Last Supper, the celebration of the sacrifice of the New Covenant remained associated with Christ's valedictory address, with His admonition to love one another, and with the celebration of a true meal. For this reason in earliest times Mass was celebrated as the conclusion of a communal meal. This practice, as St. Paul points out to the Corinthians, led to unseemly behavior (1 Cor 2: 17–34). But even after the meal was discontinued and Mass became independent, the sense that the participants in the celebration of the sacrifice constituted a community was much stronger than it is today. And so we find in the *Didache* (*Teaching of the Twelve Apostles*), for example, the following statements among instructions for celebrating Sunday Mass. "Anyone who has a quarrel with his neighbor must not be admitted until they are reconciled so that your sacrifice may not be desecrated." Today the *Confiteor,* the public confession of sins, exhorts all who assist at Mass to forgive sincerely all their fellowmen.

23. CHRIST'S SACRIFICE UPON THE CROSS: THE ONCE-FOR-ALL BLOOD SACRIFICE OF THE NEW COVENANT

UNDER THE OLD COVENANT the sacrifice of the great Day of Atonement was unique. To show this it had to be offered by the high priest himself who on this day, and on this day only, entered the Holy of Holies, to sprinkle the Ark of the Covenant with the blood from the sacrifice.

Because of its exalted rank this sacrifice constituted in a special way a prefiguring of the atoning sacrifice of Jesus Christ by which it made satisfaction to God the heavenly Father not only for the sins of Israel but for the sins of the whole world from that of Adam until the last one committed before the end of time.

But in that moment when Jesus Christ the Son of God, acting as the divine-human High Priest, initiated the final performance of the sacrifice, presenting Himself as victim, the sacrificial act was transformed from within in a unique way.

Under the Old Covenant a mortal priest offered to the one and only God a gift chosen from the creation, thereby acknowledging Him to be Lord of creation and paying Him homage. But in Jesus Christ, by contrast, there appeared a priest who, as the Son of God made man, possessed priestly dignity, not through outward appointment, but intrinsically from the very moment when He joined human nature to His divinity. In place of a gift from the creation there appeared the crown of creation, the divine-human life of Jesus Christ.

No longer do we have a sacrifice rising up from man to God: now it is being raised up by the Son of God, by the second Person of the Trinity, to the heavenly Father. Thus the sacrifice transcends human limitations: Jesus Christ the Son of God is the High Priest, offering Himself as victim, and it is God the Father to whom the sacrifice is made.

The Victim in this sacrifice — the divine-human life of Jesus Christ — had such infinite value that, by comparison, all other gifts from the creation ceased to count. In this single sacrifice all the sins of the world were atoned and the plenitude of grace which reposed in Christ the Redeemer was made available for all men. In the Epistle to the Hebrews where the superiority of the New Testament sacrificial order over that of the Old is pointed out, this transference of the locus of sacrifice from earth to heaven and the unique and conclusive effect of Christ's sacrifice is described as follows:

> Such was certainly the high priest that fitted our needs, holy, innocent, undefiled, set apart from sinners, and exalted higher than the heavens. He has no need of offering sacrifice day by day, as do the other high priests, first for their own and then for the people's sins. He did this once for all, when he offered himself (Heb 7:26–27).

> But when Christ, high priest of the messianic blessings, appeared, he entered once for all through the greater and more perfect tabernacle not made by human hands, that is, not of earthly origin. It was not the blood of goats and calves but his own blood that was the means of his entering the Holy Place and securing eternal redemption. Now if the blood of goats and calves and the sprinkled ashes of a red cow sanctify the defiled and result in outward cleansing, how much more will the blood of Christ — of him who through his eternal spirit offered himself unblemished to God — cleanse our own conscience from lifeless deeds and fit it for the worship of the living God? (Heb 9:11–14.)

> And just as it is appointed for men to die once and then to undergo judgment, so also was Christ offered only once to bear the sins of the multitude; at his second appearance he will not deal with sin, but will bring salvation to those who await him (Heb 9:27–28).

When Jesus the Son of God gave His life a sacrifice in atonement for the sins of the world, mankind entered into a remarkable situation. The old sacrifices lost their meaning and value because they had been instituted by God merely as foreshadowings of the sacrificial death of Christ. After the sacrifice of the cross no new sacrifice was ever possible again. The sacrifice of the cross had expiated all guilt and vindicated the honor of God abundantly. Any repetition of the sacrifice of the cross itself can be excluded because Jesus as true man could die only once.

Because of this the love and power of God provided that the one conclusive sacrifice of the cross should be made present in a bloodless sacrifice and men thus enabled to participate in the once-for-all sacrifice of the cross.

In His omniscience, when He made His sacrifice, Jesus did not atone sin in general but took upon Himself the particular sins of each person; and so in that hour He entered into a spiritual relationship with every individual. Now, as a consequence, every man who sins enters into a relationship with Christ in exactly the same way as a sick man does to the physician who can cure him.

And if a man wishes to pay homage to God as supreme Lord, to render thanks, and to make supplication for himself and others, then once more he enters into a relationship with Christ. For Christ has honored God infinitely with adoration and thanksgiving on behalf of all men and thus for every individual; and has made intercession in advance for everyone who shall ever pray to God. Hence the words referring to His death upon the cross, which Jesus spoke shortly before His passion, have been fulfilled. "And I, once I have been lifted up from the earth, will draw all men to myself" (Jn. 12:32).

The sacrificial death of Christ upon the cross is the blood sacrifice which fulfills the prophecies of the Old Testament and upon which the new and eternal Covenant is founded.

The reconciliation of the human race with God has been achieved through a blood sacrifice in which Jesus Christ the Son of God as High Priest and Head of the human race sacrificed Himself.

The blood sacrifice of Jesus Christ upon the cross made infinite atonement to God the Father for all the sins of mankind and made available to all men the riches of grace in Jesus Christ their head.

The Life of the Individual. Anyone who wants to assist at Mass with fitting devotion and reverence must keep constantly in mind its whole magnitude. Only so will the prayers which accompany the celebration of the sacrifice make a real spiritual impression upon him.

Because the sacrifice of the cross and the Sacrifice of the Mass are one and the same in their priest and in the gift offered, the Church requires that there should be a crucifix upon the altar when Mass is being celebrated. The altar is thus an external reminder of the hill of Calvary upon which Jesus Christ gave up His life for men and poured out His blood in sacrifice.

The Life of the Church.   In a hymn for the feast of the Sacred Heart, the heart of Jesus is depicted as the Ark of the New Covenant in which is hidden a new law, a law based on forgiveness, on the clemency of grace, on merciful love. And this heart is also the temple of the New Covenant, a temple which will never more be destroyed.

This Heart allowed itself to be pierced with a lance during the sacrificial death, to supply men with a visible image of that love with which it had always been secretly inflamed.

The sacrificial death of Jesus is therefore at once an inner sacrifice of the Most Sacred Heart and an outward blood sacrifice through which the last drop of this heart's blood was shed.

Because the Sacrifice of the Mass takes its origin from Calvary and forms a unity with it, the compassionate making present to oneself of the Passion and Death of Jesus Christ is always an indispensable prerequisite of spiritual participation in the celebration of the Sacrifice. Pope Pius, in *Mediator Dei,* draws attention to this. "The sacred liturgy puts Christ before us whole and entire, in all the phases of His life: the Christ who is the Word of the eternal Father, who is born of the Virgin Mother of God, who teaches us truth, who heals the sick and consoles the afflicted, who suffers and dies; who then triumphs over death by His resurrection, and from His throne in the glory of heaven sends down upon us the Spirit, the Paraclete, to live for ever in His Church. What Jesus Christ was yesterday, and is today, He remains for ever. And the liturgy presents Christ to us not only as an example to imitate but as a teacher for us to believe, as a shepherd for us to follow, as the advocate who saves us, as the source of holiness, and as the Mystical Head whose living members we are. . . .

"And because His cruel sufferings constitute the mystery from which our salvation chiefly springs, it is in keeping with the Catholic faith that the Passion should be emphasized; indeed it is the center of our worship, because it is what the Eucharistic Sacrifice daily represents and re-enacts, and because all the Sacraments are closely linked with the Cross."

24. THE HOLY SACRIFICE OF THE MASS: THE BLOODLESS FOOD OFFERING WITH A SACRIFICIAL MEAL AS THE SACRIFICE OF THE NEW COVENANT

FROM the boundless love which He has for men, Jesus has given us a perfect gift, Himself. This great gift is no mere commemorative celebration of the sacrifice of the cross but a memorial sacrifice in which He Himself officiates as High Priest and is the victim presented to the heavenly Father in order to preserve and increase divine life in His people.

St. Paul writes about this to the Corinthians:

> The fact is that I have received as coming from the Lord, and have passed on to you, how the Lord Jesus on the night of his betrayal took bread in his hands and after he had given thanks broke it and said, "This is my body which is given up for you; do this in remembrance of me." In the same way, after he had finished supper, he took the chalice in his hands and said, "This chalice is the new covenant sealed with my blood. Do this, as often as you drink it, in remembrance of me" (1 Cor 11:23–25).

In respect of officiating priest and victim the holy Sacrifice of the Mass is thus identical with the sacrifice of the cross.

There is, however, a real difference in the mode of offering: in its execution, the sacrifice on the cross is a blood sacrifice which consists in the giving up of life and the ritual presentation of blood to God as a symbol of life; but the Sacrifice of the Mass on the other hand is accomplished through a food offering with a sacrificial meal whose external matter is bread and wine. As well as this, the action of the Sacrifice of holy Mass begins, not directly with Christ, but with the action of the priest who acts by commission of the Church.

The Council of Trent expressly stated that the holy Sacrifice of the

Mass represents a *sacrificium visibile,* a visible sacrifice. It must be a visible sacrifice because of its nature sacrifice is visible — a visible act by which men pay solemn homage to God as supreme Lord. Such a visible sacrifice is then provided by holy Mass in the form of a food offering wherein the blood sacrifice of Christ is renewed in a sacramental fashion.

We may now ask in what way Mass becomes a visible sacrifice. During Mass the sacrifice of Christ becomes visible in that under the appearance of bread and wine, the body of Christ and the blood of Christ, sacramentally separated, are made present.

The inner unity of the sacrifice of the cross and of the Mass is the basis of the prayer of the Canon and of that part of the Mass in which the sacrifice is completed, and also of the solemn prayer known as the Preface, with which the Canon begins and by which the faithful are drawn into the sacred sacrificial transaction.

In the Preface the priest ascends in spirit into heaven on high to approach the heavenly Father. The faithful who assist at the sacrifice are to follow the priest at the altar. And when the words "Lift up your hearts," are spoken, this is no empty phrase. Hearts are to be lifted up to heaven, to that place where Jesus Christ stands before the Father.

In the Preface the Church is thinking not simply of this individual Sacrifice of the Mass now being celebrated here, but of the many Masses being offered simultaneously this day all over the world, and of all which will be offered down the years and centuries, merging together in heaven and becoming one in Jesus Christ the one and everlasting High Priest. Thus the Preface begins with the words, "It is truly meet and just, right and available to salvation, that we should *always* and *in all* places give thanks to you, O Lord, holy Father, almighty, eternal God, through Christ our Lord."

Because Christians unite in this thanksgiving and praise with the mind of Jesus Christ the true High Priest, Mass in early times was given the name "Eucharist" — a sacrifice of thanks, a sacrifice in thanksgiving for Redemption.

It is therefore a thanksgiving of the Church in the name of all participants in the Mass and a thanksgiving for Mass itself, when at the end of the Canon the Church has the priest say, as he raises the chalice and the host, "Through Him [Christ], and with Him, and in Him, is unto You, God the Father Almighty, in the unity of the Holy Spirit, all honor and glory. World without end."

These concluding words of the Canon direct our attention specifically to the supreme end which is the glory of God. This is the goal of every sacrifice; and in the Sacrifice of the Mass this goal is attained supremely.

And so, in Mass Christ offers Himself "in the midst of His Church." Should it come about that not a single priest was left on earth, then the celebration of Mass would come to an end.

The sacrificial homage to God by the redeemed is rendered through a bloodless *making present* of the blood sacrifice of Christ upon the cross.

At Mass, in the midst of His Church, Jesus Christ the glorified Son of God offers Himself up to the heavenly Father in a sacramental renewal of His sacrifice on the cross.

Jesus Christ has set the sacramental renewal of the sacrifice of the cross in the external form of a bloodless food offering with a sacrificial meal because this form gives the best symbolic expression to the intention of this sacrifice, which is to preserve, strengthen, and unfold the life of grace in the souls of His people.

When we say that Christ offers Himself in Mass "in the midst of His Church," we mean to affirm that the presentation of the sacrifice in its ritual execution is not carried out by Jesus Christ but comes from the Church which received a commission from Christ to do this.

Mass forms a unity with the sacrifice of the cross. This is made visible upon the altar when the body of Christ which was offered upon the cross, is made present under the appearance of bread, and the blood which Christ offered upon the cross, is made present under appearance of wine.

At the Consecration the best kind of prayer for the faithful to make is one which has reference to this double sacrifice. It might run something like this: "O heavenly Father, we present to You, through

Your Son Jesus Christ, that most sacred Body which He gave for us; and we offer, through Your Son Jesus Christ, that most sacred Blood which He poured out for us upon the Cross."

The Life of the Individual. Because Christ is offering Himself in Mass for the faithful, His sacrifice becomes the possession of all who are united spiritually in a sacrificing community at the celebration of Mass. All the individual homage which the worshipers offer to God the heavenly Father becomes part of His homage; His reparation becomes the possession of all and the reparations of others become incorporated into His; His petitions to the Father become petitions for all, and the petitions of all are taken into the petition of Him who is the Head and High Priest of men, ever present before the Father, ready to approach Him on behalf of men. His thanksgiving to the heavenly Father becomes the thankgiving of all, and that of all becomes part of His.

The Life of the Church. In nothing so much as in Mass does the Church reveal herself as mediator between God and man.

The rule that everyone of the faithful should appear on Sundays at the celebration of Mass is based upon the duty of every man to pay homage to God within the community of God, as the Giver of life, and to make reparation to Him, to thank Him, to ask His pardon and to pray for the gifts of His mercy. And because this is so, newly baptized heathens who have been accustomed to sacrificing to false gods often show a better understanding of the Mass than do those Christians who, proud of the outward progress of culture, think that homage paid by human society through the fulfilling of a sacrifice is obsolete.

What a misunderstanding of Mass lurks behind the idea that on Sundays a man can worship God as well in the open air! Jesus offers Himself for us upon the altars of our churches and not in the open spaces of nature.

25. THE SACRIFICIAL MEAL, HOLY COMMUNION

CHRIST, THE HIGH PRIEST of the New Covenant, performed the first celebration of Mass and of the sacrificial meal with which it concluded in circumstances which made it easy for the disciples to see that it was the fulfillment of His promise after the miracle of the loaves. At the time, the celebration of Mass formed a living unity with the celebration and partaking of the sacrifice of the Paschal Lamb. In the events of that evening the festival of the Paschal Lamb was taken over directly into the sacrifice and sacrificial meal of the New Covenant. St. Luke relates:

> When the hour had come, he took his place on the couch, and so did the apostles. "It has been my heart's desire," he said to them, "to eat this paschal supper with you before I suffer. I tell you, I shall not eat it again till it is fulfilled in the kingdom of God." And after receiving a cup and saying grace, he said: "Take this, and divide it among you. I tell you, I shall not again drink of the produce of the vine till the kingdom of God is set up."
>
> He also took bread into his hands and, after saying grace, broke it into portions, which he gave to them with these words: "This is my body, which is about to be given for your sake. Do this as my memorial." He did the same with the cup when supper was over, and said: "This cup is the new covenant sealed by my blood, which is about to be shed for your sake" (Lk 22:14–20).

In those days it was obvious to all, Jews and heathens alike, that sacrifice and sacrificial meal should be joined. It was a matter of course, therefore, for the early Christians to partake of the ritual meal whenever they attended Mass. As well as this, indeed, it was already known for Holy Communion to be received apart from Mass. The faithful were even given the Sacred Species to take home.

One who is spiritually dead can receive spiritual nourishment as little as a dead man can receive ordinary food.

To be able to receive Holy Communion it is necessary that man possess divine life, and also that the communicant show proper reverence for the approach of his divine Lord.

Mass in outward form represents a bloodless sacrifice with a sacrificial meal. The sacrificial meal is Holy Communion.

Holy Communion is the sacrificial meal in which the heavenly Father invites us to the sacrifice of His Son. In this meal we receive Jesus Christ as the bread of life. For us His brethren, Christ has offered Himself up to His Father, and so we receive Him back from the Father as the Bread of Life.

It follows from Jesus' own words that Holy Communion is a sacrament. "The Jews then had a violent discussion among themselves. 'How,' they argued, can this man give us his flesh to eat? . . . He who eats my flesh and drinks my blood is in possession of eternal life, and I will raise him from the dead on the last day" (Jn 6:52, 55).

Holy Communion has an effect upon the soul analogous to that of food upon the body.
1. Jesus unites Himself with us deeply and draws us close to the Father.
2. Jesus strengthens divine life in us and empowers us to do good.
3. Jesus shields us from sin, assures us of a glorious resurrection whose glory He increases.

Whoever receives Holy Communion while in a stage of mortal sin receives unworthily. Of an unworthy Communion St. Paul says, "Consequently, whoever eats this bread or drinks the Chalice of the Lord unworthily will be held responsible for a sin against the body and blood of the Lord" (1 Cor 11:27).

To prepare for Holy Communion spiritually one must confess mortal sins, be at least sorry for venial sins, and go to receive the Bread of Life with a deep desire for spiritual strengthening.

External preparation for Holy Communion consists in fasting for three hours from solid food and alcohol and for one hour from liquids other than water and in coming cleanly and respectably dressed.

The Life of the Individual. Cardinal Newman wrote this for those who receive Holy Communion infrequently:

The true reason why people will not come to Holy Communion is this — they do not wish to lead religious lives: they do not like to promise to lead religious lives; and they think that that blessed Sacrament does bind them to do so, bind them to live very much more strictly and thoughtfully than they do at present. Allow as much as we will for proper distrust of themselves, reasonable awe, the burden of past sin, imperfect knowledge, and other causes, still after all there is in most cases a reluctance to bear, or at least to pledge themselves to bear, Christ's yoke.

He added a warning to those who receive Holy Communion often:

As he begins to be familiar with the words of the prayers and the order of the Service, so does he both hear and receive with less emotion and solemnity. It is not that he is a worse man than he was at first, but he is exposed to a greater temptation to be profane. . . . Now is the time when he is in danger of not discerning the Lord's Body, or receiving the gift of life as a thing of course, without awe, gratitude, and self-abasement. . . .

Here too, let me mention another sin of a similar character into which communicants are apt to fall; viz. a forgetfulness, after communicating, that they have communicated. . . But consider . . . what does this imply, but that we imagine that we have received the benefit of it once and for all, as a thing done and over, and that there is nothing more to seek? . . . Surely, after so great a privilege, we ought to behave ourselves as if we had partaken some Divine food and medicine (if great things may be compared to ordinary), which, in its own inscrutable way, and in its own good time, will "prosper in the thing whereto God sends it" — the fruit of the tree of life which Adam forfeited.

The Life of the Church. With natural food, the body's own life assimilates the food and so absorbs it into itself. With the Bread of Life which the faithful receive at the sacrificial meal the reverse happens. This Bread is Itself the life and gives life — by His grace Christ so affects a man that his life is assimilated to the life of Christ.

In this way all the faithful are drawn into the life of Jesus Christ, the Head of the Church. Worthy Communion does not effect merely the union of the individual believer with Jesus, but also the union of the faithful with one another in the love of Christ and in His grace.

26. OFFERING THE HOLY SACRIFICE OF THE MASS

Reception Into the Sacrificing Society

FOR THE ISRAELITES, the whole people constituted the sacrificing society. Membership of the people of Israel carried with it the right of being able to sacrifice to the true God in the temple at Jerusalem.

Even among the heathens one could not simply go to the altar of any of the gods and offer sacrifice without more ado. First of all one had to become affiliated to the society which built and maintained the altar. Or else one sacrificed in association with a member of the society or asked special permission to do so.

The right of participating in the sacrifice of the New Covenant is acquired at the moment when a man becomes united to Christ the high priest through the sacrament of Baptism. St. Paul alludes to this fact when writing to the Corinthians:

> Does not the chalice of blessings which we bless bring us into union with Christ through his blood, and does not the bread which we break bring us into union with Christ through his body? Because the bread is one, we, the many who all partake of that one bread, form one body (1 Cor 10:16–17).

When St. Paul describes the sacrificing society of Christians as a sacrificing community in the immolated body and blood of Christ he is introducing terminology strange to the Scripture of the Old Testament; for it was not until the Redemption through Jesus Christ that a relationship between the Father in heaven and mankind arose of a kind which the Holy Scripture could describe as a society.

In the prayers of Mass the idea that the faithful form an exclusive society finds expression in phrases which say that they make sacrifice together. They are described as a *society,* a *family,* as the *servants of the Lord,* a *holy people,* and as the *people of the New Covenant.*

The way in which the faithful take part in the Holy Sacrifice is determined by the place of the priest within the framework of the sacrificial system of the New Covenant. Here the priest is God's representative before the people and the people's representative before God. But he is both by the commission of Christ and the Church. He is not a representative of the people before God by commission of the people.

After Pentecost, following Christ's command: "Do this in memory of me," the Apostles began to celebrate the Holy Sacrifice in the temple at Jerusalem. Outside Jerusalem they attended the worship of the synagogue. The worship of the synagogue was made up of two parts, a prayer service and a Bible service. The prayer service began with morning prayer, whose opening words were: "Hear O Israel: the Lord our God is one God. You shall love the Lord your God with all your heart and with all your mind and with all your strength." These words could be compared to the arousing of a right disposition in the worshipers. The Bible service consisted in the reading of passages from the Law — the five Books of Moses — and from the Prophets.

The pattern of this reading is shown in the description of Jesus' appearance in the synagogue at Nazareth.

> One day he came to Nazareth, the home of his childhood. On the Sabbath, he went according to his custom to the synagogue and stood up to read. A scroll of the prophet Isaias was handed him, and, after unrolling the scroll, he came upon the place where the following text occurs:
> "The Spirit of the Lord rests upon me,
> because he has anointed me.
> He has appointed me a messenger
> to bring the Good News to the humble;
> to announce release to captives,
> and recovery of sight to the blind;
> to set the oppressed at liberty;
> to proclaim a year of grace
> ordained by the Lord."

He then rolled up the scroll and, after handing it back to the attendant, sat down (Lk 4:16–20).

Attendance at the temple worship ceased when the temple was

destroyed; attendance at the synagogue ceased about A.D. 100 when it was in fact prohibited. Christians celebrated Mass in the evening, the time when Jesus had instituted this worship, and did so in private houses belonging to Christians. At this period an *agape* or "love feast" was joined to the Sacrifice of the Mass. And so, during this period the Church recognized a prayer and Bible service in the early morning and a sacrificial service in the evening. When first the temple sacrifices, and then the Bible services of the synagogue were abandoned, Christians began to combine their two types of service. Tertullian (c. A.D. 150) tells us that the services had been transferred to the early morning.

The three sections which once went to the formation of Christian worship still provide the best introduction to the structure of Mass.

The Celebration of the Sacrifice

The Nature of the Sacrificial Action

What was new in the Sacrifice of Mass both for Jews and for heathens was the fact that there was now only one victim. Moreover, the Mass had the outward form, not of a blood sacrifice, but of a food offering.

A fact of great significance for the structure of the sacrificial action and for the formation of the accompanying prayers in particular is that the first generations of Christians were profoundly affected by the memory of Christ's ascension into heaven and had a very lively sense of Christ's mediation in heaven. From this arose a set liturgical phraseology which was like a melodic refrain. All the prayers end with the words, "Through Jesus Christ Your Son our Lord, who lives and reigns with You for ever and ever."

The Divisions of Mass

We must divide the celebration of Mass into three sections. The second ranks higher than the first and the third than the second. The three sections are:

> I. The Prayer-Liturgy
> II. The Bible-Liturgy
> III. The Sacrifice-Liturgy

I. The Prayer-Liturgy

The Prayer-liturgy expresses sentiments of longing for God (cf. Ps 42) and of sorrow for sin. In the *Confiteor* we say, "through my fault, through my most grievous fault" and in this way confess not only our *greatest* sins, but *all* our sins.

II. The Bible-Liturgy

As a rule the first Bible lesson is taken from one of the Epistles of the Apostles; and therefore it is called "the Epistle," a reading from a letter. The second lesson comes from one of the four Gospels. The reading may be from any of the Gospels, Matthew, Mark, Luke, or John, more or less at random; but the passages are chosen so that they give us a complete picture of the life of Jesus, beginning with Christmas cycle and ending with the Easter cycle.

III. The Sacrifice-Liturgy

The Sacrifice-liturgy has three parts:
1. Preparation for the sacrifice of Jesus Christ
2. The consecration, the contemporary sacrifice of Jesus Christ
3. Holy Communion, the sacrificial feast.

1. *Preparation for the Sacrifice of Jesus Christ*

This preparation is twofold:
a) The priest's preparations at the altar
b) The preparations made by the worshiping community.

The priest's preparation consists in his setting apart with prayer, as Christ's official representative and as the representative of the people, the offerings of bread and wine which are then destined as those gifts which are to be changed into the body and blood of Christ by the word of His power, spoken through His representative.

The preparation of the faithful consists in their joining their own work and sorrow and troubles to the sacrifice of Christ, making of themselves a "holy people" dedicated to the Lord, interiorly and externally uniting themselves to the actions of Christ and His priest.

Just as the Prayer- and Bible-liturgies had ended with a prayer, so this part of the liturgy ends with a prayer, the prayer over the offerings.

In early Christian times the faithful brought bread and wine and other gifts with them to the altar for the Sacrifice of the Mass. Bread and wine for the sacrifice were then selected from these gifts. The later offertory processions at services for the dead are vestiges of this ancient custom. In general the place of these Offertory gifts has been filled today by the alms which the faithful give at Mass. These contributions should, therefore, be made in the proper spirit.

Full of concern that the faithful should take part, the Church has made of this preparation of the bread and wine upon the altar an action by which those who shall partake of the sacrifice are prepared spiritually. The priest prays at this point: "In a spirit of humility and with a contrite heart may we be received by You, O Lord; and may our sacrifice be so offered in Your sight today that it may please You, O Lord God."

"Come, O Sanctifier, Almighty, Eternal God, and bless this Sacrifice prepared for Your holy Name."

2. *The Consecration, the Contemporary Sacrifice of Jesus Christ*

At the Consecration Christ's sacrifice is made and completed (Pope John XXIII in an address to the Liturgical Congress at Assisi).

The contemporary sacrifice of Jesus Christ is accomplished at the Consecration. The actual sacrificial act is the following:

The bread becomes Christ's body, the wine His blood. Christ's first sacrifice was His sacrifice in blood upon the cross of His body and blood; and this made atonement for the world. In the Sacrifice of Mass Christ presents His glorified body and blood to His heavenly Father without making a fresh sacrificial act distinguishable from that of the cross.

That most solemn prayer with which the sacrificial action proper begins owes its origin to the Church's concern to draw the faithful spiritually into the sacrificial act. Because this prayer is intended to draw the faithful into the holy action and raise them up with it, it is called the Preface.

The Common Preface, which expresses the basic thought of all the others, runs as follows:

It is truly meet and just, right and available to salvation, that we should always and in all places give thanks to You, O Lord, holy Father, almighty, eternal God: through Christ our Lord. By Him the Angels praise Your Majesty, the Dominations adore it, the Powers tremble before it, the Heavens, the heavenly Virtues, and blessed Seraphim, with common jubilee glorify it. Together with them we beseech You that we may be admitted to join our humble voices, saying: Holy, holy, holy, Lord God of Hosts. Heaven and earth are full of Your glory. Hosanna in the highest. Blessed is He who comes in the name of the Lord. Hosanna in the highest.

After the Preface the priest then remembers the Church on earth and the saints in heaven. These prayers too are meant to give a spiritual lead to those taking part in the sacrifice. The same is true of the final prayer before the Consecration when the priest prays that the sacrifice will be pleasing to God.

At the Consecration of the offerings the priest as an individual retires; and now as Christ's representative he says:

> Our Lord Jesus Christ, the day before He suffered, took bread in His holy and venerable hands, and with eyes lifted up toward heaven unto You, O God, His Almighty Father, giving thanks to You, did bless, break and give unto His disciples, saying: Take, and eat all of this. FOR THIS IS MY BODY.
>
> In like manner, after He had supped, taking also this excellent chalice into His holy and venerable hands and giving thanks to You, He blessed, and gave to His disciples, saying: Take and drink all of it. FOR THIS IS THE CHALICE OF MY BLOOD OF THE NEW AND ETERNAL TESTAMENT; THE MYSTERY OF FAITH; WHICH SHALL BE SHED FOR YOU, AND FOR MANY, FOR THE REMISSION OF SINS. As often as you do these things, you shall do them in remembrance of me (from the Canon of the Mass).

At the words of Consecration spoken by the priest, the host is changed into the body and the wine in the chalice into the blood of Christ.

At the Consecration we should pray in the same manner as the liturgy.

Before the Consecration:

"Heavenly Father, look down upon Your Son Jesus who now offers Himself for us and with us."

At the Elevation of the Host:

"Heavenly Father,
be merciful to me for Christ's sake;
for Christ's sake forgive me my sins."

At the Elevation of the Chalice:
    "Heavenly Father,
    May I live with Jesus,
    May I die with Jesus,
    May I be blessed forever with Jesus."

After the Consecration, the prayer concludes by recalling the words of Christ: "Do this as my memorial" (Lk 22:19).

In spirit the Church approaches the throne of the Father saying, "Look, we are doing what Jesus Christ commanded us to do"; and accordingly she prays, "Wherefore, O Lord, we Your servants, and likewise Your holy people, calling to mind the blessed Passion of the same Jesus Christ Your Son, our Lord, together with His Resurrection from the grave, and also His glorious Ascension into heaven, offer to Your excellent Majesty, of Your gifts and presents, a pure Victim, a holy Victim, a spotless Victim, the holy bread of eternal life and the chalice of everlasting salvation."

And while the priest is saying this, the faithful should be calling to mind the Passion, Death, Resurrection and the glorious Ascension of Jesus Christ. Thus they will be cooperating in the sacrifice, as Christ and His Church want them to.

Following the reference to the redemptive acts of Jesus, the Church prays that the sacrifice of Christ will be accepted as the Church's sacrifice; and at the same time she makes intercession for the dead and commemorates the saints. The actual sacrificial action ends with a renewed appeal to Christ the Mediator through whom the almighty Father is given honor and glory in the unity of the Holy Spirit.

3. *The Sacrificial Meal, Holy Communion*

Both with Jews and with heathens a sacrificial meal was often joined to the sacrifice. The early Christian required, therefore, no elaborate instruction that Holy Communion constituted the sacrificial meal of Mass and that its reception was included in full participation.

The disposition in which participants should approach the holy sacrifice is expressed in the prayers before Holy Communion.

O Lord Jesus Christ, Son of the living God, who, by the will of the Father and the co-operation of the Holy Spirit, have by Your death given life to the world: deliver me by this most sacred body and blood from all my iniquities and from all evils; and make me always adhere to Your commandments, and suffer me never to be separated from You. Who with the same God the Father and the Holy Spirit live and reign God, world without end. Amen.

Let not the partaking of Your Body, O Lord Jesus Christ, which I, though unworthy, presume to receive, turn to my judgment and condemnation; but by Your mercy be it profitable to my safety and health, both of soul and body. Who with God the Father, in the unity of the Holy Spirit, live and reign God, world without end. Amen.

Because Christ made His sacrifice upon the cross as man's representative, so within the celebration of Mass it falls to the office of the priest to act *for the faithful as Christ's representative* before the Father. For the same reason the gifts of bread and wine do not fulfill the same function as, for example, the sacrificial gifts which were laid upon the altar of the Old Covenant.

The chief divisions of the Mass are:
1. The Prayer-liturgy
2. The Bible-liturgy
3. The Sacrifice-liturgy — which in turn has three parts:
    a) Preparation for the sacrifice of Jesus Christ
    b) The Consecration, the contemporary sacrifice of Christ
    c) Holy Communion, the sacrificial feast.

Preparation for the sacrifice is twofold:
    a) Through the priest at the altar
    b) By the people themselves.

The Consecration. The actual sacrifice is this: the priest, as Christ's representative, pronounces these words over the bread and wine: "This is my body which is sacrificed for you. . . . This chalice is the new and eternal Covenant in my blood which is shed for you unto remission of sins"; and after the Consecration he offers the body and blood of Christ to the heavenly Father.

Holy Communion, the sacrificial feast:
    a) At Holy Communion the priest receives the body and blood of Jesus as a sacrificial meal, and he gives the body of the Lord to the faithful as the Bread of Life.
    b) In Holy Communion the faithful receive the Savior's body as the food of their souls.

c) The faithful cooperate in Mass by praying with the priest, and by making an external offering along with him; by offering through the priest, who is Christ's representative and who speaks words of Consecration, both Christ's body and blood and themselves also to the heavenly Father.

The Life of the Individual.   Knowing all of the liturgical prayers of the Mass by heart is not sufficient to insure a proper understanding of what is happening in Mass. For a devout celebration of Mass we must possess a lively awareness that at Mass Jesus the High Priest is interceding for us and for all men with His heavenly Father. Therefore we must never forget to meditate on this fact at the beginning of Mass.

The Life of the Church.   Pope Pius XII, in an encyclical of 1947, says of the participation of the faithful in the liturgy:

We therefore highly commend the zeal which, to enable the faithful to take part more easily and more profitably in the Mass, seeks to adapt the Roman Missal to their use, so that they may join in prayer with the priest, using his very words and uttering the sentiments of the Church herself. We also approve the efforts of those who want to make the liturgy a sacred action in which, externally also, all who are present may really take a part. There are several ways in which this may be done. The whole congregation, always conformably with the rubrics, may recite the responses in an orderly manner; they may sing chants corresponding to the various parts of the Mass; or they may do both. Or, at High Mass, the people may sing the responses and join in the liturgical chants.

Their chief purpose is to foster the devotion of the faithful and their close union with Christ and His visible minister, and to arouse in them those sentiments and attitudes of mind in which they must become like the High Priest of the New Testament.

At the same time, although such methods do externally indicate that the Mass, being offered by the Mediator between God and men; is to be regarded as the act of the whole Mystical Body, it must be understood that they are by no means necessary to give it its public and communal character.

The Council of Trent laid down certain attitudes of mind which are indispensable for attendance at Mass in the right spirit. These are: a keen sense of the sovereignty of God allied to an honest desire to proclaim it and to express dependence on Him in an exterior way; a lively belief in the efficacy of Jesus Christ as High Priest and in the presence of Christ under the appearance of bread and wine; a holy awe and reverence of the unfathomable mystery of this sacrifice and a true sorrow for one's sins which matches a desire to find forgiveness in the blood of Christ.

The encyclical, *Mediator Dei,* mentions these dispositions in the following words: "Now the Apostle's exhortation, 'Yours is to be the same mind as Christ Jesus showed,' requires all Christians, so far as human power allows, to reproduce in themselves the sentiments that Christ had when He was offering Himself in sacrifice: sentiments of humility, of adoration, praise, and thanksgiving to the divine Majesty. It requires them also to become victims, as it were; cultivating a spirit of self-denial according to the precepts of the Gospel, willingly doing works of penance, detesting and expiating their sins."

27. THE LITURGICAL YEAR: THE RE-PRESENTATION OF THE WORK OF REDEMPTION THROUGH THE LITURGICAL YEAR; THE PRESENCE OF JESUS IN THE TABERNACLE

I. *The Liturgical Year*

The Lord God had appointed certain festival days for the Israelites on which they were to remember their duty toward Him. First among these was the Easter festival, which called to memory the deliverance from the yoke of Egypt. Because the Old Covenant was a covenant of promise, its festivals had a prophetic character. In the providence of God the fulfillment of the prophecies contained in the Easter festival fell at such a time as to make the feast of commemoration of the deliverance from Pharaoh coincide with the feast of commemoration of the deliverance from Satan. On Pentecost, the second great festival of the Jews, Christ sent His Holy Spirit down upon the Church; and so it appeared that outwardly the Church was retaining two of the festivals of the Old Covenant. In reality, two remembrance days of the work of redemption coincided with these two festivals.

The following feasts of our Lord stand in the closest association with Easter and Pentecost: Corpus Christi, the feast of the Sacred Heart of Jesus, and the feast of Christ the King.

Corpus Christi is the feast which commemorates the institution of the Holy Eucharist. To a certain extent it has evolved from Maundy Thursday.

The feast of the Sacred Heart reminds the faithful of the love of

240

the heart of Jesus and spurs them on to make reparation for the ingratitude which this love suffers. This feast has associations with the mystery of Christ's death and so with Good Friday.

The feast of Christ the King is intended to awake and strengthen in the faithful awareness of the fact that Christ the Redeemer is the true Lord of the world and that the span of time between His Ascension and the end of the world is the time in which men must declare themselves for Him if they wish one day to share in His glory in heaven. Even now Christ Himself is conqueror and king.

The feasts of the martyrs who gave their lives for Christ are closely associated with the feasts of our Lord. To this class belongs, for example, the commemoration of the two princes of the Apostles, SS. Peter and Paul.

A second series of feasts commemorates those events which led up to the redemption of man in the sacrificial death of Jesus. Most notable of these are the feast of the Nativity of Jesus Christ — Christmas; the feast of the Circumcision; and the Epiphany — the feast of Christ's manifestation to the Gentiles.

Associated with the mystery of Christ's birth we have the feasts in honor of the Blessed Virgin, the Mother of God. The feast of the Immaculate Conception brings to mind her election and preservation from the stain of original sin; the Assumption, her bodily reception into heaven. With the childhood of Jesus are associated the feasts of John the Baptist.

For the Church, the climax of any feast is in the celebration of Mass. Here the prayers which precede the actual sacrifice, and some of the prayers in the Canon itself will be in keeping with the mystery celebrated of the feast day. They present the Savior to those who join in the celebration as He was in the conditions or age which the feast calls to mind. For the Church, therefore, at Christmas the Savior is a child who is saluted by shepherds; at Epiphany, a hidden king recognized and adored by the wise men; in Lent, one who battles with His foes; on Good Friday, one who goes to the Mount of Olives, is scourged, crowned with thorns, condemned to death, and laid in a grave. At Easter the jubilant shout of the Church is heard, greeting His Resurrection and the completion of the work of salvation; and throughout all the Easter season the rejoicing is never silent. At

Pentecost the Church renews its prayer to the Lord that He will send down the Holy Spirit.

The Liturgical Year gives us a constantly renewed outward presentation of the act of Redemption. And all the time, this outward presentation corresponds to an inward, secret outpouring of the grace of Christ upon men. Christ Himself is operating in the Liturgical Year in a mysterious way which has some similarity to His operation in the sacraments.

II. *The Presence of Jesus in the Tabernacle*

Besides this representation of the life of Christ in the Liturgical Year the faithful are brought close to Him in another way, through the presence of Christ in the Blessed Sacrament under the appearance of the host. In this case nothing of the life of Jesus is there but His presence under the form of bread. Any believing Catholic can enter a church and, so to speak, express all his belief by a genuflection in front of the tabernacle; for belief in the presence of Jesus Christ in the Blessed Sacrament embraces a belief in the Holy Sacrifice of the Mass, in the three divine Persons of the Trinity and in the love of God for men.

It is because Christ is sacramentally present in the church that Catholic churches are open during the day and that Catholics salute a church when they pass by.

Alongside the natural and civil calendar we have the Liturgical Year.

By the Liturgical Year is understood the series of feasts of our Lord, of His mother, and of the saints and of the ordinary Sundays which brings before the minds of the faithful the accomplishment of the work of salvation through Jesus Christ and its working out in the history of the Church.

There are two cycles of feasts in the Liturgical Year: the Christmas cycle and the Easter cycle. The Christmas cycle is preceded by the preparation period of Advent and the Easter cycle by that of Lent. These periods of preparation are hallowed by penance, works of charity, and fervent prayer.

The greatest feast in the Liturgical Year is Easter, the feast of the Resurrection of our Lord and of our own resurrection. The Easter season ends with Pentecost, the feast commemorating the descent of the Holy Spirit.

The obligatory feasts of our Lord are: Christmas, the Circumcision, Easter, Ascension, Pentecost.

The chief holy days in honor of the Mother of God are: the Immaculate Conception (December 8) and the Assumption (August 15). Those in honor of the saints are: St. Joseph, SS. Peter and Paul, and All Saints.

Jesus within the tabernacle is Mediator, present for the purpose of making intercession with the Father and of imparting His grace to us.

The Life of the Individual. By its recurrence the Liturgical Year exercises a quiet but deep influence upon the faithful spirit. The Holy seasons wean us from this world and impress upon us the reality of that world which we do not see.

By meditating on each aspect of our Faith in turn, we grow in grace from one holy season to another, from one year to another in the knowledge of our Lord.

The Life of the Church. Pope Pius XII tells us: "All the year round the celebration of the Eucharistic Sacrifice and the recitation of the Divine Office revolve, as it were, about the Person of Jesus Christ; the cycle being so contrived as to be wholly dominated by our Savior in the mysteries of His humiliation, His redemptive work, and His triumph. In thus reminding the faithful of these mysteries of Jesus Christ, the sacred liturgy seeks to make them share them in such a way that the divine Head of the Mystical Body lives by His perfect holiness in each of His members."

The same Pontiff urgently recommends devotions in honor of the Blessed Sacrament: "Especially to be commended is the practice of concluding certain devotional exercises, which have become customary among Christians, with Benediction of the Blessed Sacrament. What an excellent and salutary devotion! As the faithful bow their heads in veneration the priest raises up the Bread of angels towards heaven and, making the sign of the Cross with It over them, entreats the heavenly Father graciously to look upon His Son crucified for love of us, and for His sake and through Him who willed to become our

Redeemer and our brother, to pour out His supernatural gifts upon those whom the blood of the spotless Lamb has redeemed."

In the northern hemisphere the feasts of the Liturgical Year occur so that the position of the sun and the life of nature become an allegory of the sacred events which we commemorate in the various feasts. For this reason a wealth of religious custom has gathered around the feasts.

At Christmas the sun begins to ascend; and so the struggle between light and darkness becomes a symbol of the struggle between Christ and sin. At Easter nature awakes; and so the new life of spring becomes a symbol of new life in the hearts of the faithful who have united themselves with the risen Christ by a contrite confession and their Easter Communion. Pentecost comes when all things are blooming; and so the green garment of nature becomes a symbol of the outpouring of the Holy Spirit upon all the faithful.

28. THE CONSUMMATION OF THE CHRISTIAN LIFE IN DEATH: THE HOMECOMING TO CHRIST AND THE FATHER

IN THE BEGINNING, death had been only a possibility. After Adam's sin it became for all men a terrible reality. Man was now made subject to pain as a foreboding of death, and to death as something which made life meaningless. The real tragedy lay in this, that after death men could not reach God.

By His death upon the cross Jesus atoned for sin and opened the gates of heaven once more. Now it was once more possible for men to become children of God and heirs of heaven. Thus the meaning of death has changed; it makes sense. By accepting death from God's hand a man can become like Jesus the God-man in a very special way. Death is no longer, therefore, the meaningless end of life, but the hour when the Christian completes the journey to the Father who accepted him as a child in Baptism.

St. Paul speaks exultantly of the change with regard to death which was inaugurated for all with the death of Jesus.

> "O Death, where is your victory?
> O Death, where is your sting?"
> Death's sting comes from sin;
> Sin's force comes from the Law.
> But thanks be to God, who gives us the victory
> Through our Lord Jesus Christ.
> So my beloved brothers, be steadfast, immovable. Devote yourselves fully at all times to the Lord's work, realizing that your toil in the Lord can never be in vain! (1 Cor 15:55–58.)

Guided by this thought of death as a going home to the Father, the Church is most anxious that all of her children purify themselves

245

from sin by a final contrite confession before they appear before their judge. So great is her solicitude that in case of need even a suspended and excommunicated priest has power to hear a confession and give absolution.

The priest gives the dying man the Bread of Life for the last time, saying: "Take, brother (sister), as food for the journey, the body of Jesus Christ, and may He protect you from the enemy and lead you to everlasting life."

After confession and Holy Communion the priest strengthens the sick man with the sacrament of the Anointing of the Sick so that he will accept his bodily and mental sufferings in imitation of the sufferings of Jesus Christ and thus be prepared for his homecoming to Christ. The priest prays, "Through this holy anointing, and through His most tender mercy, may the Lord forgive you whatever you have done wrong . . . through sight; by hearing; by smell; by taste or talk; by touch; by your steps."

When the anointing is over the priest exhorts the dying man to accept all his sufferings as God's will and gives him a plenary indulgence for the hour of death.

When the hour of death approaches the Church offers solemn prayer for everyone, be he a saintly man who has served God all his life or an unfortunate soul who has returned only at the last moment. The prayer begins, "Go forth, Christian soul, from this world, in the Name of God, the Father Almighty, who created you; in the Name of Jesus Christ, Son of the Living God, who suffered for you; in the Name of the Holy Spirit, who was poured forth into you; in the name of the glorious and holy Mother of God, the Virgin Mary. . . ."

This prayer is followed by the commendation of the person to Jesus Christ. It runs: "We commend to You, O Lord, the soul of Your servant; and we pray to You, O Lord, Jesus Christ, that You will not refuse to admit to the bosom of Your Patriarchs this soul for whose sake You came in mercy to this our earth. Acknowledge, O Lord, Your own creature, made by no false gods, but by You, the only true and living God, for there is none other God but You, and there is nothing to compare with Your handiwork. Give joy, Lord, to his soul in Your presence; and remember not his misdeeds of old, nor wanton sins that passion or the fever of desire may have inflamed in him. Though he has sinned, yet he has not denied the Father, the Son, and the Holy Spirit; but he has believed; and he has had zeal for God within him, and faithfully has worshipped God who made all things."

Because the Church believes in the resurrection of the body she demands that due respect be shown to the body even in death; hence her disapproval of cremation, and her insistence that interment be accompanied by suitable prayers.

After death the Church is specially mindful of the faithful as her children by offering the holy Sacrifice of the Mass for them.

The Christian life is consummated in death.

For a Christian, death is his homecoming to the Father. Up to the last moment the Church supports him with her sacraments and after his departure assists him still by prayers of intercession.

The Life of the Individual. By constantly admonishing the faithful to remember death, the Church does not intend to draw unbalanced attention to the body's dissolution. Man should rather keep in mind that at death he returns to the Lord who has made him and who loves him. Whoever regards death in this way will not be crippled by the thought but will be spurred on to fresh zeal in combating sin and in striving toward good.

The Life of the Church. How we ought to regard our last hour is shown most expressively in the Preface of the Mass for the dead. We give thanks, "Through Christ our Lord. In whom the hope of a blessed resurrection is shown to us, that they who are saddened by the certain necessity of dying be comforted by the promise of eternal life to come. For the life of Your faithful, O Lord, is changed, not taken away; and the abode of this earthly sojourn being dissolved, an eternal dwelling is prepared in heaven."

PART III

THE EXALTATION AND FULFILLMENT OF NATURAL LIFE IN THE COMMUNITY OF GRACE WITH JESUS CHRIST

BASIC INTRODUCTION

THE DOCTRINE OF THE TWOFOLD WAY

He replied: "'Love the Lord your God with your whole heart, and with your whole soul, and with your whole mind.' This is the great and first commandment. But a second commandment is like it: 'Love your neighbor as yourself'" (Mt 22:37–39).

1. CONSCIENCE AND MAN'S SENSE OF MORAL OBLIGATION

CONSCIENCE, like the capacity to love and to hate, is a part of man's nature. Every man knows that certain things are good and to be done, and certain things are bad and to be avoided. Through conscience, the majesty of God is close to every man as the supreme lawgiver. The judgment of conscience does not, however, always support one's own inclinations.

Because conscience is embedded in man's nature, all men, even the heathen, have a conscience, and all are responsible to God for their actions. St. Paul comments: "They [the Gentiles] show that the requirements of the Law are written in their hearts. Their conscience bears the same testimony, as also their thoughts, which alternately accuse or defend them" (Rom 2:15).

Because the judgments of conscience reveal the will of God, the individual is obliged to submit to the judgment of conscience. St. Paul speaks of this: "Every act that does not proceed from conscientious conviction is sinful" (Rom 14:23).

And because all men possess a God-given conscience to which they are subject, Jesus Christ, the Head and Redeemer of mankind, has declared that at the last day all men without exception will be judged by Him.

Many people, it is true, act with such little regard for any law that we might think that they had no conscience. But they have. An example of this is found in the scriptural account of Antiochus the Great.

With all the means at his command, regardless of right or wrong, this ruler sought to come to power and to increase in power. In his lust for power he wished to force religious uniformity upon all of his subjects, and he condemned to death all Israelites who refused to sacrifice to heathen gods.

Toward the end of his life he suffered defeat in a campaign against the Persians, and many people took advantage of this event to shake off the yoke of his rule. Scripture relates:

> And it came to pass when the king heard these words, that he was struck with fear, and exceedingly moved: and he laid himself down upon his bed, and fell sick for grief, because it had not fallen out to him as he imagined. And he remained there many days, for great grief came more and more upon him, and he made account that he should die.
>
> And he called for all his friends, and said to them: Sleep is gone from my eyes, and I am fallen away, and my heart is cast down for anxiety. And I said in my heart: Into how much tribulation am I come, and into what floods of sorrow, wherein now I am: I that was pleasant and beloved in my power! But now I remember the evils that I have done in Jerusalem, from whence also I took away all the spoils of gold and of silver that were in it, and I sent to destroy the inhabitants of Juda without cause. I know therefore that for this cause these evils have found me; and behold I perish with great grief in a strange land (1 Mc 6:8–13).

Conscience operates by showing that individual acts are either in conformity with the moral law and therefore to be done, or in contradiction to the moral law and therefore to be avoided. Accordingly, man's responsibility for his actions decreases or even ceases if in any way the use of reason is impaired or his freedom restricted. Thus, for example, responsibility is removed if a person's use of reason is impaired through fever or as a result of compulsive ideas. Responsibility is diminished or removed altogether if the will ceases to be free. In emotional illness, for example, responsibility can disappear. Fear diminishes the freedom of the will but does not, as a rule, remove responsibility completely. The use of force leaves it unaffected. The saying holds good: a man would be free even if born in chains.

Conscience is the foundation of religious life.

Conscience is the inner God-given voice which commands good and warns us against evil.

Man is bound to *obey* this commanding and forbidding voice. Holy Scripture says, "He who eats when he is in doubt, condemns himself because his act does not come from conscientious conviction; for every act that does not proceed from conscientious conviction is sinful" (Rom 14:23).

All men have a conscience. Holy Scripture says: "They show that the requirements of the Law are written in their hearts. Their conscience bears the same testimony, as also their thoughts, which alternately accuse or defend them" (Rom 2:15).

A good conscience makes a man happy, contented, and strong in suffering: a bad conscience makes him restless and miserable. The worst state of all is that of a man who has silenced his conscience by a life of sin and has ended up with "no conscience."

The Life of the Individual. Every Christian has the duty of forming his conscience, i.e., of gaining that competence to judge between good and evil which is required in the conditions of his life.

Conscience is in good order and *correct* if it is able, not merely to judge in general that this is good or that bad, but to say what degree of good or bad belongs to each.

If a conscience takes account of small faults and avoids them, and seizes even the slightest opportunities of doing good, it is a *sensitive* conscience.

Conscience goes wrong if it is careless or *lax,* declaring some forbidden action to be permissible without a conclusive reason or in the face of existing knowledge. And a conscience can be anxious or *scrupulous* when a person considers things to be sins which are not, or when, in judging sins, he cannot free himself from uncertainty.

If anyone is able to go on living in sin for some length of time without a pang of conscience, then by degrees he has reached a stage where his conscience is *atrophied*.

A conscience is *erroneous* when a man considers that an action which is commanded is forbidden or that a forbidden action is commanded or permitted. A genuine error exists, it is true, only when the man cannot be blamed for it. Even in such a case he is bound to follow his conscience. But if the man himself is to blame for his error, because he has refused to learn so that he might remain untrammeled, then there is no question of genuine excusable error. The degree of culpability or of pardonable ignorance is a matter which only God can judge.

A good example of how conscience operates is given by St. Thomas More, the Lord Chancellor of Henry VIII. Thomas More had to take the Oath of Supremacy, which implied that the king of England was supreme leader of the Church in a way which denied the supremacy of the Pope. At that time the doctrine of papal supremacy had not yet been defined. As Thomas More knew in advance that sooner or later the king would demand that he take the Oath of Supremacy, he sought most conscientiously to decide whether the oath was lawful or not. Once he had become convinced that the doctrine of papal supremacy was part of the doctrinal inheritance of the Church the question of how to act was settled for him: he must refuse to take the oath. He and his friends knew what that would mean for him. And the latter tried to convince him that he could take the oath like other worthy people, both lay and cleric, without committing sin. From prison Thomas More wrote these lines in answer to these suggestions. "I said that I was very sure, that mine own conscience so informed as it is, by such diligence as I have so long taken therein, may stand with my own salvation. I meddle not with the conscience of them that think otherwise. And I trust that they will use no violent forcible ways, and also that if they would, God would of his grace . . . give me strength to stand. . . . For this I am very sure, that if ever I should swear it, I should swear deadly sore against mine own conscience." And so he died a martyr.

The Life of the Church. Because through conscience man comes by nature into a personal relationship with God, the history of revelation turns out in the end to be a history of conscience.

Cardinal Newman, who by his life showed himself as few men do to be a man of clear conscience, described this inner connection between conscience and the acceptance of divine revelation in this way:

> What is the main guide of the soul, given to the whole race of Adam, outside the true fold of Christ as well as within it, given from the first dawn of reason, given to it in spite of that grievous penalty of ignorance, which is one of the chief miseries of our fallen state? It is the light of conscience, "the true Light," as the same

Evangelist says, in the same passage, "which enlighteneth every man that cometh into this world." Whether a man be born in pagan darkness or in some corruption of revealed religion — whether he be the slave of some superstition, or is in possession of some portions of Scripture, and treats the inspired word as a sort of philosophical book, which he interprets for himself . . . in any case, he has within his breast a certain commanding dictate, not a mere sentiment, not a mere opinion, or impression, or view of things, but a law, an authoritative voice, bidding him do certain things and avoid others.

And my second remark is this: that, in spite of all that this Voice does for them, it does not do enough, as they most keenly and sorrowfully feel. They find it most difficult to separate what it really says, taken by itself, from what their own passions or pride, self-love or self-will, mingles with it. Many is the time when they cannot tell how much that true inward Guide commands, and how much comes from a mere earthly source. So that the gift of conscience raises a desire for what it does not itself fully supply. It inspires in them the idea of authoritative guidance, of a divine law; and the desire of possessing it in its fulness, not in mere fragmentary portions or indirect suggestion. . . . Thus you see a religious man, who has not the blessing of the infallible teaching of revelation, is led to *look out* for it, for the very reason that he is religious. . . . Such is the definition, I may say, of every religious man, who has not the knowledge of Christ; he is on the look-out.

These words of Cardinal Newman provide the best transition to the expositions which follow. God has in fact accepted those people who were "on the look-out" in mercy and love. Even under the Old Covenant He had already given them the basic universal rules for conscience in the Ten Commandments, and in the New Covenant, through the mouth of Christ His own Son, He has revealed these Commandments in their fullness.

2. THE TEN COMMANDMENTS OF GOD: TEN FUNDAMENTAL RULES FOR CONSCIENCE, REVEALED BY GOD

AFTER THE FALL God entered into a special relation with the chosen people, and to them He gave clear, universal rules for living. Holy Scripture tells us:

> While Israel was encamped . . . in front of the mountain, Moses went up the mountain to God. Then the Lord called to him and said: "Thus shall you say to the house of Jacob; tell the Israelites: You have seen for yourselves how I treated the Egyptians and how I bore you up on eagle wings and brought you here to myself. . . ."
>
> On the morning of the third day there were peals of thunder and lightning, and a heavy cloud over the mountain, and a very loud trumpet blast, so that all the people in the camp trembled. But Moses led the people out of the camp to meet God, and they stationed themselves at the foot of the mountain. Mount Sinai was all wrapped in smoke, for the Lord came down upon it in fire. The smoke rose from it as though from a furnace, and the whole mountain trembled violently. The trumpet blast grew louder and louder, while Moses was speaking and God answering him with thunder. . . .
>
> Then God delivered all these commandments:
>
> "I, the Lord, am your God, who brought you out of the land of Egypt, that place of slavery. You shall not have other gods besides me. You shall not carve idols for yourselves in the shape of anything in the sky above or on the earth below or in the waters beneath the earth; you shall not bow down before them or worship them. For I, the Lord, your God, am a jealous God, inflicting punishment for their fathers' wickedness on the children of those who hate me, down to the third and fourth generation; but bestowing mercy down to the thousandth generation, on the children of those who love me and keep my commandments.

256

"You shall not take the name of the Lord, your God, in vain. For the Lord will not leave unpunished him who takes his name in vain.

"Remember to keep holy the Sabbath day. Six days you may labor and do all your work, but the seventh day is the Sabbath of the Lord, your God. No work may be done then either by you, or your son or daughter, or your male or female slave, or your beast, or by the alien who lives with you. In six days the Lord made the heavens and the earth, the sea and all that is in them; but on the seventh day he rested. That is why the Lord has blessed the Sabbath day and made it holy.

"Honor your father and your mother, that you may have a long life in the land which the Lord, your God, is giving you.

"You shall not kill.

"You shall not commit adultery.

"You shall not steal.

"You shall not bear false witness against your neighbor.

"You shall not covet your neighbor's house. You shall not covet your neighbor's wife, nor his male or female slave, nor his ox or ass, nor anything else that belongs to him" (Ex 19:3–20:17).

The Ten Commandments are the fundamental rules for conscience, made known by God Himself. The separate laws apply to particular matters belonging to the substance of human life and so apply to all. Because the Commandments legislate only for general situations they do not include, for example, reference to the duties of particular callings and stations in life. But these can be deduced from the Ten Commandments.

The First Commandment is the basic rule of conscience governing man's attitude to God.

The Second Commandment is the basic rule of conscience for keeping holy the name of God.

The Third Commandment is the basic rule of conscience for the sanctifying of the Lord's Day.

The Fourth Commandment contains the law of God governing our relations to parents and legitimate superiors.

The Fifth Commandment contains the law of God for the life of body and soul.

The Sixth Commandment contains the law of God governing the powers of reproduction.

The Seventh Commandment contains the law of God about property, its rights and its obligations.

The Eighth Commandment contains the law of God about speaking and keeping silent.

The Ninth and Tenth Commandments contain the law of God governing the interior world of desire.

The Commandments of God bear a close relationship to the natural law and to the demands of the moral law which is embedded in man's nature, so that neglect of them constitutes a violation of man's nature. The law of nature is as immutable as human nature itself.

The Commandments of God do not, however, enunciate the law of nature in the form of a set of guiding principles for a human ruler, but rather in the form of an obligation upon the individual to behave and act in accordance with the law of nature. In this way they lay an obligation upon secular rulers and states to pay heed to the law of nature.

The legislation of modern states expresses, in the main, the stipulations of the law of nature as state laws in the so-called basic rights of the citizen; but they very often express this in a way which suggests that these rights arise from their promulgation by the state. But whoever thinks that the state creates these basic rights will also believe that the state can change or rescind them; and once this idea has taken root it will not be long before the state is encroaching upon fundamental human rights.

When the popes exhort us to return to a recognition of God in His Commandments they are thinking particularly of this replacement of God-given natural rights by rights conferred merely by the state.

In revealing the Ten Commandments God has responded to man's need to have completely reliable rules by which to judge the rightness of particular human actions.

The Ten Commandments are ten rules revealed by God for the consciences of all men.

God gave the Ten Commandments to men out of love; by them He desires to lead man along the way by which the image of God will be unfolded within him, and to protect him from deviations into inhumanity.

The Life of the Individual. In the end everything depends upon honest effort to gain self-knowledge. We recall those mysterious words of Jesus, "The man who already has will receive yet greater wealth, while he who does not have will lose even what he has" (Mt 13:12).

Men who do not wish to see themselves by the inner light which shows them what they are avoid quiet and solitude. Pascal, the philosopher and mathematician says:

> Because men cannot mend death, misery, and ignorance, to make themselves happy it has come to pass that they refuse to think about these things. That is the only way they have discovered of comforting themselves in so many sorrows. But it is miserable comfort indeed, for it cannot begin to heal the evil, but only hides it for a while: and if man hides it, he never thinks about healing it in truth.
>
> And so it comes about through a strange reversal of nature that tedium, man's most serious evil, becomes in a way his greatest blessing, because it contributes more than anything to his seeking true salvation; and dissipation, his greatest blessing as he thinks, becomes in fact the worst thing for him, because more than anything else it keeps him from seeking true amelioration of his suffering. And both of these things are an amazing proof of man's misery and ruin and also of his greatness. Man is bored by everything and throws himself into all this activity merely because he has an idea of the happiness which he has lost and, not finding it within himself, he seeks it in exterior, perishable things without ever being able to satisfy himself; for satisfaction lies neither in ourselves nor in creatures but in God.

The Life of the Church. There are people who say "Priests ought to leave off this eternal preaching of basic truths and get onto problems which affect more advanced people. You get the impression that the Church is still stuck in the Old Testament and takes too little account of the freedom of the children of God."

The question which lies behind this sort of remark was raised by Cardinal Newman a hundred years ago. "The world is content with setting right the surface of things; the Church aims at regenerating the very depths of the heart. She ever begins with the beginning; and, as regards the multitude of her children, is never able to get beyond the beginning, but is continually employed in laying the foundation. She is engaged with what is essential, as precious and as introductory to the ornamental and the attractive. She is curing men and keeping them clear of mortal sin; she is 'treating of justice and chastity, and the judgment to come'; she is insisting on faith and hope, and devotion, and honesty, and the elements of charity; and has so much to do with precept that she almost leaves it to inspirations from Heaven to suggest what is of counsel and perfection. She aims at what is necessary rather than at what is desirable. She is for the many as well as for the few. She is putting souls in the way of salvation, that they may then be in a condition, if they shall be called upon, to aspire to the heroic, and to attain the full proportions, as well as the rudiments, of the beautiful."

The revelation of the Ten Commandments begins with the statement: "I am the Lord your God." These words are not directed, as one might at first suppose, to the people of Israel as a community, but to the people as individuals. This is exemplified well by the command, "Honor your father and mother." Father and mother can only be honored by individuals.

On Mount Sinai God was already speaking to individuals. He told the individual what he must and must not do if he wishes to remain true to human nature as created by God. From this first proclamation of God's law it already appears that its validity does not depend upon its acceptance by human societies and so cannot be invalidated by being set aside by men.

3. THE TEN COMMANDMENTS OF GOD—COMMANDMENTS OF CHRIST

WHEN JESUS APPEARED in Galilee, teaching and working miracles, news of Him spread throughout all the surrounding countryside, to the hill country of Juda in the south and to the regions in the east and north. Representatives of all the people were daily coming to the Lord.

Everyone regarded Jesus with expectancy and pressed forward to see Him face to face. Men, women, peasants, shepherds, fishermen, artisans, and merchants, all came with an unspoken question. What is the purpose of man's life upon earth? What must he do? Can he become perfectly happy forever?

To these questions which all brought with them Jesus gave an answer. The evangelist Matthew tells us:

> One day when his eyes fell on the crowd, he went up a mountainside, where he sat down, with his disciples close to him. Opening his lips he gave to his hearers a lengthy instruction, saying:
> "Blessed are the humble souls,
>   for theirs is the kingdom of heaven.
> Blessed are the meek and gentle,
>   for they will inherit the land.
> Blessed are the sorrowing,
>   for they will be consoled.
> Blessed are those who hunger and thirst after holiness,
>   for they will be fully satisfied.
> Blessed are the merciful,
>   for they will have mercy shown to them.
> Blessed are the singlehearted,
>   for they will see God.
> Blessed are the promoters of peace,

for they will rank as children of God.
Blessed are the victims of persecution for conscience' sake,
for theirs is the kingdom of heaven.
Blessed are you when you are reviled, or persecuted, or made a
target for nothing but malicious lies — for my sake. Be joyful —
leap for joy; a rich reward awaits you in heaven. So, too, were
persecuted the prophets who preceded you" (Mt 5:1–12).

If we had been able to make a film of Jesus' audience as He
began to expound the first Beatitude to them, what changes we would
have seen in their looks and expressions. What a strange road to
happiness this Jesus of Nazareth was painting. And yet He spoke with
a spiritual assurance which came right home to every listener.

The eighth Beatitude at first surprised them; and then in the concluding words He explained how it linked up with the Commandments
of God:

> "Do not think it is my mission to annul the Law or the Prophets.
> It is not my mission to annul, but to bring to perfection. I assure
> you emphatically: before heaven and earth pass away, not a single
> letter or one small detail will be erased from the Law — no, not until
> all is accomplished" (Mt 5:17–18).

> "You have heard that it was said to the men of old: 'Do not
> murder' and 'He who commits murder is answerable to the court.'
> I, on the contrary, declare to you: anyone who is angry with his
> brother is answerable to the court; anyone who says to his brother,
> 'You imbecile,' is answerable to the Supreme Council; anyone who
> says, 'You fool,' must answer for it in the fiery pit. Suppose, then,
> you are about to offer your gift at the altar, and there remember that
> your brother holds something against you: leave your gift there
> before the altar, and first go and settle your argument with your
> brother; and then come back to offer your gift" (Mt 5:21–24).

> "Again, you have heard it was said of old: 'Do not swear falsely,
> but you must redeem your promises made under oath to the Lord.'
> I, on the contrary, declare to you: do not swear at all, whether by
> heaven, for it is God's throne; or by the earth, for it is his footstool;
> or by Jerusalem, for it is the city of the Great King; nor should
> you swear by your own head, for you cannot make a single hair
> white or black. Let your speech be 'Yes,' when you mean Yes, and
> 'No,' when you mean No. Whatever is in excess of these expres-
> sions is due to the evil in the world" (Mt 5:33–37).

Using these examples, Jesus proved that in the eight Beatitudes

He was introducing no new rules for conscience, but simply unfolding thoroughly the old basic rules, the Commandments of God. In this connection He contrasts Himself with Moses: "You have heard that it was said to the men of old . . . I, on the contrary, tell you." With the words "I tell you," Jesus takes the place of God on Mount Sinai, and Jesus' audience takes the place of those who first received the Commandments of the Old Covenant.

Jesus' sermon, as He Himself emphasizes, is based as a whole and in detail upon the Ten Commandments of God. These are still to be fully observed.

Jesus solemnly declared that He had come to fulfill the Commandments of God.

Jesus made the Ten Commandments His own:

1. By revealing to men the full meaning of the commandments.
2. By promising men grace to keep them.
3. By demanding that men keep them out of love for God.
4. By giving men the most perfect example of keeping the Commandments out of the love of God. At the Last Supper He said, "I have set you an example, so that what I have done to you, you, too, shall do" (Jn 13:15).

The Life of the Individual. A prayer of Pascal shows how a man who believes fervently in God's fatherly goodness enters into a new spiritual relationship with God. "Grant, O God, that with constant calm of spirit I may face all possible occurrences, for we know not for what we should ask, and I cannot ask for one thing rather than another without presumption and becoming responsible for things which Your wisdom wishes to hide from me. O Lord, I know that I know only this: that it is good to imitate You and wicked to offend You. Apart from that I know not what is better or worse in things. I know not which is better for me, health or sickness, riches or poverty: I cannot judge at all about the value of the things of this world. To distinguish these things exceeds the power of men or of angels: it is hidden in the mysteries of Providence which I adore and desire not to fathom."

The Life of the Church. In the eight Beatitudes Jesus calls those men blessed who are always spiritually prepared for God. They must persevere on earth and they will share in the eternal vision of God. With this thought in mind the Church has the eight Beatitudes read on the feast of All Saints.

Many, it is true, are inclined to regard the Beatitudes as a kind of poetic introduction to the Sermon on the Mount, not to be taken literally as the other sayings of Jesus are.

What sort of a world would that be in which men had ceased to prize heavenly things more than earthly things, to seek comfort and not despair in sorrow, to master themselves and to strive for reconciliation between men, to follow mercy and compassion, honesty and purity of mind? What sort of world would we find if men had ceased to love peace rather than discord, had ceased to obey God and consider their fellowmen even when it did not pay them to do so?

4. THE THEOLOGICAL VIRTUES: FAITH, HOPE, AND CHARITY, THE FUNDAMENTAL FORCES IN STRIVING TOWARD GOD

MAN HAS SUCH GREATNESS that all the treasures of the world are unable to satisfy him; only God is sufficient; and only he who realizes this has a healthy spiritual vision, seeing things as they really are. In the Sermon on the Mount Jesus teaches about this:

"Do not lay up treasures for yourselves on earth, where moth devours and rust consumes, and where thieves break in and steal; but lay up treasures for yourselves in heaven, where neither moth devours nor rust consumes, nor thieves break in and steal. After all, where your treasure is, there, too, your heart is bound to be.

"The eye serves your person as a lamp; so long, then, as your eye is sound, your whole person will have light; but when your eye is defective, your whole person will grope in the dark. Consequently, if your inward lamp is darkened, how dense will that darkness be!

"A man cannot be the slave of two masters. He will either hate the one and love the other, or, at least, be attentive to the one and neglectful of the other. You cannot have money and God for masters.

"I tell you therefore: do not fret about what to eat, or what to drink, to sustain your life, or about what to wear on your bodies. Is not life more precious than food, and the body more precious than clothing? Look at the wild birds: they do not sow, or reap, or store up provisions in barns, and yet your heavenly Father feeds them! Are not you more precious than they? And which of you can by fretting add one minute to his span of life? And as for clothing, why do you fret? Observe the lilies in the field! How they grow! They do not toil or spin; and yet, I tell you, even Solomon in all his glory did not dress like one of these. Now if God so clothes

265

the grass in the field, which is there today and is thrown into the furnace tomorrow, will he not much more readily clothe you? What little faith you have!

"Therefore, have done with fretting, and do not constantly be asking; 'What are we going to eat?' or, 'What are we going to drink?' or, 'What are we going to wear?' Why, the heathen make all these things an object of eager search; besides, your heavenly Father knows that you need all these things. No, let your first concern be the kingdom of God and what he requires of you; then you will have all these things thrown in for good measure" (Mt 6:19–33).

In this beautiful exhortation Jesus points out that man as a creature of God stands above the order of plants and animals and therefore must strive toward a goal which is higher than this world. If he does not find his final rest in God he cannot be happy; first and foremost he must seek the kingdom of God.

Three things are necessary if we would find this kingdom of God and come to share in the divine life. In the Sermon on the Mount Jesus tells us what they are: *knowledge* of God, which is derived from God's own revelation; *a desire for God in hope,* which finds its guarantee in God's promises; and *devotion to God in love,* which corresponds to the love of God revealed in the incarnation of Christ. St. Paul in his letter to the Corinthians speaks, therefore, of *faith, hope,* and *love,* as three God-given powers through which man progresses toward God.

The Apostle begins with the supreme virtue, love, which is present in embryo in faith and which is finally consummated in the vision of God.

If I should speak the languages of men and of angels, but have no love, I am no more than a noisy gong and a clanging cymbal. And if I should have the gift of inspired utterance, and have the key to all secrets, and master the whole range of knowledge, and if I should have wonder-working confidence so as to be able to move mountains, but have no love, I am nothing. And if I should distribute all I have bit by bit, and should yield my body to the flames, but have no love, it profits me nothing.

Love is long-suffering; love is kind, and is not envious; love does not brag; it is not conceited; it is not ill-mannered; it is not self-seeking; it is not irritable, it takes no note of injury; it is not glad when injustice triumphs; it is glad when the truth prevails. Always it is ready to make allowances; always to trust; always to hope; always to be patient.

Love will never end. If there are inspired utterances, they will become useless. If there are languages, they will be discarded. If there is knowledge, it will become useless. For our knowledge is incomplete, and our utterances inspired by God are incomplete, but when that which is perfect has come, what is incomplete will be useless. When I was a little child, I spoke as a little child, I thought as a little child, I reasoned as a little child. Now that I am grown to manhood, I have discarded as useless my childish ways. We see now by means of a mirror in a vague way, but then we shall see face to face. Now my knowledge is incomplete, but then I shall have complete knowledge, even as God has complete knowledge of me. So, we now have these three, faith, hope, and love, but the greatest of them is love (1 Cor 13:1–13).

Because the theological virtues of *faith, hope,* and *love* enable man to put aside every worldly allurement and press on toward God, St. Paul likens these virtues to weapons with which a man fights his way to God.

But let us, who belong to the day, be alert. Let us put on the breastplate of faith and love, and for a helmet the hope of salvation. For God has not destined us to incur wrath, but to gain salvation through our Lord Jesus Christ, who died for us in order that, whether we are awake or asleep, we may find life in union with him (1 Thes 5:8–10).

The deepest longing of the human heart can only be satisfied by God. God wills, however, that satisfaction should come through the beatific vision in a way which transcends all earthly happiness. This blessedness in the vision of God is brought to men through the strength of the *graces of faith, hope, and love.*

By *faith* man sees in God the goal; by *hope* he takes hold of this goal; and in *love* union with God already begins.

Faith, hope, and *love* only grow by being active in life; and as without study and practice even the greatest mathematical talent will fall, so if they are not active in life, *faith, hope,* and *love* will eventually be lost. Jesus' saying alludes to this: "The man who already has will receive yet greater wealth, while he who does not have will lose even what he has" (Mt 13:12).

The theological virtue of *love* claims the highest place. It is contained in germ in faith, and it comes to fulfillment when faith becomes sight and hope possession; by itself it never ends. It endures forever.

The Life of the Individual.   A man may be confused about the principles according to which he lives; but it is impossible for him to live without principles. To live without principle is to live by a set of very bad principles.

We ought constantly to pray for the theological virtues, for faith, hope, and love. This petition pleases God above all others; and for this reason there is no prayer which He will grant so readily, if it be sincere. And to the one who supplicates for these gifts first of all, God will give in addition many other things he never asked for; for Jesus Himself affirmed solemnly that the man who seeks first the kingdom of heaven and its justice will receive all other things.

The Life of the Church.   A man on a journey will keep in mind his goal, especially when troubles assail him. A Christian likewise, who by faith knows that here he has no abiding city but strives for one to come, will keep in mind, especially when temptations come, his ultimate goal — eternal blessedness in the vision of God. This happens every time he thinks of God. The inestimable value of the morning offering lies in its being an inward orientation of oneself toward God.

The additions to the Rosary which are common in many places refer to the theological virtues. They consist of supplications for an increase in faith, a strengthening of hope, and a growth of love. Because the faithful ought to arouse in themselves from time to time the virtues of faith, hope, and love, appropriate prayers are attached to the central act of worship on Sundays.

5. THE FOUR CARDINAL MORAL VIRTUES: PRUDENCE, JUSTICE, FORTITUDE, TEMPERANCE— THE FOUR BASIC PRINCIPLES GOVERNING ALL HUMAN ACTION

1. Thoughtful Regard for the Divinely Appointed Overall Plan — the Virtue of Prudence

HUMAN RELATIONSHIPS, even in the simplest conditions, are complex and constantly changing. For this reason we are forever obliged to arrange our various relationships in order of importance.

In baptism a man receives a special gift from God, spiritual inclinations and capacities enabling him, in all his actions, to enter into God's plan, and in this way to help realize God's plan for the world. These inclinations and capacities are called the cardinal moral virtues of *prudence, justice, fortitude,* and *temperance.*

Faith demands that a man should follow the right goal for his life and employ the right means to reach it. The capacity which grace produced of assessing circumstances and of choosing the right means which will lead to the goal which God wills is called the virtue of Christian *prudence. Justice, fortitude,* and *temperance* cannot be possessed apart from *prudence;* and therefore St. Thomas describes *prudence* as "the mother of all virtues."

Whoever neglects important and lasting possessions and seizes upon unimportant trifles which are soon spent is not prudent. We must not make the chief thing subordinate or the subordinate the chief.

Our Lord gives an impressive exhortation to prudence in the Sermon on the Mount:

"In short, whoever hears these words of mine and acts accordingly is like a sensible man who built his house upon rock: the rain poured down and the floods came and the winds blew and beat against that house; but it did not collapse. It was founded upon rock. And whoever hears these words of mine and does not act accordingly is like a foolish man who built his house upon sand: and the rain poured and the floods came and the winds blew and beat against that house, and it collapsed. In fact, the collapse of it was complete" (Mt 7:24–27).

Christian prudence, which sees human life with all its relations as a whole, is contrasted with that prudence which detaches particular desires from the whole and pursues them for their own sakes. Both individual and society suffer when this sort of prudence prevails.

Because Christian prudence depends upon the exigencies of life at particular times, during the course of life its character alters.

Prudence in the young and spiritually inexperienced is shown specially in a readiness to listen to what is said to them. It makes them obedient and docile.

Prudence in mature age is characterized by the ability to make judgments which are uninfluenced by the maxims of the world. Adult prudence is also shown in independence of judgment and in firmness of resolve.

The prudence of old age consists in retiring more to an advisory level and allowing opportunity to those in their prime to exercise their still fresh powers. The prudence of old age knows how to impart good advice at the right time and in the right way.

2. Considerate Regard for the Rights of One's Fellowmen — the Virtue of Justice

Some of the commonest decisions which a man has to make day by day are those governing his behavior toward his fellowmen with regard to their property or what is due to them.

In the Sermon on the Mount Jesus enunciated the golden rule.

"Do to your fellow men exactly as you wish them to do to you" (Mt 7:12).

The meaning would have been the same had Jesus said, "Whatever you think that your neighbor would like do to him." Jesus reversed the rule. He put it this way to show men the way to discover most certainly and speedily how to reach a correct judgment about what they should do or forbear to do to their fellows. When it is a case of determining what demands we can make upon others, we are to show what legal experts we are. The wisdom of Jesus' golden rule works in quite the opposite way. It enables us to find ways of serving our fellowmen.

Everything which constitutes justice in the narrower sense obviously falls under the rule which Jesus proclaimed. Justice toward society and the law demand that both rulers and subjects contribute their share toward the common good. Social justice governs discharge of those duties which arise from man's social nature according to the conditions of the time. These duties may be codified in state laws; but even if they are not, they still bind groups in their dealings with one another. By virtue of their office, the leaders and rulers of the state must apportion privileges and burdens justly, and must take account of reward and punishment in the proper way. This justice can be described as juridical justice. Under the heading of justice a special place is given to just dealing in matters of earning, exchange, and buying. The Seventh Commandment, "Thou shalt not steal," applies to this sort of justice.

At first glance it might be thought that a man can possess the virtue of justice without having love. In reality, however, this is not so easy to accomplish. Without love there can be no insight into the inner value of an action. And so without love a man is not in a position to judge of an act impartially.

3. The Resolute Overcoming of Outward Adversity — the Virtue of Fortitude

As St. John says, the whole world is in the grip of evil (cf. 1 Jn 5:19). Good can prevail only in the face of manifold adversity. A good man accepts this, ready either to overcome it or to suffer it in patience.

Accordingly a good man requires strength to bear the burden which cannot be removed, and courage to fight resolutely against an obstacle which ought to be removed.

The man who knows both how to suffer in patience and how to take arms against trouble acts with courage and boldness founded upon faith and assisted by grace. It is, therefore, of the nature of Christian fortitude to go hand in hand with an awareness of one's own weakness. This fact is expressed clearly by St. Paul when he says, "When I am weak, then I am strong" (2 Cor 12:10).

In the course of His Sermon on the Mount our Lord cites examples of courage, not so much the courage of attack as the courage of endurance. He impressed His hearers by the very unfamiliarity of His phrases. He says:

> "You have heard it said: 'An eye for an eye, and a tooth for a tooth.' I, on the contrary, declare to you: do not meet evil with evil. No, if someone strikes you on your right cheek, turn to him the other as well. And if a man intends by process of law to rob you of your coat, let him have your cloak as well. And if someone forces you to go one mile with him, go two miles with him. Give to anyone who asks you, and if someone would borrow from you, do not turn away.
>
> "You have heard it said: 'Love your neighbor, and hate your enemy.' I, on the contrary, declare to you: love your enemies and pray for your persecutors, and thus prove yourselves children of your Father in heaven. He, certainly, lets his sun rise upon bad and good alike, and makes the rain fall on sinners as well as saints. Really, if you love those that love you, what reward do you deserve? Do not tax collectors do as much? And if you have a friendly greeting for your brothers only, are you doing anything out of the common? Do not the heathen do as much? Be perfect, then, as your heavenly Father is perfect" (Mt 5:38–48).

This exhortation to bear oppression patiently certainly does not mean that Jesus never demands any active striving for the kingdom of God. We learn this from the following saying.

> "Do you suppose that I came to shed peace upon the earth? No, I tell you; quite the contrary! I came to sow dissension. For example, from now on there will not be five persons in one family without a quarrel; two will be on one side, and three on the other; father will quarrel with son, and son with father; mother with daughter, and daughter with mother; mother-in-law with daughter-in-law, and daughter-in-law with mother-in-law" (Lk 12:51–53).

If our Lord did not clearly express in the Sermon on the Mount this aspect of fortitude, viz., attack in the face of danger, He had a special reason for not doing so. His hearers were all too ready to assume that fighting for the Kingdom of God was to be identified with fighting for secular freedom for Israel from the Roman yoke.

4. Resolute Mastery of Interior Adversity — the Virtue of Temperance

Since the Fall man has continually been learning that good is threatened not merely from without but also from within himself. In short, his own passions can so take possession of him that he is liable to make their satisfaction the goal of his life: he lets life take its course. But this life of self-expression leads not to fulfillment but to the destruction of life, his own and that of others. Man can insure against such destruction only through temperance and self-discipline.

In two pictures in the Sermon on the Mount, our Lord makes it plain to His audience that man has to take himself in hand. He admonishes us:

"Enter by the narrow gate; for wide is the gateway and spacious the road that leads to destruction; and many there are that enter by it! But oh, how narrow the gateway and how narrow the road that leads to life, and few there are that find it!" (Mt 7:13–14.)

As Jesus was speaking of the narrow road His audience could see the zigzag country lanes lined with thorns, threading their way up and down the hillsides.

The broad road made them think of the new paved roads laid down by the Romans where walking was easy — you could even drive a carriage on them.

In the broad gate they recognize the entrances to the palaces which allowed many people to enter together quite conveniently. The narrow gate made them think of little wicket gates. If you found one you had to put down all your luggage and squeeze through.

It is certainly more comfortable at first to take the broad street which leads you to the broad gate which can be seen easily from afar and through which you can walk without any trouble.

But whoever follows the broad road and comes through the broad gate arrives in the end at a place where life is life no longer; and he who takes the narrow road and comes through the narrow gate finds at last, after effort and sorrow, self-denial and privation, freedom and fullness of joy for all eternity.

Man's task is to place his life under the law of God and so to cooperate in realizing God's plan for the world. Various spiritual capacities are required for this. These are called the moral virtues.

The four cardinal virtues are: *prudence, justice, fortitude,* and *temperance.*

Christian *prudence* enables us to perceive, in the particular situations of life, what is in accordance with the plan of God for our life and the corporate life of mankind, and to act accordingly.

Christian *justice* consists in our willingly leaving with or rendering to every man what is his, and so contributing our share in the carrying out of God's plan for the communal life of mankind.

Christian *fortitude* consists in our persevering in the fight for God's law and in suffering hardship and danger in the same cause.

Christian *temperance* consists in our bringing God's law to bear upon our inner inclinations and passions.

The Life of the Individual. The whole of our moral task, the task of ordering our earthly life so that it pleases God, is summed up in St. Paul's advice: Use this world as though you did not use it.

The Life of the Church. The material world and the soul of man have been created by the same personal God; hence there is no division between worldly affairs and religious matters. At most we can distinguish duties which man owes immediately to God and duties which refer proximately to men, but which ultimately are founded in God.

In recent times attempts have been made to create religious attitudes apart from belief in God. In this way man was to gain independence of God without having to renounce the values attributed to religion. At times we hear of an *interior spirituality* which was to replace the God-centered piety of olden times.

That interior spirituality would make man the founder of his own religion. Such a religion would be as changeable and self-contradictory as the man who created it. Tolstoy, the Russian writer, said: "The attempt to establish morality while avoiding religion is like the action of children who want to transplant a flower which they like, but who, because the root does not appeal to them does not appear to be of any use, tear it up and stick it in the ground without the root. Without a religious basis there can be no true, genuine morality, just as there is no real plant without root."

6. THE LAW OF LOVE: THE SUMMARY OF ALL MAN'S DUTIES

ALL OF MAN'S OBLIGATIONS can be derived from the law of love, from the command to love God and our neighbor. In the time of Jesus this was already recognized.

> Presently an expert in the Law came forward to sound him out. "Rabbi," he said, "what must I do to obtain a place in eternal life?" "Well," he replied, "what does the Law say about it? What do you read in it?" He answered: "'Love the lord your God with your whole heart, and with your whole soul, and with your whole strength, and with your whole mind'; and besides, 'Love your neighbor as yourself.'" "Your answer is correct," he said to him; "act accordingly, and you will have life" (Lk 10:25–28).

"Love the Lord your God with your whole heart, and with your whole soul, and with your whole strength, and with your whole mind." This command affirms that man's thoughts must first of all be fundamentally rooted in God; then man's desires and feelings will follow suit and he will love God with his whole heart. If a man's heart is directed toward God then he will use all of his powers to live for God and what is good. Christian love is born of thought which arouses feeling and issues in deeds.

Jesus gave men an example of how they should love God before all else. On several occasions He stressed that for Him the beginning and the end was the will of His Father in heaven. "To do the will of him whose ambassador I am — this is my food!" (Jn 4:34.)

Just as clearly Jesus declared that He was the model of love to men which would bind his disciples. This occurred in the hour of farewell when, after the washing their feet, He announced:

> "And new commandment I give you: love one another; as I love you, so I want you, too, to love one another. By this token all the

275

world must know that you are my disciples — by cherishing love for one another" (Jn 13:34–35).

The Christian must also see the problem of how to love his neighbor in relation to the example of Jesus.

When a man becomes aware, by faith, that Jesus loves those whom he does not like as much as those to whom he feels attracted, he is beginning to practice a love which transcends nature.

Jesus brings this sort of love to light in the parable with which He concludes the conversation with the lawyers on the subject of the greatest commandment. After Jesus had said that whoever loves God with all his heart and his neighbor as himself will enter into heavenly blessedness, the lawyer, wishing to justify himself, as the Scripture says, asked Him: "And whom, pray, must I consider a neighbor?" (Lk 10:29.)

It was as though he had asked which of the people he met were to be excluded from this love.

Jesus showed him by a parable that true love of our fellowmen knows no exceptions. He began:

> Jesus complied with his request and said: "Once upon a time, a man who was on his way from Jerusalem down to Jericho fell in with bandits; they stripped and beat him, and then went their way, leaving him half dead. By some chance a priest was going down the same road; but when he saw the man, he made a detour. In like manner a levite came near the spot and he, too, made a detour at sight of him. Finally a traveling Samaritan came near him, and he, on seeing the man, was stirred to pity. He went up to him and bound up his wounds, pouring wine and oil into them. He then mounted him on his own beast of burden and brought him to an inn, where he took care of him. Moreover, on the morrow he produced two denarii to pay the innkeeper, and left these instructions: 'Take good care of him; and in case you spend anything over and above this sum, I will repay you on my way back.' Now which of these three men seems to you to have taken a neighborly interest in the man who had fallen in with bandits?" "The one," he replied, "who pitied him in that practical way." "Very well, then," Jesus said to him, "model your conduct on his" (Lk 10:30–37).

Jesus' words, "Model your conduct on his," apply to everyone who calls himself a Christian.

What Jesus taught in this parable was incorporated in their preaching by the Apostles. They spurred the faithful on to make the life of faith into a life of love for God and neighbor. St. Peter thus admonishes the faithful in his Second Epistle:

> For this reason, make every effort to supplement faith with moral courage, moral courage with knowledge, knowledge with self-control, self-control with patience, patience with piety, piety with brotherly affection, brotherly affection with love.
>
> If you have these virtues in abundance, they will make you both active and fruitful, and bring you to the deep knowledge of our Lord Jesus Christ. He who does not have these virtues is practically blind in his nearsightedness and forgetful that he has been cleansed from his former sins. Consequently, brothers, strive even more to make your calling and election secure, because if you do this you will never stumble. Indeed, in this way ample provision will be made for your entrance into the eternal kingdom of our Lord and Savior Jesus Christ (2 Pt 1:5–11).

In this exhortation of St. Peter the inner connection between the moral virtues and the love of God and of neighbor is pointed out in vigorous language. By means of the moral virtues a man grasps certain parts of God's plan which relate to his own life and by realizing this he participates in carrying out the great plan of God.

The sum total of human duty to God and neighbor is summed up in the Christian *law of love.*

The law of love runs: "You shall love the Lord your God with your whole heart, and with your whole soul, and with your whole strength, and with your whole mind; and your fellowman as yourself." This law asserts that the love of God must determine one's entire inner thought and volition, and must become effective in external actions.

Love of God operates in relation to *ourselves* and our *fellowmen.* According to the commandment of our Redeemer and Master we must love all our fellowmen as children of the heavenly Father, like ourselves. And we must love our relatives, our parents, brothers and sisters, for the sake of God. The commandment to love our neighbor extends for this reason even to enemies. Our Lord commanded: "I, on the contrary, declare to you: love your enemies and pray for your persecutors, and thus prove yourselves children of your Father in heaven" (Mt 5:44).

Love of our neighbor is shown by our rejoicing with him, sorrowing with him, and supporting him in his corporal and spiritual necessities.

The corporal works of mercy are: to feed the hungry, to give drink to the thirsty, to clothe the naked, to shelter the homeless, to visit the sick, to visit the imprisoned, to bury the dead.

The spiritual works of mercy are: to convert the sinner, to instruct the ignorant, to counsel the doubtful, to comfort the sorrowful, to bear wrongs patiently, to forgive injuries, to pray for the living and the dead.

The Life of the Individual.   What Jesus made plain concerning the greatest commandment in His conversation with the lawyer, St. Paul tells the faithful in these words:

> Let there be no unpaid debt except the debt of mutual love, because he who loves his neighbor has fulfilled the Law. For the commandments:
>
> "You shall not commit adultery;
> You shall not kill;
> You shall not steal;
> You shall not covet";
>
> and if there is any other commandment, all are summed up in this saying,
>
> "You shall love your neighbor as yourself."
>
> Love does no evil to a neighbor. Love, therefore, is the complete fulfillment of the Law (Rom 13:8–10).

Christian love provides motives for caring about our fellowmen which natural love by itself does not know. Christian love transforms, exalts, and purifies all natural love of person for person; love of parents for children and of children for parents, love of husband for wife and wife for husband; love between brothers and sisters; between relatives and friends.

Cardinal Newman, after pointing out that a vague comprehensive intention of goodwill is not of much use, writes:

> The real love of man *must* depend on practice, and therefore, must begin by exercising itself on our friends around us, otherwise it will have no existence. By trying to love our relatives and friends,

by submitting to their wishes, though contrary to our own, by bearing with their infirmities, by overcoming their occasional waywardness by kindness, by dwelling on their excellences, and trying to copy them, thus it is that we form in our hearts that root of charity, which, though small at first, may, like the mustard seed, at last even overshadow the earth.

We are to begin with loving our friends about us, and gradually to enlarge the circle of our affections, till it reaches all Christians, and then all men.

This exposition of Newman draws attention to a law which is of the utmost importance for the collective condition of human relationships.

As rings spread out from the center where a stone is thrown into a pool, so an effect spreads out to others from the action of any man. This is effected — if one may use such a term — by spiritual transmission. First to feel the effect are the members of the family. Each member contributes his share in the spirit which prevails in the family. As members of a family reciprocally influence one another, so do families produce the character of the larger social groups and these, in turn, that of nations, and the nations the character of mankind at a particular time. Every good or bad action penetrates the human race in such a way as to effect the further course of human history. It is no empty saying but a genuine fact that no man can be completely judged without taking into account many men who lived before and who are partly the cause of his action, and countless who will live after him, upon whom his act will have an effect. Thus from each individual lines extend into the past and into the future. On the day of judgment God will expose before all men these endless ramifications and decisions.

The truth that the times are always what people make them was expressed 1500 years ago by St. Augustine: "Brethren, it is not the times which are good or bad. As we ourselves are, so are the times. How foolish of us to transfer our guilt to the day which lightens us and to the night which quietly closes about us! Every man creates his own epoch. If he lives a good life, then the times in which he lives are good. If storms assail from without or from within, in all temporal situations a man is still able to serve God and work out his soul's salvation. Let us then wrestle with the time and mould it, and so all times will become holy."

The Life of the Church. We find that in every society provision is made for special emergencies and general distress. Hence in the very first Christian times the Apostles organized collections and assistance for those in need. St. Paul had collections carried out in Greece and in Europe for the needy Christians in Jerusalem and in Asia. In fact, this business seemed to him so important that he devoted a special section of an Epistle to it. In this he enjoins the faithful to give: but he wants them to give willingly. "Let each one give as he has determined in his heart, not grudgingly or from compulsion, for 'God loves a cheerful giver' " (2 Cor 9:7).

And St. Paul explains that such charity not only remedies the distress of the non-Christian but brings a blessing upon the giver also.

St. Paul appoints the first day of the week, i.e., Sunday, as the day for making this collection. If the faithful not only pray but also make offerings on Sunday, this is a custom which originated in the first few years after the death of Jesus.

There is one act of charity which anyone can perform at any time: that is prayer. In prayer every believer moves through the world without passport or visa, doing good.

In Pope Pius XII's encyclical on the Mystical Body of Christ we read: "In the distribution of that treasure He not only shares this work of sanctification with His spotless Bride, but wills it to arise in a certain manner of her labor. This is truly a tremendous mystery, upon which we can never meditate enough: that the salvation of many souls depends upon the prayers and voluntary mortifications offered for that intention by the members of the mystical Body of Jesus Christ."

7. SIN: MAN'S DISOBEDIENCE TO GOD

MAN POSSESSES understanding and free will. If God were to compel man to live according to his nature, He would be violating his nature. God, therefore, gives man laws or commandments which he may freely obey or not. If he disobeys, he acts against his own nature: he disrupts his own life and also helps destroy the lives of others.

In Baptism every Christian renounces the devil and chooses Christ as Lord and King. Should he thereafter transgress the laws of God, he does something which amounts to mocking Christ. In sin a Christian faces Christ, to whom he owes life and everything, and says: "I may do as I will — and so I choose whatever gives me pleasure."

The true nature of sin is brilliantly portrayed in St. Matthew's story of the mocking of Jesus.

> The soldiers of the governor now took Jesus in charge and gathered round him the entire company in the praetorium. They stripped him and put a scarlet cloak on him; next they put upon his head a plaited crown of thorns, and placed a reed in his right hand; then they knelt down before him with the mock salute: "Long live the King of the Jews!" (Mt 27:27–29.)

St. Augustine pinpoints the essence of grave sin thus: "He who sins wants to be a God himself, a little God maybe, but one who has no great God above him."

A man commits a grave sin when he transgresses a law of God in a *grave matter,* with *full knowledge* and with *full consent:* sin is disobedience. If the act has to do with a trivial matter or with serious matter not fully grasped or not done completely freely, then the sin is venial.

Disobedience, which constitutes the essence of grave sin, has characteristics which make it particularly obnoxious. Sin is hateful ingratitude. Disobedience is directed not against a harsh and loveless lawgiver but against God our Lord from whom we receive life itself and all natural and supernatural gifts, and who sent His own Son into the world to save us from the bondage of Satan.

Sin always includes contempt of God. There is no comparison between what a man gains by sin and what he gives up in the love and friendship of God. In exchange for some ridiculous trifle he gives the love of God. This essential feature of sin is portrayed by warning examples from the life of Jesus and His disciples. Judas the Apostle betrayed the Lord for thirty pieces of silver, and Peter was incited to deny the Lord by the curiosity of a servant girl.

Holy Scripture leaves us in no doubt that the man who dies in mortal sin and so out of friendship with God remains at enmity with God and goes to the place of torment known as hell. Christ Himself says, "It is better for you that one of you should perish than that you should be thrown, body and all, into the infernal pit" (Mt 5:30). Therefore He exhorts everyone most emphatically "And do not fear people that kill the body, but have no power to kill the soul; rather fear him who has power to ruin both body and soul in the infernal pit" (Mt 10:28).

The parable of the rich man and Lazarus only makes sense if we see the picture of hell which is interwoven into the story, not as a concession to popular imagery, but as a reference by Christ to the torments which hell represents. All that Jesus says about the Last Judgment is reduced to nothing if the condemnation of evil men to a place of torment in hell does not entail eternal punishment.

A venial sin is committed when the law of God is broken either in a slight matter or in a grave matter but without full knowledge or full consent of will.

He who persistently offends a friend in small things sooner or later forfeits his friendship; similarly, carelessness over venial sins leads to mortal sin. Apart from this it deprives a man of many graces, and earns for him temporal punishment and the pain of purgatory after death.

Because man has been created by God with reason and free will he is able to know God's will and yet, despite this, to oppose it and thus to sin.

A sin is committed by transgressing a commandment of God. God only commands what is in harmony with man's nature and what protects and develops the dignity of man. Every sin is also, therefore, an act of self-destruction.

All sins are not equally serious: there are *mortal sins* and *venial sins*.

One commits a mortal sin by transgressing a Commandment of God or of the Church in a grave matter, knowingly and with full consent of the will. In all circumstances we must avoid mortal sin, because it constitutes a serious injustice against God and the greatest misfortune for ourselves.

1. By mortal sin we lose supernatural life and access to heaven.
2. It deprives us of the grace of God, upon which all else depends.
3. Its punishment is the eternal pain of hell.

One commits a *venial sin* by transgressing a Commandment of God in a slight matter, or in a grave matter without full knowledge or without full consent of will. For the following reasons we ought not to be indifferent to venial sin:

1. It is an offense against God.
2. It deprives us of many graces.
3. It earns us the pains of purgatory and also temporal punishment in this world.
4. Taking venial sin lightly paves the way to mortal sin.

The Life of the Individual. Beggar and millionaire are alike in facing the same basic task in life: to avoid mortal sin. This is a task which must never be deferred until a more convenient occasion.

All grave sins, even those committed against other men, are first and foremost an offense against God and not merely some injustice to our neighbor. Correspondingly, when we are sinned against, we should not become preoccupied with the offense to ourselves but should remember that the offense is primarily against God. Such an attitude will help us to cultivate a forgiving mind. Whoever forgives is also forgiven by God. "Forgive us our trespasses as we forgive those who trespass against us."

The Life of the Church. The Church is the only society on earth which regards sin as primarily an offense against God, and tries to keep men away from it by pointing this out.

Outside the Church, sin is looked upon as stupidity: something not generally permissible, but tolerable in exceptional circumstances. Believers must be on their guard against becoming infected with such ideas. Their own secret, evil inclinations toward what is forbidden are forever wanting to seduce them into accepting a special ruling for themselves in this or that case.

Mindful of original sin, the Church never deviates from the fact that the danger of temptation has its ultimate cause in this radical inclination of man toward evil and radical apathy toward good. The influence of other men and the power of the devil have such an uncanny effect precisely because man is himself inclined to evil and feels a fatal urge not to take God's Commandments as the ground plan of his life but to judge matters for himself. Satan's suggestion to Eve to give the thing a try has lost none of its danger since the day it lured the mother of our race to destruction.

8. TEMPTATION: THE MYSTERIOUS WARFARE WITHIN THE SOUL

SIN IS A CONSCIOUS and deliberate transgression of a divine commandment. Temptation to sin arises at the moment when one becomes aware that one is drawn, in thought, desire, speech, or through negligence, to something evil. In this moment conscience, the voice of divinely guided reason, stirs and pronounces its judgment on good and evil.

It is most important to know wherein real temptation lies. In the Epistle of St. James there are a few sentences which are very much to the point:

> Blessed is the man who patiently endures trial, because after he has withstood the trial, he will receive the life-giving crown, which the Lord has promised to those that love him. No one should say when he is tempted, "I am tempted by God." It is a fact that God cannot be tempted by evil, and that he tempts no one. Rather each individual is tempted by his own passion, inasmuch as he is allured and enticed by it. Then passion conceives and gives birth to sin; and when sin has grown to maturity, it brings forth death (Jas 1:12–15).

It is never God who tempts us. Nor, indeed, is it the devil who first makes of temptation what it is to us. The primary source of temptation is our own weakness, our longing for evil. It is true that the devil's influence over imagination, and pressure from other people, can make evil appear much more enticing than it appears to be at first.

We may never assume that the devil will leave off trying to lead men astray into sin. He even approached Christ the Redeemer, who was Holiness Itself.

St. Matthew writes:

> Then Jesus was led on by the Spirit into the desert to be put to the test by the devil. Forty days and forty nights he fasted

and after that he was hungry. Now, then, the tempter approached and said to him: "If you are the Son of God, command these stones to turn into loaves of bread." But he met the proposal by replying: "It is written, 'Man does not live by bread alone: but by every word coming from the lips of God.'"

Then the devil took him up into the holy city and set him down upon the battlement of the temple. "If you are the Son of God," he said to him, "fling yourself down; for the Scripture says: 'to his angels he will give charge of you' and 'Upon their hands they will bear you up that you may not stub your foot against a stone.'" Jesus answered him: "On the other hand, the Scripture says: 'You shall not tempt the Lord your God!'"

Again, the devil took him up to a very high mountain and let him see all the kingdoms of the world and their splendor. "All these things I will give to you," he said to him, "if you go down on your knees and do homage to me." Then Jesus said to him: "Get out, Satan! The Scripture says: 'You shall do homage to the Lord your God, and him alone shall you adore!'" So then the devil left him undisturbed and, presently, angels approached and waited on him (Mt 4:1–11).

Since the Fall man's spiritual weakness has consisted in the dimming of his intellect and the instability of his will. Darkness of understanding leads to his inability to recognize the danger of temptation. Instability and weakness of will cause man to put off making spiritual decisions and to convince himself that, should any issue arise, he will automatically do what is right. All men without exception have a much too high opinion of themselves.

In war one must never allow himself to be taken by surprise, and at the onset of battle must defend himself with all possible vigor. What would we think of a soldier who saw the enemy approaching and went back to sleep, observing that he was not quite yet there? The same rule applies to spiritual warfare — temptation. If we do not heed the first warning but convince ourselves that there is no danger as yet, the preliminary skirmish is lost, and total defeat will soon follow.

Jesus gives us an example of how we should face temptation. Our Lord repulsed the tempter at once with complete firmness. His mind remained fixed upon the will of God. He did not pause and consider, He said: "Depart."

Every sin has its history, and this history begins with temptation.

By temptation is meant any inward or outward event or experience by which man is enticed toward sin. The foundation of all sin is in the inclination to evil. As St. James says: "Each individual is tempted by his own passion, inasmuch as he is allured and enticed by it. Then passion conceives and gives birth to sin" (Jas 18:14). The devil begins to work on a man when he is being tempted. St. Peter says, "Be sober, watchful! Your adversary the devil, like a roaring lion, prowls about looking for someone to devour" (1 Pt 5:8).

Man can effectively withstand his own inclination and the influence of the devil by thinking continually of God and by strengthening himself through prayer. This is St. Paul's meaning when he writes:

> Put on all the armor that God has forged, that you may be able to make a stand against the devil's cunning tricks. Our wrestling is not against weak human nature, but against the Principalities and the Powers, against those that rule the world of darkness, the wicked spirits that belong to an order higher than ours (Eph 6:11–12).

A temptation, which experience has shown to lead to sin, is called a proximate occasion of sin. To seek such an occasion or to allow it to persist without cause is already to sin. Holy Scripture says therefore, "He who loves danger will perish in it" (Sir 3:25).

The Life of the Individual. To combat man's peculiar unconcern and apathy at the approach of temptation we have our Lord's words, "Watch and pray" (Mt 26:41). Watching insures that we recognize the danger of a situation. Prayer insures that we admit the weakness of our own will. Only an honest-minded man is capable of these two things. "Whoever exalts himself will be humbled; he who humbles himself will be exalted" (Lk 14:11).

Temptations make us prudent, thoughtful, and kindly in judging others, and wise in giving advice. "One never put to the proof knows little" (Sir 34:10).

Whoever loves his own person with a right Christian love must decide honestly what people, places, and things constitute here and now an occasion of sin for him; and must avoid them.

The Life of the Church. It is part of the Church's task to make men vigilant all the time over temptation. Were the Church to neglect this she would be unfaithful to her vocation. The purer a man's mind, the more thankful will he be to God for this guidance. He who is already inclined in his heart to evil will say that this sort of exhortation is oppressive and interfering.

Many a person thinks secretly: True, there are people who have to avoid danger if they are not to fall. But this rule does not apply to me: I am capable of keeping a clear head in the face of temptation and of putting on the brake before it comes to grave sin.

Whoever speaks thus of temptations is making an assumption which is never true of temptation — if it really is temptation; for temptation consists essentially in the spiritual vision being dimmed and the will being unstable.

9. THE SEVEN CAPITAL VICES: SEVEN ROADS TO DESTRUCTION

IN SPITE OF INDIVIDUAL DIFFERENCES, all men alike inherit the effects of original sin. The powers and accomplishments of person are no longer at the command of a good will. The prophet Jeremiah says: "More tortuous than all else is the human heart" (Jer 17:9).

The first few chapters of Holy Scripture demonstrate in a few sentences how an unrestrained propensity of the heart — envy in this case — can overpower a man and bring disaster upon him and others. Here is the passage:

> Now Abel was a keeper of flocks and Cain a tiller of the soil. In the course of time Cain brought to the Lord an offering of the fruit of the ground. Abel also brought some of the firstlings of his flock with their fat portions. The Lord was pleased with Abel and his offerings; but for Cain and his offering he had no regard. Cain was very angry and downcast. The Lord said to Cain, "Why are you angry and why are you downcast? If you do well, will you not be accepted; but if you do not do well, will not sin crouch at the door! Its desire is for you, but you must master it."
>
> Cain said to his brother Abel, "Let us go out into the field." Now when they were in the field, Cain turned against his brother Abel and slew him (Gn 4:2–8).

Envy blighted Cain's life by turning him into a murderer; and there are other cardinal propensities, too, which gain power over a man's heart and drive him to wicked deeds.

We distinguish seven of these cardinal propensities: *pride, covetousness, lust, envy, gluttony, anger,* and *sloth.*

Certainly no man is enslaved by all of these basic propensities; but there is no one who is not in great danger at some time from one or other of them.

If a man is careless about a single one of these fundamental tendencies it opens out like a flower which has its roots struck deep and wide in the earth. A person who tries only halfheartedly to free himself suffers the severest reverses. Fighting passion with only half the will seems only to stimulate fresh growth.

In a parable sermon, our Lord tells us:

> "When the unclean spirit is driven out of a man, he haunts waterless regions in quest of refreshment, and, when he does not find any, says: 'I will return to the house from which I have been driven out.' Then, if on his return he finds it swept and tidy, he goes and gets seven other spirits, who are worse than himself, to join him, and they enter and make themselves at home there. Such a man is worse off in the end than he was at the beginning" (Lk 11:24–26).

Jesus compares the condition of a man who does not correct himself sincerely with that of one who is cured of demon-possession and then later becomes possessed by even worse demons.

As a man advances in cardinal sin it becomes necessary for him to justify himself; hence he is driven to deny faith in God who can make demands upon him, and in the Son of God who is able to redeem him.

Certain evil propensities are to be found in man which, if yielded to, become so strong that they control his entire life. From time immemorial seven such propensities have been distinguished and called the capital vices.

The seven capital sins are: *pride, covetousness, lust, envy, gluttony, anger, sloth.*

Christian discretion demands that each one of us make sure which propensity of the heart is specially dangerous for him. A person who leaves an evil propensity unassailed is like a ship's captain who leaves a hole unmended in the bottom of his ship through which water comes pouring in.

The Life of the Individual. As seven capital vices have been enumerated, we may well ask which of the seven is the worst. In itself, pride is the worst. It is the root of all sin, even of those with which it does not seem to have any connection.

In fact, however, for every individual, some particular vice is the most dangerous, and in a way the last listed, sloth, is the most deadly for everyone. For it is sloth — disinclination for prayer and honest endeavor — which first makes it possible for the other six to seize control or to keep it and to commandeer all the powers of a man for their own ends.

The Life of the Church. The Church keeps the possibility constantly in mind that from small beginnings and small faults a man may fall into a state in which he becomes impervious to any influence of grace, and after years of bad confessions and unworthy Communions may remain obdurate even in the face of death. But the Church never makes a particular judgment that any individual has brought this guilt upon himself. Only when a man who has belonged to the Church himself refuses to accept the consolations of the Blessed Sacrament does the Church refuse to bury him as a believer. And yet, even in such a case she affirms that no one knows what may have happened in the dying man in the last moment.

The doctrine that concupiscence is an effect of original sin saves the dignity of the human race. The human race is like a family whose history starts off with the bankruptcy of its parents. No individual can do anything about this bankruptcy; but through the redemption by Jesus Christ it is made possible for him to regain that favored position which Adam and Eve our first parents lost for themselves and their posterity.

THE COMMANDMENTS OF GOD AND OF THE CHURCH, AND THE DUTIES OF ONE'S STATION IN LIFE AS THE FULFILLMENT OF THE ONE SUPREME COMMANDMENT TO LOVE GOD AND OUR NEIGHBOR

"He who accepts my commandments and treasures them — he is the one that loves me. And he that loves me will, in turn, be loved by my Father; and I will love him, and will manifest myself to him" (Jn 14:21).

10. GOD: MAN'S CHIEF END

1. Faith

FOR THE BELIEVER, the thought that God is above him and all men is the basis of all his thinking. He judges, evaluates, and distinguishes everything from the standpoint of faith. Faith is the norm of life. Accordingly, Scripture speaks of life as a "walking before God."

Every baptized person must apply this rule to his life in each new situation, never wavering; but this does not always happen.

St. Peter's life provides an example of this. At Caesarea Philippi Peter solemnly confessed his faith in the divinity of Jesus: "You are the Messiah, the Son of the living God." For this Jesus praised him and said: "Blessed are you, Simon, son of Jona. It was my Father in heaven that revealed this to you, and not flesh and blood" (Mt 16:17).

But when Jesus, relying upon this profession, wanted to introduce His disciples to the mystery of His suffering and death, Peter failed Him.

> From that time on Jesus began to make plain to his disciples that it was necessary for him to go to Jerusalem, suffer much at the hands of the elders, high priests, and Scribes, be put to death, and on the third day rise again. At this Peter drew him aside and proceeded to lecture him. "May God spare you, Master," he said: "this must never happen to you!" But he turned on Peter with the words: "Get out of my sight; follow me, Satan! You are a stumbling block to me, for you do not take God's view of things but men's" (Mt 16:21–23).

Sternly the Lord corrects Peter, calls him, the disciple whom He had chosen to be the chief of them all, a devil, supporting His remark with the words, "You do not take God's view of things, but men's" (Mt 16:23).

The believer takes, not his own thoughts, but the thoughts of God as the basis for all his actions.

God is truth itself: He knows all things and when He speaks, He speaks the truth.

Whoever believes in God the Lord must believe all that He reveals. (*Faith must be complete.*)

He must hold fast to the truth of all His words without faltering.

He must also make his faith the foundation of his life. Faith without works is dead (cf. Jas 2:26). (*Faith must be living.*)

He must not allow men to seduce him from his faith. (*Faith must be steadfast.*)

Because faith is the beginning of God's solicitous love, to reject this love is a grave sin. "He that does not believe will be condemned" (Mk 16:16). (*Disbelief.*)

Because faith is a believing in God's word, a man may not deny separate items of revealed truth. (*Heresy.*)

Because faith is a believing in God's word, it is a grave sin to turn aside from God's word as though one did not know it. (*Apostasy, or denial of faith.*)

Because faith is a believing in God's word, it is a grave sin to doubt the truths of faith. (*Deliberate doubt.*)

It is also a sin to neglect hearing the word of God, reading good books, newspapers, and journals, or to expose faith to danger by reading books, papers, and journals which attack the faith.

2. Hope

By Christian hope the man in grace sets himself a goal which reaches far beyond this world and time itself. By God's grace he desires to have a share in the eternal vision of God. To attain this goal he must at all times cooperate with the grace of God.

Hope in God makes a man enterprising and active. It enables him to rise again after a defeat, and to lay fresh plans after victory. Hope gives to a child something of the wisdom of age and to the old man something of the zest of youth.

It is an anchor for the soul. Sure and steadfast it passes beyond the inner veil, where Jesus has entered as a forerunner on our behalf, having become forever a high priest after the manner of Melchisedech (Heb 6:19–20).

The man who lives by Christian hope can be likened to a man who walks on the waves at God's command.

An event is described in St. Peter's life where this image of walking at God's command coincides with an actual walking upon the sea. The same event shows too how a man can waver in trusting and can lose confidence. St. Matthew gives an eyewitness account:

> During the last part of the night, however, he came toward them, walking over the sea. But when they saw him walk upon the sea, they were perplexed. "It is a ghost!" they said, and from fright cried out. But Jesus at once addressed them. "Take heart," he said; "it is I! Do not be afraid."
>
> Thus reassured, Peter said to him: "Master, if it is you, tell me to come to you over the water." "Come," he replied. So Peter climbed out of the boat and, starting in the direction of Jesus, walked over the water; but when he felt the stiff breeze, he took alarm and, since he began to sink, cried out: "Lord, save me!"
>
> Jesus immediately reached out his hand and took hold of him. "How little faith you have!" he said to him; "what made you doubt?" (Mt 14:25–31.)

Full of confidence Peter got out of the boat at Jesus' word, and behold, he could walk upon water.

But what if he should sink through into the depths?

Fearfully he looked at the rolling waves.

The moment he thought of his own strength rather than the power of God he began to sink. Peter had lost firm trust.

This event in St. Peter's life is a symbol of all those situations wherein a man begins some work full of confidence in almighty God, and then loses trust in God.

This is not the only way in which a man can sin against Christian hope. He can sin against hope by completely disregarding God (indifference to God), doubting God's goodness and mercy (despair), or toying with the thought that later on he will certainly be absolved of his sin (presumption).

3. Love

In Christian love a man puts love of God before every other love and makes it the foundation of his life. This love of God is never a risk as the love of one human being for another is always said to be; for God Himself already loves every single person and never forsakes him.

Love of God is distinguished from all love between men in that man does not gain this love of God by a resolution *he* makes, but by *grace* which *God gives*. The man in love is the man in grace.

Whoever thinks he can love by his own decision and his own strength without the spiritual assistance of God, who mistakes a feeling of goodwill for love, will learn what St. Peter once learned. A few hours after he had declared vehemently that he would never leave his master in the lurch, he denied Him. We read in the Gospels:

> Under a strong escort they marched him off and took him to the palace of the high priest. Peter, meanwhile, followed at a distance. When the men had lit an open fire in the courtyard and seated themselves round it, Peter was sitting among them. As he sat with his face to the fire, a slave girl caught sight of him and, looking straight at him, said: "This man was with him." But he denied it. "Woman," he said, "I have nothing to do with him." After a little while, another person saw him and said: "You are one of them." "No, sir," Peter said, "I am not." After the lapse of about one hour, another stoutly affirmed: "This man was certainly with him. Why, he is a Galilean." "Sir," Peter rejoined, "I do not know what you are talking about." And immediately, while he was speaking, a cock crowed. Then the Master turned round and looked full upon Peter, and Peter remembered the Lord's prediction — how he had said to him: "Today, before a cock crows, you will disown me three times." And he went out and wept bitterly (Lk 22:54–62).

Peter marked well what this night taught him. After the resurrection, when Jesus asked him,

> "Simon, son of John, do you love me more than these others do?" "Yes, my Master," he replied; "you know that I really love you." "Then," Jesus said to him, "feed my lambs." He asked him a second time: "Simon, son of John, do you love me?" "Yes, Master," he replied, "you know that I really love you." "Then," he said to him, "be a shepherd to my sheep" (Jn 21:15–16).

If, for the sake of created things, we do something which God does not wish or leave undone something which He desires, we betray our love of God. Every grave sin is against love of God. That is its essence.

A man can begin to harbor aversions to God, as to men, and can even come to hate Him. Men who hate God are amazingly resourceful in devising plans against God and show an impatient zeal in carrying them out. They lack but one thing — peace of mind.

Man's ultimate end is God. Man strives toward this end with the strength supplied by grace in *Christian faith, Christian hope,* and *Christian love.*

Christian *faith* consists in our accepting the revelation of God from the mouth of its preacher as the word of God and binding our- selves by it. Thus St. Paul writes in his First Epistle to the Thessa- lonians: "For this too we give unceasing thanks to God, that when you received the word of God's message from us, you welcomed it, not as a human message, but, as it truly is, the message of God" (1 Thes 2:13).

Man must accept the revelation of God including all revealed truths with a sure, lively, and steadfast faith. He sins against faith who rejects God's revelation as a whole (unbelief), who excludes certain particular truths of revelation (heresy), who makes it appear to men that he does not believe (denial of faith), who doubts either of the whole of revelation or of parts of it (deliberate doubt).

Christian *hope* consists in our aiming for eternal life, in Jesus Christ, and through the power of His grace. Without faith this goal can neither be known nor reached. Christian hope causes us to seek the kingdom of God in our lives, faithfully and undaunted. He sins against Christian hope who forgets about God, who loses confidence in Him, who trusts presumptuously in His love or mistrusts Him.

Christian *love* consists in our making the love of God in Jesus Christ the foundation of our thought, our basic attitude, and the object of our actions. Christian love binds us to God and makes us like Him. He sins against Christian love who loves created things more than God Himself, who is ungrateful to God, who grumbles against God and hates Him.

The Life of the Individual. For one who lives by faith, hope, and love the all-important thing is no longer life in this world but life in God or, more exactly, life in Christ who leads us to the Father.

The Life of the Church. The condition of a man is determined by his possession of or lack of the three theological virtues, faith, hope, and love; and by the degree in which he possesses them if he does have them.

As a rule the inward condition of a person eludes the sight of man. There is one case, however, in which it is apparent even in this world how the three theological virtues are able to raise a man above himself and transform him. This is the case of the saint. In him faith is fully victorious, hope has taken over the leadership, and love of God and of men for God's sake has reached such a pitch that it can be seen outwardly.

Before the Church raises one of the departed to the dignity of the altar and sets him among the host of the saints, it examines above all if he possessed the three theological virtues in an extraordinary degree. If then it concedes him the dignity of being raised to the altar, it does so in order to present him as an example of these virtues for all the faithful to follow.

11. GOD, EXALTED ABOVE ALL THINGS. THE ADORATION OF GOD

MAN IS A CREATURE OF GOD. God is the Giver of his life. Man is therefore a being who has not taken existence from himself; nor has he made the world which surrounds him; and so it does not belong to him.

If a man wishes to see himself in a true light and have a proper self-respect he must recognize these facts for what they are. In other words, man must pay homage to God as Giver and Lord of life; He must pay Him the honor of adoration. As the First Commandment puts it: "You shall worship the Lord your God."

When adoration begins, man no longer questions or sets conditions: he can only surrender himself. The following passage from the prophet Isaiah describes an incident which shows how the spirit of adoration lays hold on the whole man:

> In the year king Ozia died, I saw the Lord seated on a high and lofty throne, with the train of his garment filling the temple. Seraphim were stationed above; each of them had six wings: with two they veiled their faces, with two they veiled their feet, and with two they hovered aloft.
>
> "Holy, holy, holy is the Lord of hosts!" they cried one to the other. "All the earth is filled with his glory!" At the sound of that cry, the frame of the door shook and the house was filled with smoke.
>
> Then I said, "Woe is me, I am doomed! For I am a man of unclean lips, living among a people of unclean lips; yet my eyes have seen the king, the Lord of hosts!" Then one of the seraphim flew to me, holding an ember which he had taken with tongs from the altar.
>
> He touched my mouth with it. "See," he said, "now that this has

touched your lips, your wickedness is removed, your sin purged."
Then I heard the voice of the Lord saying, "Whom shall I send?
Who will go for us?" "Here I am," I said; "send me!" (Is 6:1–8.)

Before the majesty of God the prophet felt himself to be as nothing,
felt himself to be impure and as one who dared not be seen. "Woe
is me," he cried out, but at the same time he made an interior
offering to God and was strongly drawn to God. To God's request
he replied, "Send me, Lord."

Man can sin against that adoration which he owes God in various
ways. He can worship false goods or intellectual ideas in a way which
is appropriate only to God; he can deny due reverence to God by
dishonoring sacred persons or objects, or by receiving the sacraments
unworthily, or by falling into the superstition of soothsaying and
magic in order to gain possession of powers which do not originate in
God. It is obviously also a sin against adoration to neglect prayer
and to absent oneself from Mass on Sundays and holy days without
just cause. Even under the Old Covenant God has obliged man to
worship Him on one particular day, as the Third Commandment
makes clear.

Man stands in a relation to God quite incomparable with his relation to any other being.

God is Lord, Creator, and Preserver of life. This relation has to be
recognized by man in a special act — in *adoration.*

The most sublime acts by which man can express his dependence on
God are *prayer and sacrifice.*

A man sins against adoration by:

1. Secretly resisting God's sovereignty; praying badly or not at all;
   not taking part in the sacrifice of the New Covenant
2. Practicing idolatry, superstition, soothsaying, and magic
3. Dishonoring sacred persons, places, or objects, or receiving a
   sacrament unworthily.

The Life of the Individual. As a creature of God, man is intrinsically designed to seek his Creator and to be subject to Him un-
conditionally. Thus it is the spirit of adoration which makes him
strong and at peace and forms the foundation of an invincible trust

in God. Conversely, the exclusion of a personal God and Creator from one's view of the universe brings with it disintegration of the man himself. If a man loses the spiritual center of his being, he is compelled to provide a new center for himself. And because there is no other God, the man falls into all manner of spiritual strife.

The Life of the Church.　Among the external expressions connected with adoration of God, we count especially genuflection, bowing the head, and folding hands at prayer. It is not the Church which introduced these gestures: they come rather from man's psychosomatic nature which always tends to make him express in external attitude what is within him. Holy Scripture describes how Jesus Himself at prayer — on the Mount of Olives for example — threw Himself down on the ground before the Father in heaven.

The extent to which the spirit of adoration is also the spirit of public worship can be seen by a glance at official liturgical books. In the missal the black print of the prayers is interrupted by annotations in red which tell the priest to the last detail what tone of voice he must use, what attitude he must adopt, and what actions he must perform. We look to the priest for an expression not of his personality, but rather of adoration. Those who see in these regulations of the Church only a fuss over trivialities are like people who complain of a work of art that it appears to be completely polished, down to the very last stroke of the brush.

Whenever it was a matter of making sacrifice, the ancient Romans, for example, became filled with a most unexpected scrupulosity. When a civic official made sacrifice in his official capacity, the attendant priest had to write out the prescribed prayers and then repeat them phrase by phrase for the person making the sacrifice. If the celebrant made a single mistake he had to begin all over again. It is no humiliation for man to bow down before One who is supremely great. It is only thus that he comes into union with Him.

12. KEEPING THE NAME OF GOD HALLOWED

A NAME AND A PERSON constitute a unity. Whoever utters a name with love and reverence is honoring the person himself: whoever uses a name flippantly or even in mockery is despising him. This is true of names used among men: it is even true of God and His holy name.

The man who has true reverence for God in His heart is essentially different from one who denies Him. In times of trial or testing this becomes manifest. The story of Job shows us this:

> Once again the sons of God came to present themselves before the Lord, and Satan also came with them. And the Lord said to Satan, "Whence do you come?" And Satan answered the Lord and said, "From roaming the earth and patrolling it." And the Lord said to Satan, "Have you noticed my servant Job, and that there is no one on earth like him, faultless and upright, fearing God and avoiding evil? He still holds fast to his innocence although you incited me against him to ruin him without cause." And Satan answered the Lord and said, "Skin for skin! All that a man has will he give for his life. But now put forth your hand and touch his bone and his flesh, and surely he will blaspheme you to your face." And the Lord said to Satan, "He is in your power; only spare his life." So Satan went forth from the presence of the Lord and smote Job with severe boils from the soles of his feet to the crown of his head. And he took a potsherd to scrape himself, as he sat among the ashes. Then his wife said to him, "Are you still holding to your innocence? Curse God and die." But he said to her, "Are even you going to speak as senseless women do? We accept good things from God; and should we not accept evil?" Through all this, Job said nothing sinful (Jb 2:1–10).

Job reverenced God, his wife did not.

It is a fact that Catholics use the name of God in reverence more than others do. That is a fine thing; but, sad to say, they also use it more frequently than others lightly and in anger. The bad habit of using the holy name flippantly or in anger (swearing) undermines reverence for God.

God's name is also used when a person promises on pain of sin to do something good (a vow). It is contrary to the reverence we owe to God to make vows on every possible occasion and then not to keep them, treating God like another human being whom we put off with specious promises. And so even in the Old Testament it is written:

> "When you make a vow to the Lord, your God, you shall not delay in fulfilling it; otherwise you will be held guilty, for the Lord, your God, is strict in requiring it of you. Should you refrain from making a vow, you will not be held guilty" (Dt 23:22–23).

Taking an oath, one solemnly calls God to witness that one is speaking the truth or will keep a particular promise.

The words of Jesus, "Let your speech be 'Yes' when you mean Yes, and 'No' when you mean No" (Mt 5:37), do not categorically forbid the taking of oaths. They are rather a setting of the ideal for the disciples that their word is as good as an oath.

When a high priest abjured Jesus in the name of God, i.e., with an oath, to say whether He were the Christ the Son of the living God, Jesus conceded to the demand, out of obedience. St. Matthew reports:

> Now, the chief priests — in fact, the Supreme Council as a body — were looking for false testimony, unfavorable to Jesus, in order to have him put to death; yet they did not find any although many false witnesses had come forward. Finally, however, two men advanced and said: "This man has said, 'I can destroy the sanctuary of God,' and, 'Within three days I can build it up again.'" Then the chief priest rose and said to him: "Have you nothing to say in your own defense? What about the evidence these men are furnishing against you?" But Jesus remained silent. The chief priest then said to him: "I adjure you by the living God to tell us outright, are you the Messias, the Son of God?" "I am, as you say," replied Jesus; "but I warn you: hereafter you will see the Son of

Man enthroned at the right hand of the Almighty and returning upon the clouds in the sky" (Mt 26:59–64).

Jesus Himself shows us that in case of necessity an oath is permissible. But the same incident also teaches what a shameful thing it is to use an oath to condemn an innocent man.

The majesty of God requires that man speak of Him with the reverence due to Him.

Man is obliged to honor God's name and keep it sacred.

The name of God is honored when it is uttered with reverence, when God is praised or thanked, when a legitimate oath is taken or a vow made.

The name of God is *dishonored* when it is uttered flippantly or in anger, when God or holy things are made fun of or blasphemed, when an oath is taken lightly or deceitfully or when a vow is broken. Whoever breaks a vow undermines his own trust in God.

The Life of the Individual.   Are we in the habit of using holy names flippantly or in anger? Are we given to swearing? Do we make an honest attempt to break ourselves of these bad habits? How can God's blessing rest upon the man who curses more than he prays? "Hallowed be Thy name," is what we say in the Our Father.

The Life of the Church.   In order to hallow God's name among men and to incite the faithful to keep it holy, the Church zealously furnishes her sanctuaries so that they appear to those who enter as special holy places.

The Church knows well enough that Mass can be celebrated in a cave or a cellar just as well as in the spaciousness of a cathedral. She knows that the word of God can be preached from the floor of a basement room just as well as from a high and splendid pulpit. But she knows too that a suitably furnished place attracts man's mind to what is holy and helps him to follow all sacred actions, the celebration of Mass, the preaching of the word of God, or the administration of the sacraments, with greater recollection and devotion.

13. GOD IN HUMAN CONVERSATION

IT IS APPROPRIATE for one with a living faith and healthy feelings to speak of God when occasion arises to the people with whom he shares the cares of life.

The tale of the disciples on the road to Emmaus makes wonderfully clear what happens every time like-minded men open their hearts to one another in the Lord. St. Luke relates:

> There was a new surprise, that same day, when two of their company were on the way to a village named Emmaus, sixty stadia from Jerusalem. Their whole conversation was about these recent events; and, while they were conversing and putting this and that together, who should draw near and join them on their journey but — Jesus! Their eyes, however, were prevented from recognizing him. "What is it," he said to them, "you are so earnestly discussing on your walk?" They stopped, and sadness clouded their faces. Then one of them, Cleopas, by name, spoke up.
>
> "Are you," he said to him, "the only visitor to Jerusalem that does not know what happened there these days?"
>
> "Well, what?" he replied.
>
> "Why," they said to him, "all about Jesus of Nazareth, who proved himself a prophet mighty in deed and word in the eyes of God and the mass of the people, and how the chief priests and our authorities delivered him up for capital punishment and finally had him crucified, although for our part we had hoped he might be the man destined to redeem Israel. But, in addition to all, this is the third day since these events took place! And furthermore: some women of our company, too, have upset us: they went to the tomb at dawn, and, when they did not find his body, came back saying they had actually seen a vision of angels who declared that he was alive! Then some of our company set out for the tomb and found the report of the women to be correct; but they did not see him in person!"
>
> "O how dull you are!" he then said to them; "How slow to understand when it comes to believing anything the prophets have said!

306

Was it not necessary that the Messias should undergo these sufferings and thus enter into his glory?" And now, beginning with Moses and going right through the prophets, he interpreted to them whatever is said about himself anywhere in the Scriptures.

Meanwhile, they had come near the village for which they were bound, and when he gave the impression of intending to go on, they used gentle force to dissuade him. "Please, be our guest," they said; "the day is fast declining, and it is close to evening." So he went in to be their guest. And this is what happened when he had reclined at table in their company: he took the bread into his hands and, after saying grace, broke it into portions, which he gave to them. At last their eyes were opened, and they recognized him; but he vanished from their sight.

"Were not our inmost hearts on fire," they said to each other, "as he spoke to us by the way, explaining to us the Scriptures?" (Lk 24:13–32.)

Jesus' saying, "Where two or three are assembled in my name, there I am in the midst of them" (Mt 18:20), does not apply only to actual prayer, but also to conversations in which men express themselves to one another in faith. Whenever this occurs, a special blessing is always present.

What a loss in depth it is when a man and wife, for example, although their faith does mean something to them, never say a word to one another concerning the faith in their hearts, either in times of good fortune or in times of trouble. What an irreparable loss it is when father and mother fail to tell their children about God in simple language, during those years when the burden of this falls on them alone. It is in these very years that the mind of the child is formed decisively. It is equally regrettable when people who share the same religious faith react to bereavement in the same way as do unbelievers.

The decline of religious conversation in a nation is like the wilting of grass in a drought.

One does not readily talk about a person one loves with people who hate him. A Christian should avoid, therefore, talking about religion and religious topics in a gossipy, unguarded, or argumentative way with those who are not religious or are antagonistic to religion. Following this rule, one should refrain from speaking about God and matters of faith with men whose minds are antipathetic. In particular, in their presence one should not mention or complain about real or alleged defects of the Church, be they faults of particular individuals or priests, or defects of a more general sort. This does not mean that one should not honestly face human errors in the Church, but prudence is necessary.

In the Sermon on the Mount, Jesus expressly warned us against such levity and lack of circumspection.

How often it has happened that remarks of this sort, quite innocently meant, have been used as weapons against the Faith.

One never makes what one loves the subject of jokes or puts it to ridicule in any way.

According to the same rule, a man whose faith is not a mere outward form guards in all circumstances against making anything religious appear ridiculous by his conversation. He must be careful, too, about what he says about the beliefs of those of a different religion. Whoever puts what is high and holy to ridicule shakes the foundations of human society.

One does not allow others to make fun of what one loves. Whenever somebody speaks deprecatingly of God or of sacred matters one should react in such a way that the speaker can see that he is displeasing one person anyway. A chilly ignoring is often the best rebuff.

Preserving the honor of God's name includes giving religious conversation its due place in daily life.

Religious conversations within the family and among friends are an essential part of religious life. As far as men in general are concerned, religious conversation carried out with *good taste* and *in love* is part of the exercise of the lay apostolate. We should never let it happen that we make fun of sacred matters or fail to show our displeasure when others do.

The Life of the Individual. In early childhood the foundations of man's relationship to religion are laid, in maturity a decision is made about the inner attitude to faith, and in the prime of life a comprehensive outlook on all things is formed. A young man must therefore see living religion around him; and so a grave responsibility is laid upon adult Christians. All must ask themselves this question: Do I show the young by my personal attitude day by day that I do believe in God, and turn to Him in all things?

The Life of the Church. In the life of a believing community faith should embrace everyday life and produce its own appropriate forms of life. With this in mind St. Paul wrote during the first generation after Christ's death, "Whenever, then, you eat or drink, or do anything else, do everything for God's glory" (1 Cor 10:31). As early as that he even devised new formulas of greeting from this general rule and used them to introduce every letter with the wish that the readers would share in the grace and peace of God.

14. KEEPING THE LORD'S DAY HOLY

GOD IS THE LORD OF TIME. Man can acknowledge this by setting aside a special portion of time as some kind of sacrifice to God.

For Jesus, the Sabbath was the day when men rested from work so that God could converse with them. For this reason He worked miracles especially on the Sabbath in order to prepare their hearts for the manifestations of God's grace. Jesus exhibited this conception of hallowing the Sabbath in opposition to the Pharisees who accused Him of desecrating the Sabbath by His miracle-working.

After healing the sick man at the pool of Bethsaida Jesus spoke of the mysterious activity of God which had not come to an end with the creation of the first man and of the world, but had only begun then.

St. John tells us:

> Some time later there was a feast of the Jews, and Jesus went up to Jerusalem. There is a pool near the Sheepgate in Jerusalem which in Aramaic is called Bethesda. It has five porticoes. In these a number of bedridden invalids — blind, crippled, haggard people — were always awaiting the motion of the water; for an angel of the Lord would descend into the pool from time to time and stir the water; and the first invalid then to go in after the stirring of the water would get well, no matter with what disease he was afflicted.
>
> There was a man there who had been an invalid for thirty-eight years. When Jesus caught sight of him lying on his mat, and learned of his long-standing affliction, he said to him: "Would you like to get well?" "Why, sir," replied the invalid, "I have nobody to put me into the pool the moment the water is stirred up, and by the time I get there, someone else has gone down ahead of me." Jesus then said to him: "Stand up; take your mat and walk." Immediately the man got well, took up his mat, and walked.

For this reason the Jews persecuted Jesus, namely, that he did things like this on the Sabbath. But Jesus answered their charge. "My Father," he said, "has been working to this hour; and so I, too, am working." The result was that the Jews were all the more eager to kill him, not only because he broke the Sabbath, but also because he spoke of God as his own Father, thereby claiming equality with God.

Jesus, therefore, resumed the argument and said to them. "I tell you the plain truth: the Son can do nothing on his own initiative; he can only do what he sees the Father do. Yes, what he is doing — that, and nothing else, the Son does likewise. The Father dearly loves the Son, and lets him see everything he himself is doing; in fact, he will let him see even greater exercises of power than the ones you witnessed, so that you will be astonished. For example, just as the Father raises the dead and gives them life, so, too, does the Son give life to anyone he chooses. Nor, again, does the Father judge anyone; no, the right to judge he has turned over wholly to the Son. All men are to honor the Son just as they honor the Father. He who does not honor the Son does not honor the Father, whose ambassador he is.

"Yes, I tell you frankly: he who heeds my message and believes him whose ambassador I am, is in possession of eternal life, and is not liable to judgment. On the contrary, he has once for all passed out of the realm of death into that of life" (Jn 4:1–9, 16–24).

These words answer the question about the meaning of Sunday. It is a day when man appears before God and when God reveals Himself and imparts Himself to man as the Father, the Son, and the Holy Spirit.

Being the first day of the week, Sunday reminds us of that moment when God first said, "Let there be"; as the day of the Resurrection it reminds us of the completion of the work of redemption through Jesus Christ; as the day when the Holy Spirit descended it reminds us of the day when the Church began its independent life in the world. Hence Sunday is the day of God's Covenant with men, the day when the Covenant is renewed, which the children of God keep holy, the day when God comes down to men.

Because this is the day when the people of God give honor to God it is indeed the "day of the Lord Jesus Christ" and of His mediatorship. The celebration of Mass is the climax of the day on which Jesus represents His people before the Father and makes their prayers His own.

And because it does unite men before God, Sunday is also the day of the love of men for one another, a day of love within the family, within the neighborhood and the congregation. Holy Scripture describes it as a day of love, St. Paul appointing it as the day when collections should be taken for the distressed brethren.

The hallowing of Sunday is the foundation of Christian life.

Sunday is *hallowed* by resting from servile works, assisting at Mass, hearing the word of God, and taking seemly recreation. Sunday should be a day of reflection upon the past and of prospect into the future, in the presence of God.

We sin against the sanctity of Sunday by:

1. Absenting ourselves by our own fault from Mass
2. Working when not in great need or making our subordinates work
3. Desecrating the Lord's day by dangerous or evil entertainment.

Servile work is permitted on Sunday when demanded by real necessity or when permitted by ecclesiastical authority because of generally applicable reasons.

Desecration of Sunday undoubtedly leads a man sooner or later to forget about God and his own spiritual life.

The Life of the Individual. That modern life makes it impossible for men to keep Sunday holy is a prejudice which fools many. Life in Ireland and in Canada is not so very different in essentials from life in other civilized lands. In Ireland and Canada 90 percent of the men attend Sunday worship. The way a Christian keeps Sunday shows what his faith is like.

What part does Sunday play in our life? Is it the day of the spirit? Do we assist at Mass? Do we make use of a prayer book suitable to our age and requirements? Do we use Sunday as a day to avoid the danger of indulging in immoderate bodily recreation at the expense of strengthening ourselves for the battle of life?

The Life of the Church. Sunday is a fresh creation of the spirit of Christianity. As such it became known among the early Christians as "the day of the Lord." By "Lord" is meant Christ. In this connection the faithful were thinking first and foremost of the Resurrection of Christ by which He sealed His work of redemption and manifested Himself as Lord of life and Victor over death.

The manner in which Sunday as the day of the Lord, the day of Christ, supplanted the Jewish Sabbath is a good example of living development. Only Jewish Christians could feel obliged to keep the Sabbath. Gentile Christians were under no obligation to the Sabbath. The Gentile Christians from the beginning felt much more inclined to gather for worship on that day upon which Christ rose from the dead and sealed the work of redemption by His Resurrection, and upon which, after the Ascension, He sent down the Holy Spirit.

As the number of Gentile Christians increased the celebration of the Jewish Sabbath disappeared in the congregations and was replaced by the celebration of Sunday. The first reference we know to the celebration of Sunday is in the Epistle to the Corinthians, written about twenty years after Christ's death, when St. Paul says that the offering for the congregation in Jerusalem is to be taken up on that day. In the Acts of the Apostles a particular Sunday service is mentioned when they were met together for the breaking of bread (at Troas) and when St. Paul gave a farewell address. On this occasion St. Paul's sermon dragged on until nearly midnight when a youth named Eutychus who was sitting on a window seat fell asleep and crashed down from the third story. St. Paul went down to him, threw himself upon him, and embraced him saying, "Do not be alarmed; life is still in him." Then he went up again to the third story and after the breaking of bread remained with the faithful until it was almost dawn (cf. Acts 20:7–12).

In the *Didache,* the first prayer book, which belongs to the year A.D. 100 or thereby — the time of St. John's death — we find this direction, "Assemble on the Lord's day, break bread and give thanks after having confessed your sins so that your sacrifice may be pure."

15. HEARING THE WORD OF GOD: A DUTY FOR ALL THE FAITHFUL

THE CHURCH lays an explicit obligation upon all the faithful to assist at Mass on Sundays and holy days of obligation. And the Fathers of the Second Vatican Council decreed that a homily, or sermon, be an integral part of Mass on Sundays and holy days of obligation.

The celebration of Mass can be compared with no other part of Christian worship. In Mass, Christ Himself acts as the glorified high priest. In Mass, the sacrifice of the cross, by which all graces were won for men, is made present sacramentally. Those present receive the graces which they need specially in their particular state of life. The Mass is thus an act of Christ Himself.

The preaching of the word of God is now an essential part of Sunday Mass. Jesus said: "He who listens to you listens to me and he who despises you despises me; but whoever despises me despises him whose ambassador I am" (Lk 10:16). The word of God is preached by the priest by Christ's commission.

This commission to preach the word of God to the faithful corresponds to a duty on the part of the faithful to listen to it. What must each believer do to fulfill this obligation? Under pain of grave sin, he is bound to acquire such knowledge of religion as is appropriate to his standard of education and his station in life.

With greater education and the raising of living conditions the obligation to acquire an appropriate degree of religious knowledge becomes more serious. A peasant in a lonely village can get along with a more restricted religious knowledge than one who works in a job where he meets many people with different philosophies of life; and a scholar who is well versed in the intricacies of scientific knowledge, to gain a proper balance, will have to acquire much more religious knowledge than an artisan.

In these circumstances the Church therefore demands that every man hear the word of God. She does not prescribe the place to which each must go or the priest he must hear. For most men, their condition in life dictates that it is sufficient if they listen to the sermon included in Sunday Mass and on holy days of obligation.

Once again he set himself to teach by the seaside; and so great was the concourse of people that he went into a boat and sat down, off the shore, while the whole throng was on land, by the water's edge. And he taught them many lessons in parable style. For instance, he said to them in the course of his teaching: "Listen! Look, the sower goes out to sow. As he sows, it happens that some of the seed falls close to the footpath; and the birds come and eat it up. Other seed falls on the stony ground, where it does not have deep soil and, because it has no soil of any depth, shoots up at once; but by the time the sun has climbed the heavens, it is scorched and, because it cannot strike root, withers away. Other seed, again, falls among the thorns; and the thorns come up and utterly choke it; and it produces no fruit. Still other seed falls on the right kind of soil; and this at last produces fruit, because it sprouts and keeps on growing; and it bears fruit thirty-, sixty-, or a hundredfold." He then added: "Let everyone heed what he has heard."

When he was alone, those around him, including the Twelve, asked him for an explanation of the parables. He said to them: "You are privileged to know the mystery of the kingdom of God; but to those outside your group all instruction is given in parable style so that as a result

'for all their looking they do not see,
and for all their hearing they do not understand;
and so they are not converted and forgiven.'"

He then said to them: "If you do not know the meaning of this parable, how, then, will you understand the parables in general? The 'sower' is he who sows the message; the words 'close to the footpath' describe those in whom the message is sown; but, as soon as they hear it, Satan comes and steals the message in them. In like manner, the ones described by the words 'sown in the stony places' are such as receive the message with joy as soon as they hear it; but they do not let it strike root in them; on the contrary, they are timeservers and, when distress or persecution comes, are at once upset. The words 'sown among the thorns' describe another class; they are such as hear the message, but then the cares of this world and the deceitful attractions of wealth and the other allurements to passion creep in and utterly choke the message; and it

turns out barren. Finally, those described by the words 'sown in
the right kind of soil' are those who warmly welcome the message
they hear, and bear fruit thirty-, sixty-, or a hundredfold" (Mk
4:1–20).

Every artisan must have technical knowledge: every Catholic must
have knowledge of his religion.

Every one of the faithful is bound to reach a standard of instruction
in the Catholic Faith comparable with his general education.

Most people will be able to do this by attending to the sermons
accompanying the Sunday services. It is true of all sermons that
none is so good as to be of any use to a man lacking goodwill,
and seldom is one so bad that a man of goodwill cannot gain
something from it.

The Life of the Individual. The following statement was made by
Volta, the discoverer of electric current and inventor of the apparatus
for measuring electrical potential; and every educated Catholic ought
to be able to apply it to himself.

I am forever indebted to God for having given me a faith, in
which I firmly intend to live and to die, securely hoping to share
eternal life by its means. Although I regard faith as a supernatural
gift of God, I have never neglected the human means of confirming
myself in faith and of removing all doubts which have emerged
and which could have confused me.

The Life of the Church. Cardinal Newman once made an observation which is equally important for both preacher and hearers. He
said that religious instruction should be couched in language which
the whole congregation can understand. The more educated among
them ought to listen to simple instruction in all humility. We are all
members of the same Church.

If you find that the sermons of many priests leave much to be
desired, then pray for the priests. St. Paul laid great store by the
prayers of the faithful and fervently requested them: "Pray . . .
particularly for me that I may be given words to speak with bold
confidence and to make known the mystery of the gospel" (Eph 6:19).

Retreats provide a notable stimulus to instruction and the devout
life, and through these many today will find it possible to gain

spiritual disentanglement from the harassing pressures and impulses of everyday life and so become recollected. The crucial thing is that the faithful should be led by spiritual exercises to a more fervent participation in the liturgy and to an increased desire to receive the sacraments. This kind of spiritual exercise is of great use — is indeed almost a necessity today — in implanting the spirit of true piety in the heart and leading men to a holy life.

16. THE LAW OF GOD AND THE FAMILY

IN THE BIBLICAL STORY of creation, God reveals in a few sentences why He created man. We read:

"God created man in his image. In the image of God he created him. Male and female he created them. Then God blessed them and said to them, 'Be fruitful and multiply; fill the earth and subdue it'" (Gn 1:27–28).

These words point basically not to marriage as the lifelong partnership of man and wife — conjugality — but to marriage as a foundation of the family — parenthood. "Be fruitful and multiply" means nothing other than "found families."

From God, father and mother receive the office of representing God to their children. Under the New Covenant this commission is part of the sacrament of Matrimony. This sacrament obliges the bridegroom and bride, who are members of Christ by Baptism, to make their children the children of God. At the same time Christ promises to give them the special help they need to fulfill all of the duties which this task imposes.

In the Scriptures of both the Old and the New Covenant there are references to the law of God according to which father and mother constitute a society along with their children, so that the children as well as the parents have their respective duties:

> Observe, my son, your father's bidding,
> and reject not your mother's teaching;
> Keep them fastened over your heart always,
> put them around your neck;

318

For the bidding is a lamp, and the teaching a light,
and a way to life are the reproofs of discipline.

(Prv 6:20–23)

For a father's blessing gives a family firm roots, but a mother's curse uproots the growing plant.

Glory not in your father's shame, for his shame is no glory to you! His father's honor is a man's glory; disgrace for her children, a mother's shame. My son, take care of your father when he is old; grieve him not as long as he lives. Even if his mind fail, be considerate with him; revile him not in the fullness of your strength. For kindness to a father will not be forgotten, it will serve as a sin-offering — it will take lasting root. In time of tribulation it will be recalled to your advantage, like warmth upon frost it will melt away your sins. A blasphemer is he who despises his father; accursed of his Creator, he who angers his mother.

My son, conduct your affairs with humility, and you will be loved more than a giver of gifts (Sir 3:9–17).

Year after year his parents went to Jerusalem for the feast of the Passover. And so, too, when he was twelve years old, they went up according to their custom at the time of the feast. After spending there the required number of days, they prepared to return, but the child Jesus remained behind at Jerusalem, without his parents knowing it. Supposing him to be in the caravan, they finished a day's journey, and began to search for him among their relations and acquaintances. When they did not find him, they retraced their steps to Jerusalem, there to renew their search for him. It was only on the third day that they discovered him in the temple, seated among the rabbis, now listening to them, now asking them questions, while all those that heard him were charmed by his intelligence and answers. They were overjoyed to see him.

His mother said to him: "Child, why did you behave toward us in this way? Oh, our hearts were heavy — your father's and mine — as we searched for you!"

He said to them: "Why did you search for me? I had to answer my Father's call, and did you not know it?" But they did not grasp the meaning of the reply he made to them (Lk 2:41–50).

To Mary's question why He had waited behind in the temple, He answered that for Him His Father's will was supreme. Even today there are cases where children have to obey the will of God in opposition to their parents, holding to the word of Scripture: "Peter and the apostles answered, 'One must obey God rather than men' " (Acts 5:29).

The Fourth Commandment is founded upon ties of blood and so in a sense is easier to keep than the others. On the other hand, unfortunately, parents and children, for the same reason, do not shrink from disobeying it. Outward conditions of life today contribute more than formerly to the dissolution of the ties between parents and children. Children begin to earn early; and often receive almost as much as their fathers. Very seldom, however, do they work at home with their own father as their employer; but this does not mean that the consequences of disobeying this commandment fail to arise. Wherever this commandment loses its force, the family disrupts, and where many families disrupt, society too begins to disintegrate.

When society had its foundations in peasant communities the honoring of the Fourth Commandment, as already hinted, was encouraged to some extent by economic considerations. These times are past. Today it is only by the power of religion that the Fourth Commandment can be validated as a means of blessing for parents and children.

The Fourth Commandment is the foundation of Christian family life. The following things govern the relationship between parents and children:

As the representatives of God, *children* must show love, honor, and obedience to their parents; and the *parents,* as God's representatives, must care for the temporal and eternal good of their children.

In *receiving the sacrament of Matrimony,* Christian parents accept the *duty* of educating their children in Christian life by word and example. By this sacrament they also receive special help to discharge this duty.

Children sin against the Fourth Commandment when they fail to love and honor their parents and disobey them.

Parents sin against the Fourth Commandment when they are careless about the temporal and spiritual welfare of their children, fail to correct their faults, and set them a bad example. They sin especially if they do not fulfill their duty of providing religious education.

In educating their children parents must take care that the education is suited to age. Little children must be made to obey as children, sons and daughters of riper years must be educated in the right use of freedom and should be told the reason for their parents' orders and views. Adult sons and daughters should be treated as companions, bound to their parents in weal and woe.

Sons and daughters who are adults should remember that there is a special blessing attached to the Fourth Commandment, and that they will receive temporal blessings and heavenly grace more than ever from God if they bear patiently with the faults of their parents. At the same time they must always bear in mind that in all circumstances their parents are in advance of them in one thing — experience of life.

If parents command something sinful, the words of Scripture apply: "One must obey God rather than men" (Acts 5:29).

The Life of the Individual. What is your relationship with your parents and superiors? How do you treat them? Do you always wait until expressly ordered before doing anything? Do you try to pass the tasks given you on to others? Are you indifferent to their troubles? Do you intend to reward your parents in their old age for what they have done for you? Do you make fun of old people? Do you honor pastors and teachers or do you aid and abet those who ridicule those in positions of authority?

What is your relationship to your children? If you want to maintain your influence over your children in later years you must be as much with them in their preschool years as your occupation allows.

Do you let your children see that it is a pleasure to you to have them? Children need signs of affection just as plants need the sun.

Never punish in anger. All children feel that as an injustice. Beating in education often produces the most fatal effects of all with those children who appear to accept it with greatest patience.

It is natural that in school and in classes of religious education the duties of children toward parents are emphasized. For most of the faithful, however, after leaving school there comes no supplementary instruction which stresses parental duties. Many parents are thus unaware that their duties toward their children are much more serious and difficult than those of the children toward them. What could be more rigorous than the commission to represent God to one's children!

The Life of the Church.   As in early times, the Church today sees in the keeping of the Fourth Commandment the foundation of successful education of youth, of contentment in home life and of the solution of the social problem. By stressing these principles constantly she does not thereby detract from the value of the measures taken by the state and the public for the welfare of the family: on the contrary she intends by this to direct the attention of all in responsibility first and foremost to the family, the ultimate cell of human society, in all their management of moral, social, and economic problems. The fortune and well-being of any state depends above all upon the ratio of happy families to broken families. No healthy life can emerge from sick cells. As the proverb has it: "The hand that rocks the cradle rules the world."

17. THE LAW OF GOD AND THE STATE

NATURE COMPELS MEN to associate in larger community groups in order to unfold their capacities fully.

1. The Law of God and the Individual State

Ideally, every state should be illumined with a heavenly radiance. Whenever called upon to do so, it should be quick to advance the well-being of the subject and to protect his spiritual and temporal goods. The citizens should be taught by it how to treat one another. St. Thomas says therefore: "Because human sovereignty originates in the divine it is obliged to imitate it."

There are many sayings in both the Old Testament and the New which refer to the law of God regarding the structure of the state. The duty of rulers:

A wise magistrate lends stability to his people, and the government of a prudent man is well ordered. As the people's judge, so are his ministers; as the head of a city, its inhabitants. A wanton king destroys his people, but a city grows through the wisdom of its princes (Sir 10:1–3).

I have seen under the sun another evil, like a mistake that proceeds from the ruler: a fool put in lofty position while the rich sit in lowly places. I have seen slaves on horseback, while princes walked on the ground like slaves (Eccl 10:5–7).

The following words of St. Paul refer to the duties of the citizen:

Let everyone submit himself to the ruling authorities, for there exists no authority not ordained by God. And that which exists has been constituted by God. Therefore he who opposes such authority resists the ordinance of God, and they that resist bring condemnation on themselves. Rulers are not a source of fear in regard to good actions, but only in regard to evil ones. You wish, then, not to fear the authority? Do what is good and you will have praise from him. For he is God's minister for your benefit. But if you do evil, fear, for not without reason does he wear the sword. He is God's minister, an avenger to inflict punishment on evildoers. Accordingly we must needs submit, not only out of fear of punishment, but also for conscience' sake. This is why you pay tribute, for they are public ministers of God, devoting their energies to this very thing. Render to all men their due: tribute to whom tribute is due; taxes to whom taxes are due; respect to whom respect is due; honor to whom honor is due (Rom 13:1–7).

Christ not only gave us an example of how we must keep the Fourth Commandment by honoring father and mother: He took up His public ministry as a commission to the people of Israel to whom He belonged. When it became evident that the people rejected His ministrations, He shed bitter tears for them. Scripture tells us:

> When at last he came near enough to have a view of the city,
> he sobbed out his grief over it, saying:
> "O if you, too, did know,
> at least on this your day,
> what makes for peace!
> But alas, it is hidden from your eyes!
> Days are coming upon you
> when your enemies
> will throw a rampart round you,
> and encircle you,
> and press hard upon your every side;
> and they will dash to the ground
> both you and your children within,
> nor will they leave stone upon stone
> within your walls;
> because you did not recognize
> the time of your visitation" (Lk 19:41–44).

Never at any moment, however, when the people showed themselves antipathetic did Jesus once entertain the thought that He should be unfaithful to the commission of His Father in order to curry favor with the people.

Jesus became in this way a model of how a man ought to love his country but must never break faith with God for its sake.

It is the duty of *those who rule* to protect citizens from injury and to preserve their just freedom. They must also represent the whole people and not partisan interests which arise within society; and yet this does not mean that they represent the sum total of individuals, but rather the people in their communal structure. In *Peace on Earth* Pope John XXIII had the following to say about public authority and the common good: "It is agreed in our time that the common good is chiefly guaranteed when personal rights and duties are maintained. The chief concern of civil authorities must therefore be to ensure that these rights are acknowledged, respected, coordinated with other rights, defended, and promoted, so that in this way each one may more easily carry out his duties. For to safeguard the inviolable rights of the human person and to facilitate the fulfillment of his duties should be the essential office of every public authority."

In every undertaking, therefore, the government must bear in mind the common good. For this reason states are bound to respect and to maintain men's natural rights and to apportion burdens and duties justly. In certain matters, questions of education and laws governing marriage, for example, they must achieve their end in cooperation with parents and with the Church, who have an interest in both of these things.

If rulers, ministers, or party leaders look more to their own advantage than to the common good, that is an abuse of delegated power.

The common good can also be damaged from the side of the citizens. This happens when they do not make conscientious use of their rights.

It is the duty of citizens to elect as representatives of the people only such as are fitted by capabilities and character to look after those things which are entrusted to the guardianship of the state. Because religion represents the highest value of all, Catholics will vote for those who know how to defend this value. The duty to vote arises from the fact that the fate of a land depends upon this.

Pope Pius XII alludes to these contingencies in an address delivered in 1948:

> The centre of gravity of a properly constructed democracy lies in the people's representation. For this political stream issues into all areas of the public life, for good or for ill. Therefore, the moral stature, the practical vision, and the mental capacities of the elected

representatives in parliament, is a question which bears very closely upon the life and death, the prosperity or decline, the ascent or the inevitable collapse of any people ruled by a democrary.

The exercise of the *franchise* is an act of great moral responsibility. This is so especially when it is concerned with electing those who are to control legislation governing, for example, the observance of holy days, marriage, the family, education and generally obligatory measures for the solution of the social problem. The Church therefore has the right to instruct the faithful in the moral duties which arise from the right to vote.

Everyone has to vote according to the judgment of his own conscience. It comes about automatically, therefore, that every Catholic will be urged by the voice of his own conscience to vote for that candidate or that party which offers a real and thorough guarantee that the rights of God and of the soul, the true welfare of the individual, the family, the community will be protected in accordance with the law of God and Christian moral teaching.

Under contemporary circumstances a serious obligation to vote is laid upon every franchised man and woman. If anyone abstains out of laziness or cowardice, he commits a mortal sin.

The extent to which a person is responsible in casting his vote depends upon his degree of understanding.

Because there will always be evil in the world, there can never be a state without imperfections. It is therefore against Christian ideals and notions to withdraw from public life, pleading this lamentable fact in excuse.

2. God's Law and the Mutual Relationships of Peoples and States

In these days the responsibility both of individual citizens and government toward the citizens and governments of other countries is becoming of increasing importance.

Technical advance has produced a situation where questions of politics, economics, social welfare, and intellectual life can now be solved only through widely extended cooperation which a hundred years ago was not only unnecessary, but impossible.

The press and commerce bring ordinary people directly in touch with one another far more thari formerly. It is much more likely nowadays for people of different countries to meet one another than it was formerly for people in different parts of the same land to meet.

This gives rise to new responsibilities within civic life for rulers and people, responsibilities relating to international life.

The duty of striving for peaceful coexistence of nations within a world community lies specially upon governments and those in power, upon the members of the various parliaments, on the directors of press and broadcasting, and most of all upon those who represent one state to another. All their efforts will be seriously endangered or brought to nothing if individual men do not remain aware of the fact that membership of a particular nation never dispenses from the duty toward our fellowmen which nature itself demands of us.

Pope John XXIII, in his magnificent encyclical *Peace on Earth,* spoke of the obligation of international harmony and justice among nations in these terms:

> We must remember that, of its very nature, civil authority exists, not to confine its people within the boundaries of their nation, but rather to protect, above all else, the common good of that particular civil society, which certainly cannot be divorced from the common good of the entire human family. . . . It is obvious that individual countries cannot rightly seek their own interests and develop themselves in isolation from the rest, for the prosperity and development of one country follows partly in the train of the prosperity and progress of all the rest and partly produces that prosperity and progress.

The following rules govern the relationship between secular rulers and citizens:

The Fourth Commandment prescribes that a Christian respect the government, submit to the laws, and fulfill his civic duties conscientiously. The citizen's most important duties are: to pay taxes, to vote, and to defend his native land against unjust attack.

The fulfillment of these obligations is not affected by the type of state. In his encyclical on the origin of the authority of the state Leo XIII expressly stated that the Church recognizes all types of state which further the common good and respect the personal rights of man.

Both government and subjects are obliged to consider the common good. The common good suffers damage if government or representatives of the people set individual or party advantage above the well-being of all. The same happens if citizens by their apathy or neglect of duty allow individuals or groups to gain undue influence. The common good will be utterly submerged if basic human rights are set aside.

Concerning the coexistence of peoples and states, the rulers and the citizens of the separate states must always remember that all men are one large family. Nations must have mutual respect and must try to understand each other's peculiarities.

The words of the prophet Malachy in the Old Testament are much more applicable under the New Covenant: "Have we not all the one Father? Has not the one God created us? Why then do we break faith with each other, violating the covenant of our fathers?" (Mal 2:10).

The Life of the Individual. The Roman orator Cicero expounded the duties of rulers and representatives of the people in this way: "First of all, they must keep in mind the good of the citizens in such a way that in all their activities they consider only this and forget their own interests; second, they must remain faithful to the totality of common interests; they may not, by paying heed to one section, fail toward the rest.

"Whoever represents only some of the citizens and does not bother about the rest introduces something pernicious into society, the spirit of unrest and schism."

George Washington, first president of the United States, wrote these words to the governors in his circular letter of 1783: "I now make it my earnest prayer, that God would have you, and the State over which you preside, in his holy protection; that he would incline the hearts of the citizens to cultivate a spirit of subordination and obedience to government . . . and finally, that he would most graciously be pleased to dispose us all to do justice, to love mercy, and to demean ourselves with that charity, humility, and pacific temper of mind, which were the characteristics of the Divine Author of our blessed religion, and without an humble imitation of whose example in these things, we can never hope to be a happy nation."

Do you try, as much as your avocation demands, to get to know your native land, its institutions and traditions? Without some grasp of a country's history it is impossible to understand its present condition properly and to find remedies for its besetting difficulties confronting the common good.

Have you acquired the bad habit of accepting as absolute truth everything you hear said at your work or in the street concerning the general defects or particular unpleasant occurrences in public life, and of repeating these things concerning prominent people in company, without seriously inquiring if these assertions are true and if you know enough about the circumstances to form a judgment?

Do you pray for your rulers? St. Paul insists upon this, although he himself was persecuted and repeatedly arrested. If people would only devote a fraction of the time they spend in complaining and talking about the government to praying for it, much would be accomplished.

Are you aware that the community is affected for good or ill by voting, and that all who refrain from voting withhold the contribution which is theirs to make to the community for weal or woe?

The Life of the Church. Since Leo XIII the popes have spoken out on the principles of a Christian world order in a series of encyclicals.

On the relation of the state to the Church Leo XIII says: "The same men who are subjects of the state are also members of the Church, but not all members of the state are members of the Church as well. The ideal relationship between Church and State consists in their mutual recognition of each other's special objectives and spheres of power, and in their co-operating in certain questions such as legislation concerning marriage, protection of the family, welfare, social institutions, and public morality." The same Pope referred also to the duty of the faithful to make conscientious use of their political powers.

Pius XI calls to mind that apathy among citizens becomes all the more portentious the more rights they have. "That state fares best," he says, "whose citizens have the clearest consciences."

Of love of one's own country Pius XI says: "For, though love of country and race, guided by Christian law, becomes a spur to many deeds of virtue and of heroism, it may also become the seed of widespread injustice and iniquity when, transgressing the bonds of right justice, it develops into immoderate nationalism. Those who are carried away by such considerations assuredly forget, not only that all the peoples, as parts of the universal human family, are joined together as brothers among themselves, and that other nations too have the right to live and prosper, but also that it is never lawful or expedient to separate what is useful from what is right. Advantages gained for the family, State or public power to the detriment of others may seem great and magnificent achievements, but St. Augustine wisely shows that they are not lasting and always carry with them fear of disaster: they are a bright joy as brittle as glass accompanied by the haunting fear of a sudden break."

In his Christmas address in 1942 Pope Pius XII enumerated a list of objectives which *Christian citizens could and ought to strive for, each according to his position and personal capacities.* He says: "He who would have the star of peace to shine permanently over society must do all in his power to restore to the human person the dignity which God conferred upon him from the beginning; he must resist the excessive herding together of human beings, as though they were a soulless mass.

"He must foster the observance and practical implementing of the following fundamental rights of the person: the right to maintain and develop physical, intellectual, and moral life, and in particular the right to a religious training and education; the right to worship God, both in private and in public, including the right to engage in religious works of charity; the right, in principle, to marriage and to the attainment of the purpose of marriage, the right to wedded society and to home life; the right to work as an indispensable means for the maintenance of family life; the right to a free choice of a state of life, and therefore of the priestly and religious state; the right to a use of material goods, subject to its duties and to its special limitations."

Looking back on the past we are compelled to say that with modern means of communication, the difficulties in the way of establishing a world order and creating world justice are, from the technical point of view, considerably less than those obtaining at the time of the creation of Roman law which embraced a host of national laws and related them to the universally applicable law under the following conditions: "All peoples which have laws and customs follow in part their own law and in part that which is common to all peoples; that is to say, whatever each nation has formulated for itself as law will be known as the civil law of this state; but what has been formulated for all men by natural reason will be observed in exactly the same way by all peoples and, as a law of the people, will be known as a law which all follow."

Finally, the late Pope John XXIII, writing in *Peace on Earth,* had this to say: "Any human society, if it is to be well ordered and productive, must lay down as a foundation this principle, namely, that every human being is a person, that is, his nature is endowed with intelligence and free will. Indeed, precisely because he is a person he has rights and obligations flowing directly and simultaneously from his very nature. And as these rights and obligations are universal and inviolable they cannot in any way be surrendered. . . . Every man has the right to life, to bodily integrity, and to the means which are necessary and suitable for the proper development of life; these are primarily food, clothing, shelter, rest, medical care, and finally the necessary social services. Therefore a human being has also the right to security in cases of sickness, inability to work, widowhood, old age, unemployment, or in any other case in which he is deprived of the means of subsistence through no fault of his own. The natural law also gives man the right to share in the benefits of culture, and therefore the right to a basic education and to technical and professional training in keeping with the stage of educational development in the country to which he belongs."

18. THE LAW OF GOD AND THE CHURCH

THE CHURCH WAS FOUNDED by Jesus Christ the God-man; within it He continues His life and work. As an independent society with its own purposes it has authority within its own sphere to command, to judge, and to punish. Thus the Lord said to St. Peter: "Whatever you bind on earth will be bound in heaven" (Mt 16:19).

The leaders of the Church and the faithful are dependent on each other. St. Paul exhorts:

> Obey your superiors and be subject to them, since they keep watch over your souls, mindful that they will have to render account. It will be to your advantage if they can do this joyfully, and not with deep sighs (Heb 13:17).

As the incarnate Son of God, Jesus was independent of all secular or spiritual authority; but in order to be like us in all things He emptied Himself of all power, and in His life submitted to the law. He submitted to the religious regulations of the chosen people fully aware that He was Lord of this law and therefore not bound to submit to it. This is demonstrated by the following incident related by St. Matthew:

> When they had entered Capharnaum, the collectors of the temple dues interviewed Peter and said: "Does not your Rabbi pay the temple dues?" "He certainly does," he replied. But as soon as he came indoors, and before he had said a word, Jesus asked him: "What do you think, Simon? On whom do earthly sovereigns levy custom dues or the poll tax? On their own children or on outsiders?" When he replied, "On outsiders," Jesus said to him: "Then, evidently, the children are exempt! However, we must give them no offense. Go down to the sea, throw in a hook, and land the first fish to come up. Then open its mouth, and you will find a stater. Take that, and give it to them to pay for me and you" (Mt 17:24–27).

In this manner Jesus Himself sets an example. It is not surprising, therefore, that He should affirm the duty of obedience to the Church. He says quite simply: "If he pays no attention to the Church, then treat him as a heathen and tax-collector" (Mt 18:17).

The faithful owe to their ecclesiastical superiors, their parish priest, the bishop of the diocese, the pope in Rome, respect, obedience, and love. But they may not allow respect, obedience, and love to be dependent upon their own relationship to those in authority. If one were to decline obedience in a case where one found fault with a superior, there would soon be none left on earth who thought that they were bound by any obedience.

The touchstone of an obedient mind is very often found in a person's attitude to his immediate ecclesiastical superiors — to his parish priest.

The following rules govern the relation between ecclesiastical superiors and the faithful:

Ecclesiastical superiors have a duty to care for the salvation of men entrusted to them.

The faithful must show respect, obedience, and love to their ecclesiastical superiors.

The Life of the Individual. Education for the professions today is so extensive that everybody, we might say, excels priests, who are God's representatives, in some field of knowledge. We need only consider how much knowledge is demanded by education for technical professions, for various manual skills, for teaching, or for the civil service.

Men being what they are, there is always the danger that if a man knows more than the priest in some subject, he will think he is superior to him in everything. This danger can only be avoided by remembering always that there are different degrees of knowledge and that religious knowledge, i.e., knowledge from revelation, is superior in degree and in breadth to all other knowledge.

If worldly knowledge were sufficient to assure human happiness, the happiness and well-being of mankind would have increased in a quite unheard-of degree during the past century, but, in fact, paradise has not arrived.

However, priests should certainly take note that their people are in many ways more knowledgeable than they. Indeed, many of the faithful have now acquired a high state of theological knowledge. This requires priests to continue their own studies in Scripture and theology, to wrestle with the problems posed by contemporary science and philosophy, for only in this way can they truly speak to men today. Theirs should be a true pastoral spirit, a kindly but not condescending attitude to the people committed to them.

The Life of the Church.   The activity of the Church in advancing the kingdom of God is always an ordered activity undertaken under the leadership and guidance of the divinely appointed pastors of the Church. At the same time this activity is shared by every single member of the laity — more so today than perhaps ever before. This is the day of the lay apostolate, of Catholic Action. Successive popes in recent times have stressed the importance of this orderly lay activity and have given guidance on how it can best be exercised.

19. THE LAW OF GOD AND LIFE ON EARTH

THE PROPER SIGNIFICANCE of man's life within the Creation is made plain by the words of Holy Scripture. In the Book of Genesis we read:

God said, "Let us make mankind in our image and likeness, and let them have dominion over the fish of the sea, the birds of the air, the cattle, over all the wild animals and every creature that crawls on the earth.

God created man in his image. In the image of God he created him. Male and female he created them.

Then God blessed them and said to them, "Be fruitful and multiply; fill the earth and subdue it. Have dominion over the fish of the sea, the birds of the air, the cattle and all the animals that crawl on the earth" (Gn 1:26–28).

God's solemn declaration concerning the first pair applies not to those alone whom He called into being by a direct act of creation, but to all Adam's posterity. The life of every single man is at once a gift and a task from God. Every man has a duty to preserve and develop this God-given life with all its power and faculties, and to place himself at the service of his fellowmen according to the will of God. Every man must also permit all the men around him to preserve and develop their powers and faculties, and assist them to do so.

Earthly life is not, however, man's highest good. It is, therefore, permissible for men to give up life and bodily health for possessions of a high order. In certain circumstances to do this may even become a duty. At other times to give up one's life is a noble act of sacrificial love. With this in mind Jesus said to Himself:

335

"I am the good shepherd. A good shepherd lays down his life to save his sheep. If a hired man, who is not a shepherd and has no sheep of his own, sees the wolf coming, he abandons the sheep and runs away; and the wolf carries them off or scatters them" (Jn 10:11–13).

As one's own life, so are the lives of one's fellowmen a gift from the hand of God. It is an assault upon the law of God to take another man's life or to impair his strength.

If a man seeks to take another's life it is always because in some way he hopes to gain some advantage for himself. This is clearly shown in King Saul's attempt to kill the young David:

> And it came to pass, when he had made an end of speaking to Saul, the soul of Jonathan was knit with the soul of David, and Jonathan loved him as his own soul. And Saul took him that day, and would not let him return to his father's house. And David and Jonathan made a covenant, for he loved him as his own soul. And Jonathan stripped himself of the coat with which he was clothed, and gave it to David, and the rest of his garments, even to his sword, and to his bow, and to his girdle. And David went out to whatsoever business Saul sent him, and he behaved himself prudently: and Saul set him over the soldiers, and he was acceptable in the eyes of all the people, and especially in the eyes of Saul's servants.
>
> Now when David returned, after he slew the Philistine, the women came out of all the cities of Israel, singing and dancing, to meet king Saul, with timbrels of joy and cornets. And the women sung as they played, and they said Saul slew his thousands, and David his ten thousands. And Saul was exceeding angry, and this word was displeasing in his eyes, and he said: They have given David ten thousands, and to me they have given *but* a thousand; what can he have more but the kingdom? And Saul did not look on David with a good eye from that day and forward.
>
> And the day after the evil spirit from God came upon Saul, and he prophesied in the midst of his house. And David played with his hand as at other times. And Saul held a spear in his hand, and threw it, thinking to nail David to the wall, and David stepped aside out of his presence twice (1 Sm 18:6–11).

God gives life: He alone is Lord of life and death. Man's bodily life has its seat in the soul and from it derives its ultimate worth. In this respect there is no distinction between the life of a child in the womb and that of a man in full maturity or that of an old man incapable of working. In no circumstances, therefore, is it lawful to kill a man. It is a direct attack upon the prerogative of God's majesty — a sin crying to heaven.

In contemporary literature, it is hard to trace signs of any upholding of the sanctity of life in every phase and in all circumstances. Compared with this, the expression of the sanctity of life, contained in the physician's oath of the great Greek physician Hippocrates (460–356 B.C.), is most moving. The oath runs: "Nor will I give to any man, though I be asked to give it, any deadly drug, nor will I consent that it should be given. Likewise I will not procure abortion but purely and holily I will keep guard over my life and my art."

In the encyclical on the Mystical Body of Christ we read: "We see to our profound grief that death is sometimes inflicted upon the deformed and mentally defective, and those suffering from hereditary disease, on the plea that they are an intolerable burden upon society; and, moreover, that this expedient is hailed by some as a discovery made by human progress and as greatly conducive to the common good. Is there any man of sense who fails to see that this is not only contrary to the natural and divine law written on the hearts of all, but also an outrage upon the noblest instincts of humanity? The blood of these unhappy creatures, especially dear to our Redeemer and especially to be pitied, 'cries to God from the earth.' " The killing of the unborn child is not mentioned specifically by the Pope because from time immemorial this has incurred ecclesiastical punishment.

The Church can never ally itself with any eugenic which advocates killing of the sick and afflicted out of consideration for healthy, vigorous people. At the same time there is no Catholic book dealing with problems of marriage which does not point out that all prospective married couples ought to ask themselves whether or not healthy progeny is to be expected from their union.

It is contrary to the Fifth Commandment to give fatal poison to a sick person in order to shorten the duration of an illness or to ameliorate its pain (euthanasia). God remains the Lord of life and whoever does such a thing attacks God's sovereignty.

In a just war a soldier is permitted to take the enemies' life as an act of self-defense. The ill-treatment or killing of defenseless prisoners, however, is forbidden.

The Fifth Commandment also forbids all interference with the proper functioning of reason, will, and imagination.

The taking of alcoholic drink in excess is an obvious example. It is quite possible for the temperate use of wine to have a beneficial effect. The excessive use of alcohol, however, always has an injurious effect. First the man becomes drunk; he loses self-control and says and does things of which he would be ashamed when sober. Apart from complete intoxication, excessive drinking causes damage to the nervous system, the digestive organs, and to the heart. Alcoholic poisoning also severely damages the genes.

The same thing applies in the same way or in a greater degree to all pills and drugs which disturb or suspend the natural interaction of reason, will, and imagination. Such drugs are designed only as medicines and permitted only for the good of the person involved and must be given only by experts.

The Fifth Commandment also limits the application of hypnosis to therapeutic purposes and only experts may practice hypnosis.

Any person who culpably shortens another's life, or exposes him to danger, sins against the law of God. This can arise on the one hand through injury and harsh treatment, or on the other from the toleration of conditions of work and livelihood which are seriously detrimental to health.

A life in harmony with the ordinance of God shows a balanced alteration between work and recreation, between rest and activity, between attention to business and play. Sport ought to provide a counterbalance to a man's usual work. Sport has thus quite another meaning for the factory worker and mental worker than for the peasant. Even for artisan and mental worker it is not quite the same; but all require some sort of healthy recreation.

The following rules apply to bodily life and the preservation of health according to the law of God:

By the Fifth Commandment God requires that we value our own life, develop our faculties and place them at the service of our fellowmen. Similarly we must value the lives of others and allow and help them to develop their own natures. Man's life is made up of bodily life as well as that of the soul.

A man sins against his own life:

1. By neglecting to look after his health;
2. By taking his own life or running into unnecessary danger;
3. By shortening life through intemperance or other passions.

To expose one's own life to danger is, nevertheless, a noble act if one is trying to save another's life. Jesus says, therefore, "This is the greatest love a man can show, that he should lay down his life for his friends" (Jn 15:13).

A man sins against the bodily life of another:

1. By unjustly killing him — murder is a sin crying to heaven for vengeance;
2. By wounding or striking him;
3. By making life miserable or shortening it.

According to our Lord's words, sins against the life of our fellowmen *originate in the heart;* in envy and hatred, in quarrelsomeness and anger, in enmity and revenge, in self-assertion and the inordinate desire to have one's own way.

Killing a man is only permitted to the individual or state in carrying out a sentence in the name of authority and in just self-defense.

Within the Christian moral code the use of sport has a definite place. Intelligent and regular indulgence in sport helps develop and restore the faculties and can be regarded as part of fulfilling of the Fifth Commandment. There is always the presumption, of course, that it is carried out in accordance with the ever applicable rule of moderation.

The Life of the Individual. Concern to procure sufficient food and clothing for oneself, one's dependents, and the community in general is a most laudable thing. The provision of a decent home is also basic. And this is especially necessary for families deprived because of minority status, such as race. A decent home is indispensable for true Christian life. Without it, education becomes more difficult and the dangers of delinquency are increased. All have an obligation to remove any injustices in the field of housing and to work for the promotion of the common good.

Provision of the greatest possible number of family houses is one of the first tasks of social welfare. It is against the Christian spirit, when letting a house, to exclude families with many children — or simply with children.

Smoke in moderation. Even more, drink temperately. If you get drunk, then keep away altogether from bars for a spell.

Make sure that you get regular healthy recreation. Guard against overstrain.

Keep to a strict daily routine and a definite plan of work. Order in daily work is an excellent exercise in self-discipline. People who leave everything to the mood of the moment never have their work done in time.

The Life of the Church.   The various provisions for the safeguarding of bodily life have had a very different significance for the Church according to the cultural condition of different peoples. In far-off days, when civilized peoples were still living in conditions such as those we find today among African tribes, the Church had to help the people in a motherly way in matters of feeding, clothing, and housing. Today, in places where there is no real civilization, the missionaries are still obliged to undertake these same tasks.

In lands where civilization has advanced the Church no longer has the task to the same extent as before of helping the faithful economically. In place of this a much more difficult task has emerged: she must instill into these people solicitude for their own lives and for the lives of their fellowmen.

20. THE LAW OF GOD AND THE LIFE OF GRACE IN THE SOUL

MAN'S BODILY LIFE is the outward, visible shell of a life of quite another sort — the mysterious life of the soul, of spirit which consists in a participation in the divine life. Man, therefore, has a responsibility for his soul and the souls of his fellowmen which is immeasurably greater than the responsibility for his body and those of his fellows.

Each man must be of the greatest possible assistance to his fellowmen upon their way to God. He fulfills this responsibility chiefly by showing an example to them. The Lord says:

> "You are the salt of the earth. But suppose salt should lose its savor, what is there to restore its nature? It is no longer good for anything except to be thrown out of doors and trampled upon by passers-by!
>
> "You are the light of the world. It is impossible for a city to escape notice when built on a mountain top. Nor do people light a lamp and then hide it under a bushel-basket. No, it is set on a lampstand that it may give light to all in the house. Just so let your light shine before your fellow men, that they may see your good example and praise your Father who is in heaven" (Mt 5:13–16).

It is not hard to resolve to do a good deed when one is in a mood of exaltation. Indeed, there is probably no man so bad but will show traces of some such noble impulse. But it requires faith and the power of faith to be like a light which always shines, or to be like a city set on a hill. St. Paul, therefore, exhorts the faithful to be steadfast:

> Let us cling without faltering to the hope which we profess, for he who has given us the promise is faithful. And let us take thought for one another in view of rousing one another to acts of love and good deeds (Heb 10:23–24).

Scandal is the lamentable opposite to a life which is a model to

341

others, and unfortunately most people are led into sin by the bad example of someone else. Jesus was aware of this dreadful law, and so He adjured men never to give scandal.

> "On the other hand, he who has been an occasion of sin to one of these little ones that believe in me, it would be better for him if he had a large millstone hung around his neck and were drowned in the depth of the sea. Cursed is the world because of its temptations to sin! It is unavoidable, to be sure, that temptations should come; for all that, he is doomed through whom the temptation comes.
>
> "But if your own hand or foot leads you to sin, cut it off and throw it away; it is better for you to enter life crippled or lame than to keep both hands or both feet and be consigned to the everlasting fire. And if your eye leads you to sin, pluck it out and throw it away; it is better for you to enter life deprived of one eye than to keep both eyes and be consigned to the fire of the eternal pit" (Mt 18:6–9).

Scandal can be given thoughtlessly. A person may behave in a way which does great damage to others and never give it a thought.

There is also premeditated scandal. This consists in a deliberate incitement to commit sin, for example, to tempt someone to desecrate the Sunday or to sin against the Sixth or Seventh Commandments.

Greater intercourse between people has at once increased the possibilities of giving scandal and of being affected by it, and lessened the sense of responsibility for it. All too easily do we succumb to the delusion that what so many others are doing cannot be too bad.

The law of God provides the following rules for the spiritual life of man:

One person endowed with a soul is of more value in the eyes of God than all the rest of creation. Every man must, therefore, regard his own soul as the most priceless thing of all, for which he is responsible to God. Every man has the duty also of developing the powers of his soul and so of being a light to others upon the way of life.

A man injures his *own* soul, his own being, by committing a sin; by committing a mortal sin he destroys the life of grace within him.

A man injures his *neighbor's* soul by leading him to sin by bad example or direct temptation. Jesus warned us against scandal in these words: "He who has been an occasion of sin to one of these little ones that believe in me it would be better for him if he had a large millstone hung around his neck and were drowned in the depth of the sea. Cursed is the world because of its temptations to sin!" (Mt 18:6.) Whoever injures another's spiritual life must repair the damage as best he can.

The Life of the Individual. Remember that you will be held responsible for your fellowmen. Not only must you avoid giving scandal, but you must set a good example to others. Your fellowmen are principally those with whom you come in contact daily, at your place of work and in your home. In the love of Christ men are closer to you the more they need your help in their temporal or spiritual troubles. The growth or decline of the Church depends very much upon the good or the bad example given by the faithful.

Do not show approval if sin is spoken of as something trivial or even as a kind of accomplishment.

Determine never to tempt another to sin or to be an occasion of sin by your behavior.

The Life of the Church. The moral law has this one thing in common with the laws of inanimate nature: its infringements always take their revenge upon men. First they take revenge upon the individual who is guilty; but they only begin to take revenge in real earnest upon a society which has more or less declared the law to be no longer applicable.

At the International Congress of Psychiatrists in 1948 the following question was put: "What is the use of conferring about sick people individually when whole nations are showing the same symptoms of illness? What good is done by looking after the individual if we are confronted by a general condition from which the individual cannot break free? What value has the education of children if the family is breaking up and the nation turning into an amorphous mass without any nucleus?"

For such great ills the only effective remedy is possessed by Him who said, "The sick have need of a physician, not the healthy" (Mt 9:12). And this remedy can but direct the sick to the Church to which He said, "Go, therefore, and make all nations your disciples" (Mt 28:19).

The Church fulfills this mission in a way which appears to have no prospects at all. She persists in turning to the conscience of individuals and demanding that they always put God's will before their own. And she makes individuals responsible before God for their neighbors. By doing this she is, however, doing exactly what she was doing almost 2000 years ago in the ancient Roman world; and when she was acting thus it seemed as ineffectual as it does today. In fact, it was thus that the Church renewed society.

The revival of the society of the declining Roman empire by Christianity came from within. We saw this by reference to a particularly difficult question in the letters of St. Paul. Christianity saw that by expanding it would be facing a world in which slavery was an accepted practice. Christianity brought about the disappearance of slavery, but this was accomplished not by the issuing of prescripts and orders, but by spreading abroad a new conception of the value of man. The preachers of this doctrine declared that both masters and slaves had been redeemed in the same way by the blood of Christ and therefore masters and slaves both had Jesus Christ as their common Lord and Judge above them (cf. Eph 5:5–9). In this way, first of all the basic relationship between masters and slaves was altered, and then finally the change became expressed in an alteration of the law and slavery became abolished.

21. THE LAW OF GOD AND THE GENERATIVE POWERS OF FATHER AND MOTHER

WE READ in the narrative of the creation:

> God created man in his image. In the image of God he created him. Male and female he created them.
> Then God blessed them and said to them, "Be fruitful and multiply; fill the earth and subdue it. Have dominion over the fish of the sea, the birds of the air, the cattle and all the animals that crawl on the earth" (Gn 1:27–28).

When the lawyers were interrogating Jesus on the subject of marriage, He pointed to these early pages of Scripture and asserted:

> "At the beginning of creation God made human beings male and female; and for this reason a man must leave his father and his mother, and the two are to become one, so that they are no longer two persons but one. Consequently, what God has yoked together man may not separate" (Mt 10:6–9).

The faith teaches that soul and body form a unity and in this unity are designed some day to share in the vision of God. Faith teaches further that the germ of this elevation of man to heaven is already planted in this life; that man is already incorporated in the divine life and has been made God's dwelling place.

These truths form the basis of God's law concerning the male and female generative powers in man.

In his first Epistle to the Corinthians, St. Paul sets out the design of God concerning the Sixth Commandment:

> The body is not for immorality but for the Lord, and the Lord is for the body. Just as God raised the Lord, so he will raise us by his power.
> Are you not aware that your bodies are members of Christ's body?

345

Shall I then take the members of Christ and make them the members of a prostitute? Never! Are you not aware that he who unites himself to a prostitute becomes one body with her? So says the Scripture, "The two shall become one flesh." But he who unites himself to the Lord, forms one spirit with him. Shun immorality. Every other sin a man may commit is outside the body, but the fornicator sins against his own body. Are you not aware that your body is the temple of the Holy Spirit? Him you have received from God! You are not your own masters. You have been bought, and at a price! So then, glorify the God in your body (1 Cor 6:13–20).

The way in which sin against the Sixth Commandment can pervert and destroy the good in a man is shown most strikingly in the story of King David.

Scripture, unerringly and unsparingly, depicts how David's first sin urges him on to further sins which formerly would have horrified him. The Bible wishes to warn everyone who reads the tale against similar calamities:

> And it came to pass at the return of the year, at the time when kings go forth to war, that David sent Joab and his servants with him, and all Israel, and they spoiled the children of Ammon, and besieged Rabba, but David remained in Jerusalem.
> In the meantime it happened that David arose from his bed after noon, and walked upon the roof of the king's house; and he saw from the roof of his house a woman washing herself, over against him; and the woman was very beautiful. And the king sent, and inquired who the woman was. And it was told him, that she was Bethsabee the daughter of Eliam, the wife of Urias the Hethite. And David sent messengers, and took her, and she came in to him, and he slept with her: and presently she was purified from her uncleanness, and she returned to her house; having conceived. And she sent and told David, and said: I have conceived.
> And David sent to Joab, saying: Send me Urias the Hethite. And Joab sent Urias to David. And Urias came to David. And David asked how Joab did, and the people, and how the war was carried on. And David said to Urias: Go into thy house, and wash thy feet. And Urias went out from the king's house, and there went out after him a mess of meat from the king. But Urias slept before the gate of the king's house, with the other servants of his lord, and went not down to his own house. And it was told David by some that said: Urias went not to his house. And David said to Urias: Didst thou not come from thy journey? Why didst thou not go down

to thy house? And Urias said to David: The ark of God and Israel and Juda dwell in tents, and my lord Joab and the servants of my lord abide upon the face of the earth; and shall I go into my house, to eat and to drink, and to sleep with my wife? By thy welfare and by the welfare of thy soul I will not do this thing. Then David said to Urias: Tarry here today, and tomorrow I will send thee away. Urias tarried in Jerusalem that day and the next. And David called him to eat and to drink before him, and he made him drunk. and he went out in the evening, and slept on his couch with the servants of his lord, and he went not down into his house.

And when the morning was come, David wrote a letter to Joab, and sent it by the hand of Urias, writing in the letter: Set ye Urias in the front of the battle, where the fight is strongest, and leave ye him, that he may be wounded and die. Wherefore as Joab was besieging the city, he put Urias in the place where he knew the bravest men were. And the men coming out of the city, fought against Joab, and there fell some of the people of the servants of David, and Urias the Hethite was killed also. Then Joab sent and told David all the things concerning the battle.

And the wife of Urias heard that Urias her husband was dead, and she mourned for him. And the mourning being over, David sent and brought her into his house, and she became his wife, and she bore him a son. And this thing which David had done, was displeasing to the Lord (2 Sam 11:1–18, 26–27).

And the Lord sent Nathan to David. And when he was come to him, he said to him: There were two men in one city, the one rich, and the other poor. The rich man had exceeding many sheep and oxen. But the poor man had nothing at all but one little ewe lamb, which he had bought and nourished up, and which had grown up in his house together with his children, eating of his bread, and drinking of his cup, and sleeping in his bosom, and it was unto him as a daughter. And when a certain stranger was come to the rich man, he spared to take of his own sheep and oxen, to make a feast for that stranger, who was come to him, but took the poor man's ewe, and dressed it for the man that was to come to him.

And David's anger being exceedingly kindled against that man, he said to Nathan: As the Lord liveth, the man that hath done this is a child of death. He shall restore the ewe fourfold, because he did this thing, and had no pity. And Nathan said to David: Thou art the man. Thus saith the Lord the God of Israel: I annointed thee king over Israel, and I delivered thee from the hand of Saul, and gave thee thy master's house and thy master's wives into thy bosom, and gave thee the house of Israel and Juda; and if these things be little, I shall add far greater things unto thee. Why therefore hast thou despised the word of the Lord, to do evil in my sight? Thou hast killed Urias the Hethite with the sword, and hast taken his wife to be thy wife, and hast slain him with the sword of the children of Ammon. Therefore the sword shall never depart from thy house, because thou hast despised me, and hast taken the wife of Urias the Hethite to be thy wife (2 Sm 12:1–10).

This story reveals truths which, in every age, come home to each individual. Sins against the Sixth Commandment are not the worst sins of all. Any sin which is aimed directly against God exceeds them in evil. Nevertheless it is true that sins against the Sixth Commandment have a peculiarly fateful effect. This is so because they constitute an abuse of the generative powers.

To protect purity God Himself has given man a special sense which announces threatening danger. This is the sense of shame. Any man who is honest with himself looks upon this feeling as a help not unlike the warning of sirens before an air raid. He pays heed and forthwith takes cover.

The law of God provides the following rules governing the generative powers in man and woman:

Within the realm of nature the human body is the dwelling and the instrument of the soul; in the realm of grace it is designed to be the temple of the Holy Spirit and to share in the eternal vision of God in glory. In a special way this dignity is violated by sin against the Sixth Commandment.

In the plan of God the generative powers of man and woman are designed to provide human life with progeny and so to ensure the continuance of the human race. In the first pages of Holy Scripture it is written: "Male and female he created them" (Gn 1:27).

Any use of these powers which is contrary to their purpose opposes God's intention in creating them. As a result, any deliberate indulgence in sexual desire outside marriage, and any desire within marriage which involves frustration of the purpose of marriage, is sinful. Our Lord says this about it in the Sermon on the Mount: "Anyone who looks at a woman with a lustful intention has already committed adultery with her in his heart" (Mt 5:28). This is called the sin of impurity.

A person sins against purity by seeking to indulge sexual desire unlawfully and by taking pleasure in it. The sin of impurity has a fateful effect. It spreads like a spark in a heap of straw; it perverts goodness, estranges from God, and frequently destroys much temporal happiness and health.

A person sins against purity — as all catechisms put it in almost identical words — by indulging impure desire in thought or wish, by reading or looking at something impure, by listening to or saying something impure, by permitting impurity, by doing some impure act alone or with others.

God has given mankind a sense of shame to protect purity. It is shameless to expose or to touch one's body wantonly, or to speak of sexual matters without proper reverence.

According to Pius XI's encyclical on education, parents should, when possible, undertake to instruct their children in sexual matters themselves. This must be done gradually. If parents have never uttered a word to their sons and daughters upon this subject which is of such importance when maturity comes, this neglect can lead to a spiritual estrangement between parents and children. It is impossible to keep a reciprocal silence on such a serious subject without in some way losing contact. The personal instruction of children by parents is also the best way of insuring that when it comes to chosing a bride or a bridgegroom, the parents can support their children with frank discussion. Parents must never forget that even more important than timely instruction is the strengthening of the will.

The Life of the Individual. It is quite impossible to employ leisure hours in reading magazines and novels, in seeing films which in their whole scheme deny the sanctity and indissolubility of marriage or jeer at it, and which represent love as a game of the heart or with hearts, without suffering lasting damage. Whoever fills his imagination with such images will sooner or later — mostly sooner — and without being aware of it, come to accept the same ideas. In a special address Pius XII called attention to these dangers to the preservation of a healthy family life.

The Life of the Church. The Church well knows that the erection of prohibition by itself is only a defense against evil and does not directly foster good. That is why the Church tries to educate the faithful in various good habits which are not immediately connected with the mastery of the life of passion, but which are kept in evidence by the Church precisely in order to strengthen the faithful in the battle for purity. In this connection we think of the exhortation to practice daily prayer; to respect and obey parents and superiors; to receive the sacraments of Confession and Holy Communion regularly; and we think also of the way in which the Church is constantly displaying to the faithful the lives of holy men and women who have been victorious in this battle against heavy odds, so that they will be ready to make the sacrifice which their own position demands of them.

Unfortunately we are not nearly careful enough about the things which children overhear concerning sexual matters, and children pick things up as riddles which later on they try to unravel for themselves. It would be wrong of parents if, in view of such possibilities, they were to make it a rule to remain absolutely silent on these matters. By doing this they would exclude this whole sphere of life from the children's mental growth. The correct attitude is to speak openly of these things, with due seriousness and in a Christian spirit, as opportunity arises. In this way the separate pieces of the puzzle in the child's mind will be slowly pieced together into a beautiful, complete picture.

22. PRESERVING THE SPIRIT'S CONTROL OVER THE SENSES

THE STORY OF JOSEPH in Egypt contains teaching which is quite as applicable today as it was then, for all men who wish to lead a pure life. Scripture relates:

He left everything he had in Joseph's charge, and having him, was concerned about nothing except the food he ate.
Now Joseph was well formed and handsome. Some time afterward, the wife of his master cast her eyes on Joseph and said, "Lie with me." But he refused, saying, "Because of me, my master is not concerned about anything in the house, but has put all that he owns in my care. He exercises no greater authority in this house than I, nor has he withheld a single thing from me, except yourself, because you are his wife. How then can I commit this great crime, and sin against God?" She urged Joseph day after day, but he would not consent to lie with her, or to be with her. On one such day, Joseph went into the house to do his work, while none of the household servants was at hand. She seized him by his garment and said, "Lie with me." But Joseph left his garment in her hand, and fled outdoors (Gn 39:6–12).

Joseph said to Potiphar's wife, "How can I sin before God?" If Joseph had not already become accustomed to keeping God always in mind, in the decisive moment he would not have spoken thus.

The following tested rules of life apply to all who wish to preserve purity according to their state in life.

1. *Do not limit your view to earthly life.*

Modern life, which seems to broaden man's outlook, involves, in fact, a narrowing of vision; for one's view of life is not broadened by a constant stream of never ending experience. We must recognize the implications which underlie the various facts of life. For example, if young people get the idea from novels and films that free, sensual love without any inhibitions is the only thing which makes life worthwhile,

that is the very worst kind of limitation. Such a view would presume
to count the lives of children and old people worthless. In the end such
principles prepare the way in civilized countries for men who assert
that it is lawful to kill others — children and old people, for example.

2. *Do not be led away from looking up to higher things.*

A man's outlook is only truly broad when he knows about the
most important laws of life in their totality. If a man reviews earthly
life in all its fullness but excludes these truths of faith which reveal
to us that life which lies hidden within the earthly life, then life is not
so worthwhile that it can provide men with complete happiness.

Only in contemplating God does man gain a sound viewpoint from
which he can review the whole of life and appoint to each power in
man its proper, fixed place.

3. *Be on guard against beginnings.*

Holy Scripture says: "Danger loved is death won" (Eccl 3:27).
This saying will be valid as long as there are men. The danger can
be a friendship, a book, a picture, an entertainment, a movie, or a
play. The Lord knew about these things when He said, "What will it
profit a man to gain the whole world when his life is forfeited?" (Mt
16:26).

4. *Persevere in the fight.*

Many people are quite prepared to take part in a short, fierce
struggle to gain some great end. In life's warfare, and in the fight
for purity, there is, unfortunately, no final conquest. The pattern of
the fight may change, but there is never a time when we can say that
victory is now assured for good. We must persevere in the struggle,
but only those can do this who receive strength from above.

5. *Persevere in prayer and in the regular reception of sacraments.*

In prayer a man turns to God and rises high above all earthly things.
In this way prayer has a beneficial effect. Because his heart was directed
toward God at all times, Joseph in Egypt immediately thought of the
presence of God in the moment of temptation. In response to prayer,
moreover, God's grace descends upon a man and gives him strength.

One of the long-approved means of guarding purity is devotion to
the Mother of God. As no other devotion, this devotion is able to give
a man fresh courage in the fight and prevents him from giving up.

To this commandment applies specially what must always be noted in the struggle against any deep-rooted evil inclination. It can happen that a person has seriously resolved to mend his life, and yet from weakness later falls again into a sin from which he had turned away. In the circumstance he may not commit a grave sin by this lapse. Such a person must not yield to the mood of the moment and say: I have fallen again; it is all the same if I consent to the sin a second time. On the contrary. Certainly, the first lapse is possibly no grave sin, but merely an act committed by a kind of compulsion as a result of earlier bad habits. But the second sin cannot be judged so leniently; it could inaugurate a new series of sins. Things which occur in sleep or in half sleep are apart from a man's free will and therefore are not grave sins.

6. *Look after your health.*

We are kept healthy by nourishing, plain fare, by a well-ordered daily routine, by regular fresh air and exercise and systematic hardening, by avoiding undue excitement, by strict moderation in the use of alcohol and in smoking.

7. *Never be idle.*

Diligent work takes soul and body under control. If in addition one has a favorite leisure occupation, that is a great advantage.

8. *Be modest.*

Do not accept everything that is offered in books, papers, and pictures. Take care on your own and with others.

9. *Be ready to learn.*

Be ready to learn from experienced and conscientious people of your own sex what you ought to know. Accept instruction specially about the damage which is caused by sins of impurity.

Temptations against the Sixth Commandment are particularly dangerous.

Sensual desire limits knowledge and impairs the will. With reference to the Sixth Commandment, therefore, it is specially necessary to avoid the proximate occasions of sin, and to resist immediately and resolutely the temptations which in spite of this will present themselves. Jesus mentions the necessity of doing this when He says: "And if your eye leads you to sin, pluck it out and throw it away; it is better for you to enter life deprived of one eye than to keep both eyes and be consigned to the fire of the eternal pit" (Mt 18:9).

Everyone must at all times be careful to insure that the spirit has control over his sensual impulses:

To maintain control by the spirit, he must pay heed to the following:

1. He must view life as a whole and turn his mind toward heaven.
2. He must be modest and ready to be taught.
3. He must instantly resist temptation.
4. He must rise up again after every fall.
5. He must receive the sacraments of Penance and Holy Communion worthily and regularly, and cultivate devotion to Mary.

The Life of the Individual. Control of sexual desire always demands of a man a certain amount of honest purpose and of deliberate consideration of himself. If one or other is lacking it will not be long until a man loses control over his impulses.

Many people make a habit of performing some gymnastics every day in order to keep their bodies fit. This is good; and it is good also — even better — daily to practice doing something which is irksome in order to establish control over oneself. Here are a few practices which one can carry out with profit:

1. Rise every day at the same hour.
2. On reading a book, pause for a moment when the excitement is at its greatest pitch.
3. Resist making the witty remark which occurs to you in the course of conversation.
4. Be kind to people you cannot bear.
5. Eat things which you dislike without comment and without a wry face.
6. Carry out your resolves even when you suffer a change of mood.
7. Stand up for a person in public whom others have vilified.
8. Avoid bad language when angry.
9. Do not hurry your prayers.

The Life of the Church. Out of its millenial experience the Church keeps before our minds that the guarding of moral purity is one of the most important tasks in the education of the young. The exposition of education in chastity takes up much space, therefore, in the encyclicals on Christian education. As we have already noted, in these it is pointed out emphatically that parents themselves have to instruct their children step by step, prudently, in all that they ought to know. Nor do the popes neglect to stress at the same time that instruction without a corresponding religious training is of little avail. On the contrary, recommending well-produced books with attractive titles to young people as a natural means of self-education may have a pernicious effect. The young person may possibly commit himself, body and soul, to advice which demands little self-control, and may no longer believe that he should depend upon religious means which demand more self-control.

23. THE LAW OF GOD AND PRIVATE PROPERTY, ITS RIGHTS AND OBLIGATIONS

THE STORY OF CREATION tells that God said to Adam and Eve:

Then God blessed them and said to them, "Be fruitful and multiply; fill the earth and subdue it. Have dominion over the fish of the sea, the birds of the air, the cattle and all the animals that crawl on the earth" (Gn 1:28).

God installed Adam and Eve as the first parents of the human race and made them and their progeny the lords of the earth.

This lordship of the earth was transmitted not to any individual but to the whole human race in all its members.

The following passages of Scripture deal with property and its right use:

For we brought nothing into this world, and certainly we can take nothing out of it. But let us be content if we have food and clothing. Those who seek to become rich fall into temptation and a snare and many senseless and harmful desires, which plunge men into ruin and destruction. The love of money is the root of all evils, and some in their eagerness to get rich have strayed from the faith and have found themselves pierced with many a pang of sorrow. Charge those blessed with the riches of this world not to be proud, or to trust in the uncertainty of riches, but in God, who provides all things in rich abundance for our enjoyment. Let them do good and be rich in good deeds; let them be liberal in sharing their goods with others, and thus provide for themselves a good foundation for the time to come, in order that they may lay hold on the true life (1 Tim 6:7–10, 17–19).

Jesus too appears as a teacher about the law of God concerning human property. To demonstrate the folly of avarice He depicted this scene:

He then spoke to them in parable style: "Once upon a time," he said, "there was a rich man whose land yielded an abundant crop. So he soliloquized as follows: 'What shall I do since I have no place to store my crops?' Finally he said: 'This is what I will do: I will pull down my barns and build larger ones; and there I will store my wheat and all my goods; and then I will say to myself: My good fellow, you have many possessions laid up to last for many a year; take life easy now: eat, drink, and enjoy yourself.' But God said to him: 'You fool! This very night your soul will be demanded from you: who is then going to get what you have provided?' It is the same with anyone who hoards to indulge himself and does not think of God in amassing wealth" (Lk 12:16–21).

Related to this teaching is the rule by which men will be judged at the Last Day. Those who have used their possessions to do good will be rewarded; those who selfishly withheld their goods from the poor will be punished as though they had shut their hearts to the Savior Himself. Then Jesus will say: "I tell you the plain truth; inasmuch as you failed to render here services to one of these least ones, you also failed to render them to me" (Mt 25:45).

According to God's design all men are to share in this world's goods in a manner which assists the preservation and development of their personal, bodily, and spiritual life.

Because every man has a right to life and its preservation, every man has also the God-given right to work, for it is only by working that he can acquire the necessities of life for himself and his dependents.

But because a man has a right not merely to preserve bodily life but also to develop his spiritual life, the full equipment of a man's nature includes at least a modicum of personal property or the possession of rights which are the equivalent of possessing property.

Without personal property which is his to manage and increase, a man loses the *incentive to work*. This fact is confirmed today.

Men with no possessions at all are in the greatest danger of losing personal freedom as well — of losing even the will to freedom. He who owns nothing is dependent upon others all the time in all that he does. The man who endures this without losing his spiritual freedom is an exception.

Definite delimitation of property between men is necessary because otherwise there would be no end to quarreling and plunder among individuals, families, and communities. For this there is no remedy save the recognition of the rights of private property.

The right of private property is admittedly limited from the start in two ways. God remains the supreme Lord of all possessions, and private ownership owes duties to the community. The more a person possesses, the greater are his obligations to assist those who possess little or nothing. The state has the right to levy taxes and, it may be, to prescribe a capital levy for the relief of distress.

From generation to generation the human race is obliged to stand up for a law of property which corresponds to the law of nature. The problem of how this goal is to be achieved takes on ever new forms as the conditions of life change.

With modern techniques and with goodwill it is possible to make the lot of man in this world much better than was ever dreamed before.

To property, the acquisition of property, and the use of property, the following rules apply:

The law of God ordains that property shall contribute to the preservation, development, and security of the bodily and spiritual life of all men in their successive generations. All property has thus the character of a lease with certain obligations. The superior is God; the obligations are in favor of our fellowmen.

Every man has the right to work, to an adequate wage, and to a modest property. Individual possessions ought, therefore, never to be so great that there is not sufficient left for those around to make their lives secure. The prophet Isaiah was already saying:

Woe to you who join house to house, who connect field with field, till no room remains, and you are left to dwell alone in the midst of the land! In my hearing the Lord of hosts has sworn: Many houses shall be in ruins, large ones and fine, with no one to live in them (Is 5:8–9).

The Life of the Individual.

Put falsehood and lying far from me,
give me neither poverty nor riches;
[provide me only with the food I need;]

Lest, being full, I deny you,
saying, "Who is the Lord?"
Or, being in want, I steal,
and profane the name of my God.

(Prv 30:8–9)

This prayer is essentially the same as the fourth petition of the Our Father, "Give us this day our daily bread." Both riches and poverty spell danger to all men without exception. The rich man says all too readily, "I have no need of God" and becomes proud. The poor man is filled with dark defiance and says, "As God has given me so little of this world's goods, I will bother no more about Him."

In judging questions of property, it is only with the greatest difficulty that a man can keep above self-interest. The rich incline to advocate an unlimited right of private property. The poor, on the other hand, fall into the trap of demanding shortcut solutions to standing abuses. As soon as rich and poor cease to show moderation in their respective tendencies, human society as a community is in danger, even if the country is rich in natural resources. On the other hand, abundance of brotherly love could result in the solving of these social problems which arise along with technical advance, and could prevent really sinister tension from arising at all.

The Life of the Church. The right to hold private property has always been recognized by the Church. It does this in the same way as Holy Scripture does. The right to private property is set out as a right which each individual must see for himself and apply to his own case.

Even the early Christians in Jerusalem who put their goods or their cash equivalent at the disposal of the congregation were aware that this represented a free offering and that no one could compel them to make it. St. Peter, therefore, told Ananias, who had handed over only half the price of the sale, asserting that it was the whole sum:

"Ananias," said Peter, "why has Satan filled your heart, that you should lie to the Holy Spirit and keep back part of the price of the land? While it remained unsold, did it not remain yours; and after it was sold, was not the money at your disposal? Why have you conceived this plan in your heart? You have not lied to men but to God" (Acts 5:3–4).

24. THE LAW OF GOD AND WORKING FOR OTHERS

AT THE TIME OF CHRIST agriculture was the only industry in the East. Thus the pronouncements of Holy Scripture concerning the duties of the big landowner are applicable to any business undertaking. In St. James' Epistle we read:

> Come now, you who say, "Today, or tomorrow, we will go and spend a year in such and such a city, carry on business, and make money," when you do not know what tomorrow will bring. Why, what is your life? You are but a puff of smoke that appears for a little while and then disappears. You should rather say, "If it is the Lord's will, we shall be alive and do this or that." As it is, you are complacent in your boasting. All such complacency is evil. Whoever, therefore, knows how to do good but leaves it undone is guilty of sin.
>
> Come now, men of wealth, weep and howl over your impending afflictions. Your wealth has rotted; your clothes are moth-eaten. Your gold and silver have rusted, and their rust will give evidence against you and will feed on your flesh as does fire. You have laid up treasures for the last days. Mark my words: the wages of which you have defrauded the workmen who mowed your fields cry aloud, and the cries of the reapers have reached the ears of the Lord of Hosts. You have led a soft life on earth and have indulged in pleasure. You have fed yourselves well for the day of slaughter. You have condemned, you have murdered the innocent man, even though he is not your adversary (Jas 4:13–5:6).

In hardheartedness toward laborers the Apostle sees the effects of an uncontrolled absorption in business, and an unrestrained thirst for power. This impulse intoxicates a man and makes him forget that the true Lord of life and possessions is not himself but God the Creator.

Within the past century, technical progress has provided man's thirst for power and impulse to dominate others with new and hitherto undreamed of possibilities. Technical progress is spreading over the whole earth and is altering the conditions of man's life. This development is affecting all lands more or less simultaneously — lands with an old established civilization and young colonies likewise. Social problems are therefore international.

In view of this fact, the popes since Leo XIII have raised their voices constantly and have pointed out in encyclicals the duty of all the faithful to labor, in their own spheres of life with a sense of Christian responsibility, for the resolution of social antagonisms.

According to the Church the following headings form the basis of social coexistence:

1. *Every man has a right to live and a right to the necessities of life — to food, clothing, and a home.* As these are only acquired through work, these rights imply the duty to work and the right to find work which provides a corresponding wage.

In *Mater et Magistra* Pope John XXIII wrote:

> The remuneration of work is not something that can be left to the laws of the marketplace; nor should it be a decision left to the will of the more powerful. It must be determined in accordance with justice and equity; which means that workers must be paid a wage that allows them to live a truly human life and to fulfill their family obligations in a worthy manner. Other factors too enter into the assessment of a just wage; namely, the effective contribution which each individual makes to the economic effort, the financial state of the company for which he works, the requirements of the general good of the particular country — having regard especially to the repercussions on the overall employment of the working force in the country as a whole — and finally the requirements of the common good of the universal family of nations of every kind, both large and small.

2. *Because the founding of a family constitutes a natural development of life, the normal adult has a right to a wage which will enable him, using appropriate industry, to maintain a family and by thrift to acquire modest possessions.*

In consonance with this idea, Pius XI affirmed in his encyclical on marriage:

> In the first place, every effort must be made to implement the provisions set forth by Our predecessor Leo XIII, namely, that

economic and social conditions in a country should make it possible for every father of a family to earn such a wage as suffices, in the conditions and in the locality in which he lives, for the support of himself, his wife, and his children: 'The labourer is worthy of his hire.' (Lk. 10, 7.) To refuse this hire, or to pay less than what is right, is a grave injustice and is numbered in Holy Scripture among the greatest of sins.

Pius XII said in an address to workers (June 13, 1943):

Our Predecessors and We Ourselves have lost no opportunity of making all men understand by our repeated instructions your personal and family needs, proclaiming as fundamental prerequisites of social justice those things which you have so much at heart — a wage which will cover the living expenses of a family, and such as will make it possible for parents to fulfill their natural duty to rear children who will be healthily nourished and well clothed; a dwelling worthy of human beings; the possibility of securing for the children sufficient instruction and a becoming education; of foreseeing and forestalling times of stress, sickness and old age.

3. *Because at all events social renewal ought to preserve and advance the integrity of the families of working people, employers must provide conditions of work which do not disrupt family unity, but which make employment in industry itself one of the elements which gives security to the home.*

In an address given in June, 1949, Pope Pius XII said:

Without in any way limiting our view to particular instances, we can formulate the task, which it is our duty to solve, in these terms. We have to guarantee to countless families the preservation of their natural, moral, legal and economic integrity, by providing them with that living space to which they have a just claim, and which meets adequately, if modestly, the requirements of human dignity.

In our present state of technical knowledge it is possible to produce much more than formerly and to distribute these goods to separate nations much more equably than before. As soon as this becomes possible its realization becomes an obligation.

The right solution of the social question is to be found between two extreme cases, in one of which the individual is allowed unlimited property with unrestricted rights, and in the other is granted no right to property at all.

In social reform how is caution to be exercised? Social reforms must be carried through in a spirit of sacrifice and with vigor, but also with the greatest circumspection and a step at a time. Social reforms are like repairs carried out on machines which cannot be allowed to stop working.

What are the employers' obligations? Employers are bound to:

1. Control their lust for profit and power.
2. See their workers as cooperatives, be considerate of them, and care for their lives as human beings.
3. Pay a just wage — for adults, a just family wage.
4. Maintain a high standard of production and a high — if possible an expanding — level of employment.

What are the obligations of the workers? The workers are bound to:

1. Use their working time fully.
2. Use the machinery and other instruments with due care and not to waste materials.

The Life of the Individual.   The social questions of our day do not touch only the workers: they demand a revolution in everyone's way of thinking, and this alone will determine whether the solution we arrive at is inward and therefore permanent, or merely external and ephemeral. It is not a question of the worker acquiring influence, but of providing work itself with a soul again. The industry to which he is tied for his existence must begin to appear as part of his natural security and not as a prison from which there is no escape.

The Life of the Church.   As Pius XII has said, "The Church is the life principle of human society." As the soul is one and undivided and as such binds the body with its many members into a unity, so the Church must permeate human society and transform it from within by her God-given powers. She does this by displaying the true principles of life for the individual himself and for his natural relationship to the community in all its modes, and by pouring out the power of grace in all human activity.

25. UNLAWFUL GAIN AND RESTITUTION

BECAUSE BY NATURE man has a right to private property, anyone who takes away from a man what belongs to him or fails to give him what is his due sins against the law of God. Accordingly, anyone who steals, plunders, cheats, practices any kind of usury or profiteering, or attempts to make money by a planned bankruptcy, contravenes the law of God. In addition it is a sin to keep goods found or not to return what has been borrowed.

It is an ominous hour when for the first time, a man deliberately takes something belonging to another. He bids farewell to himself and becomes another person. The case is not altered in the slightest by the fact that many men do such dishonest things.

Judas knew such a day: a day when he appropriated for his own use some of the money which Jesus put in his charge. The second time he felt less uneasy about it; then it was not long until he became quite used to regarding every contribution to Jesus as a gift from which he could deduct something for himself. We see this at the meal at Bethany. St. John the Evangelist tells us:

> Six days before the Passover, Jesus came to Bethany, where Lazarus, whom Jesus had raised from the dead, was living. Here a dinner was given in his honor, at which Martha acted as hostess, while Lazarus was one of the guests reclining at table with him. On this occasion Mary took a pound of perfume made of very costly spikenard, anointed the feet of Jesus, and wiped his feet with her hair. The whole house was filled with the fragrance of the perfume. But Judas Iscariot, one of his disciples, who intended to betray him, said: "Why was not this perfume sold for three hundred denarii and the money given to the poor?" He said this, however, not because he was interested in the poor, but because he was a thief and used to pilfer what was put into the purse, which he

carried. Jesus then said: "Let her have her way. It will turn out that she has reserved this perfume for the day of my anointing" (Jn 12:1–7).

A few days later it was this same Judas who went to the high priest and asked, "What will you pay me for handing him over to you?" (Mt 26:15.)

Whoever has unjustly acquired goods must restore them to the rightful owner. As long as he keeps them he perpetuates the theft. Few things are so hard for men to do as to restore unjustly acquired goods. It makes him feel what he is — a thief. But with God's grace, that which the evangelist Luke relates of the chief tax-gatherer is always possible again:

> He now entered Jericho. As he made his way through the town, there was a stir: a man named Zaccheus, a high official among the tax collectors and rich as well, was curious to find out who Jesus was, but owing to the press of people had no chance to do so, for he was small of stature. In order, therefore, to get a glimpse of Jesus, he ran ahead and climbed up into a sycamore tree, because he was expected to pass that way. When Jesus came to the spot, he looked up. "Zaccheus," he said to him, "come down quickly; today I must be your guest." And, coming down quickly, he welcomed him joyfully. But a murmur ran through the crowd of spectators. "He has turned in," they commented, "to accept the hospitality of a sinner!" Then Zaccheus drew himself up and addressed the Lord: "Upon my word, Lord, I will give to the poor one half of my possessions and, if I have obtained anything from anybody by extortion, I will refund four times as much." Then, in his presence, Jesus said: "Today salvation has visited this household, because he, too, is a son of Abraham. After all, it is the mission of the Son of Man to seek and save what is lost" (Lk 19:1–10).

God's grace still strengthens all those who wish to clear their consciences and put right any injustice.

Because restitution of unjustly acquired goods is part of true contrition and determination of amendment, confession without it is ineffective. It makes no difference whether one conceals the sin in advance or declares one's readiness to make restitution to the confessor while secretly intending never to do so. Such behavior often leads the person never to return to confession or to repeat the same behavior on subsequent occasions.

But there is no doubt that in many cases it is often confession which leads to the restitution of unjustly acquired goods. Furthermore, there is no doubt that an honest confession to the priest of the first grave sin against the Seventh Commandment brings to many a deep realization of what such a sin means and so has the result that no more follow.

The law of God forbids the unlawful acquisition of goods. The sin of unlawful acquisition is committed by:

1. Stealing another's property or damaging it.
2. Keeping what is found or borrowed.
3. Robbing or cheating another, or harming them by thoughtless debt.

A person shares the guilt of unlawful acquisition if he counsels the deed, assists with it, commands it to be done, or receives and buys stolen goods.

The prohibition of unjust acquisition applies to companies and economic combines just as it applies to exchange and selling for private purposes. Business representatives, if they transgress the Seventh Commandment on behalf of their companies, are as guilty as if they were acting for their own private advantage. Faults of this sort have a particularly fateful effect because they destroy the whole basis of business life.

Whoever has acquired goods unjustly or has in some way injured another materially is bound to restore the other's property as soon as possible and make good the injury as far as is in his power.

The Life of the Individual.   Beware of the first theft, the first cheating in business, the first fraud at work.

If some unjustly acquired possession is not restored and the person who has a right to it is unable to recover it legally he is permitted to recompense himself by means of what is called "secret compensation." Secret or occult compensation is permitted only if money or goods due to a person for work done or for some other just reason are withheld despite demand. It must be remarked, however, that resort may not be had to this procedure at will, and that even when it is permissible its practice can blunt the sense of a distinction between "mine" and "thine."

The sense of right and wrong is suspended, as it were, with many people when the matter has to do with public property, the property of the community, the country, the state, or the Church. But whoever does not respect the right of property in these realms will soon be making exceptions in other cases as well.

For example, this applies to the use of public utilities without paying the prescribed charge. The man who makes a habit of traveling without a ticket will soon be making other "economies" in his private life. The same holds true of bypassing the electricity meter.

The Life of the Church. Taxation also belongs to the sphere governed by the Seventh Commandment. Citizens are bound to declare their incomes, and not to hide sizable sums. The authorities, however, are bound to refrain from unnecessary taxation, to apportion taxes equitably, and to administer the revenue conscientiously and economically.

The bad effects of a taxation policy which feeds upon confidence of the taxpayer was pointed out seriously by Pius XII to the members of the International Congress of Public Finance in 1948. Among other things he said,

> Many people, too many people, guided by interests and by party spirit, or by considerations more of sentiment than of reason, as improvised economists and politicians, deal and treat with financial and fiscal questions with more ardour and earnestness, and with more assurance and nonchalance, according to the greatness of their incompetence. Sometimes these men do not even seem to suspect the necessity of solving the questions by careful study, prolonged observation, and investigation and experience.
>
> The needs of nations, great or small, have formidably increased. The fault is not alone due to international complications or tensions. It is also, and even more probably, due to the unmeasured extension of the activity of the State, activity which, dictated too often by false or unhealthy ideologies, makes of financial policy, and particularly of fiscal policy, an instrument at the service of interests of a completely different order. The state will be surprised, after that, by the danger in which the science and art of public finance finds itself, of sinking, through lack of fundamental, clear, simple

and solid principles, into the role of technique and of purely formal manipulation.

Such a state of things influences more seriously the mentality of individuals. The individual, little by little, is losing his understanding of the financial affairs of the State. Even in the wisest policy, he always suspects some mysterious manoevres, some malevolent *arriere-pensee,* for which he should be on the watch to defend himself. . . .

How could the Church contemplate with indifference this crisis, which in reality is a crisis of conscience? In the name of human conscience, do not ruin morale from above. Abstain from those measures which, despite their technical virtuosity, hurt and wound the people's sense of justice and injustice, or which relegate as secondary his vital force and his legitimate ambition to harvest the fruit of his own work — all considerations which merit the attention of the legislator's mind in the first place, not in the last place.

26. THE INNER DESIRE FOR TRUTH, THE PREREQUISITE OF ALL TRUTHFULNESS

IN MANY PLACES Scripture shows how human speech is meant to serve the interests of truth and love:

"Brood of vipers! How can you say anything good when you are wicked! After all, a man's speech is but the overflow of his heart. A good man dispenses what is good from his store of good things, and a wicked man dispenses what is wicked from his store of wicked things. I tell you, moreover, that of every loose and random word which men speak they must give an account on Judgment Day. Yes, by your word you will be pronounced innocent, and by your word found guilty" (Mt 12:34–37).

We all commit many faults. If a person does not commit faults in speech, he is perfect and capable of controlling his whole body. Now if we put bits into horses' mouths to make them obey us, we direct their whole bodies. Consider ships also. Large as they are and driven by strong winds, yet by means of a very small rudder they are steered wherever the will of the pilot determines. So too the tongue is a small member, yet it can boast of great achievements. See how great a forest is set ablaze by a very small fire. The tongue is a fire; it makes wickedness attractive. Among our members it is the tongue that defiles the entire body and sets on fire the whole course of our life, as the tongue in turn is set on fire by hell. Human ingenuity is able to tame and has tamed every kind of wild beast and bird, reptile and sea animal; but no man can tame that restless evil, full of deadly poison, the tongue! With it we bless the Lord and Father, and with it we curse men who are made in the image of God! Out of the same mouth come blessing and cursing. It is not right, my brothers, that it should be so. Does the spring gush forth fresh and bitter water from the same outlet? Can a fig tree, my brothers, produce olives, or a grapevine, figs? Neither can salt water produce fresh water (Jas 3:2–12).

369

Man's relationship to the Eighth Commandment depends peculiarly upon his interior intention. If the interior intention to be truthful is lacking, everything — even truth itself — can be turned to the service of untruthfulness, lying, and deceit. Gifted and educated people are especially able to disguise this interior resistance to truth with every kind of cunning excuse, both from themselves and from others. On the other hand, if a man is permeated with the desire for truth, many temptations lose their power over him.

The importance of the interior desire for truth is a basic theme running through the Gospel of St. John. There is one account there of how two sorts of men — the simple and honest, and the clever and dishonest — approach Jesus simultaneously and, because of the differences in their inner attitude, become involved in a fruitless quarrel with one another. This happened over the healing of the man born blind. St. John relates:

> One day he saw, in passing, a man blind from birth. So his disciples asked him: "Rabbi, who has sinned, this man or his parents, to account for his being born blind?" "Neither this man has sinned," replied Jesus, "nor his parents. No. God simply wants to make use of him to reveal his ways. Our duty is, while it is day, to conform to the ways of him whose ambassador I am. Night is coming on, when no man can do anything. As long as I am in the world, I am the light of the world." With these words spoken, he spat on the ground, and by means of the spittle made a lump of mud, and then spread the mud over his eyes, and said to him: "Go, and wash in the pool of Siloam" — a word which in our language means "Ambassador." So he went, and washed, and came back able to see.
>
> Now the neighbors and the people who had seen him before — for he was a beggar — said: "Is not this the fellow who used to sit and beg in such and such a place?" Some said: "This is the man." Others said: "Not at all; he only looks like him." He himself declared: "I am the man." They asked him therefore: "How, then, were your eyes opened?" "The man called Jesus," he replied, "made a lump of mud and spread it over my eyes and said to me: 'Go to Siloam and wash.' So I went and washed, and got my sight." When they asked him: "Where is this man?" he replied: "I do not know."
>
> The man who had been blind was then taken before the Pharisees. Now it happened that the day on which Jesus had formed the lump of mud and opened his eyes was a Sabbath. So the Pharisees, for

their part, asked him how he had obtained sight. He replied: "He put a lump of mud on my eyes, and I washed, and now I see."

Then some of the Pharisees said: "That man has no authority from God; he does not observe the Sabbath." Others argued: "How can a sinner give such proofs of power!" As a result, there was disagreement among them. So they asked the blind man again: "What do you say about him, because he opened your eyes?" He answered: "He is a prophet."

The Jews, therefore, did not believe that he had been blind and then obtained sight, until they summoned the parents of the man himself who had regained his sight, and put this question to them: "Is this your son? And do you say he was born blind? How, then, is he at present able to see?" His parents gave this explanation: "We know that this is our son, and that he was born blind; but how he is now able to see we do not know, nor do we know who opened his eyes. Ask him himself; he is old enough; he will give his own account." His parents said this because they were afraid of the Jews; for the Jews had already agreed among themselves that, if anyone should acknowledge Christ as the Messias, he should be put out of the synagogue. That was why his parents said: "He is old enough; ask him himself."

So they summoned a second time the man who had been blind, and said to him: "Give glory to God! We know that this man is a sinner." "Whether or not he is a sinner I do not know," he replied; "one thing I do know: I was blind and now I see." Then they asked him: "What did he do to you? How did he open your eyes?" "I told you already," he replied, "and you did not take my word for it. Why do you want to hear it again? Do you, too, perhaps, want to become his disciples?" Then they heaped abuse on him. "You are a disciple of that man," they said; "we are disciples of Moses. We know that Moses is God's spokesman, but whose mouthpiece this man is we do not know." "Why," the man retorted, "the strange thing is that you do not know whose mouthpiece he is when, as a matter of fact, he has opened my eyes! We know that God does not listen to sinners; but when one is God-fearing and does his will, he does listen to him. Since the world began, it is unheard of that anyone opened the eyes of one born blind! If this man had no mission from God, he could do nothing!" By way of answer they said to him: "You were wholly born in sin, and you mean to teach us?" And they expelled him.

Jesus was informed that they had expelled him. When he met the man, he said: "Do you believe in the Son of God?" "Well, who is he, sir?" the man answered; "I want to believe in him." "You are now looking in his face," replied Jesus; "yes, it is he who is now speaking to you!" "I do believe, sir," he said; and he fell on his knees before him. Jesus continued: "To be the parting of the way — that is my mission to the world: henceforth the sightless are to have sight, and those who see are to become blind." Some of the Pharisees, who happened to be near, heard this and said to him: "Maybe we, too, are blind, are we?" "If you were blind," replied Jesus, "you would have no sin; as it is, you claim to have sight. Your sin remains" (Jn 9:1–41).

The Pharisees are educated people who do not want to know anything about Jesus and who therefore use all their wit attempting to justify themselves before others. The man born blind is one without any education: in place of that he has an interior desire for truth which strives honestly and fearlessly toward its goal.

The underhand excuses of the dishonest Pharisees and the courageous protestations of faith of the blind man recoil upon one another repeatedly. The Scribes had decided in advance: we will not recognize Jesus as the Messiah — for ourselves or for anyone. They do not care what means they employ to gain this end. As if it would do them any good! First they try to deny the fact that the man really was born blind. Then they call in question Jesus' honesty. Finally they expel the cured man from the synagogue. The cured man has no education but he does not fear them. What is true is true and remains true, no matter how many Scribes put forward their objections.

Speech has been given to men by God in order that they may communicate with one another: it is governed by the law of truth and of love.

Through speech and gesture man reveals his inner self. Men have received from God the priceless treasure of speech through which to make known to one another their thoughts and wishes and so to be able to establish a spiritual community.

The use of speech intended by God presupposes an interior desire for truth. Man's relation to God, to himself, and to his fellowmen is determined by the will to be truthful. The duty of being truthful applies equally to the spoken, the written, and the printed word.

The Life of the Individual.   Jesus says: "If you make my teaching your rule of life, you are truly my disciples; then you will know the truth, and the truth will make you free men" (Jn 8:32).

An interior relationship to what is recognized as true and right, and being a man of one's word makes a man calm and composed. Such a man can respect himself. Conversely, striving against the consequences of known truth or avoiding the presentation of truth itself and breaking one's word make a man suspicious and touchy. He loses all regard for himself and is sensitive to everything that is said.

What has been said applies to dealings between men, neighbors, and communities. Within these smaller spheres the consequences of untruthfulness are likewise limited in scope. But representatives of large private businesses and of states are also bound to be truthful in their dealings with the corresponding representatives of other businesses or states. Speech was not given by God to disguise thoughts but make them intelligible.

The Life of the Church. In his address at the beginning of 1946, Pius XII speaks of the dire effects upon men's relations with one another which result from the want of the inner will to be truthful. He explains:

> The sign which our age bears upon its forehead is the ever-increasing tendency to dishonesty. It is not simply a case of sinning against honesty with the object of getting out of trouble or sudden difficulties in individual instances. It is, rather, that dishonesty is being elevated into a system and practised as an art in which the lie, twisting of words and deeds, and deceit, become regular weapons of attack which one uses with skill and pride in one's own cunning.
>
> It is not now our intention to describe in detail what devastation results in public life from this game of dishonesty. But We have a duty to open the eyes of the Catholics of the whole world and of all who share Our belief in Christ and a transcendent God, to the danger which this domination of lying brings to the Church, to Christian culture and to the whole religious and human heritage.

27. THE LAW OF GOD ABOUT SPEAKING AND KEEPING SILENT

ORIGINALLY God gave speech to men so that they might communicate their thoughts and feelings to one another. With sin, the urge came into the world to use words to conceal truth, to make out that one was innocent oneself while others were guilty. It is uncanny, the way in which this urge appears even in little children. A man who does not take himself in hand can become so accustomed to lying that he no longer realizes that he is doing it; and while lying himself, he gives vent to exasperated complaint over the deceit of others.

It was the lies of false witnesses which sent Jesus to His death. Holy Scripture relates:

Now, the chief priests — in fact, the Supreme Council as a body — were looking for false testimony, unfavorable to Jesus, in order to have him put to death; yet they did not find any although many false witnesses had come forward. Finally, however, two men advanced and said: "This man has said, 'I can destroy the sanctuary of God,' and, 'Within three days I can build it up again.'" Then the chief priest rose and said to him: "Have you nothing to say in your own defense? What about the evidence these men are furnishing against you?" But Jesus remained silent (Mt 26:59–62).

It was a lie which hindered the spread of the news that God had risen from the dead. Scripture tells us:

As they were going on their errand, some of the guards quite unexpectedly turned up in the city and reported to the chief priests what had taken place. The latter at once arranged a meeting with the elders and, after holding a consultation, gave the soldiers a considerable sum of money with these instructions: "This is what you must give out: 'His disciples came by night and stole his body while we were asleep.' And in case this is reported at the gover-

374

nor's headquarters, we will satisfy him and see that you have nothing to worry about." They accepted the bribe and did as they had been directed. Accordingly, this version of the story was circulated in Jewish communities and is current to this day (Mt 28:11–15).

And so, lies and betrayal have a place not only at the beginning of Jesus' Passion but also at the empty tomb. Since that time the world has not changed.

People lie from sheer loquacity (jocose lies); they lie in order to save themselves (lies of excuse); in order to harm others (malicious lies); in order to boast (exaggeration); and in order to help others (officious lies).

The following rules are intended by God's law to protect truth and love in speech:

By the Eighth Commandment God protects honesty and truth. He sins against truthfulness who lies or dissembles, who breaks a promise or a contract.

A man is certainly bound to be truthful when he speaks; but he is not always bound to speak — his duty may possibly be to remain silent, and speech would be a sin. For example, a person commits the sin of detraction if he makes known the real faults of another.

A man sins against his neighbor by lying if he arouses suspicion about him, makes a rash judgment against him, injures him by gossip or calumny.

The Eighth Commandment applies to the press, radio, and TV in a higher degree; for the readers of a book or a newspaper are numbered in thousands, and listeners to radio and TV viewers in hundreds of thousands — in millions.

Whoever injures another person's good name must make good the damage as far as possible. He must retract calumny.

The Life of the Individual. If you hear it said that a certain man never lies, he has already gained your profound regard and your affection. Be such a man yourself. If you want to get to know yourself, find out where you are most inclined to lie. Is it in boasting, in self-esteem, or in harming others?

Do you take trouble to think before you speak?

In almost everyone there is an ineradicable urge to appear very shrewd before one's fellowmen. The easiest way to achieve this is to show all other men up as stupid and to criticize all their doings in a superior manner. Half annoyed and half amused, St. Augustine writes about this malpractice: "Much more serious than many another misdeed is the sin of shutting our eyes to our own faults and backbiting and slandering our neighbor. In this way we despise men and hold them as of little account — even the most virtuous. We find fault with everyone, we meddle in everything although none has invited us. Although we ourselves have learned nothing, we would teach others. . . . Such simple souls are like boys who sit in a boat in the harbor, enjoying to row around near the shore; but in retrospect they pride themselves on having braved the fiercest storms."

The urge to talk about the faults of others is so deeply ingrained in fallen man that none can overcome it by a single resolve.

The Life of the Church. The Church has often been reproached for encouraging untruthfulness by permitting so-called "mental reservation."

A statement with mental reservation is understood to be a statement whose literal wording bears another meaning than that which is intended. When, for example, an official is asked about a matter on which he is not permitted to speak — as the questioner well knows — then he may reply: "I cannot really say anything about that."

Such statements containing mental reservation may not be used as we please. There must be a lawful reason for their use. Mental reservation is always excluded, therefore, when the questioner has a right to know the truth — as have, for example, parents, superiors, and judges. And again, mental reservation is not permissible in concluding a contract.

28. THE LAW OF GOD AND KEEPING FAITH IN CONFIDENCES AND CONTRACTS

IN ALL LANGUAGES, the word "trust" is hard to define.

If we trust a man we will reveal secrets to him which otherwise would remain hidden. We believe what such a man says without troubling to verify it, and in time of distress we rely on him.

Besides the trust which one individual places in another, there is the trust which the community places in individuals. Upon such trust depend all sorts of public arrangements — from the parks with their flower beds which are left undisturbed to the assurance that people will not deceive by making false statements in schedules. Because such arrangements are always increasing this sort of trust becomes ever more important.

Trust also constitutes the trusts of bargains and contracts between individuals, between groups, and between states.

By the Eighth Commandment God is guarding human contracts. Whoever breaks a contract transgresses God's law.

In the Scripture narrative of Absalom's revolt against his father King David two men appear, one of whom presents a fine example of faithfulness while the other presents an example of shameful unfaithfulness.

The man who remained true to David was Ethai the non-Israelite; the man who broke faith was his friend and counsellor Achitophel. The mentality of both became obvious when David fled in haste from Jerusalem with his faithful followers while Absalom with the insurgents moved up from the south. Scripture relates:

> And there came a messenger to David, saying: All Israel with their whole heart followeth Absalom. And David said to his servants

that were with him in Jerusalem: Arise and let us flee, for we shall not escape *else* from the face of Absalom. Make haste to go out, lest he come and overtake us, and bring ruin upon us, and smite the city with the edge of the sword. And the king's servants said to him: Whatsoever our lord the king shall command, we thy servants will willingly execute. And the king went forth, and all his household on foot. And the king left ten women his concubines to keep the house. And the king going forth and all Israel on foot, stood afar off from the house; and all his servants walked by him, and the bands of the Cerethi and the Phelethi, and all the Gethites, valiant warriors, six hundred men who had followed him from Geth on foot, went before the king.

And the king said to Ethai the Gethite: Why comest thou with us? Return and dwell with the king, for thou art a stranger and art come out of thy own place. Yesterday thou camest, and today shalt thou be forced to go forth with us? But I shall go whither I am going. Return thou, and take back thy brethren with thee, and the Lord will show thee mercy and truth, because thou hast shown grace and fidelity. And Ethai answered the king, saying: As the Lord liveth, and as my lord the king liveth, in what place soever thou shalt be, my lord, O king, either in death or in life, there will thy servant be. And David said to Ethai: Come, and pass over. And Ethai the Gethite passed, and all the men that were with him, and the rest of the people.

And they all wept with a loud voice, and all the people passed over: the king also himself went over the brook of Cedron, and all the people marched towards the way that looketh to the desert (2 Sm 15:13–23).

But David went up by the ascent of mount Olivet, going up and weeping, walking barefoot, and with his head covered, and all the people that were with them, went up with their heads covered weeping. And it was told David that Achitophel also was in the conspiracy with Absalom, and David said: Infatuate, O Lord, I beseech thee, the counsel of Achitophel (2 Sm 15:30–31).

The history of mankind everywhere reveals traitors who play the same role as Achitophel did toward David. But alongside men who default there are always men and women who show a shining example of faithfulness. One of the most sublime and rewarding tasks of education is to place these examples of faithfulness before young people and so to arouse in them that sense of faithfulness which lies dormant in the nature of every man.

Whoever becomes the confidant of another binds himself to silence. If he does not keep silent, then he sins against truthfulness — slightly or seriously, according to the circumstance. Likewise, a person sins who uses the confidence placed in him for his own ends or who uses the influence which he has over the person who trusts him to this person's disadvantage. Again, a man sins against good faith if he leaves the person who trusts him in the lurch or exploits him in any way. And obviously a man sins in a much greater degree if he sets out to gain another's confidence so that he can make use of him.

The Eighth Commandment obliges us to be reticent and to keep faith.

Whoever discloses confidences to others commits sin. If this disclosure concerns serious matters, especially if they are official secrets, the sin is grave.

Bargains and contracts must be kept in the spirit in which they were made. In this there is no distinction between private relations, business affairs, and state contracts.

The Life of the Individual. Nearly all who are in business today complain about the unreliability of people. If all who complained would begin improvement with themselves, all would share in the benefit.

If we inquire into the ultimate cause of the war in which millions lost their lives, breach of faith and of contracts would be found high on the list. As the feeling for the sacredness of a contract diminishes, so does the possibility fade of reaching a peace settlement which is more than a truce.

The Life of the Church. The popes of the past decades have repeatedly pointed out the dire result in the destruction of mutual trust, which follows from the attempt to erect human society upon a foundation which excludes belief in God and the demands of conscience.

29. THE LAW OF GOD IN THE REALM OF DESIRES

THE WORLD cannot call a man to account for what goes on within his heart; but he is answerable to his own conscience and before God for his thoughts and desires. As far as his own well being is concerned, every man accepts this principle. For example, if a man learns that another desires his death, he does not say that he doesn't mind at all because he has not actually murdered him.

The Ninth and Tenth Commandments indicate specifically that God's laws are binding before God Himself and not merely before the rulers of any state. These two Commandments assert that the desire to perform some impure act and the desire to appropriate another's property are transgressions of God's law. That is to say, something is being declared unlawful which cannot be proved and established either by men or by any authority.

As God has decreed, these two Commandments form the transition from merely civic proscriptions, with their defined contents and corresponding punishments, to a judgment of human actions which takes account of sinful desire in itself. Jesus was only developing fully the implications of the Ninth and Tenth Commandments when He said:

> "What comes out of a person is the thing that defiles a person. Yes, it is from within, out of the hearts of men, that evil intentions proceed — fornication, theft, murder, adultery, greed, malice, fraud, wantonness, envy, profanity, pride, folly. All these wicked things come from within and defile a person" (Mt 7:20–23).

A warning example of where sinful desire leads is given by an incident in the life of King Achab.

> And after these things, Naboth the Jezrahelite, who was in Jezrahel, had at that time a vineyard near the palace of Achab king of Samaria. And Achab spoke to Naboth, saying: Give me

thy vineyard, that I may make me a garden of herbs, because it is near, and adjoining to my house, and I will give thee for it a better vineyard; or if thou think it more convenient for thee, I will give thee the worth of it in money. Naboth answered him: The Lord be merciful to me, and not let me give thee the inheritance of my fathers. And Achab came into his house angry and fretting, because of the word that Naboth the Jezrahelite had spoken to him, saying: I will not give thee the inheritance of my fathers. And casting himself upon his bed, he turned away his face to the wall, and would eat no bread.

And Jezabel his wife went in to him, and said to him: What is the matter that thy soul is so grieved? And why eatest thou no bread? And he answered her: I spoke to Naboth the Jezrahelite, and said to him: Give me thy vineyard, and take money for it; or if it please thee, I will give thee a better vineyard for it. And he said: I will not give thee my vineyard. Then Jezabel his wife said to him: Thou art of great authority indeed, and governest well the kingdom of Israel. Arise, and eat bread, and be of good cheer. I will give thee the vineyard of Naboth the Jezrahelite. So she wrote letters in Achab's name, and sealed them with his ring; and sent them to the ancients, and the chief men that were in his city, and that dwelt with Naboth. And this was the tenor of the letters: Proclaim a fast, and make Naboth sit among the chief of the people, and suborn two men, sons of Belial, against him, and let them bear false witness: that he hath blasphemed God and the king. And then carry him out, and stone him, and so let him die.

And the men of his city, the ancients and nobles that dwelt with him in the city, did as Jezabel had commanded them, and as it was written in the letters which she had sent to them. They proclaimed a fast, and made Naboth sit among the chiefs of the people.

And they sent to Jezabel, saying: Naboth is stoned, and is dead. And it came to pass, when Jezabel heard that Naboth was stoned and dead, that she said to Achab: Arise and take possession of the vineyard of Naboth the Jezrahelite, who would not agree with thee, and give it thee for money, for Naboth is not alive, but dead. And when Achab heard this, to wit, that Naboth was dead, he arose, and went down to the vineyard of Naboth the Jezrahelite, to take possession of it.

And the word of the Lord came to Elias the Thesbite, saying: Arise, and go down to meet Achab king of Israel, who is in Samaria. Behold he is going down to the vineyard of Naboth, to take possession of it, and thou shalt speak to him, saying: Thus saith the Lord: Thou hast slain, moreover also thou hast taken possession.

And after these words thou shalt add: Thus saith the Lord: In this place, wherein the dogs have licked the blood of Naboth, they shall lick thy blood also (3 Kgs 21:1–12, 14–19).

Every good deed, every evil deed — the greatest heroism or the worst iniquity — has its origin in the secret places of the heart.

But more powerful than any impulse toward evil is the grace of God. The man who has been incorporated by Baptism into the life of Christ adopts a new relationship to his own evil concupiscence. He has been called to live by God and in God and has been equipped with God's help to master his evil desires.

Thus St. Peter writes:

> It is a fact that his divine power has bestowed on us all needed aid for our spiritual life and piety, by imparting the deep knowledge of him who called us by his own glory and power. Through these manifestations he has bestowed on us precious and very great promises, to enable us to escape the corruption which lust causes in the world, and become partakers of the divine nature (2 Pt 1:3–4).

> I know that the time is near at hand for the removal of my tent, as also our Lord Jesus Christ indicated to me. But I will also take care that after my death you may at all times have the means to recall these instructions.

> We were certainly not following cunningly devised myths when we made known to you the power and coming of our Lord Jesus Christ. On the contrary, we were eyewitnesses of his majesty (2 Pt 1:14–16).

From wishes and desires arise words and deeds. Before God a man is just as responsible for deliberate wishes and desires as he is for deliberate words and deeds.

The particular prohibition by the Ninth and Tenth Commandments of impure desire and the coveting of another's goods has a special significance. Even under the Old Covenant God marks out two examples, viz., the unlawful desire for another's property and the sinful desire for another man's wife, so that even sins of thought, which are not judged by human courts of law, appear as under God's judgment. The Sixth and Seventh Commandments are thus adduced because their subject matter is so important for the social life of men.

The Life of the Individual. A man's secret, unspoken wishes give the truest picture of his true self. Be aware of the true nature of your secret desires or else they will betray your purpose if you are not vigilant. Pray that God will protect you from yourself.

What is true of the individual is true also of the life of nations. Through their untamed desires and wishes they become a prey to discontent, and discontent is the chief cause of war.

The Life of the Church. The success of many books is due to their putting into words, and declaring to be good and true and beautiful, these things which pander to the common desires of the age. Such books, whatever subject they deal with, constitute a danger to the faith and the life of the faithful. All the more so because today nearly everyone is literate. The Church makes use of the same fact — that all are literate — in combating open and insidious errors. More frequently than in earlier days, the popes publish general encyclicals which explain how various problems are to be solved in the spirit of faith. And these encyclicals are couched in language suited not only to the learned professor, but to all of mankind.

30. THE COMMANDMENTS OF THE CHURCH: THE MORE PRECISE REGULATIONS FOR CARRYING OUT THE VARIOUS COMMANDMENTS OF GOD

FROM THE VERY OUTSET Jesus had been determined to give the Church juridical power. This is shown by the fact that He initially described the men whom He chose to be its leaders as *shaliach* — apostles or ambassadors. A *shaliach* is a man who has received authority from another to command and to make decisions in his name. To explain this Jesus said later on to His Apostles: "He who listens to you listens to me, and he who despises you despises me; but whoever despises me despises him whose ambassador I am" (Lk 10:16).

The Church exercises the power given by the Lord in His name and in His Spirit. That is to say: she uses this authority only to apply the basic rules of conscience, which have already been laid down, to particular significant cases and to formulate them in set definitions.

Thus the Commandments of the Church do not lay new obligations upon the faithful but are merely the regulations for carrying out the divine Commandments. They are described as such by Pius XI in his encyclical of March 14, 1937. With changing conditions these Commandments can, therefore, assume new forms. For example, the stipulation about contributing to the needs of the Church are today taken more and more into account in the Commandments of the Church.

Along with the power of legislating within her own sphere the Church has also received the power of administering punishment. A juridical power which is unable to judge and to punish transgression of the law is no power at all but at most an expression of opinion.

Jesus Himself asserted, therefore: "If anyone refuses to listen to the Church, then treat him as a heathen and tax collector" (Mt 18:17).

The First Commandment of the Church

Even under the Old Covenant other days besides the seventh day of the week were observed as days of rest and of festival. These days commemorated the various manifestations of God's grace to the people of Israel. Among these were numbered especially the Easter festival, Pentecost, the Feast of Tabernacles, and the dedication of the second temple. St. Luke tells us how Jesus went up to Jerusalem with Mary and Joseph when He was twelve years old to the Easter festival.

In like manner, as well as sanctifying the weekly day of rest which now falls upon Sunday, the Church celebrates certain feasts which call to mind the manifestations of God's grace in the establishment of the new scheme of salvation. From the very beginning, Easter became the commemoration of the Resurrection of Jesus, and Pentecost that of the descent of the Holy Spirit.

The First Commandment of the Church prescribes, then, that the appointed feast days must be kept holy in the same way as Sundays.

The First Commandment of the Church also explains the way in which all Christians must observe Sundays and feast days.

All Christians who have reached the age of reason are bound under pain of mortal sin to hear Mass on these days, not merely externally and in the physical sense, but so that they actively participate in the spiritual action. They must at least follow the chief parts of the Mass — the Offertory, the Consecration, and the Holy Communion — and unite themselves with the priest who offers the Holy Sacrifice in the name of the congregation.

Those who are infirm or sick, and those who are prevented through a work of charity or of public necessity, are excused attendance at Mass. Anyone who cannot attend Mass without risking damage to his health is also excused. The same applies to those whose work cannot be interrupted on Sunday without harm to the common good. Railway workers and those engaged in industries which demand their service on Sundays are guilty of no sin if they fail to attend Mass because of the demands of work. But even those must find a way of attending Mass occasionally during the year — during holidays most likely. It is not possible to fulfill one's attendance at Mass through the radio or television.

The Second Commandment of the Church

The second commandment of the Church prescribes certain acts of penance. Days of abstinence are those days upon which we must abstain from flesh-meat: fast days are days when we may eat only one full meal. There are days of fast and abstinence, when we must both abstain from flesh-meat and eat only one full meal. Jesus Himself prepared for His public life by fasting for forty days (cf. Lk 4:1 ff.).

Each diocese or province settles for its own region which days of the year shall be set aside for fasting or abstinence of both together.

In the encyclical of Pius XI on the reparation due to God it was expressly emphasized that all the faithful are bound to do penance and make reparation. The Church therefore demands that penance and reparation be part of the life of the faithful, and be not regarded as merely the concern of the specially devout.

The Third and Fourth Commandments of the Church

Jesus instituted the Holy Eucharist so that He might affect man's spirit through the appearances of bread and wine just as food and drink affect a healthy man.

"He who eats my flesh and drinks my blood is in possession of eternal life; and I will raise him from the dead on the last day; for my flesh is real food, and my blood is real drink. He who eats my flesh and drinks my blood is united with me, and I am united with him. As the living Father has appointed me his ambassador, and I live because of the Father, so, too, he who eats me will have life because of me" (Jn 6:54–57).

In the Fourth Commandment, the Church does not state how often a person must receive Holy Communion. She states rather that a man who does not receive the Body of the Lord as the food for his soul at least once in the year, during the Easter time, can no longer be numbered among the community of the faithful in Christ until he shows some sign of having changed his outlook.

It is the Church's desire that the faithful should receive the sacraments of Penance and Holy Communion frequently and regularly. One is obliged to receive the sacrament of Penance before Holy Communion only if one is not in a state of grace.

The Fifth Commandment of the Church

The Fifth Commandment obliges all to support the clergy and the Church buildings and furnishings, according to their means.

The obligation to support the Church is simply the contemporary application of those words which Jesus spoke on first sending out the seventy-two disciples. He directed them to turn to their hearers for sustenance while they were doing His work proclaiming the good news of the kingdom of God; and He added, as the reason: "The laborer is entitled to his wages" (Lk 10:7). Similarly St. Paul says: "Those who preside at the altar share the altar's offerings" (I Cor 9:13).

We ought to think of gifts to the Church as gifts to Christ Himself. He who gives cheerfully will in turn be rewarded by Christ with precious gifts.

The Sixth Commandment of the Church

The Sixth Commandment of the Church comprises all the regulations which the Church has made governing the sacrament of Marriage. The Church takes every precaution that no marriage be contracted which could never be valid because the basis for the marriage vows was lacking. For this reason she lays down in advance the conditions which make marriage impossible. She would like to insure that in these cases no relationship at all should ever begin to exist. By acting in this way the Church follows the mind of the Lord who laid down as the fundamental law for marriage: "What God has yoked together no man may separate" (Mt 19:6).

The Church also wishes to limit as far as possible the number of marriages where family life would seem from the outset to be gravely endangered. She therefore erects impediments to marriage which make a marriage irregular but not absolutely invalid. In this case the Church demands that the couple declare the reason why they desire to marry in spite of these considerations; and they must promise to respect the assurances in terms of which the Church permits them to marry.

Christ Himself gave the Church authority to make laws. The Church makes use of this authority to break down various Commandments of God into more precise regulations.

The most important Commandments of the Church are:

1. To keep the Sundays and holy days of obligation holy, by hearing Mass and resting from servile works.
2. To keep the days of fasting and abstinence appointed by the Church.
3. To go to confession at least once a year.
4. To receive the Blessed Sacrament at least once a year and that during the Easter season (Septuagesima Sunday to Trinity Sunday).
5. To contribute to the support of our pastors.
6. Not to marry within certain degrees of kindred, nor to solemnize marriage at forbidden times.

All the faithful who have reached the age of reason must assist at the offering of the holy Sacrifice of the Mass on Sundays and holy days of obligation unless prevented from doing so by some serious reason. It is, therefore, a sin against the First Commandment of the Church:

1. To miss Mass wholly or partially on a Sunday or feast day through one's own fault; and
2. To hear Mass without devotion and reverence.

The Life of the Individual. Reception of the sacraments of Penance and Holy Communion and attendance at Sunday Mass are always a most reliable index of the religious condition of any parish. That is not to say that all who receive the sacraments regularly and attend Mass on Sundays are already saints, and that those who do not do this are already lost: but it is impossible to find a parish in which the spirit of religion prevails where the sacraments are not being received and where people are not attending Sunday Mass. And again it is impossible to find people diligent in attendance at Mass and eagerly receiving the sacraments in a parish in which there is no true religious spirit.

The Life of the Church. The Church also has the right to forbid the reading of books which are a danger to the faithful or to the preservation of good order. But it would be a great mistake to suppose that the reading of all books not specifically prohibited is permitted. All of the faithful are bound, by reason of Christian self-love, to avoid reading any book which is likely to harm them. People who have lost faith through imprudent reading are to be counted in thousands.

There are other rules which can be described as Commandments of the Church. No one is allowed to join any sect or forbidden society or attend spiritualist seances; to contract a mixed marriage; to arrange to be cremated or to join a cremation society. Marriage must be solemnized according to the rites of the Church, children must be baptized and educated as Catholics, and in danger of death a Catholic must receive the sacraments.

The early Christians liked best to think of the Church as a maternal lawgiver. This was expressed in countless representations. In this Christians made no distinction between enactments which were directly derived from words of Christ and those which the Church made autonomously; for they regarded the Church as the mother who had reborn them into everlasting life and who thus could exercise motherly rights over them.

31. DUTIES OF VOCATION AND STATION: THE COMMAND TO LOVE ONE'S NEIGHBOR APPLIED TO PARTICULAR SPHERES OF ACTIVITY

THE TEN COMMANDMENTS OF GOD all derive from the twin commandment, to love God and our neighbor; but they contain only such regulations as bind all men without any exception. Similarly the duties of various stations in life derive from this twin commandment; but because they apply only to those in a particular state they could not be included in the Commandments of God. If this had happened they would have now been out of date because the number of avocations has increased and the types of obligations have changed. The fact that the duties of the various stations derive from the chief Commandments is demonstrated by the conversation which John the Baptist had one day with tax collectors and soldiers on the banks of the Jordan.

> Also tax collectors came to be baptized by him. "Rabbi," they said to him, "what are we to do?" "Exact nothing," was his answer to them, "in excess of the rate prescribed to you." Also men of the police force consulted with him. "And for our part," they said, "what are we to do?" He replied: "Browbeat no one; blackmail no one; and be content with your pay" (Lk 3:12–14).

In questioning John the men had stressed the word "we." What must *we,* the tax collectors, and what must *we,* the soldiers, do? Is it possible for us ever to remain in our jobs?

The tax collectors had plenty of opportunity for cheating and extortion — and they often took it, so that the word "tax collector" had become a term of abuse. The soldiers were in a similar position.

390

They served not only as soldiers but also as armed police, and thus had opportunities of making money.

John told the tax collectors and soldiers not to leave their jobs but to take care to preserve justice and love of their neighbors. He said to the tax collectors: "Do not go beyond the scale appointed you." To the soldiers he said: "Do not use men roughly, do not lay false information against them." This admonition applied to them as police officers. Then he added: "Be content with your pay." Discontent with pay was very often the cause of all sorts of extortions.

A man's job determines his external way of life. This cannot be altered. But every man certainly has it in his own power of turning his job into something which has to do not merely with hand or head but with the heart and with the heart's impulse to love. The picture of a mother cleaning and mending her children's clothes shows us this union of work and love. There is no job whatsoever which a man cannot use as a means of developing his own personality. In this way the external performance of his job can become a morally good act. The workman who accepts his daily work in this spirit gains more from it, it may be, than he for whom he is working. In the heat of toil he matures like fruit in sunshine and earns from his labor a reward which endures to eternal life.

For thirty years Jesus the Son of God practiced the craft of a joiner in the little town of Nazareth to show us all how our attitude ennobles work.

For all Christians life has the same high and clear goal:

For a Christian, life is the time when he is able to work with all his powers and gifts for the kingdom of God. He does not know how long this time will be.

The duties of station in life and of avocation arise from the demands of justice and love of one's neighbor.

Members of the same class and profession have a duty to avoid dishonest competition and to cooperate in advancing the common good.

The various groups must practice mutual respect and regard one another as members of the same community, apportioning burdens justly.

All trades and professions represent services to the community.

The Life of the Individual.   Pope John XXIII's words opening the Second Vatican Council have relevance here:

The great problem confronting the world after almost two thousand years remains unchanged. Christ is ever resplendent as the center of history and of life. Men are either with Him and His Church, and then they enjoy light, goodness, order and peace. Or else they are without Him, or against Him, and deliberately opposed to His Church, and then they give rise to confusion, to bitterness in human relations, and to the constant danger of fratricidal wars. . . . In the daily exercise of our pastoral office we sometimes have to listen, much to our regret, to voices of persons who, though burning with zeal, are not endowed with too much sense of discretion or measure. In these modern times they can see nothing but prevarication and ruin. They say that our era, in comparison with past eras, is getting worse and they behave as though they had learned nothing from history, which is, none the less, the teacher of life. They behave as though at the time of former Councils everything was a full triumph for the Christian idea and life and for proper religious liberty.

We feel we must disagree with these prophets of doom who are always forecasting disaster, as though the end of the world were at hand.

In the present order of things, Divine Providence is leading us to a new order of human relations which, by men's own efforts and even beyond their very expectations, are directed toward the fulfillment of God's superior and inscrutable designs. And everything, even human differences, leads to the greater good of the Church.

It is easy to discern this reality if we consider attentively the world of today, which is so busy with politics and controversies in the economic order that it does not find time to attend to the care of spiritual reality with which the Church's *magisterium* is concerned. Such a way of acting is certainly not right, and must justly be disapproved. It cannot be denied, however, that these new conditions of modern life have at least the advantage of having eliminated those innumerable obstacles by which at one time the sons of this world impeded the free action of the Church. . . .

Our duty is not only to guard the precious treasure of the faith, as if we were concerned only with past, but to dedicate ourselves with an earnest will and without fear to that work which our era demands of us, pursuing thus the path which the Church has followed for twenty centuries.

The Life of the Church. The cultivation of the right attitude to one's job is more important for social life than the advancement of vocational training. Without a proper attitude to work the specialist's activity can be perverted to a purpose quite the opposite of that for which it is designed. A well-educated merchant, for example, finds far more opportunity to enrich himself dishonestly than does a stupid one. The phrase "a good businessman" is very often equivocal. The same sort of thing happens in other callings.

The supreme model which the Church sets before the faithful of how to fulfill one's daily task in love for God and man is Jesus, the incarnate Son of God who for thirty years plied the trade of a carpenter in Nazareth, and thereby spiritually ennobled and sanctified work.

32. THE PRIESTLY AND RELIGIOUS STATE: THE SPECIAL VOCATION TO SERVE CHRIST AND HIS CHURCH

AS WELL AS ORDINARY WORKERS all large undertakings must have their specialists. Men who are specially trained for particular jobs are appointed only in a certain proportion. As a rule they have their own place of work and hours of work, and they are superior in rank to the ordinary workers. No one imagines that there is anything objectionable in this.

What has just been said holds true of the Church. It is possible to think of the Church as the largest undertaking which the world has ever seen. She is now almost two thousand years old and embraces millions of people from over the whole world. In this mighty undertaking there are jobs to which specialists — extraordinary workers — must be appointed.

These specialized vocations which the Church cannot do without are those of priests and religious who put themselves at God's disposal in a way which compels them to avoid all purely secular callings.

During His earthly life our Lord designated certain functions in His service as vocations which consist in making oneself free to do the service of the kingdom of God and of love for God, and in following, not one's own will but the directions of the Church.

Scripture tells us:

> When he had finished speaking, he said to Simon: "Launch out into the deep water, and have your men lower the nets for a haul." "Master," Simon explained, "we worked all night without catching anything. However, since you tell me to do so, I will have the nets let down." When they had done this they caught, in a single haul,

an extraordinary number of fish; in fact, their nets threatened to break. Then they beckoned their partners in the other boat to come and lend them a helping hand. They came, and both boats were filled so that they were on the point of sinking.

When Simon Peter saw what had happened, he threw himself down at the feet of Jesus. "Lord, leave my boat," he said; "I am a sinful creature." A feeling of awe had gripped him, as it had all his associates, because of the number of fish caught in the haul; so, too, it had seized James and John, the sons of Zebedee, who were Simon's partners. Jesus then said to Simon: "You have nothing to fear. Hereafter you will be a fisher of men." When they had brought the boats to shore, they abandoned everything and became his followers (Lk 5:4–11).

The invitation "Follow me," which Jesus addressed to Peter and his companions who hitherto had been free to do as they pleased, implied that from now on they were bound to follow His instructions, and included also the duty of obedience.

If anyone solemnly binds himself to obey the leaders of the Church or the superior of a religious order, this is known as taking the vow of obedience. This vow is a matter of free choice: it cannot be imposed upon all.

When Jesus was asserting that the marriage vow is indissoluble, He also pointed out that His disciples could resolve to lead a celibate life with the intention of dedicating themselves wholly to the service of God. It was, in fact, at the very moment when the disciples observed that if marriage be indissoluble it were better to remain single, that Jesus upbraided them for these hasty words and said with some animation:

"Not all master this lesson," he said to them, "but only such as have received a special gift: as there are those barred from marrying by a natural defect, and those barred by an act of man, so there are those who bar themselves from marrying for the sake of the kingdom of heaven. Only a strong soul should try to master this lesson" (Mt 19:11–12).

By this answer Jesus expressly referred to the fact that among the unmarried there are those who are so for the sake of the kingdom of God — for the love of God. From the context we understand that these serve the kingdom of God, that is the Church, in the same way as married people serve their families. This group devoted to special work will always constitute a minority — as Jesus makes plain when He says: "Take this in, you whose hearts are large enough for it."

A person who renounces marriage forever is said to take a vow of celibacy or chastity.

There is yet another saying of Jesus, which St. Matthew adds to the address on marriage, and which shows how Jesus Himself had in mind a connection between chastity, poverty, and obedience.

> Here Peter took occasion to say to him: "We, you see, have given up everything and become your followers. What, then, are we to get?" Jesus said to them: "I tell you with assurance: in the final regeneration, when the Son of Man takes his seat on a throne befitting his glory, you, my followers, will, in turn, be seated on twelve thrones and have jurisdiction over the Twelve Tribes of Israel. And so in general: whoever gives up home, or brothers, or sisters, or father, or mother, or children, or lands, for the sake of my name, will receive a hundred times as much and inherit eternal life" (Mt 19:27–29).

Here Jesus is promising to all who forsake family and possessions for His sake a place of special honor in heaven.

Priests and religious can be likened to specialists in a great business undertaking. Like these, they have their own work and their own sphere of operation.

Priests are obliged to place themselves immediately at the service of God and of men.

No one may be compelled to enter the priesthood or the religious life; and no one should be prevented from doing so. There are several ecclesiastical punishments for both of these actions.

All of the faithful must respect priests and religious and must see them as people who serve the good of all, under God's commission.

The Life of the Individual. No one is obliged to take all or any one of the vows of chastity, of poverty, and of obedience. But those who make the doctrines of faith the basis of their judgment must not withhold proper respect from those who do take these vows. Sad to say, there are people who in time of need will turn to a priest, and in time of illness will prefer to enter a hospital staffed by nuns, but who afterward applaud or even indulge in frivolous and malicious talk about priests and nuns. Many incipient vocations to the priesthood and to the religious life are certainly obstructed by such talk.

The Life of the Church. The Church is most anxious to have as many good priests as possible, and to discourage from entering the priesthood all who are not fit to fulfill the obligations of the priesthood.

As well as this, the Church is always on the lookout for dedicated men and women who will serve the poor; the sick and the abandoned, under her leadership. In this connection, these words of Jesus apply to all the faithful without exception: "The harvest is plentiful, but the laborers are few. Pray the owner of the harvest, therefore, to send out laborers to do his harvesting" (Lk 10:2).

It is a matter of honor that Christian parents should keep a watchful eye on any of their children who show a disposition toward the priestly or the religious life. One of the finest prayers for young married people is the prayer that from their marriage God will raise up children who will dedicate themselves to Him in the priesthood or in a religious order. Pius XII said in an address during 1942:

> Never forget, beloved sons and daughters: the family which is founded, according to God's will, upon the proper union of man and wife, has to supply Christ and His Church with servants and apostles of the Gospel, has to provide priests and heralds to care for the Christian flock, to traverse the oceans bringing light and salvation to souls.
>
> What will you do if some day the divine Master comes and asks you for His first-fruits, i.e., demands back from you one of your children, a son or a daughter — it was He who gave them to you in the first place — to make of him a priest or religious? What will you say to your children if with childlike trust they open their hearts to you and tell you of the divine longing in their souls wherein a soft, sweet voice has implored them, "Wilt thou?"?
>
> We beseech you in God's name: do not obstruct the entry of the divine call into any soul with your rough and selfish attitude.

Adult men and women who have never married or who are childless may be able to support students for the priesthood and so assume a spiritual parenthood over them.

33. AWAITING CHRIST THE LORD

LIFE IS A GIFT and a commission. It belongs also to God's undisputed sovereignty over life to determine the hour when each individual shall die. Eternal salvation or damnation depends upon whether, in that hour, a man is a child of God or not. Thus Jesus likens men living upon this earth to servants who must await their master's return.

"Keep your loins girt and your lamps burning. Yes, be like men who are on the lookout for their master, uncertain when he starts for home from the wedding feast. Thus, the moment he arrives, they will at once open the door for him. Well for those slaves whom the master on his return finds awake. I assure you, he will gird himself and bid them recline at table and personally wait on them! And whether he returns before midnight or after, well for those slaves if he finds them so engaged! Of one thing you are sure: if the owner of a house knew at what hour the thief was coming, he would stay awake and not let his house be broken into" (Lk 12:35–39).

We can react in several ways to the knowledge that a particular person is coming. We can wish earnestly that he will not come; we can note the fact that he is to arrive and think no more about it; or we can make his expected arrival the center of all our desire.

If we act thus, then we think of the one who is to come every day. We do certain things and refrain from others, all on account of the one we await. Many things which others take up with a will have no charm for us because they cannot be associated with the person whose arrival we long for, or because we are fully satisfied with the thought of his coming. In our longing we wish that the sun would run his course more quickly and the years follow one another with greater haste.

When we hear someone speaking about the one whom we await, we listen and our expectancy increases with all we hear. The one we await is the subject of our first thoughts in the morning and our last at night. We prepare in advance all that we are going to tell him when at last he arrives. In a sense he is already with us.

It is such a mood that Jesus wants us to have when He says that we should be like those who are waiting for His return. We should be thinking every day about the approach of our Lord. We should put away certain things and begin to apply ourselves to other things, all on account of His approach. Many things which seem important to others should appear quite meaningless to us when we think of Jesus who is drawing near. Longing for Him we shall see in death a beginning rather than an end. When we hear someone speaking about Jesus we should attend carefully and intensify our expectancy with any new thing which we are able to learn about Him.

And if we act thus, Jesus the One who is to come is already present with us in spirit, and when He comes in reality it will be a meeting in which we recognize the Lord as the long-awaited One and He greets and rewards us who have waited for Him.

In the light of faith we see that every man's life has an intrinsic, eternal value which is independent of all the external circumstances of life.

Life upon this earth is our probation in God's service. Whoever serves God in grace can never be really unhappy, and whoever lives apart from the grace of God can never be described as a truly happy man. For the faithful, life upon this earth is a waiting for ever-lasting life in the world to come.

The Life of the Individual. In this world no man can release himself from dependence upon sensory perception; and it is charac-teristic of all the senses that they tire of receiving impressions. And so, in this world there is no delight whatsoever which does not pall after a certain time.

When a person contemplates God he gazes upon One who never passes away but who exists in Himself and gives existence to all other beings including man himself. God is not merely eternal beauty but is also infinite beauty. And man will never weary of gazing upon Him. To the vision of God there is thus no end in the sense that one will at some time have seen all there is to see, or that one has tired of what one is beholding.

Being in such a condition, a person will look back upon this life with all its struggles and pain as upon a fraction of a second which is past: but eternity before it is seen as joy without end. Only one man knew of this blessedness in heaven: Jesus Christ the Son of God who came down from heaven and returned there. From His own knowledge of this blessedness of heaven He exhorted His people: "Be joyful — leap for joy — a rich reward awaits you in heaven" (Mt 5:12).

The Life of the Church. It is possible that some of the faithful do not always look forward to the Lord's coming as they ought to: they may even forget about it all together in their immersion in earthly things. But the Church herself, as the community in whom the Holy Spirit dwells, is always on the watch. This character of her being is expressed very specially in her title "The Bride of Christ." This description must on no account be regarded as a pretty, poetic expression: it is derived from Scripture. John the Baptist says that Jesus is "the bridegroom who possesses the bride" (Jn 3:29). Jesus Himself took up this imagery and spoke of the community of disciples as a bride who must spend a long weary time separated from the bridegroom and longingly await His return (cf. Mk 2:19-20).